GENDERING THE CROWN IN THE SPANISH BAROQUE *COMEDIA*

The Baroque Spanish stage is populated with virile queens and feminized kings. This study examines the diverse ways in which seventeenth-century *comedias* engage with the discourse of power and rulership and how it relates to gender.

A privileged place for ideological negotiation, the *comedia* provided negative and positive reflections of kingship at a time when there was a perceived crisis of monarchical authority in the Habsburg court. Author María Cristina Quintero explores how playwrights such as Pedro Calderón de la Barca, Tirso de Molina, Antonio Coello, and Francisco Bances Candamo—taking inspiration from legend, myth, and history—repeatedly staged fantasies of feminine rule, at a time when there was a concerted effort to contain women's visibility and agency in the public sphere. The *comedia*'s preoccupation with kingship together with its obsession with the representation of women (and women's bodies) renders the question of royal subjectivity inseparable from issues surrounding masculinity and femininity.

Taking into account theories of performance and performativity within a historical context, this study investigates how the themes, imagery, and language in plays by Calderón and his contemporaries reveal a richly paradoxical presentation of gendered monarchical power.

New Hispanisms
Cultural and Literary Studies

Series editor: Anne J. Cruz

New Hispanisms: Literary and Cultural Studies presents innovative studies that seek to understand how the cultural production of the Hispanic world is generated, disseminated, and consumed. Ranging from the Spanish Middle Ages to modern Spain and Latin America, this series offers a forum for various critical and disciplinary approaches to cultural texts, including literature and other artifacts of Hispanic culture. Queries and proposals for single author volumes and collections of original essays are welcome.

Gendering the Crown in the Spanish Baroque Comedia
María Cristina Quintero

Reading Inebriation in Early Colonial Peru
Mónica P. Morales

Gendering the Crown in the Spanish Baroque *Comedia*

MARÍA CRISTINA QUINTERO

LONDON AND NEW YORK

First published 2012 by Ashgate Publishing

Published 2016 by Routledge
2 Park Square, Milton Park, Abingdon, Oxon OX14 4RN
711 Third Avenue, New York, NY 10017, USA

Routledge is an imprint of the Taylor & Francis Group, an informa business

Copyright © 2012 María Cristina Quintero

María Cristina Quintero has asserted her right under the Copyright, Designs and Patents Act, 1988, to be identified as the author of this work.

All rights reserved. No part of this book may be reprinted or reproduced or utilised in any form or by any electronic, mechanical, or other means, now known or hereafter invented, including photocopying and recording, or in any information storage or retrieval system, without permission in writing from the publishers.

Notice:
Product or corporate names may be trademarks or registered trademarks, and are used only for identification and explanation without intent to infringe.

British Library Cataloguing in Publication Data
Quintero, María Cristina.
Gendering the crown in the Spanish Baroque comedia. – (New hispanisms)
   1. Spanish drama – Classical period, 1500–1700 – History and criticism. 2. Spanish drama (Comedy) – History and criticism. 3. Baroque literature – History and criticism. 4. Kings and rulers in literature. 5. Queens in literature. 6. Women and literature – Spain – History – 17th century.
   I. Title II. Series
   862.3'09352621–dc23

Library of Congress Cataloging-in-Publication Data
Quintero, María Cristina.
  Gendering the crown in the Spanish Baroque Comedia / by María Cristina Quintero.
    p. cm. — (New hispanisms: cultural and literary studies)
  Includes index.
   1. Spanish drama—Classical period, 1500–1700—History and criticism. 2. Sex role in literature. 3. Kings and rulers in literature. I. Title.

PQ6105.Q56 2012
862'.3093521—dc23
                                                                                      2012003111

ISBN 9781409439639 (hbk)

To Roland

Contents

List of Figures		*ix*
Acknowledgments		*xi*
Introduction		1
1	Women and Drama in Early Modern Spain	11
2	Beauty and the Machiavellian Beast	47
3	Transgendered Tyranny in *La hija del aire*	91
4	English Queens and the Body Politic	123
5	Christina of Sweden and Queenly Garb(o)	169
Epilogue		215
Works Cited		*223*
Index		*239*

List of Figures

2.1	Juan Carreño de Miranda. *King Charles II*, 1673. Madrid, Museo del Prado. (Photo: Erich Lessing/Art Resource, NY)	60
2.2	Antonis Mor. *Queen Mary of England*, 1554. Madrid, Museo del Prado. (Photo: Erich Lessing/Art Resource, NY)	62
2.3	Raphael (Raffaello Sanzio). *Joanna of Aragón, Queen of Naples*, 1518. Paris, Louvre. (Photo: Réunion des Musées Nationaux/Art Resource, NY)	63
4.1	Anonymous. *Ann Boleyn*, late 16th century. London, Ann Ronan Picture Library. (Photo: HIP/Art Resource, NY)	136
4.2	George Gower. *The Armada Portrait of Elizabeth I*, 1588. Bedfordshire, Great Britain, Woburn Abbey. (Photo: Scala/White Images/Art Resource, NY)	153
5.1	Diego Velázquez and others. *Margarita of Austria, Wife of Philip III, on Horseback*, ca. 1631. Madrid, Museo del Prado. (Photo: Erich Lessing/Art Resource, NY)	170
5.2.	Diego Velázquez and others. *Equestrian Portrait of Queen Isabel of Bourbon, Wife of Philip IV*, 1635–1636. Madrid, Museo del Prado. (Photo: Erich Lessing/Art Resource, NY)	171
5.3	Diego Velázquez and others. *Philip III on Horseback*, ca. 1631. Madrid, Museo del Prado. (Photo: Erich Lessing/Art Resource, NY)	172
5.4	Diego Velázquez. *Philip IV on Horseback*, 1631–1636. Madrid, Museo del Prado. (Photo: Scala/Art Resource, NY)	173
5.5	Diego Velázquez. *Gaspar de Guzmán, Count-Duke of Olivares, on Horseback*, 1635. Madrid, Museo del Prado. (Photo: Scala/Art Resource, NY)	175
5.6	Sébastien Bourdon. *Queen Christina of Sweden on Horseback*, 1653–1654. Madrid, Museo del Prado. (Photo: Erich Lessing/Art Resource, NY)	177

5.7   Greta Garbo and Elizabeth Young in *Queen Christina* [DVD]/
      Metro-Goldwyn-Mayer. Directed by Rouben Mamoulian,
      screenplay by H.M. Harwood and Salka Viertel,
      produced by Walter Wanger. Burbank, California,
      Warner Home Video, 2005.   212

5.8   Greta Garbo and John Gilbert with Painting of Philip IV
      in *Queen Christina* [DVD]/Metro-Goldwyn-Mayer. Directed
      by Rouben Mamoulian, screenplay by H.M. Harwood
      and Salka Viertel, produced by Walter Wanger. Burbank,
      California, Warner Home Video, 2005.   213

5.9   Greta Garbo and John Gilbert in *Queen Christina* [DVD]/
      Metro-Goldwyn-Mayer. Directed by Rouben Mamoulian,
      screenplay by H.M. Harwood and Salka Viertel,
      produced by Walter Wanger. Burbank, California,
      Warner Home Video, 2005.   214

Acknowledgments

This book has been a long time in the making, punctuated as it was with all kinds of interruptions, both happy and not. Throughout it all, I have been fortunate to have had generous interlocutors—family, friends, colleagues, and students—who provided conversation, laughter, support, and sustenance of all kinds: Gro Aarnes, Penny Armstrong, Inés Arribas, Teresa Caballero, Nancy Dersofi, Alice Donahue, Rob Gregg, the Hall family—Anna Maria, Carter Jr., Carter III, and (especially) Patricia; Augusto Jiménez, Kate Heston, Alani Hicks-Bartlett, Rhonda Hughes, Sharon James, Nadia Kale, Eyda Merédiz, Carlos Ortiz, my artist sister Clemencia Quintero and my talented nephew Daniel; my always-supportive parents, Maria Santos and Manuel Quintero, and the rest of the Quintero clan: Manny, Debbie, Amanda, and Melissa; Roberta Ricci, Enrique Sacerio-Garí, Azade Seyhan, Ingrid Sidirov, and Rosi Song; the amazing Wedgwood women—Barbara, Helen, Katherine, and Sarah; Peter Wedgwood, H. Roland Wedgwood, and Nick Young. David Cast and Gridley McKim Smith have been generous colleagues, always ready to share bibliography and their vast knowledge of early modern art. Gridley has provided vital help at various points in the development of the manuscript. Special thanks must go to Madhavi Kale for years of stimulating conversation and long walks. I owe a particular debt to Oliva Cardona for providing practical, technical, and moral support to all my teaching and research endeavors. For over three decades, Anne J. Cruz has provided friendship and inspiration, and I am very pleased to be part of her new series at Ashgate.

I am grateful to the Provost's Office at Bryn Mawr College—especially Provost Kim Cassidy and Assistant Provost Beth Shepard-Rabadam—for their academic and financial support. The library and technical staff at Canaday Library have responded promptly to my many requests for information and technical assistance during the preparation of the manuscript. John O'Neal of the Hispanic Society of New York was helpful in tracking down a document at a crucial moment in my research. I take this opportunity to also thank the anonymous readers of the manuscript: their suggestions and bibliography have made this book stronger. The students in my graduate seminars at the University of Maryland and the University of Pennsylvania allowed me, with their insightful comments and questions, to refine some of the ideas in the book. I also want to express my gratitude to Erika Gaffney and Kathy Bond Borie at Ashgate Publishing for their help during the editing process.

Shorter versions of Chapters 3 and 4 and a small section of Chapter 1 have appeared previously: "'The Body of a Weak and Feeble Woman': Courting Elizabeth in Antonio Coello's *El conde de Sex*," *Material and Symbolic Circulation between Spain and England, 1554–1604*, ed. Anne J. Cruz (Aldershot, UK: Ashgate, 2008), 71–87; "Gender, Tyranny, and the Performance of Power in

Calderón's *La hija del aire*," *Bulletin of the comediantes* 53.1 (2001): 155–78; and "English Queens and the Body Politic in Calderón's *La cisma de Inglaterra* and Rivadeneira's *Historia Eclesiástica del Scisma del Reino de Inglaterra*," *MLN* 113 (1998): 259–82. I am grateful to the editors for permission to reprint this material.

My wonderful sons, Diego and Cristián, have regaled me over the years with their wry sense of humor, eclectic music, and preternatural wisdom. This book is dedicated to my husband, Roland Wedgwood: excellent musician and chef, perceptive reader and critic, and splendid travel and life companion: *cuanto tengo confieso yo deberos.*

Introduction

The drama of early modern Spain offers the modern reader a memorable if ambivalent performance of power. In the last decades, the facile one-sided view of the *comedia* as nothing more than a monolithic and systematic propaganda machine—a view held for a long time by literary critics and historians alike—has been decidedly put to rest.[1] This corrective approach, however, cannot entirely negate the fact that the purpose of much of this drama—particularly the plays written for the palace theaters of the Habsburg court—was to celebrate monarchical authority and further encode certain societal assumptions about the proper roles of men and women within that power structure. What makes the *comedia* so remarkable is that the dynamics of power and gender reproduced in these plays are infinitely complex, especially when we consider that at this time the monarchy—then universally accepted as the most natural and valid type of government—was consistently perceived to be in crisis. Playwrights such as Lope de Vega, Tirso de Molina, Pedro Calderón de la Barca, and Francisco Bances Candamo found themselves writing and producing plays at a time of considerable social upheaval, particularly in the second half of the seventeenth century.[2] Their drama responded to a generalized perception of decline and the need to maintain and even rescue a system of symbols of monarchical authority through performance and public spectacle. At the same time, the *comedia* also became a chronicle of societal anxieties or tensions and a tentative vehicle for critique. The seventeenth-century Spanish stage was a fluid and dynamic space (even an unstable one) where the immediate affirmation of a certain ideology often went hand in hand with the questioning and even the contestation of the status quo.

---

[1] Perhaps the most important book in this regard is Melveena McKendrick's *Playing the King: Lope de Vega and the Limits of Conformity* (London: Tamesis, 2001). McKendrick's detailed and insightful analysis of what she calls the "relentless demystification of monarchy" found in Lope's plays has inspired my own thinking about the topic in Calderón and other playwrights. Although the British critic does not deal specifically with queens in Lope, it seemed superfluous for me to incorporate his plays in this study.

[2] The bibliography on the state of the monarchy in Spain during the seventeenth century is vast. Among the most useful books, see Henry Kamen, *Spain in the Later Seventeenth Century, 1665–1700* (London: Longman, 1980); R.A. Stradling's *Philip IV and the Government of Spain 1621–1665* (Cambridge: Cambridge UP, 1988); and J.H. Elliott's *The Count Duke of Olivares: the Statesman in an Age of Decline* (New Haven: Yale UP, 1986). While many of these studies, as the title of Elliott's book indicates, tended to emphasize the decline of Spain, especially during the reign of Charles II, recent books such as Christopher Storrs's *The Resilience of the Spanish Monarchy 1665–1700* (Oxford: Oxford UP, 2006) provide a more nuanced account of the state of affairs in Spain during the second half of the seventeenth century.

This study will concern itself with the works by playwrights—prominently Pedro Calderón de la Barca—who directly deal with the ambivalent discourse of dominance and rulership and how it relates to gender, specifically through the representation of imagined gynocracies, or the reign of women. In the Baroque *comedia*'s multivalent performance of power, the compulsive representation of kingship goes hand in hand with an obsession with the representation of women (and women's bodies), rendering the question of royal subjectivity as it related to the monarch's body on stage inseparable from issues surrounding masculinity and femininity. Indeed, it would not be an exaggeration to state that the construction of monarchy in many seventeenth-century plays is in fact gendered. The *comedia*'s preoccupation with kings and monarchy in general has long been recognized and studied by prominent critics such as Dian Fox, Melveena McKendrick, Robert ter Horst, and recently by Alban Forcione, among others;[3] but it can be argued that not enough attention has been paid to the genre's obsession with women who assume and wield political authority. This may seem a surprising claim, given that the representation of gender and women in early modern Spanish drama has been an insistent concern of literary critics and historians.[4] After all, Melveena McKendrick's indispensable and seminal *Woman and Society in the Spanish Drama of the Golden Age* appeared well over 30 years ago, providing an exhaustive study of strong female characters, including different types of female leaders that appear on the early modern stage.[5] While deeply indebted to McKendrick and other scholars, I am interested in extending the study of these powerful feminine figures and interrogating the claim that dramatists in the seventeenth century never really question a woman's ability to lead. McKendrick, for example, has stated that "… as one reads more and more of these plays it becomes apparent that the problem of female government was not one with which most seventeenth-century dramatists were particularly concerned" (*Women and Society* 188).

---

[3] See Dian Fox, *Kings in Calderón: A Study in Characterization and Political Theory* (London: Tamesis 1986); Melveena McKendrick, *Playing the King*; Robert ter Horst, *Calderon: The Secular Plays* (Lexington: UP of Kentucky, 1982); Alban Forcione, *Majesty and Humanity: Kings and Their Doubles in the Political Drama of the Spanish Golden Age* (New Haven: Yale UP, 2009). Other recent books on the monarchy are Jodi Campbell's *Monarchy, Political Culture, and Drama in Seventeenth-Century Madrid: Theater of Negotiation* (Aldershot, UK: Ashgate, 2006) and Anita Howard's *The King Within: Reformations of Power in Shakespeare and Calderón* (Bern: Peter Lang, 2010).

[4] In addition to Melveena McKendrick's *Women and Society in the Spanish Drama of the Golden Age: a Study of the* mujer varonil (Cambridge: Cambridge UP, 1974), the extensive bibliography on gender and the *comedia* includes books, articles, and anthologies by Ruth El Saffar, Anne J. Cruz, Anita Stoll, Teresa Soufas, Georgina Dopico Black, and Laura Bass, among many others. I will allude to specific studies in the course of my analysis.

[5] See especially chapter 6 of *Women and Society*, "The Amazon, the Leader, the Warrior," where, despite her caveats, McKendrick analyzes plays such as Lope de Vega's *La reina de Nápoles* that engage directly with what she terms "the variety of dilemmas latent in female rule" (197).

The British scholar also tells us that the presentation of negative examples of queenly behavior was a way of deflecting attention from criticism of the current monarchy, and that often the fascination with individual and sexual identity "elbows out any concern with the very concept of female leadership" (187). In my view, however, the portrayal of queens and the feminization of defective rulership in Calderón and other playwrights reflect a real ideological ambivalence toward female agency in general and feminine rule in particular. In the face of a political and historical reality where women had often assumed the throne in multiple principalities throughout Europe, there was still serious anxiety surrounding female sovereignty. The plays examined here are indicative of a particular society's attitudes toward women in general and women as political players, specifically; and there are questions raised by the staging within the *comedia* of extraordinary women wielding power that remain to be addressed. I would also claim that it is difficult in these plays to separate individual and sexual identity from political concerns; and the fascination with sexual identity does not preclude deeply felt concerns over the rule of women. In a recent article, Elizabeth Lehfeldt has suggested that the experience and critique of their country's decline led Spaniards to "craft a distinct discourse of masculinity in the seventeenth century" ("Ideal Men" 463). The presentation of feminized kings and women as bodies of authority in so many *comedias* was one public manifestation of this anxiety over gender dissonance and its relationship to political ideology.

Female monarchs and women in positions of leadership are everywhere in the *comedia*: from the eponymous character in Lope de Vega's *La reina Juana de Nápoles* [Queen Juana of Naples] to Semíramis in Calderón's *La hija del aire* [*The Daughter of Air*] to Tirso de Molina's María de Molina in *La prudencia en la mujer* [*Prudence in Woman*] to Francisco Bances Candamo's Princess Iberia, the allegorical personification of Spain in *La piedra filosofal* [*The Philosopher's Stone*]. It seems contradictory that we would find such an insistent fascination with the figure of a female leader at a time when there were resolute attempts to circumscribe women's behavior in conduct books, from the pulpit, and through social regulation. There is an intrinsic paradox in this repeated performance of powerful women since, after all, the female body was considered—almost by definition—to be a subjected and submissive body, one that needed to be kept away from societal gaze as much as possible. Where sermons and treatises were concerned with providing acceptable models of femininity, the *comedia* proffered a different type of exemplarity.

We know that Spanish dramatists—especially those working within the court—often took advantage of the conditions of performance in the palace theater to present what we can call an aesthetics of monarchy that belied a political/didactic intentionality. Exemplarity was one of the expected ingredients of this drama, with many of the plays providing models of princely behavior taken from history, legend, and popular traditions. Critics such as Fox and Stephen Rupp, among others, have suggested that the plays of Calderón de la Barca, for example, should be studied within the tradition of *de regimine principum*.[6] This term, which originates with a treatise by Thomas Aquinas, referred primarily to critical and theoretical works whose stated purpose was to provide counsel and guidance to a prince. Although it was not initially applied to drama, the term can be extended to the *comedia*; and in fact, plays whose purpose was to provide lessons in kingship enjoyed a long, distinguished tradition. Aristotle, for one, had suggested that tragedy could serve as a school for princes and specifically, as a corrective for the abuses by tyrants. Despite the significant chronological distance between Attic tragedy and the *comedia*, the two genres shared the recognition that drama provided a most propitious opportunity for imparting lessons on rulership. According to R.A. Stradling, "the production of an *ideal* Christian prince was a *raison d'écrire*" (*Philip IV* 13) during the sixteenth and seventeenth centuries in Spain. At a time when the centrality of a *male* prince is not in question, it is curious that so many of these plays engage with the figure of a woman in a position of authority, often juxtaposed with a feminized male monarch. The Horatian ideal of *prodessere et delectare*, or "enseñar deleitando [to teach while entertaining]," and the construction of an ideal prince assumed a problematic dimension when the political lessons of the plays were directly or indirectly embodied by feminine figures.

The exemplarity that was at the heart of these plays was always potentially dangerous and destabilizing, for it put the structures of power literally into play, often transforming them and presenting fictional alternatives on stage. The danger in this performance was recognized by the *tratadistas* at the time, as José Pellicer del Tovar, for example, demonstrates:

> Hay sucesos en las historias y casos en la invención incapaces de la publicidad del teatro, como son tiranías, sediciones de príncipes y vasallos, que no deben proponerse a los ojos de ningún siglo, ni menos inventar ejemplos de poderosos libres que fiados en la majestad se atreven absolutos a las violencias y a los insultos, violando su gravedad a vueltas de sus torpezas.
> [There are events in history and cases in fiction that should not be shown openly in the theater; for example, tyrannies, sedition on the part of rulers or their vassals. These should not be placed before the eyes in any era; and even less should there be fictionalized examples of powerful men who, confident in their absolute majesty, dare to engage in violence and insults, violating their own gravity with their loutish behavior.] (Qtd. in Sánchez Escribano and Porqueras Mayo 37)[7]

---

[6] See the introduction to Fox's *Kings in Calderón*. Also, Stephen Rupp's *Allegories of Kingship: Calderón and the Anti-Machiavellian Tradition* (Philadelphia: U of Pennsylvania P, 1996) studies with more specificity the impact of anti-Machiavellian treatises such as Diego de Saavedra Fajardo's *Idea de un príncipe político* on Calderón's drama.

[7] The translations from English to Spanish in this book are mine, unless otherwise noted.

Of course, the taboo subjects that Pellicer lists are precisely the topics repeatedly represented in the *comedia*. The fictional monarchies on stage embody and affirm a certain ideology of power and what an ideal monarchy might look like, but at the same time the theater offers a long list of tyrannical and loutish monarchs who inspire sedition. Often, and this is the subject of the present study, these disturbing manifestations of power are directly related to questions of gender, masculinity, and femininity. While it is perhaps impossible to fully gauge the intentionality of the playwright or the actual impact on his audience, we can safely conjecture that these dramatic versions of monarchy implicitly invited a comparison with the contemporary monarchical structure. Several critics—prominently N.D. Shergold, John Varey, John Elliott, Jonathan Brown, and Margaret Greer—have commented on how the conditions of representation and performance in the court provide important insights on the complicated "play of power" (to use Greer's term). Describing the seating arrangements at the palace theater, these critics tell us that the king was seated in the most privileged position, one that provided the optimal perspective for viewing the plays. His courtiers sat along the sides of the room with their eyes fixed on the monarchs as much as on the play; and, in many respects, the king and queen were part of the spectacle.[8] It was no coincidence that the king's throne was called a "theatro," reminding us of the etymological meaning of the word as "the place to see." Greer has stated that "in the specific context of a court representation, [the experience of the spectators] is directly influenced by the conspicuous presence of the ruling figures, which, given the appropriate cues in the drama, would encourage a political interpretation as one possible world construct suggested by the action on stage" (*Play of Power* 102–3).

Because the *comedia* repeatedly presented monarchs—both male and female—as central characters in the dramatic plots, the result of these conditions of spectatorship was a complicated and gendered doubling of performances of kingship. Current theories of performance and performativity, which have been recently applied to early modern texts, may provide a new vocabulary for approaching the dynamics of the *comedia* and help us gain valuable insights into the fictional doubling of the body of the monarch on stage. In the work of critics such as Elin Diamond and Josette Féral, "theater" and "performance" appear not as synonyms but rather as almost opposites. According to Féral, *theater*, as commonly understood, displays an "obeisance" to structures and conventions, and also highlights and promotes a playwright's authority. *Performance*, on the other hand, dismantles textual authority and illusionism. Invoking concepts taken from psychoanalysis, particularly Jacques Lacan, Féral states that theater inscribes the subject in the law and in preestablished theatrical codes—in other words, in the symbolic associated with masculine preeminence; whereas performance

---

[8] See Jonathan Brown and John Elliott's *A Palace for a King: The Buen Retiro and the Court of Felipe IV* (New Haven: Yale UP, 1980), 46, and Margaret Greer's *The Play of Power: Mythological Court Dramas of Calderón de la Barca* (Princeton: Princeton UP, 1991), 83.

"highlights the realities of the imaginary" and allows flows of desire—often associated with the feminine—to speak ("Performance" 178).

While for some other critics this opposition may seem extreme,[9] most theorists of performance theory, such as Barbara Freedman, agree that performance can become "that within theater which deconstructs it" ("Frame-Up" 71). Freedman adds that "theater provides the tools—the stages, the mirrors, or reflecting gazes—through which perspectives are fragmented, shattered, and set into play against one another" (74). We could apply this opposition between the apparent rigidity of theatrical "law" and the fluidity of performance to those *comedias* that deal specifically with the question of monarchy, particularly those presented at the palace before the actual monarchs. I am referring not only to the *comedias de palacio*, such as the mythological plays studied by Greer, but also to those plays that had their beginnings in the *corrales* and were later transposed to the palace at the request of members of the court. Court plays, we know, were often highly stylized and subject to strict codes and conventions, and their immediate purpose and message, as I have already suggested, were the promotion of the ideals and values of hereditary masculine monarchy. As such, theater assumed the characteristic of the "law," as described by Joseph Roach, for example: "As a cultural system dedicated to the production of certain kinds of behaviors and the regulation or proscription of others, law functions as a repository of social performances, past and present" (55). That is, theater, like the law, reproduces to a great extent the social behavior of performances based on tradition and actual practice. Nevertheless, in an actual staged performance, different meanings that may interrogate the dominant discourse are created through the interplay of gestures, costumes, actors, and the presence and participation of the audience. One example of how a performance might have put authority into play can be found in that most commonplace of *comedia* conventions: the betrothal or wedding at the end, a union (or unions) often engineered and blessed by a fictional monarch.[10] This obligatory denouement was meant to reestablish order and reincorporate the characters (especially women, many of whom had been temporarily truant) into the law and ideals of the symbolic. Often, however, these conjugal pairings were deeply troubling.

---

[9] Indeed, Feral herself has attenuated her views as shown, for example in the foreword to a special issue of *SubStance*, where she states, "any spectacle ... is an interplay of both performativity and theatricality" (5). See *SubStance* 31.2/3, Special Issue on Theatricality (2002): 3–16. Féral's earlier views can be found in "Performance and Theatricality: The Subject Demystified," *Modern Drama* 25 (1982): 170–81.

[10] For a provocative discussion of the marriage convention in the *comedia* and its relation to the law, see María Mercedes Carrión's *Subject Stages: Marriage, Theater, and the Law in Early Modern Spain* (Toronto: U of Toronto P, 2010). See also Catherine Connor's "Marriage and Subversion in *Comedia* Endings: Problems in Art and Society," in *Gender, Identity, and Representation in Spain's Golden Age*, eds Anita Stoll and Dawn L. Smith (Lewisburg: Bucknell UP, 2000), 23–46.

A case in point is Calderón's famous *El médico de su honra* [*The Physician of His Honour*], which ends with the hasty betrothal of Gutierre and Leonor mandated by King Pedro I. This union, within the context of the plot, is Pedro's attempt to restore some measure of order, and it also simultaneously complies with the "law" of the theater that prescribes resolution. This restoration, however, requires that the king condone the chilling murder of an innocent woman, Mencia, by her husband, Gutierre (whose obsession with honor is in itself a manifestation of a pathological crisis of masculinity). Mencia's death, as Fox, Ruth El Saffar, and Georgina Dopico Black have suggested, is meant to remove the threat of the feminine imaginary (desire and the threat of adultery) from Gutierre's household and from the kingdom (treason and fratricide/regicide).[11] The performance of the play—which included not only the horrifying final display of Mencia's body drained of blood but also repeated enactments of the king's lack of discretion and wisdom—would have graphically dismantled any semblance of order suggested by the play's technically conventional ending. Thus, the conventions of the *comedia* (in this case, the proverbial happy nuptials at the end) and the belief in the monarch as the ultimate source of justice are ironically deconstructed in the performance of the play. In other even more overtly political plays staged at the palace, the very presence of the king in the audience would have at least partially destroyed the illusionism surrounding the fictional monarch within the theatrical space. As McKendrick suggests: "every such play the king saw must, as he sat watching, have stirred in his mind some sort of dialectic between his own situation and the events he was witnessing on stage … self-consciousness and identification were unavoidable" (*Playing the King* 31). How much more complex this interaction must have been when the monarchy enacted on stage was embodied by a woman. We can only guess as to what a performance of feminized power (either as a fictional queen on stage or as an effeminate king) might have meant to an audience watching the actual king watching the action.

An important characteristic of performance in general, according to contemporary critics, is that it always represents repeated or restored behavior. As such, performances are also about the dialectics of presence and absence and of past and present (Franko and Richards 2). The *comedia*'s repeated staging of fictional monarchies suggests layers and degrees of absence. For one thing, the intrinsic nature of any performance is that of a temporal and temporary event— experienced at a specific place with a limited duration—in the process of continual disappearance. Once the performance is over, there is no indelible, complete record of the elements that made it unique from other similar events. Working with a genre that flourished almost 400 years ago, it is difficult to fully reconstruct what

---

[11] See Dian Fox's "*El médico de su honra*: Political Considerations," *Hispania* 65.1 (1982): 28–38; Ruth El Saffar's "Anxiety of Identity: Gutierre's Case in *El médico de su honra*," in *Studies in Honor of Bruce W. Wardropper*, eds Dian Fox, Harry Sieber, and Robert ter Horst (Newark, DE: Juan de la Cuesta, 1989), 105–24; and chapter 3 of Georgina Dopico Black's *Perfect Wives, Other Women: Adultery and Inquisition in Early Modern Spain* (Durham: Duke UP, 2001), 109–64.

the performance of any of these plays was truly like, despite the excellent work by critics such as N.D. Shergold, J.E. Varey, John Allen, and José María Ruano de la Haza, among others.[12] We have information about the configuration of the theaters and descriptions of the staging, scenery, costumes, and even the seating arrangement for particular plays; but we can only conjecture about other aspects of the performance. We are missing much of the non-verbal dimension of the plays and even some of the verbal aspects: the use of movement, the gestures—all of which would have conveyed meaning independently of language—plus the timbre and inflections of the actors' voices. According to Mark Franko and Annette Richards, "performances of the distant past raise with particular urgency the issue of absence" (1), and, certainly, the effect of the performance and the relationship between performers and the audience is forever lost to us. We can never know, for example, how the audience would have experienced the figure of the king as a character on the stage and the actual monarch sitting on that second stage that was his throne. In Guillén de Castro's *El curioso impertinente* [*Impertinent Curiosity*], one of the characters exclaims about another:

> Hace [el actor] un rey con tal afeto,
> Que me parece de España,
> De suerte que a mí me engaña
> Y obliga a tener respeto.
> [(The actor) plays the part of the king with such success that he seems to be the king of Spain, so much so that he deceives me and forces me to show him respect.] (Qtd. in Fox, *Kings* 6)

There is no indication that most or any of the members of the *comedia* audience were as willing as this character to suspend their disbelief and to get so caught up in the action that the fictional king would be confused with the real one.[13] Nevertheless, the performance of kingship must have impacted viewers in positive

---

[12] The volumes in the series *Fuentes para la Historia del Teatro en España*, published by Tamesis Books and prepared by N.D. Shergold, J.E. Varey, and, more recently, Margaret Greer, are indispensable for the study of the theater of early modern Spain. See also John Allen, *The Reconstruction of a Spanish Golden-Age Playhouse: El Corral del Príncipe 1583–1744* (Gainsville: UP of Florida, 1983); and José María Ruano de la Haza and John Allen, *Los teatros comerciales del siglo XVII y la escenificación de la comedia* (Madrid: Editorial Castalia, 1994). The database prepared by Teresa Ferrer Valls, *Diccionario biográfico de actores del teatro clásico español* (DICAT) (Kassel: Reichenberger, 2008), is a recent and essential resource for information on the staging of seventeenth-century plays.

[13] This is not to say that there weren't plays that overtly or indirectly established correspondence between a fictional character and the actual king. This seems to have been particularly the case with the mythological court plays, as studied by Margaret Greer in the introduction to her edition of Calderón's *La estatua de Prometeo* (Kassel: Edition Reichenberger, 1986) and more fully in *Play of Power*. Indeed, as Greer has suggested: "Even in plays not written with a specifically political intent, audiences of the period were known to construct political readings in suggestive circumstances" (*Play of Power* 104).

and negative ways, particularly within the theatrical spaces at the royal palaces; and it is fruitful to speculate what this impact might have been when the monarch on stage was a woman.

Beyond the absence implied by our inability to fully understand what an audience might have seen or felt in an actual performance, another absence is suggested in these performances. Joseph Roach tells us that performance stands in—becomes a surrogate—for an elusive entity that it is not, but that it must vainly aspire both to embody and replace (xi). I would argue that one important absence implied in the *comedia*'s performance of kingship during Calderón's time would have been the absence of a strong monarchy and a concomitant crisis of masculinity. In the *comedia*'s obsessive repetition of the same motifs surrounding the idea of the monarchy, there was an implicit attempt to construct an ideal monarchical identity or subjectivity. Reading plays such as *La gran Cenobia* [*The Great Zenobia*], *La cisma de Inglaterra* [*The Schism in England*], *La hija del aire* [*The Daughter of Air*], *Afectos de Odio y Amor* [*The Emotions of Hate and Love*], and many others, one is struck by the reiterability of the same dramatic situations; the same characters and plot twists turn up again and again. The lack of "originality" is not coincidental but rather part of the overall effect, as the plays "aspire to embody and replace" (to use Roach's words), through sheer repetition, certain monarchical values and virtues that were absent or had been perhaps forgotten. We know from contemporary accounts, for example, that there were serious reservations about Philip IV as an effective king—not only when he was a callow young man given to the pleasures of the *corrales* and women of easy virtue, but also later, when he came under the influence of his *privado*, the formidable Count Duke of Olivares. The situation of the monarchy became particularly precarious after Philip died and his second wife, Mariana of Austria, assumed the regency during the minority of their only surviving son, the future Charles II. Given Charles's physical illnesses (and possible mental disabilities) and the suspicion directed at his mother and her circle before and after he assumed the throne, the concerns over the lack of a strong ruler became singularly intense in the last half of the seventeenth century.[14]

According to Carmen Sanz Ayán in *Pedagogía de Reyes: El teatro palaciego en el reinado de Carlos II*, theater acquired a specifically pedagogical dimension during the second half of the seventeenth century:

> En la Monarquía Hispánica durante la segunda mitad del siglo XVII, este fenómeno cultural y festivo de exaltación del poder real que fue la fiesta teatral palaciega presentó un componente añadido. Dadas las limitaciones físicas e intelectuales que desde el comienzo de su existencia demostró Carlos II,

---

[14] The negative assessment of Charles II's monarchy has been subject to recent revisions by historians, including Christopher Storrs in the previously cited book *The Resilience of the Spanish Monarchy 1665–1700* and Luis Ribot García in *Carlos II: el rey y su entorno cortesano* (Madrid: Centro de Estudios Europa Hispánica, 2009). These avoid the often-repeated portrayal of Charles as a mentally deficient and completely incapable ruler.

comenzó a contemplarse la posibilidad explícita de que el teatro representado en Palacio cumpliera una función pedagógica en la formación del Rey.
[In the Spanish monarchy during the second half of the seventeenth century, the cultural and festive phenomenon of exalting royal power that characterized theatrical celebrations in the palace gained an added component. Given the physical and intellectual deficiencies that Charles II had displayed since the beginning of his life, the possibility that palace theater could acquire a pedagogical function in the formation of the king began to be contemplated.] (21)

Indeed, Charles—the product of generations of inbreeding among the Habsburgs—seemed like the embodiment of the crisis of masculinity and monarchy that so many *arbitristas* warned about.[15] The *comedia*, with the reiterability of dramatic situations—again, an intrinsic characteristic of performance—would have offered the opportunity to provide idealized alternatives and proffer warnings about the precarious nature of the monarchy and the absence of certain values. That these dramatic situations involved the performance of feminine power within an environment as fraught as that of the Habsburg Court is a central concern of this study.

Through the analysis of the themes, imagery, and language of a number of Baroque *comedias*, it becomes clear that the construction, mythification, and mystification of monarchical power was a complex process inseparable from considerations of gender. Specifically, women's bodies are deployed in the service of bolstering absolutist power, and at the same time they are used—overtly or implicitly—to call the structures of power and gender categories to account.

---

[15] A major concern surrounding Charles II's visible frailty was that he was impotent and therefore unable to engender an heir to the throne. The obsession with the topic of succession would appear in the *comedia* with increasing frequency during his reign. We will return to this topic in subsequent chapters.

Chapter 1
Women and Drama in Early Modern Spain

Performing Gender in the *Comedia*

A remarkable feature of the *comedia* of the Golden Age is that the behavior of feminine characters is consistently at variance with the ideals of containment, silence, and chastity promoted for women in conduct books such as Juan Luis Vives's 1524 *Instrucción de la mujer cristiana* [*The Education of a Christian Woman*], Antonio de Guevara's 1529 *Relox de príncipes* [*The Dial of Princes*], Luis de Leon's 1584 *La perfecta casada* [*The Perfect Wife*], and countless other treatises. In fact, the most compelling feminine characters in the *comedia* are transgressors who are invariably negotiating their identity in an endless game of disguises, inversions of gender roles, and the undermining of societal expectations. In many plays it is, paradoxically, the loss of honor (through seduction or rape) that instigates agency in the female protagonists, forcing them to leave their homes, explore different identities (famously by disguising themselves as men), and acquire speaking and writing voices in order to seek redress for their lost reputations.[1] Thus, in spite of the sharply contained theatrical space and fundamentally conventional and conservative nature of these plays, there is always possibility for mobility and contestation, if not actual subversion.[2] In these plays, suppositions about the proper

---

[1] The bibliography on cross-dressing women and gender fluidity in early modern drama is extensive, starting with Melveena McKendrick's *Women and Society in the Spanish Drama of the Golden Age. A Study of the* mujer varonil (Cambridge: Cambridge UP, 1974), and her *Identities in Crisis: Essays on Honor, Gender and Women in the Comedia* (Kassel: Reichenberger, 2002). See also the two anthologies edited by Anita K. Stoll and Dawn L. Smith, *The Perception of Women in Golden Drama* (Lewisburg, PA: Bucknell UP, 1996) and *Gender, Identity, and Representation in Spain's Golden Age* (Lewisburg, PA: Bucknell UP, 2000); and Javier Aparicio Maydeu's "The Sinful Scene: Transgression in Seventeenth-Century Spanish Drama (1625–1685)," in *Bodies and Biases: Sexualities in Hispanic Cultures and Literature*, ed. David William Foster and Roberto Reis (Minneapolis: U of Minnesota P, 1996), 24–36. On the topic outside Spain, see Marjorie Garber's *Vested Interests: Cross-Dressing and Cultural Anxiety* (New York: Routledge, 1992). For a theoretical discussion of gender fluidity, see Judith Butler's *Bodies That Matter: On the Discursive Limits of Sex* (New York: Routledge, 1993); *Gender Trouble: Feminism and the Subversion of Identity* (New York: Routledge, 1990); and "Performative Acts and Gender Constitution: An Essay in Phenomenology and Feminist Theory," *Theater Journal* 40.4 (1988): 519–31.

[2] The term "subversion" has perhaps been used too carelessly in discussions of women in early modern Spain, as Helen Nader convincingly argues in the introduction to *Power and Gender in Renaissance Spain: Eight Women of the Mendoza Family, 1450–1650* (Urbana: U of Illinois P, 2004).

roles for men and women are repeatedly negotiated, and this negotiation frequently goes hand in hand with negotiations of political power.

The *comedia* became a particularly potent site for performing gender, especially when we take into account the ideology of enclosure that governed early modern society's attitudes toward women. It must be emphasized that I am referring here to the *ideology* of enclosure and silence, not to the historical reality of women's lives. Literary scholars and historians in the past decades have done much to correct the idea that women in Spain were uniformly oppressed, contained, and restrained within the home and convent during the sixteenth and seventeenth centuries. Through the work of Elizabeth Perry, Helen Nader, Anne J. Cruz, and Theresa Earenfight, among others, we know that the lives of early modern women in the Iberian Peninsula were much more complex and productive than was previously recognized.[3] There was, then, a conflict between the "official" move to limit a woman's range of activities, as manifested in conduct books and in the general misogynist stance taken by most male writers on the one hand, and the often-silenced history of what women really accomplished on the other. It is likely, in fact, that the strident rhetoric against the public role of women was a defensive response to the increasingly visible activity on the part of women.

When studying the *comedia* and indeed any other Golden Age genre, we have to keep in mind this paradoxical situation with regard to real women and their literary/symbolic portrayal. We have to confront, first of all, the dominant narrative that attempted to systematically relegate women to the domestic, private sphere, making them silent and invisible. Thus we find in Juan Vives an exaggerated, even paranoid, belief that a woman endangered her honor every single time she stepped out of her house into the public sphere: "cada vez que la doncella sale de casa pone en el peso de las lenguas a su hermosura, y su crianza, su saber y bondad, comoquiera que no hay cosa hoy en el mundo tan tierna ni tan delicada ni tan frágil como es la honra y reputación de la mujer, en tanto grado que parece estar colgado de un cabello [each time that the maiden leaves her home she puts her beauty, her upbringing, her knowledge, and her goodness at the mercy of wagging tongues since there is nothing in the world more tender or delicate or fragile as a woman's honor and reputation, to the point that they seem to be hanging by a hair]" (137). The world outside the walls of the convent or the family dwelling is conceived as a constant threat, presenting nothing but terrors lurking and waiting to pounce on the helpless and hapless maiden:

> Mas antes que saque el pie de casa, apercíbase en su corazón como que sale a la batalla del mundo. ¿Piense qué es lo que verá? ¿Qué oirá? ¿Qué dirá? Considere que a cada paso, como detrás cantón, le saldrán cosas que le harán traspié, por hacerla estropezar.

---

[3] See Mary Elizabeth Perry's *Gender and Disorder in Early Modern Seville* (Princeton: Princeton UP, 1990); Nader's collection of edited essays, *Power and Gender*; the anthology edited by Anne J. Cruz and Mihoko Suzuki, *The Rule of Women in Early Modern Europe* (Chicago: U of Illinois P, 2009); and Earenfight's collection *Queenship and Political Power in Medieval and Early Modern Spain* (Aldershot, UK: Ashgate, 2005).

[Before she sets foot outside the house, let her understand in her heart that she is about to enter battle in the world. Let her think about what she will see, what she will hear, and what she will say. Let her consider that with each step, behind every corner, things will be there to trip her up and make her fall.] (138)

In the very public space of the *comedia*, however, strong and active female characters, embodied by "real" flesh-and-blood actresses, were prominently featured both in the popular *corrales* and in the more rarefied setting of the *palacio*. As Teresa Soufas points out in her pioneering study of women playwrights: "[t]he drama as a visual and verbal representation makes particularly complex the presence of women on stage who are not silent or enclosed" (*Dramas of Distinction* 21). The presence of the actresses on stage would be, in fact, the converse of a presumed feminine absence in the public sphere; and while it is true that the display of women opened them up to an erotized surveillance, the ostentatious display of the feminine body also had the potential to contest the sexist attitudes and conventions of this society. Furthermore, seventeenth-century plays offer daring versions of feminine behavior in characters that take charge (if only temporarily) of their own destiny, and fill the stage with a performance of agency and with the protean flexibility of roles and identities. Not surprisingly, this agency was considered pernicious; and critics of the theater in the seventeenth century repeatedly railed against the presence of women both on the stage and in the audience.[4] The numerous treatises criticizing the theater were singularly concerned with the dangers of the female body on stage and its negative effect on the audience, both male and female.

We find in these documents a remarkable emphasis on the actual dynamics of performance—a concern with the bodies moving, acting, and gesturing on the stage. Juan Bautista Fragoso, among others, highlights the perils of the kinetic female body in performance itself:

En las comedias escritas en nuestra vulgar se mezclan muchas cosas impúdicas y obscenas, porque se introducen mujeres de no mucha edad á danzar y cantar, las cuales con su garbo y movimiento y con la desenvoltura de su semblante introducen en los que las ven y oyen el amor torpe.
[In the plays written in our vernacular many shameful and obscene things are mixed together, for they present very young women dancing and singing and they, through their lively movements and the shamelessness of their gestures, introduce impure love in all who see and hear them.] (*Bibliografía* Cotarelo y Mori 320)

---

[4] See the introduction to Soufas's *Dramas of Distinction: a Study of Plays by Golden Age Women* (Lexington: UP of Kentucky, 1997). Basing herself on Cotarelo y Mori's indispensable history and anthology of anti-theatrical treatises, *Bibliografía de las controversias sobre la licitud del teatro en España* (Madrid: Rev. de archivos, 1904), Soufas provides a good summary of the negative attitudes toward women in the theater, both as actresses and members of the audience. My study inevitably draws on many of the same sources.

Emphasis is placed on the appearance ("desenvoltura de su semblante") and movement ("danzar," "cantar," "movimiento"), and the ability of their performance to inspire unsanctioned feelings and behavior in an audience. Pedro de Rivadeneira echoes this sentiment regarding actresses in a treatise entitled *Tratado de la tribulación* [*Treatise on tribulations*]: "enterviniendo en las representaciones palabras lascivas, hechos torpes, meneos y gestos provocativos á deshonestidad, de hombres infames y mujercillas perdidas, y habiendo exceso y demasía en las comedias que cada día se representan, son ilícitas y perjudiciales ... [lascivious words, coarse acts, provocative undulations, and gestures to the point of obscenity are introduced in the performances by villainous men and lost women; and because these *comedias* that we see every day are characterized by excess and extremes, they are illicit and harmful]" (Cotarelo y Mori 523). Again, in the treatises of the time the concern was with enclosing women and keeping them behind walls (those of the family home, the convent, and even the brothel), as far away from public view as possible. In the spirited performances of the *comedia*, an audience made up of both men and women is confronted with not only a body which by its very nature should be kept from public view but one which is constantly moving, further defying the limits of any type of enclosure. The mobility purportedly forbidden to women by this "política del encierro [politics of enclosure]"[5] is thus circumvented.

Another serious concern for the critics of the theater was the danger of mimetic response. It was believed that women in the audience would be corrupted and enticed to replicate the lascivious behavior witnessed on the stage, as the following quote from José Saenz de Aguirre makes evident:

> A cada paso sucede que los que van al teatro honestos y continentes salen absolutamente trocados. ¡Cuántas doncellas y castas matronas que sostuvieron íntegra su virtud se ven allí arder en el amor impuro, del que antes no habían sufrido sensación alguna, y perdiendo insensiblemente el pudor y recato, llegan á corromperse! Pocos son, pues, si es que hay algunos, que á vista de aquellas expresiones amorosas, ademanes é invenciones no se sientan heridos de algún efecto impúdico.
> [It happens all the time that those who attend the theater as modest and contained folk leave it absolutely transformed. How many virgins and chaste matrons who had maintained their virtue intact find themselves there burning with impure love, of which they had never had inkling, and foolishly losing their modesty and reserve, they are corrupted! There are few, if any, who, within sight of those amorous expressions, gestures, and tricks, would not be hurt by some shameless effect.] (Cotarelo y Mori 49)

Saenz de Aguirre here emphasizes the transformative power of performance. These seventeenth-century theorists, interestingly, ignore the denouement of the typical Baroque play, where "order" or the "law" (as described by Joseph Roach,

---

[5] The term "política del encierro" is used by Francisco Vázquez García and A. Moreno Mengíbar in their *Sexo y razón: una genealogía de la moral sexual en España (siglos XVI–XX)* (Madrid: Ediciones Akal, 1997), 372.

for example) is reinstated with women conveniently reintegrated into society through marriage or betrothal. That is, they intuit the dangers of the performance itself despite the playwright's adherence to the laws and conventions of the theater, as discussed in the introduction. One would think these self-appointed guardians of morality might have taken some solace in the fact that whenever truly transgressive women are introduced as characters in a play such as Calderón's *La hija del aire* [*The Daughter of Air*], their punishment is inexorable and terrible, providing a semblance of restored order through the eradication of a disturbing female presence.

Thus, the preoccupation with the movements of actresses on the stage and the possibly destructive power of their performances, while ignoring the expected affirmation of the status quo at the end, underscores the opposition between theater and performance that some contemporary critics have established. While the overt "message" of this theater ultimately affirmed certain dominant values of the society, the individual performances in all their kinetic complexity—especially as they concerned the female body—presented a threat to those very values. Again, we return to Josette Féral's view that while *theater* seemingly inscribes the subject in societal laws and theatrical codes, *performance* allows the flow of desire to speak. The *comedia*, then, provided the space for a performance that had the potential for putting conventional gender attributes into "possibly disruptive play," as Judith Butler describes it (*Gender Trouble* 4). While a play such as Calderón's *La Cisma de Inglaterra* [*The Schism in England*], for example, contains a condemnation of the role that the historical Anne Boleyn played in Henry VIII's break with Rome, the seductive presence and actions of the actress who played her would have no doubt put into play those sensations of desire and transgression that Butler, Féral, and the seventeenth-century moralist Saenz de Aguirre describe.

Sixteenth- and seventeenth-century accounts of the *comedia* also suggest that the theatricality on the stage was matched by the theatricality of the audience. The *comedia* represented a unique opportunity for both the actresses and the women in the audience to perform their femininity and even their sexuality. The following quote from Juan de Pineda alludes to the extended theatricality inspired by the *comedia*: "las mugeres que dicen ir por ver las tales representaciones, más van por representarse á sí mesmas y ser vistas de los que allí se hallaren [The women who claim they go only to see the performances, actually go to represent themselves and to be seen by those gathered there]" (Cotarelo y Mori 506). It is interesting to note that the women in the audience often themselves adopted a type of disguise—capes and masks—when attending performances of the *comedia*. Soufas claims this was a way of assuming, somewhat anonymously, the role of observer and "thus remain a step beyond the male control that sought to monitor and enclose them" (*Dramas of Distinction* 27). The *comedia*, then, inspired women to violate the repeatedly promoted ideals of silence, enclosure, and chastity and allowed them to achieve a degree of visibility, to be both subjects and objects of the gaze. José de Barcia y Zambrana addresses fathers and specifically warns them against this visibility:

> ¿No *viste* á tu hija antes que *viese* comedia con una dichosa ignorancia que vivía como inocente paloma? ¿No la *viste* después, que *abriendo los ojos* á la malicia, supo lo que debiera ignorar? ya pide gala, ya desea salir, ya *quiere ver y ser vista* ... .
>
> [Did you not *see* your daughter before she *saw* a play, how she lived in blissful ignorance like an innocent dove? Did you not *see* her afterwards, when, by *opening her eyes* to malice, she learned what she should not have known? Now she requests adornments, now she wants to go out, now *she wants to see and to be seen* ... .] (Cotarelo y Mori 83, emphases added)

The question of seeing and being seen with regard to women acquired, according to Francisco Vázquez García and A. Moreno Mengíbar, an ontological dimension during the seventeenth century. Invoking the philosopher George Berkeley on the relationship between being and perception, the Spanish theorists state: "Si [George] Berkeley definió al Ser en función de la capacidad de percibir o de ser percibido (*percipere aut percipi*) habrá que afirmar que el *status* de la mujer durante los siglos XVI y XVII radicaba en un *No-Ser* cimentado por ese círculo de invisibilidad construido en torno a su cuerpo y su voluntad [If (George) Berkeley defined Being as a function of the capacity of perceiving and being perceived, then we would have to affirm that the status of women during the sixteenth and seventeenth centuries was based on a Non-Being solidified by the circle of invisibility that was erected around her body and her volition]" (375).

Participation in theatrical experience provides, then, a direct portal to a visibility that countered that "*No-Ser [Non-Being]*," and to a transgressive knowledge explicitly associated with sight.[6] According to feminist critics, masculinist societies often manifest a paranoia surrounding women who both possess and hold the look, and the reaction of these male authors to the *comedia* reveals at its most blatant the fear of this double peril. The plays literally engendered a crisis of sexuality, for not only did the *comedia* threaten the proper behavior of women, but the very idea of sexual difference and differentiation was at risk. Indeed, a common belief was that theater had the effect of feminizing the male viewers. According to Pedro de Rivadeneira, for example: "no solamente se estragan las costumbres y se arruinan las repúblicas ... con esta manera de representaciones; pero hácese la gente ociosa, regalada, afeminada y mujeril [Not only are customs corrupted and republics ruined by this manner of performances, but the people become idle, spoiled, effeminate,

---

[6] Vázquez and Mengibar also state that "El mayor peligro para una mujer y, en definitiva para todo el orden cósmico, era que pudiese 'Ver y Ser Vista,' que rompiese los muros del encierro simbólico y material en el que debía vivir y que pudiese disponer libremente de su persona, de su voluntad y de su cuerpo por encima de las restricciones familiares y sociales [The greatest danger for a woman, and indeed to the whole cosmic order, was that she would 'see and be seen,' that she could tear down the walls of that symbolic and material enclosure in which she had to live and that she could dispose freely of her person, her will, and her body beyond family and societal restrictions]" (376).

and womanly]" (Cotarelo y Mori 522). Of interest in this view is the equation between nationhood ("república") and masculinity. Rivadeneira goes on to say:

> Y por esta misma razón los príncipes y repúblicas bien ordenadas, aun las que carecieron de la lumbre de la fe ó no admitieron jamás semejantes comedias en sus repúblicas, ó conocido el daño, después las desterraron, ó á la menos no consintieron que mujeres se hallasen presentes á ellas.
> [And for that very reason rulers and well-governed republics, even those that did not possess the light of faith, either did not permit such plays in their realm, or once aware of the danger, removed them later, or at the very least, never allowed women to attend.] (Cotarelo y Mori 522)

Ignacio de Camargo, one of the most intemperate enemies of the theater, not surprisingly states this danger even more emphatically:

> Mas, ¿quién jamás pensara ver á los hombres nacidos solo para nobles y varoniles empresas abatidos á tan bajos y afeminados empleos que apenas se distinguen de las mugeres? ... De dónde pueden nacer estos viles y afeminados afectos sino del centro de las delicias sensuales, que son los patios de las comedias, fuente universal de todos los vicios.
> [Now, who would have thought it possible to see men who were born for noble and manly enterprises degraded to such lowly and effeminate uses that they are barely distinguishable from women? ... Where can these vile and effeminate affectations come from but from that center of sensual delights, the courtyards of the *comedias*, universal wellspring of all vices.] (Cotarelo y Mori 126)

Taking pleasure in theater was, therefore, an intrinsically feminine and feminizing experience. Elizabeth Lehfeldt has recently suggested that the economic and political decline of Spain in the seventeenth century led to a critique of diminished masculinity ("Ideal Men"), and it is this crisis of manhood that Carmargo anticipates in his comments. Ironically or self-consciously, the *comedia* often overtly dramatizes this crisis in the action presented on stage.[7]

The threat that theatrical activity might have to a society's clearly differentiated gendered behavior and classification is, in fact, an old concern. Plato, for example, was wary of drama because, like desire, drama led to the disintegration of the self. In her book *Tragedies of Tyrants*, Rebecca Bushnell has studied the classical roots of Renaissance political thought as it pertains to English tragedies and traces the link between tyranny, theatricality, and femininity. For one thing, Socrates, as reported by Plato, warned against imitation because it might lead men to imitate lesser beings, namely slaves, madmen, or women (Bushnell 17). The greatest danger lay in the mimetic production of multiple selves. Furthermore, feminization and theatricality were often viewed as a danger to kings as well:

---

[7] For a thought-provoking perspective on how this crisis of masculinity manifested itself in the *comedia*, see Sidney Donnell's *Feminizing the Enemy: Imperial Spain, Transvestite Drama, and the Crisis of Masculinity* (Lewisburg, PA: Bucknell UP, 2003).

"The marks of the feminine in Greek culture—irrationality, appetite, and the power of mimesis—are also the tyrant's characteristics. The tyrant is attacked by being theatricalized and implicitly feminized" (Bushnell 20). It is perhaps no surprise, then, that within the Spanish context, Philip IV—considered by many to be one of the weakest Habsburg kings—was often associated with theatricality in its multiple connotations.[8] For one thing, Philip was an enthusiastic participant in theatrical activity; in addition to consorting with actresses and players, he was reputed to have written several plays and often performed in palace masques. Beyond that, for some critics and historians, this particular king led an intensely theatricalized existence. In *A Palace for a King*, Jonathan Brown and John Elliott, for example, have said of Philip IV that he was in many ways an actor, directed by complex rules of protocol and public expectation, under the constant direction of his *privado*:

> The court of the King of Spain resembled a magnificent theater in which the principal actor was permanently on stage. The stage instructions were meticulously detailed; the scenery was imposing, if a little antiquated; and the supporting cast was impressively large. All that was needed was a director of genius to orchestrate the action and make the necessary dispositions to secure the most brilliant scenic effects. In the Count-Duke of Olivares ... the perfect director was ready to hand. (31)

While historians such as R.A. Stradling have strongly contested the negative portrayal of Philip IV as nothing more than an obedient actor or a puppet in the hands of the powerful minister,[9] the theatricality and self-indulgence (characteristics associated with women) that some identified with the monarch would become repeated themes in the *comedias* under consideration; and plays like *La gran Cenobia* [*The Great Zenobia*] and *La hija del aire* [*The Daughter of Air*] deal in one way or another with the feminization of the monarchy and its concomitant crisis of masculine power.

The negative views of the *comedia* held by Barcia y Zambrana and Rivadeneira vividly express the enormous anxiety surrounding the theater and the impact of the public visual display of the female body on its audience. Ironically, women were seen simultaneously as weak creatures and as terrifying forces whose influence needed to be controlled. The presence of women and women's bodies on the stage, a performance already burdened with questions concerning decorum and morality, becomes even more problematic when the dramatic characters being portrayed

---

[8] Theatricality had a multiplicity of meaning. According to Tracy C. Davis and Thomas Postlewait in *Theatricality* (Cambridge: Cambridge UP, 2003), it is "a mode of representation or a style of behavior characterized by histrionic actions, manners, and devices, and hence a practice; yet it is also an interpretive model for describing psychological identity, social ceremonies, communal festivities, and public spectacles, and hence a theoretical concept" (1). Throughout my discussion, I take advantage of the various meanings of the word while attempting to clarify in each instance the sense I am invoking.

[9] See Stradling's *Philip IV and the Government of Spain 1621–1665* (Cambridge: Cambridge UP, 1988), especially chapter 10.

are women who assume and wield political power and control. How much more discomfiting it must have become when this by turns submissive and transgressive "body natural" was presented time and time again as a body of authority and the bearer of political power—a body politic. In terms of the actual performance of the plays, beyond the problematic notion of female rule within the fiction of the plays, there is the added complication that it was an actual actress who embodied the often-exalted symbolic royal body upon a public stage. Actresses were routinely considered not much more respectable than "mujeres públicas" or common prostitutes, as Rivadeneira states:

> las mujercillas que representan comunmente son hermosas, lascivas y que han vendido su honestidad, ... á manera de sirenas encantan y transforman los hombres en bestias, y les dan tanto mayor ocasión de perderse, cuanto ellas son más perdidas, y por andar vagueando de pueblo en pueblo menos se echa de ver su perdición.
> [the hussies who regularly perform (in these plays) are beautiful, lascivious, and have sold their chastity, ... like sirens, they enchant and transform men into beasts and they give them the optimal opportunity to doom themselves, although they themselves are even more lost, but because they wander from town to town, their perdition is not as obvious.][10] (Cotarelo y Mori 523)

That such women could assume the role of a sovereign would, at some level, create a paradoxical situation for the viewing public, even one more tolerant of actresses than someone like Rivadeneira. The *comedia* in its totality, as stated before—with its conventional denouement of order reestablished—would seem to represent the status quo, the symbolic, the law, or the reproduction of values and precepts of the dominant social system. Nevertheless, in the actual "live" performance—with the presence of real women making themselves visible and wielding political (albeit fictional) power—there is an implicit questioning and negotiation of the symbolic, that is, the gender restrictions imposed by the reigning ideology. Women were the negative other; and yet, many of these fictional feminine characters embodied on the early modern Spanish stage were, in fact, not only dramatically appealing (and no doubt visually fetching to the masculine viewer) but also exemplary. Such is the case of the eponymous heroines in Calderón's *La gran Cenobia* [*The Great Zenobia*] and Tirso's Empress Irene in *La república al revés* [*The Republic Upside Down*].

---

[10] There were many regulations in place meant to contain the possibly disruptive behavior of actresses. Indeed, any woman involved in the theater in any capacity was required to be under the protection of a male figure, as Lola González tells us: "En la mayoría de los casos la vinculación de una mujer al oficio teatral dependía ... de su vinculación a una figura masculina, cónyuge en caso de estar casada y el padre o tutor en caso de ser menor y soltera [In most cases, the connection of a woman to the theatrical profession depended on her connection to a masculine figure, her husband if she was married and her father or tutor in the case of a minor or unmarried woman]." See "Mujer y empresa teatral en la España del Siglo de Oro: el caso de la actriz y *autora* María de Navas," *Revista sobre teatro áureo* 2 (2008): 137.

Feminine Exemplarity

It is possible to identify in the *comedia* a rhetoric of exemplarity applied to women in positions of power; and indeed, we find in these plays both positive and negative examples of female rule. These plays proffer alternative performances of the female royal body, what we might call a *speculum reginae* or "mirror of queens." In some ways, these *comedias* seem to hark back to an earlier tradition of feminine exemplarity and to the debate on women's role (or the *querelle des femmes*, as it is best known) that originated in the late Middle Ages throughout Europe.[11] The fascination with strong women certainly is not exclusive to the *comedia*, and any well-read Spaniard of the sixteenth and seventeenth centuries would have been familiar with the tradition of feminine exemplarity. We need only mention the popularity of Boccaccio's *De claris mulieribus* [*Concerning Famous Women*], translated into Spanish in 1494 but known in Spain earlier, which presented positive and negative female models of rulers such as Penthesilea, Queen of the Amazons,[12] and Lavinia, Queen of Laurentaum, in addition to the better-known Dido, Zenobia, and Semiramis.[13] Indeed, alongside overtly misogynist texts such as Alfonso Martínez de Toledo's *Corbacho*, for example, we find in Spain a number of treatises that defend and even exalt women. Some critics, such as Jacob Ornstein, have even claimed that the prevalence in the fifteenth century of pro-feminist treatises far exceeded that of anti-feminist texts.[14] One early Spanish treatise in praise of women was *Jardín de las nobles doncellas* [*The Garden of Noble Damsels*], written by Fray Martín de Córdoba and dedicated to none other than the young Isabel of Castile. In this work, the author affirms that women possess

---

[11] For a general discussion of the *querelle des femmes* in Europe, see Joan Kelly, "Early Feminist Theory and the 'Querelle des Femmes,' 1400–1789," in *Signs: Journal of Women in Culture and Society* 8.1 (1982): 3–28; and the anthology edited by Thelma S. Fenster and Clare A. Lees, *Gender in Debate from the Early Middle Ages to the Renaissance* (New York: Palgrave, 2002).

[12] On the figure of the Amazon in Spanish literature, see Harriet Goldberg's "Queen of Almost All She Surveys: The Sexual Dynamics of Female Sovereigns," *La corónica* 23.2 (1995): 51–63.

[13] Another notable medieval treatise is the famous *The Book of the City of Ladies* by Christine de Pizan, inspired in part by Boccaccio's *De mulieribus*.

[14] For a good summary of these treatises, see Rina Walthaus, "Classical Myth and Legend in Late Medieval and Renaissance Ideas of Gender: The Use of Classical Examples in Spanish Treatises for Women," *Crítica Hispánica* 18.2 (1996): 361–74. Jacob Ornstein is quoted by Walthaus on p. 326. The presence of so many documents in favor of women should not deceive us, however, as Dawn Smith cautions: "It is important not to confuse a writer's ability to create strong-minded and independent female characters with a pro-feminist attitude." See "Women and Men in a World Turned Upside-Down: An Approach to Three Plays by Tirso," *Revista canadiense de estudios hispanicos* 10.2 (1986): 256. Although she does not deal with Spain, Constance Jordan's *Renaissance Feminism: Literary Texts and Political Models* (Ithaca: Cornell UP, 1990) also provides an excellent discussion of the debate.

all the necessary characteristics to be successful monarchs and identifies specific "feminine" characteristics that make women good rulers: compassion, piety, and generosity, for example. In addition, he urges Isabel to overcome the weakness of her sex and to call upon the "manly spirit" that she, as a royal princess, possesses.[15] Nevertheless, as Barbara Weissberger has shown, this text is far from being a true defense of female sovereignty, and *Jardín de las nobles doncellas* ultimately proves to be an attempt to control and contain Isabel's power and fashion her into an ideal consort to a *male* king (xxiii). Indeed, the exemplarity invoked had less to do with political ability than with emphasizing the accepted traditional feminine virtues, particularly chastity.

Other prestigious models of feminine behavior are also provided by texts such as Diego de Valera's *Tratado en defensa de las virtuosas mujeres* [*Treatise in Defense of Virtuous Women*] (c.1445) and *Libro de las virtuosas e claras mujeres* [*The Book of Virtuous Women*] by Alvaro de Luna. Many of these texts were written in the late fifteenth or early sixteenth century, inspired perhaps by the still-vivid memory of the Catholic queen. Closer to Calderón's time, we find Cristóbal de Villalón's *El Scholastico* (1530–1540), Cristobal de Castillejo's 1544 *Diálogo de las mujeres* [*Dialogue of Women*], Juan de Espinosa's 1580 *Diálogo en laude de mugeres* [*Dialogue in Praise of Women*], Juan Pérez de Moya's 1583 *Varia historia de sanctas e ilustres mugeres en todo género de virtudes* [*Varied History of Saintly and Illustrious Women with All Types of Virtues*], Antonio de Guevara's 1574 *Epístolas familiares* [*Familiar Epistles*], and Juan de la Cerda's 1599 *Vida política de todos los estados de mujeres* [*The Political Life of Every Class of Woman*]; all texts which adopt a position that can be plausibly described as "pro-feminist." One of the figures Villalón praises, for example, is the Roman matron Clarichee, who, in a speech before the emperor Trajan and the Roman senate, insists that both sexes are equally adept at rulership: "No nos disteis lugar a que nosotras hiciéramos pragmáticas y constituciones, que también supiéramos hazer lo que nos cumpliera como vosotros hezistes en vuestro favor [You did not allow us to formulate rules and constitutions, but we would have known how to do so to our benefit in the same way you did it to yours]" (qtd. in Redondo, *Images de la femme* 293). This is the same complaint voiced, in one of many examples, by a character in Lope de Vega's *La vengadora de las mujeres* [*The Avenger of Women*]:

> Desde el principio del mundo
> se han hecho tiranos grandes
> de nuestro honor y albedrío,
> quitándonos las ciudades,
> la plata, el oro, el dinero,
> el govierno, sin que baste
> razón, justicia ni ley

---

[15] See Elizabeth Howe's "Zenobia or Penelope? Isabel la Catolica as Literary Archetype," in *Isabel la Católica, Queen of Castile: Critical Essays*, ed. David A. Boruchoff (New York: Palgrave Macmillan, 2003), 91–102.

[Since the beginning of the world, {men} have made themselves powerful tyrants of our honor and our will, taking away the cities, the silver, the gold, the money, the government, all without reason or justice or law.] (616)

The same arguments would be echoed in the seventeenth century by women writers such as María de Zayas and Sor Juana Inés de la Cruz.

Villalón also invokes the models of Semiramis and Zenobia. The former was a more ambiguous and often negative version of a female leader, but the latter became a frequently invoked figure of feminine exemplarity in the context of monarchical power. In addition to making an appearance in Vives's *Instrucción de la mujer cristiana*, Zenobia figures prominently in several treatises and is frequently cited as the model of wisdom and virtue in a queen. For example, Fernán Pérez de Guzmán, in his 1450 *Generaciones y semblanzas* [*Generations and Portraits*], wrote a chapter dedicated to Zenobia called "Quien fue Zenobia y de sus fazañas e de su gran coraçon en todos sus fechos [On who was Zenobia and her accomplishments and the courage she displayed in all her deeds]." "Zenobia" was one of the monikers applied to Isabel of Castile. And, in England, Thomas Elyot compares Catherine of Aragon, Isabel's daughter, to the legendary leader in his 1532 *Defence of Good Women* (written, perhaps, as a refutation of Vives's negative portrayal of queens in positions of power).[16] Later in the seventeenth century, Rodrigo Mendes Silva repeatedly compared the prudence of Empress Maria (Philip III's grandmother and—due to the intricate matrimonial practices of the Habsburgs—also his aunt) to that of Zenobia in his biography of the monarch (Sánchez, *Empress* 147).

Henry Kamen's assertion that "the exercise of power by women at every level was widely accepted in early modern Europe" (*Early Modern* 171) is no doubt correct. In Spain, as Earenfight has recently demonstrated, the role of queens during the Middle Ages was more active than it was in any other part of Europe:

> The active and visible political careers of Spanish queens from the thirteenth through the seventeenth century were fostered by a combination of forces—on the one hand, territorial expansion and conquest, and on the other, a political culture that did not explicitly prohibit queens from active participation in the governance of the realm. (Earenfight xiv)

Likewise, Cruz reminds us that "from the late fifteenth to the mid-sixteenth century, Spain was led by a series of female sovereigns" ("Juana of Portugal" 103), although Earenfight is right when she tells us that "none of the queens after Isabel of Castile and her daughter, Juana, ruled in their own right" (xxv). The anxiety surrounding the rule of women never abated, however, and female exemplarity often becomes a double-edged sword. For one thing, in the *de regimine principum* treatises that proffer detailed advice regarding all aspects

---

[16] For a comparison of Thomas Elyot's treatise to Vives's, see Constance Jordan's "Feminism and the Humanists: The Case of Sir Thomas Elyot's *Defence of Good Women*," *Renaissance Quarterly* 32.2 (1983): 181–201.

of kingship, we find few references to the rule of women despite the historical realities in the Iberian Peninsula and, indeed, in all of Europe. When feminine rule is invoked, it is couched in cautionary language. As an example, we might take Juan de Mariana's well known and influential 1598 *Del rey y de la institución real* [*On the King and the Royal Institution*], in which he briefly addresses the question of women as heads of state in his discussion of inherited monarchy. He begins by making a misogynist analogy to the undesirability of having a woman as head of a household:

> Ocurren también dudas sobre si deben ser llamadas á suceder las hembras cuando hayan muerto todos sus hermanos y no hayan quedado de ellos sino hijos varones. En muchas naciones está ya determinado que no sucedan fundándose en que no sirve una mujer para dirigir los negocios públicos, ni es capaz de resolverse por sí misma cuando ocurran graves acontecimientos en el reino. Si cuando mandan en familias particulares anda perturbada la paz de todo el hogar doméstico, ¿qué no sería, dicen, si se las pusiera al frente de toda una república? [There are doubts as to whether women should be called upon to succeed when all the brothers are dead and they left only male children. In many nations, it is determined that a woman may not succeed based on the fact that she is unable to conduct public business and is incapable of acting on her own when serious circumstances beset the kingdom. If when women rule over private families, they perturb the peace of the domestic home, what might it be—they say—if one were to put them at the head of an entire republic?] (475)

Nevertheless, he goes on to acknowledge that in the different kingdoms of Spain, the rule of women has been a reality, and he even turns to the Bible to cite some models for this practice:

> En los diversos reinos de España no se ha seguido siempre ni una misma costumbre ni una misma regla. En Aragón unas veces han sido admitidas á la sucesion, otras excluidas. Como empero leamos en las sagradas escrituras que Débora gobernó la república judía, y veamos adoptado por muchas naciones que pase la corona á manos de las hembras cuando no haya varones que puedan ceñirlas, y en Castilla, que es la mas noble region de España, sin que en nada ceda a las extrajeras, y hasta entre los vascos vemos seguida desde los tiempos primitivos la costumbre de no distinguir para la sucesion varones ni hembras; no creemos que puedan ser vituperadas con razon las disposiciones de nuestras leyes respecto a este punto ... .
> [In the diverse kingdoms of Spain, there has been no uniformity in tradition or law with respect to this question. In Aragon, sometimes women have been allowed to succeed the throne, other times they have been excluded. However, since we see in the sacred scriptures that Deborah ruled the Jewish nation, and we see that many countries have adopted the practice of letting the crown pass to the hands of a woman when no man is available to wear it, and that in Castile— which is the noblest region of Spain, with nothing to cede to other nations—and even among the Basques, we see the practice from primitive times onward of not distinguishing between men and women in succession, we do not believe that the disposition of our laws with regard to this issue can be criticized.] (475)

Despite the precedence and even prestige of the models invoked, and despite the fact that female rule was in evidence in the political reality of Europe during the Middle Ages and the Early Modern period, we find in theorists like Mariana a deep suspicion of feminine power. The women rulers they mention almost always come across as usurpers, as agents of chaos and disorder.

Mariana limits himself to alluding to anonymous or Biblical queens. Vives, in the earlier *Instrucción de la mujer cristiana* (1524), provides a particularly equivocal discourse over the notion of women taking the throne. This work was commissioned by Catherine of Aragon, then the wife of Henry VIII of England, as a guide for the education of their daughter, Mary Tudor.[17] Vives's treatise had made abundantly clear that he did not consider a woman able to function as a ruler because she is first and foremost subject to her husband, who replaces all loyalties: "Mas siendo acompañada con su marido, dondequiera que estuviere tiene patria, casa, padres, parientes, riquezas y bienes [But as long as a woman is accompanied by her husband, wherever she goes she has a country, a home, parents, relatives, riches and possessions]" (220). Vives is also fond of offering historic or legendary queens as supreme examples of the extreme fealty a woman owes her husband: "Ejemplo de esto tenemos en Hipsicratea, mujer de Mitrídates, rey de Ponto, la cual en toda la guerra que su marido tuvo con romanos ... le siguió trasquilada los cabellos y vestida como hombre ... huyendo delante de los enemigos, teniendo por sabido que allí era su reino y riquezas y patria, donde su marido [A good example would be Hypsicratea, the wife of Mithridates, king of Pontus, who, during the wars her husband waged against the Romans ... followed him with her hair shorn and dressed as a man ... fleeing enemies and knowing for certain that wherever her husband was she would have her kingdom and riches and country]" (220). The treatise, as Gloria Kaufmann, among others, has pointed out, is decidedly ambivalent toward women, particularly compared with the more enlightened views of his contemporaries, Thomas More and Erasmus (896). Vives fluctuates between providing an enlightened attitude toward the education of women (following Erasmus's lead) and articulating a certain repugnance toward women's nature, one he considers entirely unsuitable for public life. Vives's ideological quandary must have been singularly difficult since he was familiar with women, such as Isabel I and his patron, Catherine herself, who were significant and visible political players in Spain and abroad. Furthermore, Vives finds it necessary to emphasize the traditional virtues of chastity and obedience: "De las cuales cuatro hermanas podemos averiguadamente decir: ningunas otras mujeres en memoria de hombres haber sido honradas de más limpia fama, ningunas de más pura castidad, ningunas

---

[17] For the reception of Vives in England, see the section titled "Woman's Rule: The Tudor Queens" in Constance Jordan's *Renaissance Feminism*, 116–21. Jordan points out that the problem of succession during the reign of Henry VIII made gynocracy—the command of a woman over men—a topic of heated discussion. Indeed, under Henry's Third Act of Succession, both Mary Tudor and Elizabeth were considered legitimate heirs to the English throne (116–17).

más queridas de sus pueblos, ningunas más admiradoras de sus maridos, ningunas a ellos más obedientes ... [Of these four sisters we can state with authority that no other women in the memory of man could surpass them in their impeccable reputation, no other in their pure chastity, no other more beloved by their people, no other more admiring of their husbands, none more obedient of them ...]" (54). Elizabeth Howe has pointed out, for example, that the Catholic monarch and her four daughters are described as "latter-day Penelopes" who "exemplify faithful wives and mothers busy at their looms, rather than with statecraft" (97).

The important political roles that these women had to play—the younger Isabel (and, later, her sister María) married Manuel of Portugal, Juana was the proprietary queen of Spain until her death, and Catherine was queen consort of England—are ignored by Vives and reduced to a passing mention of the love and admiration they earned from the populace precisely for conforming to and performing before the public certain feminine virtues. Their social position may have placed Isabel I and her daughters at the very center of political power, but because of their sex, they and their bodies never cease to be subjected to specifically prescribed behavior. This is the leveling effect that Soufas has identified in these treatises, where no differentiation is made among women of different social classes. It is an example of what Soufas has called "a conceptual commonality with regard to the gender constructs" (*Dramas of Distinction* 18). In another often-cited passage juxtaposing women's speech with political activity, Vives states: "Pero en la mujer nadie busca elocuencia, o grandes primores de ingenio, o administración de ciudades, o memoria o liberalidad. Sola una cosa se requiere de ella, y ésta es la castidad [But no one would look to a woman for eloquence, or great signs of cleverness, or the administration of cities, or memory or liberality; only one thing is required of her, and that is chastity]" (79). A woman need only maintain her body pure, away from the profanation that public display and action might bring about.

For a long time, it was easy for critics and historians to accept views such as these as a credible indication of the limited role allowed to women in early modern Spain. As stated before, however, recent scholarship has provided a corrective to the narrow view of female activity in the public sphere. Women in early modern Spain participated in a multiplicity of civic, commercial, legal, and political activities, despite these official admonitions. There is in Vives's *Instruccion*, as in other similar texts, a tension and an intrinsic contradiction between the ideal of womanhood as prescribed in the treatises and the much more complex reality of public and political life.

By contrast, in the *comedia*—that singularly privileged site of society's self-imagining—we discover the repeated representation of women wielding power in the administration of a state. Feminist critics have stated that one way of excluding women from authority is by rendering female power invisible. In Golden Age *comedias*, feminine power was made visible by being literally embodied in the actual performance of the play, a performance that frequently took place in the politically conspicuous space of the court. The *comedia*'s insistent enactment of female rule shares with other performances, as described in modern criticism, two characteristics: it is repeated behavior and it represents a complex dynamic of presence and absence. For one thing, the absence of a queen regnant in the audience of the court (that is, as opposed to a consort or regent) would provide visible contrast against the presence of these formidable feminine rulers onstage.[18] At the same time, the *comedias* were, perhaps unwittingly, reflecting the complex real situation of women, who were much more active in the public and political sphere than the prescriptive literature would allow. In the *comedia*, the repeated presentation of women exercising the supposedly masculine privilege of political and monarchical power would seem to be a challenge to the dominant ideology and rhetoric of masculine dominance.

The Body Politic

I have made frequent references to the importance of the body in performance. The staged royal female body on stage must be considered also in view of the corporeal metaphors of power that originated in ancient and classical sources, became prevalent during the Middle Ages, and were still widespread during the sixteenth and seventeenth centuries. In early modern Europe, the human body was considered the measure of all things; and there was an insistent association between the body and the state. To take only one example, the sixteenth-century physician Jerónimo Merola establishes correspondences between the republic and the body, "siguiendo en todo la cifra de nuestro cuerpo cuyo bivo retrato es nuestra república [following in every respect the sum total of our body whose living portrait is the republic]" (qtd. in Redondo, "La métaphore" 47). He adds later:

> Quanto más me voy metiendo en las cosas de nuestro cuerpo, y por sus partes voy midiendo las de la República, más a las veras me voy maravillando de ver lo mucho que se parecen. La Analogía de más calidad, y en la qual más que en otra ninguna se funda todo este libro, es lo que ay entre la República y el cuerpo. [The more I become immersed in matters related to our body, and as I compare the parts of the Republic against the parts of the body, the more I marvel at how much these two entities are alike. The most valuable analogy on which, more than any other, this book is based is the relationship between the Republic and the body.] (47)

In medieval and early modern Spain, this association and the centrality of the body of the king was made in virtually all the political treatises and in numerous legal documents. As early as Alfonso the Wise's *Segunda Partida* [*Second Law*] we find the following: "Dijeron los sabios que el Rey es cabeça del reino ... de

---

[18] This was true of classical theater as well. Evidence suggests that women did not attend plays in Athens despite the fact that, as Arlene W. Saxonhouse points out, "female characters appeared on stage—often in major roles, often giving the lie to themes of male potency" (24). See *Women in the History of Political Thought: Ancient Greece to Machiavelli* (New York: Praeger, 1985).

la cabeça nascen los sentidos porque se mandan todos los miembros del cuerpo [Wise men have said that the King is the head of the kingdom ... from this head all the senses are born from which all the members of the body are ruled]" (qtd. in Civil 13). Centuries later, Baltasar Álamos de Barrientos claims in his 1614 *Tacito español* [*The Spanish Tacitus*] that "Ay tanta trauazón y dependencia entre el Príncipe y su República que no le puede acontecer a vno dellos cosa, que el daño, o prouecho della, no toque al otro; siendo el Príncipe el alma, y la República el cuerpo [There is so much interconnectedness and dependence between the Prince and his Republic that nothing of harm or benefit can happen to one without affecting the other, the Prince being the soul and the Republic the body]" (qtd. in C. Davis 34).[19] There are numerous allusions to the king as the head or the heart or the soul, and to the idea that each part of the state corresponded to a part of the body that receives from the monarch its unity.

The metaphor of the political body was a popular and politically useful one because, as Charles Davis tells us, it helped establish two fundamental principles: 1) the primacy of the figure of the prince and thus, the superiority of the monarchy as a system; and 2) the coherence and interdependence of every element in this monarchical system. Again, Álamos de Barrientos:

> El cuerpo de la República es vno solo, y no se pueden apartar sus miembros sin daño irreparable suyo; y por eso ni diuidirse ni darse a muchos: y assí se rige mejor por el ánimo e entendimiento de uno solo: y por eso es mejor govierno el de la Monarquía.
> [The body of the Republic is one only, and its limbs cannot be detached without causing irreparable damage; and for that reason, it cannot be divided nor distributed among many: therefore, it functions best through the will and understanding of one entity, and for that reason, the best form of government is a monarchy.] (Qtd. in C. Davis 34)

Saavedra Fajardo states the inseparability of the state from the body of the king even more emphatically:

> No ha de haber exceso ni daño en el Estado, que luego no llegue fielmente a la noticia del príncipe; no hay sentimiento y dolor en cualquier parte del cuerpo que en un instante no toque y informe el corazón, como á príncipe de la vida, donde tiene su asiento el alma.
> [There will be no excess or harm in the State that does not get ultimately noticed by the prince; there is no sensation or pain in any part of the body which does not instantly touch and alert the heart, which is like the prince of life, where the soul has its abode.] (*Idea* 79)

---

[19] The articles by Augustin Redondo, Pierre Civil, and Charles Davis all appear in the excellent anthology on the early modern body edited by Redondo, *Le corps comme métaphore dans L'Espagne des XVIe et XVIIe siècles: du corps métaphorique aux métaphores corporelles* (Paris: Sorbonne, 1992).

According to Pierre Civil, the association of the king's body with the divine, although occasionally invoked, was greatly attenuated in Spain. Also, unlike England and France, medieval and early modern Spain did not fully develop a doctrine of the mystical dual bodies of the king, a doctrine famously summarized in the following passage:

> For the King has in him two Bodies, *viz.*, a Body natural, and a Body politic. His Body natural (if it be considered in itself) is a Body mortal, subject to all Infirmities that come by Nature or Accident, to the Imbecility of Infancy or old Age, and to the like Defects that happen to the natural Bodies of other People. But his Body politic is a Body that cannot be seen or handled, consisting of Policy and Government, and constituted for the Direction of the People, and the Management of the public weal and this Body is utterly void of Infancy, and old Age, and other natural Defects and Imbecilities, which the Body natural is subject to ... (Qtd. in Kantorowicz 7)

Civil tells us that there is, in fact, no Spanish treatise that makes a similar *legalistic* separation of the two bodies, nor is there an emphasis on the notion of the *corpus mysticum*, that to which the king is married as Christ is married to the church.[20] We do encounter in Spanish treatises allusions to a binary conception of kingship in the reference to two types of majesty, as Antonio de Guevara states: "La magestad eterna ... dio a los principes magestadad temporal [The eternal majesty ... gave the princes a temporal majesty]" (qtd. in Civil 18). More to the point, perhaps, Álamos de Barrientos states, "El Principe tiene dos personas, de particular y de Rey [The Prince has two persons, a private one and that of a King]" (22). What is repeatedly emphasized in treatises on kingship and the theater, then, is the separation of the private self of the monarch from his public persona. Equally important is the understanding that the body as a political metaphor had clearly gendered connotations. In the evocation and invocation of a body politic, a male body is assumed throughout, and the virtues assigned to a prince are understood to be "masculine."[21]

---

[20] On the other hand, the notion of the republic (not specifically the monarch himself) as a *corpus mysticum* seems to have been prevalent from the Middle Ages on in Spain, as J.A. Maravall demonstrates in his "La idea del cuerpo místico en España antes de Erasmo," in *Estudios de historia del pensamiento español* (Madrid: Ediciones Cultura Hispánica, 1967), vol. 1, 179–200. Also, in *Orígenes de la monarquía hispánica: propaganda y legitimación, ca. 1400–1520* (Madrid: Dykinson, 1999), José Manuel Nieto Soria reminds us that in the Middle Ages, we can find allusions to the mystical body of the republic applied to different political groups. He quotes, for example, the following, in which members of the nobility identify themselves as "miembros del cuerpo místico de la cosa pública destos Reynos de Castilla e de León, tanto principales como demuestra la esperiencia de nuestros linajes, estados e casas e faciendas e naturaleza [members of the mystical body of the republic of these kingdoms of Castile and Leon, as important as is demonstrated by the experience of our lineage, our estates, our domains, and our nature]" (85).

[21] It is nevertheless interesting that it was precisely during Queen Elizabeth's reign in England that the doctrine of the king's two bodies became established/accepted.

As stated before, these treatises established correspondences between various segments of the state and different parts of the body. Not only was the king the head or the soul, but the nerves were the law, the brains the church, the military the heart, and the royal counselors the eyes. Saavedra Fajardo states in his "Empresa LV" that the king's ministers "son sus ojos, su piés y sus manos; con que vendrá á ver y oir con los ojos y orejas de muchos, y acertará con los consejos de todos [they are his eyes, his feet, and his hands, with which he will be able to see and hear with the ears of many, and he will make the right decisions heeding the counsel of all]" (*Idea* 145). This elaborate figuration of power, however, did not seem to allow for any meaningful incorporation (in its double meaning) of a woman's body into the body politic. Indeed, if anything, the only "anatomical" role assigned to woman at the time was that of "costilla," or rib, man's companion originating from and destined to function at his side, as the following verses from an anonymous *romance* remind us:

> Que fue la mujer primera
> Formada de una costilla,
> Para darnos a entender
> La inmensa sabiduría,
> Que la mujer no es cabeza
> Sino amable compañía
> Como la ley de Dios manda
> Y la Iglesia nos avisa.
> [The first woman was formed from a rib so that we would understand the immense wisdom that woman is not the head but rather the agreeable companion as the law of God commands and the Church tells us.] (qtd. in Monet 84)

Juan de Mariana underscores woman's corporeal incompleteness when he states that God "a la hembra sujetó al imperio y potestad del varon como formada de su costado, y ordenó que le obedeciese á la manera que la parte obedece al todo [(God) subjected woman to the rule and power of man since she was formed from his flank, and ordered that she obey him in the way the part obeys the whole]" (426). Thus, corporeal images or analogies, when used on women, were generally meant to emphasize their weak, subservient state, as Vives, among many others, makes perfectly clear, even going so far as to insinuate that the man has given birth to woman:

Indeed, it was used as a way of justifying and perhaps limiting female rule. See Ernst H. Kantorowizc's *The King's Two Bodies: A Study in Medieval Political Theology* (Princeton, Princeton UP: 1957); and Louis Montrose's *The Subject of Elizabeth: Authority, Gender, and Representation* (Chicago: Chicago UP, 2006) and his articles "Idols of the Queen: Policy, Tender, and the Picturing of Elizabeth I," *Representations* 68 (1999): 108–61, and "'Shaping Fantasies': Figurations of Gender and Power in Elizabethan Culture," in *Representing the English Renaissance*, ed. Stephen Greenblatt (Berkeley: U of California P, 1988), 31–64.

> [L]a mujer es hija del marido, porque salió de su costado, es más inclinable y flaca, y menos aparejada para sostener las flaquezas que acarrea la vida humana, a cuya causa ha menester defensa y amparo; y siendo desamparada del marido, queda, desnuda, y sola y puesta a los vaivenes de las mudanzas injuriosas.
> [(T)he woman is the daughter of her husband, because she came from his rib, and as such is more susceptible and weak, and less able to withstand the weaknesses that human life brings about. As such, she needs defense and protection; and if she were left unprotected by her husband, she would be left naked, alone, and exposed to the vagaries of harmful circumstances.] (220)

Paradoxically, although woman is excluded from the political body, she is, in fact, repeatedly associated with the sinfulness and passions of the natural body. Later on, Vives states:

> Como el hombre es formado de ánima, y cuerpo, así el matrimonio consta de hombre y mujer, pero él es el ánima, y ella es el cuerpo. Es necesario que el alma mande, y el cuerpo obedezca si el hombre quiere vivir.
> [Just as man is made up of soul and body, so, too, matrimony is made up of man and woman, but he is the soul and she is the body. It is necessary that the soul be in charge and that the body obey if mankind is to survive.] (227)

Women, then, were seen as the direct opposite of spirit and intellect and were routinely associated with the "body natural," making them inadequate for positions of power.

The prejudice against women in authority was extended naturally to royal and noble women as well. In her book on Juana the Mad, Bethany Aram quotes the fourteenth-century Catalan author Francec Eiximenis as claiming that, in fact, "The effeminate and weak [body politic] is governed by women and by other people similar to them and worse, who have no shame or determination or virtue in their affairs or who care for useless things" (6). This attitude did not coincide, as stated before, with the political reality of Spain. Women in the Middle Ages in Spain occupied prominent and powerful offices, such as the regency in Castile and the lieutenancy in the Crown of Aragon. Spain was ruled continuously by women, in some form or another, beginning in 1474, when Isabel la Católica assumed the throne of Castile, until the mid-sixteenth century (Cruz and Suzuki 103). In addition to Isabel, queen regnant until 1504, the following women exercised significant authority: Isabel's daughter Juana of Castile was legally considered the queen until her death, despite her purported mental incapacities;[22] Isabel of Portugal became empress when she married Charles V and acted as his "lieutenant and governess of the realm" during his frequent absences; and finally, there was Juana of Portugal (also known as Juana of Austria), Charles's daughter, who, at the request of her brother Philip II, served as regent between 1554 and 1559 while Philip was in England. We could also mention that in the second half of

---

[22] Bethany Aram calls Juana a "proprietary queen who never ruled" in *Juana the Mad: Sovereignty and Dynasty in Renaissance Europe* (Baltimore: Johns Hopkins UP, 2005), 4.

the seventeenth century, the rule of women continued intermittently when Isabel of Bourbon, Philip IV's first wife, served as regent during the Catalan Revolt, and later, when Philip's second wife, Mariana of Austria, became regent after the king's death.

Historians have, until recently, tended to ignore these and other powerful women in early modern Spain. Even some of the best historians of early modern Spain—Henry Kamen, John Elliott, and (to a lesser extent) R.A. Stradling—have relegated these queens to being shadowy background figures. Recent studies, such as those already mentioned by Cruz and Earenfight, and, notably, Magdalena S. Sánchez's *The Empress, the Queen, and the Nun*, seek to partially "re-dress" (as it were) this neglect.[23] Sánchez's book addresses the important role played by three prominent Habsburg women during Philip III's reign: the Empress Maria of Austria (Philip's grandmother, who served as regent of Spain until his majority), Margarita of Austria (his formidable wife), and Margarita de la Cruz (Empress Maria's daughter and Philip's aunt; who, significantly, opted for the life of a nun over that of queen). Sánchez's book documents both the attitudes toward women in power in general and the actual contributions of these particular feminine figures to the dynamics of monarchy. A good queen, Sánchez tells us, satisfied the requirements expected of a good wife, supervising the retinue of servants and making her husband's court the model for a peaceful and orderly realm.

Within the context of the court, therefore, the feminine sphere of household management served as a parallel or analogy to the masculine sphere of the political realm (Sánchez, *Empress* 66). Moralists such as Jerónimo de Florencia wrote that if a wife fulfilled her duties faithfully, this would communicate itself into a peaceful household and furthermore into a peaceful state. Thus, Sánchez quotes him as saying that "the husband of a valorous woman will have no need of plunder (*despojos*) nor of going to battle ... because God will give peace and tranquility to his kingdoms on account of *her* merits" (83). It was said of Margarita of Austria that "she frees the republic from vices; she desires and procures the best and the most useful (things) for the government" (97). Many of the same feminine virtues promoted by patriarchal ideology could be used by women as weapons to subvert the status quo. Ostentatious displays of piety, for example, inspired admiration for a queen and this reverence could, in turn, be translated into power and influence in political matters. In Sánchez's words, "women often exploited the female image presented by men in order to further their own goals" (84). Indeed, the performance of feminine virtue (which is, of course, not the same as intrinsic virtuous behavior) was an important vehicle for securing a measure of political visibility. Religion and religiosity became areas that could be exploited for their

---

[23] In addition to Magdalena Sánchez's seminal history, *The Empress, the Queen, and the Nun: Women and Power at the Court of Philip III of Spain* (Baltimore: Johns Hopkins UP, 1998), see the anthologies edited by Anne Cruz and Mihoko Suzuki and by Theresa Earenfight, and Bethany Aram's *Juana the Mad*; see also María José Rubio's *Reinas de España: Las Austrias* (Madrid: La Esfera de los Libros, 2010).

performative impact. Religious patronage and other acts or rituals "were inherently expressions of power relationships" (Sánchez, *Empress* 13). Women established female communities (particularly the convent) that provided a counterbalance to the male-oriented palace. By cherishing and maintaining the virtues of virginity and chastity, a woman supposedly raised herself up to the moral level of a man. Indeed, the pursuit of these feminine virtues led to a kind of transgendering. After all, none other than Saint Augustine had argued that by choosing to live as a virgin, a woman showed virility and masculine strength. Other less admirable (at least, to the modern eye) behavior often invoked to limit women's influence could also be turned into a strategy for assuming power. For example, melancholy and illness became ways of manipulating the king and the court (Sánchez, *Empress* 169). The Spanish queens were political creatures keenly aware that they were vital players in marriage, alliances, succession, and as diplomatic representatives for their countries and royal line. The Habsburg dynasty relied on informal networks revolving around relatives, primarily women, to pursue their interests; and it is quite possible that some of the wives of the Spanish kings may have even acted as spies for their Austrian relatives (Sánchez, *Empress* 113).

Returning to the political use of body imagery, Earenfight suggests that the monarchy during the Middle Ages and the Early Modern period was, in fact, a "corporate" enterprise. That is, monarchical power was not wielded by one individual alone but was rather "a multiplicity of power relations that are not separate entities, but rather elements contained within a network" (xvii). Perhaps it is in this notion of a monarchy as corporate that we can reconcile the rhetorical absence of women in the imagery of the body politic. Even when women did not have a visible, unambiguous role, they almost always wielded informal but important power. Earenfight provides a suggestive definition of queenship itself: "It is a repertoire of collective norms, institutional structures, and strategies for participation within the political sphere of monarchy that included, but was not limited to, governance" (xvi). At the same time, there is no avoiding the fact that, despite the overwhelming feminine presence and influence in the Spanish court, official recognition and respect were hard to come by. Treatises such as Pedro Luján's *Coloquios matrimoniales* make clear that "por grande que sea en estado, y por generosa que sea en sangre una mujer, tan bien le parece en la cinta una rueca, como al caballero una lanza, y al letrado un libro, y al sacerdote su hábito [no matter how noble a woman's state may be or how generous her lineage, the distaff suits a woman best, like the lance to a knight, the book to a learned man, and the habit to the priest]" (80). In *La perfecta casada*, Fray Luis de León offers the following advice: "Así que traten las duquesas y las reinas el lino, y labren la seda, y den tarea a sus damas, pruébense con ellas en estos oficios, y pongan en estado y honra aquesta virtud; que yo me hago valiente de alcanzar del mundo que las loe [Therefore, let duchesses and queens work with flax and let them embroider silk, and let them give their ladies-in-waiting similar tasks, thereby giving them example by raising these virtuous activities in prestige and honor; and I will be so bold as to win praise for them from the rest of the world]" (27).

Regulatory manuals like Luján's and León's tended to eliminate all class differences among women, as Ruth Kelso demonstrates in *Doctrine for the Lady of the Renaissance*, a study of Renaissance conduct manuals.[24]

Another more specific example of the expected subordination of royal wives to their husbands can be found in Vives's description of the marriage between the Habsburg Emperors, Maria and Maximilian:

> La reina doña María, mujer del emperador Maximiliano, como hubiese sucedido heredera de su padre Carlos en la tierra y condado de Flandes y los flamencos no tuviesen en tanta estimación al dicho emperador como deberían, por verle tan humano y benigno, traían todos los negocios del estado delante la dicha reina doña María como a su principal señora, y ella jamás quiso determinar cosa alguna de poder absoluto sin consultarlo primero con su marido, cuya voluntad tenía por ley ... y de esta manera puso a su marido en muy gran autoridad con los pueblos de Flandes.
>
> [Queen Mary, wife of the emperor Maximilian, had inherited the land and county of Flanders from her father, Charles, and the Flemish did not have the great appreciation for the emperor that they should have. Since they saw him so human and benign, they would bring all state business to queen Maria as their sovereign, but she never agreed to reach any determination requiring absolute power without first consulting with her husband, whose will she deemed law ... and in this manner, she placed her husband in a position of great authority before the people of Flanders.] (257)

Thus, even while recognizing that a woman was clearly more wise and gifted in the art of government and that the real power emanated from her, she still had to publicly perform her subservience to her husband.

The one distinct and celebrated political function that the royal feminine body had was to provide an heir to the throne. In a fascinating but little-studied play by Lope de Vega, *El animal de Hungría* [*The Beast from Hungary*], we find the following dialogue between the former queen of Hungary and a naïve young girl on what it means to be a queen:

---

[24] See Kelso, *Doctrine for the Lady of the Renaissance* (Chicago: U of Illinois P, 1978). For a more recent consideration of these manuals within the Spanish context, specifically the Marcela episode in Cervantes's *Don Quijote*, see Emilia Navarro's "Manual Control: 'Regulatory Fictions' and their Discontents," *Cervantes: Bulletin of the Cervantes Society of America* 13.2 (1993): 17–35. Navarro states: "It is easy to see why the majority of the conduct manuals, and most especially those directed at the women of the upper and middle classes, should choose to gloss over the class factor: if they are to serve their very purpose as exemplars, it is imperative that they delve into the commonality of woman, in order to validate the model of behavior that they uphold, a model which must be made to seem plausible, and to constitute a worthy and attainable aspiration for their intended readers. To emphasize class closure would, in fact, potentially discredit their very purpose as exemplars" (19).

ROSAURA: ¿Qué es 'reina'?
TEODOSIA: Mujer del rey.
ROSAURA: ¿Pues qué hace?
¿De qué sirve?
TEODOSIA: De dar reyes
para que den esas leyes;
porque desta otro rey nace;
y de aquel, otro; y ansí
se va el gobierno aumentando.
ROSAURA: Ser reina voy deseando.
TEODOSIA: Más dichosa que yo fui.
ROSAURA: Paréceme lindo oficio
hacer reyes; por mi vida,
que me dejéis que al Rey pida,
pues es común beneficio,
haga que nazcan de mí
treinta reyes o cuarenta.
[ROSAURA: What does "queen" mean? TEODOSIA: Wife of the king. ROSAURA: What does she do? What is she good for? TEODOSIA: She creates kings so that they can create laws; because from her another king is born, and from him another; and so the kingdom grows. ROSAURA: I'm beginning to want to be queen. TEODOSIA: May you be luckier than I was. ROSAURA: It seems to me that creating kings is a beautiful occupation; truly, let me request the king, since it would be mutually beneficial, that he let me give birth to thirty or forty kings.] (458–74)

A woman's ability to bear children increased her intrinsic worth and necessarily made the royal consort a central political player; and it is not surprising that we find an almost morbid obsession with the queen's reproductive capabilities.[25] Philip III, for example, writes to his daughter Ana, asking how often her husband Louis shares her bed and stating: "… ya querría que acabásedes de ser mujer, que para eso y otros os aprovecharía y para que me dieses presto un nieto [I wish you were already a woman, since I could use you for these and other purposes, and so that you could quickly give me a grandson]" (qtd. in Sánchez, "Pious and Political" 101). Isabel of Valois's onset of puberty was eagerly awaited and documented via letters to her mother, Catherine de' Medici, queen of France, and other *memoriales*. Catherine demanded frequent reports on Isabel's health while she was pregnant, even sending her packages "où il y a tout plein de recettes, donc elle peut avoir de besoin [where there are many types of prescriptions which she may need]" (qtd. in Hume 305). María José Rubio calls the Spain of this time "un reino pendiente de los embarazos reales [a realm preoccupied with royal pregnancies]" (339).

---

[25] For the iconography related to childbearing, see María Cruz de Carlos Varona's "Representar el nacimiento: imágenes y cultura material de un espacio de sociabilidad femenina en la España Altomoderna," *Goya* 319 (2007): 231–45.

Thus, while we know relatively little about the daily activities of queens or about their political interventions, we do possess ample documentation on when someone like Isabel of Valois first got her menstrual period and all the gory details of each of her childbirths. There was, then, a paradoxical attitude toward the queen's body. For one thing, the female sovereign was occasionally imbued with a quasi-divine status, and anything hinting of carnality was avoided in visual representations, for example. Hidden behind splendid dresses of rich cloth—damask, lace, velvet, brocade—and forced to wear layers of clothing, including the voluminous "guardainfante," any intimation of the real flesh underneath was eliminated. One anecdote is telling in this regard: during Mariana of Austria's long trip to Spain to marry Philip IV, she arrived in a town famous for its silk stockings and was given as a gift a basket with several pairs. The majordomo immediately returned the gift, exclaiming; "Habéis de saber que las reinas de España no tienen piernas [You should know that the queens of Spain do not have legs]" (Ríos Mazcarelle 36).

At the same time, given this apparent desire to deny a real body to the female monarch, it is paradoxical that the queen's biological functions—her mortal and biological self—were so public a topic, commented in the court and recorded in writing and in the city squares. Indeed, public opinion was aggressively vigilant about the sexual politics that were being played out to maintain the dynasty. Jerónimo de Barrionuevo, whose *Avisos*—letters informing his patron, the Déan of Zaragoza, of the comings and goings of the members of the royal family—represent a valuable, if idiosyncratic, source of information on the royal pregnancies, among other things. He reports, for example, the following on September 23, 1654: "Dícese tiene la Reina sospechas de preñada. Dios lo haga, y si ha de ser hija, ¿para qué la queremos? Mejor será que no lo esté, que mujeres hay hartas [It is said that the queen suspects that she is pregnant. May God will it so, and if it is to be a daughter, what do we want her for? It would be better that she not be [pregnant], for we have enough women as it is]" (I. 61). Another entry for February 13, 1658, informs us that "La Reina (Mariana de Austria) tiene diez y ocho días de falta. Paréceme que segun va, parirá cada año [The queen is eighteen days late. It seems to me that if things continue like this, she will give birth once a year]" (II. 162).[26]

The vigilance toward the queen's body also manifested itself in more popular forms, including satirical *pasquines* and *letrillas*. When Charles II, Mariana of Austria's son, married Maria Luisa of Orléans, the young woman's ability to provide an heir became a public matter of concern, as indicated by the following popular quatrain:

---

[26] Barrionuevo's *Avisos* has been edited in the twentieth century by A. Pay y Melia and published in two volumes (Madrid: Ediciones Atlas, 1968); my citations indicate the volume and the page number. More intimate details appear occasionally in Barrionuevo, such as: "También se dice no está bueno [el Rey], por haberse anticipado á dormir con la Reina sin estar del todo evacuada, resultando en las partes bajas un achaque [It is also said that the king is not well because he hastened to sleep with the queen without her being completely purged, and this resulted in some aches in his lower parts]" (II, 159).

> Parid, bella flor de lis
> que en aflicción tan extraña
> si parís, parís a España
> si no parís, a París.
> [Give birth ("Parid"), beautiful fleur de lis, because your affliction is so bizarre that if you do give birth ("parís"), you give birth to Spain. If you don't give birth ("si no parís") then back to Paris you go.] (Qtd. in Kamen, *Spain* 373)

The last line wittily not only suggests that the queen should be returned to her native country if she fails to produce an heir; it also expresses the prevalent fear that Spain itself would fall prey to France should there be no successor. Giving birth and meeting subsequent maternal responsibilities represented, according to Magdalena Sánchez, areas of political leverage and influence for the royal consorts. Thus, these women were able to use their importance as the mothers or future mothers of heirs to the throne to influence the court (*Empress* ix–x). The same Maria Luisa addressed above, for example, seems to have been quite adept at exploiting the sexual politics of reproduction and the authority they afforded her, as the following letter from Alexander Stanhope, the British ambassador to Madrid during Charles II's reign, attests:

> February 22, 1695
> I can inform you a little more of the affairs of this court than by my last [letter], only that it is agreed on all hands that the young queen carries all before her, since His Majesty's confessor has told him he is obliged on conscience to do whatever she will have him, which [the confessor] proves thus: upon the satisfaction of her mind depends the good disposition of her body; upon that the hope of succession; upon that the happiness of the monarchy, which His Majesty is obliged in conscience to do all things to procure. (Cowans 188)

Maternity, however, had negative consequences and enormous personal costs as well. For one thing, motherhood was considered to be antithetical to the wisdom and physical conditions necessary to enter the political sphere, as Juan Huarte de San Juan makes clear:

> Luego la razón de tener la primera mujer no tanto ingenio, le nació de haberla hecho Dios fría y húmida, que es el temperamento necesario para ser fecunda y paridera, y el que contradice al saber; y si la sacara templada como Adán, fuera sapientísima, pero no pudiera parir.
> [The reason the first woman was not born with much intelligence is that God created her cold and moist, the necessary temperature for women to be fecund and suitable for childbirth, but inimical to knowledge; for if He had made her temperate like Adam, she would have been very wise but not fecund.] (374)

The reality, of course, was that women such as Margarita of Austria and Isabel of Bourbon played central political roles that required the use of their intellectual faculties, wisdom, and common sense, all the while complying with their dynastic/biological responsibilities, often to the detriment of their health. It is hard to apprehend the tremendous psychological and physical demands placed on these women. Bartolomé Bennassar, for one, has harrowingly summarized the human cost to these women in *La España del siglo de oro*:

> [E]l oficio de la reina consistía en tener muchos hijos: era preciso que una reina de España trajera al mundo a numerosos príncipes y a una gran cantidad de infantas para asegurar la sucesión y para ofrecer abundantes posibilidades a la estrategia matrimonial del monarca y sus consejeros. De esta manera, de la sucesión de matrimonios procedía la acelerada sucesión de nacimientos, ciclo interminable de intensos regocijos y de funerales desolados porque la mayoría de estas criaturas principescas moría a temprana edad ... desde 1527, fecha del nacimiento del futuro Felipe II, hasta 1661, año en el que nace el futuro Carlos II, y sin tener en cuenta los embarazos interrumpidos, las reinas o futuras reinas de España tuvieron treinta y cuatro infantas o infantes, uno cada cuatro años por término medio. Ahora bien, diecisiete de ellos, exactamente la mitad, no alcanzaron su décimo año de vida.
> [The function of the queen consisted in having many children: it was crucial that the queen of Spain brought forth numerous princes and a good quantity of princesses to assure the succession and to offer abundant possibilities for the matrimonial strategies of the monarch and his advisors. Thus, from the succession of weddings there came the accelerated succession of births, an endless cycle of intense rejoicing and desolate funerals, since most of these royal creatures died at an early age ... Beginning in 1527, the date of the birth of the future Philip II, until 1661, the year in which Charles II was born, and without taking into account the miscarriages, the queens or future queens of Spain gave birth to thirty-four princes or princesses, an average of one every four years. Of course, seventeen of them, exactly half, never reached their tenth year.] (23)

R.A. Stradling speculates that at least one queen, Isabel of Bourbon, may have died of the sheer physical exhaustion resulting from trying to fulfill her numerous duties as regent (when Philip IV was at war during the Catalonian revolt), all while recovering from a difficult pregnancy: "who can doubt ... that one of the causes of Felipe's bereavement was the sheer overwork of his spouse" (*Philip IV* 241).[27]

The difficult childbearing responsibility of the Habsburg queens is not a topic directly dramatized by the *comedia*, although we do find frequent references to the thorny topic of succession. It is clear that the quotidian experiences of royal women were not the concern of seventeenth-century playwrights, but at the same time, "real" queens, whether contemporary or historic, had a profound influence on the production of the *comedia* in a variety of ways.

---

[27] Similarly, Ríos Mazcarelle states: "Isabel de Borbón se había echado la obligación de encargarse de una gran parte del trabajo burocrático, así como despachar con los ministros y atender a los diplomáticos. Su delicada salud no pudo resistir tanta acumulación de obligaciones [Isabel of Bourbon had assumed the obligation of taking on a great deal of the bureaucratic work, such as dealing with the ministers and taking care of the diplomats. Her delicate health could not endure this great accumulation of duties]" (19).

Historical Queens and/in the *Comedia*

In his book on Calderón's secular plays, Robert ter Horst tells us that "in a very specific sense, woman is sovereign in the theater of Calderón. The female who literally rules fascinates him ..." (38). At the same time, the playwright and his contemporaries seem to have been more comfortable portraying legendary or mythic queens, such as the aforementioned Zenobia and Semiramis, rather than actual historical figures.[28] Indeed, only two of the Calderón plays studied in subsequent chapters deal with historical queens: *La cisma de Inglaterra* counts among its characters Catalina de Aragón, Ana Bolena, and Maria Tudor; and *Afectos de odio y amor* [The Emotions of Hate and Love] has as its protagonist a fictionalized version of Queen Christina of Sweden, who was still alive when the play was written. The most conspicuous absences in Calderón's oeuvre are the two most famous "Isabels"—Isabel of Castile and Elizabeth I of England—and the playwright's silence represents two eloquent omissions or erasures. Isabel of Castile's almost total absence in plays by Calderón and infrequent portrayal in other Baroque *comedias* is particularly surprising since, as we have seen, she provided a unique historical model for a monarch. The playwright does include her briefly in *La niña de Gómez Arias* [Gomez Arias's Maiden], where she appears as a *dea ex machina* who metes out justice to the villainous Gómez Arias at the end of the play. Lope de Vega was the playwright who incorporated the figure of Isabel most frequently into his plays. Not only does she appear at the denouement of one of his most famous plays, *Fuenteovejuna*, but she is also one of the main characters in *El niño inocente* [The Innocent Child] and notably in *El mejor mozo de España* [*The Best Boy in Spain*]. And yet, it is fair to say that Isabel is not featured prominently as a protagonist or major character in early modern Spanish *comedias*. Indeed, Maria Caba tells us that in those plays where the Catholic queen plays "un papel digno de mención [a role worth mentioning]," her portrayals "hacen hincapié en esos rasgos de la personalidad de la Reina que podían ser utilizados para presentarla como una mujer dócil y por tanto, femenina y virtuosa [emphasize those characteristics of the Queen's personality that could be used to show her as a docile woman, feminine and virtuous]"[29] (26). Indeed, in the opening scene of Lope's *El mejor mozo de España*, Isabel appears spinning and declaring: "Tres cosas parecen

---

[28] There are, of course, exceptions. Lope de Vega's 1615 *La reina Juana de Nápoles* [Queen Juana of Naples] is based on the story of the fourteenth-century queen. Tirso de Molina's remarkable play *La prudencia en la mujer* [*Prudence in Women*] deals with María de Molina, queen regent of Castile and Leon after the death of her husband, King Sancho IV, in 1295. Ruth Kennedy deems the latter one of the best historical plays produced in Golden Age Spain, in "*La prudencia en la mujer* and the Ambient that Brought it Forth," *PMLA* 63 (1948): 113–90. Another late seventeenth-century play based on a historical queen is *La reina María Estuarda* [*Queen Mary Stuart*] by Juan Bautista Diamante, published in 1674.

[29] See *Isabel la Católica en la producción teatral española del siglo XII* (Woodbridge, England and Rochester, NY: Tamesis Books, 2008), 26. Caba deals with plays written by Lope de Vega, Tirso de Molina, and Luis Vélez de Guevara.

bien: / el religioso rezando, / el gallardo caballero / ejercitando el acero, / y la dama honesta hilando [Three things seem right: a religious man praying, a gallant knight wielding the sword, and a virtuous woman spinning]" (36–40).[30]

Isabel was an exemplary, powerful ruler, and yet, as Barbara Weissberger documents, there was always a deeply felt ambivalence toward her rule. For some, she was the epitome of feminine virtue. Others ascribe to her some masculine characteristics. For Fernán Pérez de Oliva, she was the synthesis of the ideal of "armas y letras [arms and letters]." Juan de Lucena describes her in laudatory terms and portrays her engaged in heroic masculine behavior: "asentado nuestros reales, ordenando nuestras batallas, nuestros cercos pasando; oyendo nuestras querellas; nuestros juicios formando … rodando sus reinos; andando, andando y nunca parando [pitching our camps, leading our battles, breaching our sieges; hearing our complaints; informing our moral judgment … circling her kingdoms, traveling, traveling, never stopping]."[31] Often, however, what made Isabel an acceptable exemplar of monarchical power was that she became a symbol of the "feminine" principle that, united with Fernando, the "masculine" principle, achieved an ideal platonic unity. It is perhaps her political "partnership" with her husband that allowed her to become the perfect model for the political woman. Baltasar de Gracián in *El político* [*The Politician*] sums up this attitude toward the Catholic monarchs: "Fuera rara y singular entre todas la Católica reina doña Isabel, de tan grande capacidad, que, al lado de la de un tan grande rey, pudo, no sólo darse a conocer, pero lucir. Mostrose primero en escogerle, y después en el estimarle. Cada uno de los dos era para hacer un siglo de oro y un reinado felicísimo, cuanto más entrambos juntos. [The Catholic queen, doña Isabel, was rare and unique among all women, of such great ability that, at the side of so great a king, she not only made herself known, but was also able to excel. She showed [her excellence] first by choosing him, and then by esteeming him. Each one of the two was capable of creating a golden age and a most fortunate reign, how much more so the two of them together]" (61).

This "shared sovereignty," as Lehfeldt has called it, inspired debates among chroniclers who were trying, in essence, to determine the gender of this joint crown.[32] Nevertheless, there appeared extremely negative and satiric portrayals of the Catholic queen as well. Some, including one written by her own royal

---

[30] Lope's play includes praise for the Catholic queen and she is occasionally seen as a strong and resolute woman, but *El mejor mozo* ends up being—as the title indicates—about the search for the perfect husband, to whom she will bear children to ensure the continuation of their glorious legacy.

[31] These quotes are taken from Barbara Weissberger's *Isabel Rules: Constructing Queenship, Wielding Power* (Minneapolis: U of Minnesota P, 2004). The Spanish quote appears on p. 242, note 48; Weissberger's English translation appears on p. 83.

[32] See Lehfeldt's article "The Gender of Shared Sovereignty: Texts and the Royal Marriage of Isabella and Ferdinand" in *Women, Texts, and Authority in the Early Modern Spanish World*, ed. Marta V. Vicente and Luis R. Corteguera (Aldershot, UK: Ashgate, 2003), 37–55.

chronicler, place her in the tradition of Eve and La Cava, a dangerous and even whorish woman.[33] Equally telling is the fact that, closer to Calderón's time, Saavedra Fajardo, in his brief "Política y razón de estado del Rey Don Fernando el Católico [Politics and Reason of State of King Fernando el Católico]," barely mentions Isabel, minimizing her importance in order to present Fernando as a worthy exemplar for Philip IV, to whom the essay is dedicated.

The other notorious "Isabel" was much more diligently ignored on the Spanish stage, and not just by Calderón. With the exception of Antonio Coello's *El conde de Sex* [*The Earl of Essex*] (analyzed in the third chapter in conjunction with Calderón's *La cisma de Inglaterra*), I know of no other Spanish play that deals overtly with the figure of Elizabeth I of England. The Protestant queen was a decidedly transgressive figure in the Spanish imagination and, much more so than Isabel la Católica, was an example of a particularly troubling female body. For one thing, it is well documented that the Protestant queen consciously cultivated androgyny and thus represented a lack of differentiation between social, gender, and even kinship categories. Indeed, the imagery surrounding Elizabeth portrayed her as male/female, king/queen, mother/son. She is famously credited with saying, "I know I have the body but of a weak and feeble woman; but I have the heart and stomach of a king."[34] Elizabeth was remarkable for the manner in which she was able to control the visual representation of herself as a female monarch. She shrewdly exploited the concept of the king's two bodies and applied it to herself, arguing, in essence, that the eternal body politic (understood to be male) was only temporarily embodied in the weak vessel of a woman. Furthermore, it is generally agreed that Elizabeth consciously engaged in theatricality in the sense that she was aware of the roles she needed to play or represent before her people and foreign dignitaries. Not only did she adopt many names—Queen Bess, Astrea, Elisa, the Virgin Queen—and guises, but she also brilliantly manipulated and controlled visual depictions of herself.[35] And yet, she is barely mentioned by name in the *comedias*, not even in the play that dramatizes the schism in England.

---

[33] For a comprehensive discussion of the myth of La Cava and its historical and political implications, see chapter 4 of Weissberger's book and Patricia Grieve's *The Eve of Spain: Myths of Origins in the History of Christian, Muslim and Jewish Conflict* (Baltimore: Johns Hopkins UP, 2009).

[34] This quote has long been attributed to Elizabeth as part of a speech she gave at Tilbury in 1588. Historians are not in agreement, however, as to whether she actually said these very words. Nonetheless, the phrase has become part of the English queen's legend. See Carole Levin, *The Heart and Stomach of a King: Elizabeth I and the Politics of Sex and Power* (Philadelphia: U of Pennsylvania P, 1994).

[35] The bibliography on the topic of Elizabeth's self-representation is impressive. Particularly helpful in this regard are Carole Levin's *The Heart and Stomach of a King*; Susan Frye's *Elizabeth I: the Competition for Representation* (Oxford: Oxford UP, 1993); Theodora A. Jankowski's *Women in Power in the Early Modern Drama* (Urbana: U of Illinois P, 1992); and the articles by Louis Montrose.

One area that has yet to be explored in *comedia* studies is whether the Spanish fascination with transgressive queens may not in fact have been a way of symbolically confronting the national trauma created by the enmity between Spain and England, particularly during the reign of Elizabeth I. McKendrick informs us that the "feminist theme" of the *mujer varonil*, or manly woman (and its variations: *mujer esquiva, mujer soldado,* and so on), does not seem to be present in plays written before 1570 (*Women and Society* 51). Elizabeth reigned as queen of England from 1558 to 1603, and while it would be difficult to prove categorically that the various women rulers who populated the Spanish stage are allegories of Elizabeth, it does seem curious that the appearance of this dramatic type coincided precisely with her reign. Juan de la Cueva and Cristobal de Virués were the first playwrights to intuit the dramatic possibilities of presenting strong female characters. McKendrick herself states that the late appearance of this topic may have to do with the fact that "interest in woman and her position had had time (since Erasmus) to gather momentum" (*Women and Society* 51). But perhaps the immediate historical circumstance of having a living example of a woman who had transgressed the limitations of her sex in order to become a powerful monarch influenced the creation and ultimate popularity of this dramatic type. Consciously or not, there was a need for the repeated performance of female rule on the seventeenth-century stage.

Although Baroque playwrights were more comfortable depicting legendary queens, there is no doubt that actual (living or not) queens had direct or indirect influence or presence in the production of plays. The five queens who were on the throne during Calderón's lifetime, for example—Margarita of Austria, Philip III's wife; Isabel of Bourbon and Mariana of Austria, consorts of Philip IV; and Maria Luisa of Orleans and Maria Anna of Neuburg,[36] who were married to Charles II —were involved, invoked, or inscribed in subtle manners in the plays that deal directly with monarchy. They served as inspiration, as spectators, as patrons, and even as actual performers. We know for one thing that many *comedias* were written to commemorate marriages, birthdays, christenings, or even to celebrate recovery from illnesses. In this manner, royal women often became the pretext for the theatrical composition, even when there were no characters on the stage that directly corresponded to the living queens. The *comedia* can be considered part of the official record of important events during the reign of the Habsburg dynasty. For example, when Maria Luisa of Orleans wed Charles II, there was a flurry of activities celebrating the event, including the performance of several *comedias* such as Calderón's *Afectos de odio y amor*.

Some of the Habsburg queens, like Isabel of Valois (Philip II's third wife), Margarita of Austria (Philip III's wife), the Empress María, and Isabel of Bourbon (Philip IV's first consort) were keenly interested in the theater and assumed the role of patrons, often commissioning original plays or requesting the restaging

---

[36] In this study, I will refer to Charles II's second wife using her German name, Maria Anna, instead of the Spanish "Mariana," to differentiate her from her mother-in-law, Mariana of Austria.

(often with the original cast) at the palace of plays originally presented in the *corrales*. Indeed, the Cuarto de la Reina [Queen's Chamber] was one of the spaces where *comedias* were presented with regularity.[37] Incidentally, more money was charged for presentations in the queen's quarters, "por causa de ser siempre en el inbierno con las malas noches de hielo y agua y tener algo mas de descomodidad las compañías [the reason being that (the performances) took place in the winter, with its awful icy and damp nights, and because they implied greater discomfort to the theater companies]" (Shergold and Varey, *Representaciones* 20). The very existence and survival of the *comedia* were at times the purview of the queen, the most significant instance taking place in the second half of the seventeenth century when theatrical production was for all intents and purposes at the mercy of Queen Mariana of Austria. In September 1665, she had prohibited the presentations of all *comedias* after the death of her husband, Philip IV, curiously decreeing that the prohibition would last "hasta que el rey mi hijo tenga edad para gustar de ellas o yo mandare otra cosa [until the king, my son, is old enough to enjoy them or until I decree otherwise]" (qtd. in Sanz Ayán 23). The order was rescinded in 1670, but even afterwards, according to Sanz Ayán, "la continuidad de los espectáculos teatrales palaciegos después de la representación de *Fieras afemina Amor* dependía de la actitud que mostrara Mariana de Austria a partir de entonces [the continuity of palace spectacles after the performance of *Love Feminizes Beasts* depended on the attitude displayed by Mariana of Austria]."[38]

We know also that royal women participated as players within the theatrical spectacle. Although I have not been able to find evidence that royal women acted in the specific plays studied here, ladies of the court (including queens and princesses) often took part in the *mascaras* [masques], *desfiles* [processions], dances, and other acts that were part of theatrical performances in the palace. Teresa Ferrer Valls has published documents on some of the events organized at the court between 1535 and 1622, one of which was a contest of *invenciones*— ornate tableaux, with elaborate costumes and music—in which Isabel of Valois and Philip II's sister, Princess Juana, both participated. The *relación*, or description, for this particular *máscara* begins as follows:

> Las invençiones que sacaron la reina y la princesa, año de mil quinientos y sesenta y cuatro, fueron desta manera: la reina y siete damas de una parte, y la princesa y otras tantas de la otra. El preçio fue un escritorio que valía mil quinientos ducados, por parte de la reina, y la princesa puso un arquita, que costó dos mil y quinientos, llena de guantes, gorgueras y lienços de cadenetas y muchos perfumes, primero que se començase el juego.

---

[37] The first volume of *Fuentes para la Historia del Teatro en España. Representaciones palaciegas: 1603–1699*, ed. N.D. Shergold and J.E. Varey (London: Tamesis Books, 1982), deals with several documents related to the productions in the Cuarto de la Reina, among other palace performances.

[38] See Carmen Sanz Ayán, in *Pedagogía de Reyes: El teatro palaciego en el reinado de Carlos II* (Madrid: Real Academia de la Historia, 2006), 39.

[The tableaux presented by the queen and the princess in the year 1564 were organized as follows: the queen and seven ladies-in-waiting on one side, and the princess and the same number of ladies on the other. The prize was a jewelry case valued at one thousand five hundred ducats on the queen's side; and the princess put a small chest, valued at two thousand five hundred, filled with gloves, ruffs, embroidered handkerchiefs, and many perfumes, all displayed before the contest began.] (Ferrer Valls, *Nobleza* 183)

Even when the queen herself did not participate directly, the members of her household took part in theatrical representations, as, for example, when the attendants to Princess Ana of Austria (Philip III's daughter and the future wife of the French Louis XIII) performed all the parts in Lope de Vega's *El premio de la hermosura* [*Beauty's Reward*] or when the ladies-in-waiting of Mariana de Austria performed Bances Candamo's *¿Quién es quien premia al amor?* [*Who Is It Who Rewards Love?*]. It is clear from these examples that royal and aristocratic women were very visible and active participants in the theatrical rituals of the court.

At the same time, beyond some passing statements in some extant documents, we have few accounts of the queens' reactions to specific plays. In fact, Simon Palmer has gone so far as to suggest that some of the Habsburg queens (notably María Luisa of Orleans and Maria Anna of Neuburg, the two wives of Charles II) may not have been all that interested in the *comedias* because they did not understand Spanish sufficiently well. Sanz Ayán points out, however, that a knowledge of Spanish was not necessary for someone like Maria Luisa of Orleans to enjoy a production like Calderón's *Psiquis y Cupido* [*Psyche and Cupid*], produced to celebrate her engagement to Charles:

Tratado con profusión en todas las cortes europeas, los personajes y la trama eran suficientemente conocidos por los que pertenecían a aquel universo cultural sin distinción de fronteras. Si tenemos en cuenta que la Reina no hablaba español y que casi todo lo que le rodeaba le resultaba extraño, lo más cercano a sus gustos y a su entendimiento debió ser la "lengua franca" de los espectáculos palaciegos. [Frequently invoked in all the European courts, the characters and plot were sufficiently known by all those who belonged to that cultural milieu without the distinction of national borders. If we take into account that the queen did not speak Spanish and that everything that surrounded her was strange to her, the "lingua franca" of the palace spectacles would have been most pleasing and understandable to her.] (92)

Indeed, María José Rubio tells us that as María Luisa became more familiar with the culture and language of Spain, she actually tested her mettle as

actriz protagonista en la representación de una obra teatral ante la corte. El 12 de junio de 1688 María Luisa y sus damas dan vida a una divertida comedia, con motivo del cumpleaños de Mariana de Austria. Para sorpresa de todos, la reina sale al escenario vestida de caballero. La expectación y el éxito de la obra, que muestra a una soberana nunca vista de esta guisa, hace que tenga que

representarse dos veces, ante Carlos II y su madre, los altos cargos de palacio y los grandes de España.
[principal actress in the performance of a theatrical piece at the court. On June 12, 1688, María Luisa and her ladies bring to life an entertaining comedy, on the occasion of Mariana of Austria's birthday. To everyone's surprise, the queen appears on stage dressed as a knight. The anticipation and success of the play, showing a sovereign queen in this guise, makes it necessary to perform the play twice, before Charles II and his mother, the top officials of the court, and the grandees of Spain.][39] (409)

Spectacle was a central activity at the court and, as the quotes attest, these royal women were implicated in theater—and theatricality—in multiple ways.

Much harder to ascertain is the playwright's intentionality in composing, revising, and staging certain plays in the court. Was Calderón interested, for example, in communicating certain messages or specific lessons to the queens rather than the king? Could plays that deal with tyrannical female rulers be interpreted as a questioning or critique of the queens' loyalty to the Austrian dynasty above and beyond the interest of Spain? This was an accusation launched against both Mariana of Austria and Maria Anna of Neuburg during their lifetimes and interrogated by historians ever since. Rubio tells us, for example, that:

Las princesas de Austria tienden siempre a comportarse en política como embajadoras de su dinastía natal. Todas fomentan la unión de las dos ramas Habsburgo de España y Austria y defienden los intereses familiares frente a otros reinos, a veces con instrucciones precisas de sus hermanos y padres, reyes de España o emperadores de Alemania.
[The princesses of Austria tend to always behave politically as ambassadors of their native dynasty. All of them promote the union of the two Habsburg branches of Spain and Austria and they defend the family interests vis a vis other principalities, at times under the precise instructions of their brothers, fathers, Spanish kings, or German emperors.][40] (337)

---

[39] Unfortunately, Rubio does not give us the name of the play, and I have not been able to identify it. Shergold and Varey refer to an unnamed *comedia* performed in the Cuarto de Príncipes on May 20, 1688, by "la Reina y sus damas," but they don't provide any more details (*Representaciones palaciegas* 255).

[40] To illustrate this point, Rubio tells us that the formidable Mariana of Austria opposed the marriage of the Infanta María Teresa to Louis XIV of France and promoted instead the alliance with her brother, Leopold I: "Mariana se opone radicalmente al estrecho acercamiento que se maquina entre Francia y España, así como al desaire infligido a su hermano el emperador. Instigada por los embajadores de Alemania en España, se esfuerza en promover la alianza de la casa de Austria frente a Francia, aunque sea en contra de los intereses inmediatos de la corona de España [Mariana is unwaveringly opposed to the rapprochement that is being engineered between France and Spain and to the insult inflicted on her brother, the emperor. Encouraged by the German ambassadors in Spain, she endeavors to promote an alliance with the Austrian house against France, although it would go against the immediate interests of the Spanish crown]" (337–8).

These were, after all, women who were politically well connected throughout Europe and who had had very little say in the marriage negotiations that often took them far from their homes at a very early age. Nevertheless, it would be difficult to prove conclusively any topical implications or the intention on the playwrights' part vis a vis the historical "real" queens in the audience.

At the same time, Margaret Greer has convincingly established connections between the plot of mythological plays such as *Las fortunas de Andromeda y Perseo* [*The Fortunes of Andromeda and Perseus*] and *Fieras afemina Amor* [*Love Feminizes Beasts*] and specific situations that concerned a specific Habsburg queen, Mariana of Austria. In this particular play, Juno's jealousy and rage toward Perseo (the product of Jupiter's adulterous affair) could be interpreted as a reflection of Queen Mariana's hostility toward Don Juan José, the product of Philip's adulterous dalliance with the actress known as La Calderona.[41] We know that, historically, Mariana saw the dashing Don Juan José as a threat to her own sons, Felipe Prospero and Charles.[42] Another example of how the general thematic concerns of the plays were made to coincide with contemporary circumstances involving the queens was *El mayor monstruo del mundo* [*The Greatest Monster in the World*], a play published in 1637 but revived (and revised) between 1667 and 1672 by Calderón—in part, perhaps, because the name of one of the characters, Mariene, was a homonym for Mariana.[43] Even when a play itself did not present

---

[41] There continues to be a great deal of speculation as to the true identity of La Calderona and as to when her affair with the king began. Many sources identify her as María Calderón while others call her María Inés Calderón. Don W. Cruickshank in his authoritative biography of Calderón de la Barca, however, tells us that there were in fact two actress sisters—Inés and María—whose last name was Calderón (no relation to the playwright). Although he doesn't clarify where the information comes from, he tells us that Inés was the royal mistress and mother of Philip's illegitimate son (*Don Pedro Calderón de la Barca* (Cambridge: Cambridge UP, 2009), 88.

[42] In addition to chapter 4 ("The Problem of Don Juan José") in Margaret Greer's *The Play of Power: Mythological Court Dramas of Calderón de la Barca* (Princeton: Princeton UP, 1991), see also the introduction to her edition of *La estatua de Prometeo* (Kassel: Edition Reichenberger, 1986) for additional discussions of the political dimension of Calderón's mythological plays.

[43] *El mayor monstruo del mundo* is not included in this study because, despite the homonymous echo in the name of this character with that of the queen, the play itself does not deal primarily with feminine monarchical power. In *The Drama of the Portrait: Theater and Visual Culture in Early Modern Spain* (University Park: Penn State UP, 2008), Laura Bass dedicates chapter 4 to a discussion of *El mayor monstruo*. Dealing with a similar but earlier context, Elizabeth Wright has suggested that Lope's *La hermosa Ester* contains echoes of the struggles between Margaret of Austria and the Duke of Lerma: "Though surviving documents do not permit more than an inference, the political allusions built into the Queen Esther story do suggest possible channels from Margaret of Austria's court network to the playwright [Lope de Vega]." See *Pilgrimage to Patronage: Lope de Vega and the Court of Philip III 1598–1621* (Lewisburg: Bucknell UP 2001), 116–17.

any direct correspondences between stage and court players, the playwrights engaged the queen directly through the *loas* [prologues] and even the décor.

The *loas* to the plays of Francisco Bances Candamo, for example, directly addressed Charles II's consorts—first Maria Luisa of Orleans and then Maria Anna of Neuburg—in order to remind them that the proper biological function of the queen's body is to provide a dynastic heir to ensure, in turn, the proper functioning of the body politic. In the *loa* to Bances's *Cómo se curan los celos* [How Jealousy Can Be Cured], the playwright presents a fictional onomastic genealogy based on Charles's name (Carlos) that includes the names of historical and legendary monarchs whose names begin with the letters of the king's name (for example, C for Charles I and Charlemagne, R for Ramiro, S for Sancho and Segismundo). The *loa* also pointedly addresses Maria Anna of Neuburg, reminding her of her duty to continue the royal line: "Y Mariana divina / a España alegre / le duplique este nombre en descendientes [And may divine Maria Anna duplicate for a joyous Spain that name through descendants] (*Cómo se curan los celos* 111).[44] Often, plays and *autos sacramentales* [religious plays] dealt specifically with events related to a particular queen, as, for example, Calderón's *La segunda esposa y triunfar muriendo* [*The Second Wife and Triumph in Death*], which celebrated Philip IV's betrothal to Mariana of Austria, not coincidently (given the *auto*'s title) his second wife.[45]

Given the scarcity of detailed information surrounding the staging of the plays studied here and their reception by specific members of the royal audience, it will be difficult to establish clear correspondences between the plots and actual situations or players in the court. The analyses of the plays that follow will focus, therefore, primarily on how these works engage with the notion of monarchy in general and with fantasies of female rule specifically. As mentioned in the introduction, Joseph Roach alludes to the process of surrogation in performances: that is, the attempt to supplement a lack, an absence, or a cultural memory. At a time when the legitimization of power often involved a search for origins and models of behavior, it is very suggestive that often this surrogation materialized through the presentation of women in power on the *comedia* stage. The questions and contradictions that we find in these plays point to deep anxieties about the gendering of power.

---

[44] For more information on Bances Candamo, see Ignacio Arellano's "Teoría dramática y práctica teatral. Sobre el teatro áulico y político de Bances Candamo," *Criticón* 42 (1988): 169–93; and Quintero's "Political Intentionality and Dramatic Convention in the *teatro palaciego* of Francisco Bances Candamo," *Revista de Estudios Hispánicos* 20.3 (1986): 37–53 and "Monarchy and the Limits of Exemplarity in Francisco Bances Candamo's *La piedra filosofal*," *Hispanic Review* 66 (1998): 1–21.

[45] See the first chapter of Stephen Rupp's *Allegories of Kingship: Calderón and the Anti-Machiavellian Tradition* (Philadelphia: U of Pennsylvania P, 1996) for a detailed study of *La segunda esposa*.

Chapter 2
Beauty and the Machiavellian Beast

> It is all the hurt that evil men can do to Noble Women and Princes, to spread abroad lies and dishonourable tales of them and ... we of all Princes that be women, are subject to be slandered wrongfully of them that be our adversaries.
> —Catherine de' Medici[1]

Calderón's *La gran Cenobia*

Pedro Calderón de la Barca occupied an ambivalent but strategic position within the political climate of the Spanish court. Like other playwrights who wrote for the court, he was indebted to the monarchy and depended on its support for his livelihood and social standing. At the same time, his occupation necessarily made him an active participant in the political community of the court, not just as panegyrist for the king, but also as a commentator. Critics such as John Elliott, Jonathan Brown, and Margaret Greer have studied Calderón's extensive involvement in the preparation and production of elaborate courtly spectacles, but not enough has been written in more general terms about the difficult situation that Calderón and all court playwrights found themselves in.[2] Theirs was an ill-defined status among the other courtiers, for while they were not typically members of the powerful nobility, neither were they mere servants or entertainers. Calderón was named Knight of the Order of Santiago in 1637; but like so many artists working within the patronage system of early modern Spain, he seems to have spent an inordinate amount of time petitioning for pensions and official court posts.[3]

---

[1] Qtd. in Montrose, "Idols of the Queen Policy, Tender, and the Picturing of Elizabeth I," *Representations* 68 (1999), 118.

[2] For discussions of the role of poets and playwrights vis a vis their patrons, see Jonathan Brown's *Velázquez: Painter and Courtier* (New Haven: Yale UP, 1986); Margaret Greer's *The Play of Power: Mythological Court Dramas of Calderón de la Barca* (Princeton: Princeton UP, 1991); Jonathan Brown and John Elliott's *A Palace for a King: The Buen Retiro and the Court of Philip IV* (New Haven: Yale UP, 1980); and Elizabeth Wright's *Pilgrimage to Patronage: Lope de Vega and the Court of Philip III 1598–1621* (Lewisburg: Bucknell UP, 2001).

[3] In his excellent biography of Calderón, *Don Pedro Calderón* (Cambridge: Cambridge UP, 2009), Don Cruickshank describes Calderón's struggles for recognition and remuneration at the court. He quotes the following from a *memorial* the playwright wrote to the king in 1648:

> Y assi suplica a V.M. que en consideracion destos seruicios, y otros particulares, de que no haze mencion en este Memorial, por ser menores, y no de esta calidad, no dignos de ponerse en el, aunque lo sean de traerlos a la memoria de V.M. sea seruido de q[ue] la satisfacion que se le dè sea vna llave de Ayuda de Camara de V.M.

Norbert Elias's work, particularly *The Civilizing Process*, has brought attention to court society as a historically important site of social organization and has invited us to rethink the role of courtiers in settings such as the court of Louis XIV. For one thing, Elias applied the term *homo clausus* to nobles in early modern Europe (particularly France) who relinquished their own material and political interests in order to conform to a central absolutist monarchy. Inspired by Elias's term, Mark Franko has coined the term *homo strategicus* in his study of French Baroque dance to refer to individuals—for example, choreographers, musicians, librettists, and professional dancers—who, working within the rarefied atmosphere of Versailles, occupied an intermediary position similar to that of playwrights such as Calderón in the Spanish court.[4] According to Franko, a *homo strategicus* is someone "who can suggest change playfully, resisting the status quo by feigning to play" (10), and this may be an apt description of Calderón and other palace playwrights. The practitioner of a singularly accessible and visible art form, Calderón had the unique opportunity of "educating" an audience that included the king himself while providing a popular form of entertainment. Despite being economically dependent on the Crown and ideologically supportive of the regime, he was able to take strategic advantage of the conditions of play (both as drama and as ludic activity) in order to suggest change or reform in a manner that did not threaten the prince or the institution of the monarchy.

Calderón did not leave an *ars dramatica* describing his political strategies as playwright for the Habsburg court; but in a treatise titled *Theatro de los theatros de los passados y presentes siglos* [*Theater of Theaters of the Past and Present Centuries*], his follower Francisco Bances Candamo eloquently describes the dual (even duplicitous) role of the playwright as both entertainer and also preceptor

---

> [And so he begs Your Majesty that it may please him that the settlement he should be given should be the key of an assistant in Your Majesty's privy chamber, in consideration of the services and of other special ones not mentioned in this memorial because they are lesser ones and not of this quality, nor worthy of being listed in it, although they are worthy of being brought to Your Majesty's memory.] (272; the translation is Cruickshank's)

[4] In *Dance as Text: Ideologies of the Baroque Body* (Cambridge: Cambridge UP, 1993), Franko uses this term as a category to supplement what he sees as the two "critically dominant historical visions of Renaissance and baroque society" (10): Norbert Elias's notion of the *homo clausus* and Mikhail Bakhtin's *homo ludens*. Elias tells us that the *homo clausus* acceded to a political, "civilized" resignation and self-control that was in keeping with ideas of contemporary (that is, seventeenth century) absolutist state formation. See *The Civilizing Process: The History of Manners* (New York: Urizen, 1986). At the other end of the social spectrum, Franko speaks of Bakhtin's *homo ludens*, attributing to the Russian critic a term usually associated with Johan Huizinga in his classic book *Homo Ludens: A Study of the Play-Element in Culture* (Boston: Beacon Press, 1955).

to the prince.[5] Bances understood the civic obligation implicit in his salaried position as court playwright to Charles II. His responsibility was to inform, alert, and educate the monarch in the art of kingship. In *Theatro de los theatros*, Bances states:

> ... me hallo elegido de su Magestad por su Real decreto para escriuir vnicamente sus festejos, y con renta asignada por ello, he juzgado tocarme por muchos títulos estudiar *ex profeso* quanto pudiese conducir a hacer arte áulica y pollítica la de festejar a tan gran Rei, cuios oídos se me entregan aquellas tres horas, siendo ésta vna de las maiores confianzas que se pueden hacer de vna doctrina.
> [... I find myself elected by his Majesty's royal decree to be the sole author of his festivities, with a stipend set apart for that very purpose, and I have deemed it my *ex profeso* responsibility to study in my texts all that would be useful in producing a courtly and political art out of celebrating such a great king, whose ears are mine during those three hours; this being one of the greatest uses that can be made out of doctrine.] (56)

The *comedia*, according to Bances, is the perfect didactic vehicle "donde insensiblemente se le puede dar a veber [al Rey] la doctrina bañada en la dulzura de los números [where, without his realizing it, one can offer [the king] the drink of doctrine immersed in the sweetness of its parts]" (57). Most remarkably, he forcefully states that a playwright's loyalty to the king should not make him forget his responsibility to the welfare of the realm: "Ni aun en la diuersión se han de apartar del bien público los Monarchas, porque han de descansar de obrar aprendiendo a obrar. Quien diuierte mal a un Príncipe soberano, todo aquel tiempo que le ocupa se lo hurta al bien público [Not even in moments of leisure should monarchs disengage themselves from the public good, for they should learn how to dispatch their duties while resting from their duties. Whoever entertains the sovereign prince badly is stealing from the public good during the entire time he entertains him]" (57).

Although Calderón never produced a similar theoretical treatise on his dramaturgy (nor, indeed, did he ever hold the official title of court playwright, as Bances Candamo did), it is clear that he, too, recognized the need to forge a strategy for both celebrating the monarch (*festejar*) and providing lessons

---

[5] Bances Candamo has received steady critical attention over the last decades. In addition to the articles by Arellano and Quintero cited in Chapter 1 (note 44), see also Santiago García Castañón's "La autoridad real en el teatro de Bances Candamo" in *Looking at the comedia in the Year of the Quincentennial*, ed. Barbara Mujica, Sharon D. Voros, and Matthew Stroud (Lanham, MD: UP of America, 1993), 229–34; and Juan Sánchez Belén's "La educación del príncipe en el teatro de Bances Candamo," *Revista Literaria* 49.97 (1987): 73–93. All owe a great debt to Duncan Moir, who, in the introduction to his excellent edition of Bances Candamo's *Theatro de los Theatros de los passados y presentes siglos* (London: Tamesis Books, 1970), provides the first serious study of this previously neglected playwright.

(*arte áulica y pollítica*) in leadership and statecraft.[6] It is, furthermore, possible to establish a correspondence, as several critics have done, between Calderón's plays and the *de regimine* treatises of *arbitristas* and theorists who were more overtly critical of the Crown and its policies.[7] The seventeenth century saw the appearance of numerous treatises that endeavored to alert the monarch to a wide variety of real and perceived crises. Political theorists such as Diego Saavedra Fajardo and *arbitristas* such as Miguel Alvarez Osorio and Juan Baños de Velasco (among many others) addressed the crisis of the monarchy directly and provided in their treatises specific plans to resolve the various problems facing the nation at the time. The work of the *arbitristas*—"los intelectuales de la monarquía [the intellectuals of the monarchy]," as Lisón Tolosana calls them (60)—was meant to provide an inducement to action and change during an extraordinarily vulnerable time for the Spanish monarchy and empire. In addition, as Lehfeldt has claimed, these writers were also singularly concerned with a crisis of masculinity among the aristocracy that, in their view, accounted for much of the decline of Spain.

Dramatists, equally aware of the calamities that beset the nation, had at their disposal the exceptionally effective theatrical space for displaying a mirror of kingship through representations of gender on the stage, among other strategies. For Calderón and *calderonistas* like Bances Candamo, theater became an extension of political thought, an acting-out of contemporary theories of state.[8] We might even

---

[6] Calderón would allude to this strategy of "decir sin decir" in his play *Darlo todo o no dar nada* [To Give All or To Give Nothing] (electronic text prepared by David Hildner, n.d., Web. 4 Sept. 2010, <*comedias.org/calderon/DARLO.pdf*>) when Alejandro praises Apeles for painting a portrait of the king in profile, thereby neither falsifying nor displaying the imperfections in his appearance: "Buen camino habéis hallado / de hablar y callar discreto [You have found the right path in discretely speaking and staying silent]" (547–8). Later, he calls the work "político ejemplo / de que ha de buscarse modo / de hablar al rey con tal tiento / que ni disuene la voz / ni lisonjee el silencio [a politic example of how to find a way of speaking to the king with such discretion that the voice does not offend him nor the silence flatter him]" (564–8).

[7] The word *arbitristas* was used to describe reformers who were concerned with the dire state of affairs in the country. Some of their suggestions were utopian and outlandish, thus earning frequent ridicule from writers, prominently Francisco de Quevedo. For two interesting discussions of the *arbitristas*, see Melveena McKendrick, *Playing the King: Lope de Vega and the Limits of Conformity* (London: Tamesis, 2000), especially chapter 2, and J.H. Elliott's article "Self-Perception and Decline in Early Seventeenth-Century Spain," *Past and Present* (1977): 41–61.

[8] Dian Fox, in *Kings in Calderón: A Study in Characterization and Political Theory* (London: Tamesis, 1986), was perhaps the first to suggest the view of this theater as a forum for staging some of the same theories espoused by the *arbitristas* (17). Fox's work has been influential in the development of my ideas. More recently, Carmen Sanz Ayán, in *Pedagogía de Reyes: El teatro palaciego en el reinado de Carlos II* (Madrid: Real Academia de la Historia, 2006), has given a more specific example of the relationship between theatrical presentations and some theories proposed by the *arbitristas* in the second half of the seventeenth century, "… algunos de los que pretendían comunicar propuestas de carácter económico para cambiar o a su juicio mejorar, algún aspecto relativo al comercio o la navegación, conscientes de

claim that the *comedia* represented an *aesthetics* of monarchy that complemented the corpus of political thought found in the treatises written by the *arbitristas*. Specifically, Calderón's dramas often become enactments of tyrannies, theatrical manifestations of anti-Machiavellian political thought, among other things. This is not to suggest that the drama was *only* an illustration of the views of political theorists, but rather to assert that the plays went beyond mere entertainment and became useful and creative tools in the ongoing debate on the monarchy.

Both the *comedia* and didactic literature often depended on the dialectical presentation of good and bad models of monarchy. The two genres displayed the humanist interest in exemplarity, taking models from the classical tradition in order to offer commentary on the contemporary political situation and the nature of the monarchy in general. Timothy Hampton has stated that humanist writing on exemplarity "was marked by a series of rhetorical and epistemological paradoxes involving the interpretation of the past and its application to practical political action" (x); and certainly the same can be said of many of the plays and political tracts that appeared at this time of social and political upheaval in Spain. Through the dramatization of historical and mythic figures, these texts enact genealogies of monarchy and engage the past in order to fashion both positive and negative, both male and female exemplars of kingship. With regard to history, for example, Juan de Mariana states: "No deje pues nunca de la mano el príncipe la lectura de la historia, revuelva constantemente y con afán los anales nacionales y extranjeros, y encontrará mucho bueno que imitar de ciertos príncipes, mucho malo que evitar, si no quiere llevar una triste y desgraciada vida [The prince should never abandon the reading of history; let him constantly and with interest mull over national and foreign annals, for he will find therein much good to imitate in certain princes and much to avoid, if he does not want to lead a sad and unfortunate life]" (513). Antiquity provided a wealth of models to "imitar [imitate]" and "evitar [avoid]"; and it also allowed for a distancing mechanism that allowed a *homo strategicus* such as Calderón to communicate his didactic message effectively in a non-threatening manner—thus reworking on the palace stage the Horatian ideal of "prodesse et delectare [teaching and delighting]," what Bances Candamo would call "decir sin decir [to say without saying]."

This chapter undertakes a comparison of two plays that exploit Classical legends as a means of exploring the workings of gender and its connection to ideologies of power and authority: Calderón's *La gran Cenobia* [The Great Cenobia] and Tirso de Molina's *La república al revés* [The Republic Upside Down]. One of the earliest plays by Calderón dealing with feminine sovereignty,

---

que estas cuestiones se hallaban en un segundo plano de interés respecto a la actualidad política, concluyeron que serían más y mejor escuchados si traducían su arbitrio a comedia *a la italiana en nueve escenas* [… some of those who hoped to communicate proposals dealing with economic matters meant, in their judgment, to improve or change some aspect related to commerce or navigation, conscious that these questions were of secondary interest with regard to the political reality, concluded that they would get more and better attention if they translated their ideas to a *comedia* in the Italian manner, with nine scenes]" (59).

La gran Cenobia (first performed in 1625 and published in 1636), has been for the most part ignored by literary critics until recently. Indeed, Valbuena Briones called it "de segunda fila [of second rank]" and Melveena McKendrick deemed it "defective."[9] A more generous assessment, and one that coincides partially with the approach I am taking in this study, has been provided by Rina Walthaus, who considers the play a *speculum principis* [mirror of princes] whose purpose was to instruct the young Philip IV on the virtues required to become a good king ("Representar tragedias" 399). What is instructive for our purposes is that the model chosen for the ideal prince is a woman.

La gran Cenobia takes its name from a legendary queen of Palmyra (Syria) who was born around 241 A.D. and whose story was recorded in the *Historia Augusta* (c.395) and in numerous other classical sources.[10] Zenobia also appeared prominently in various medieval and early modern treatises dealing with exemplary feminine figures taken from antiquity, from Boccaccio's fourteenth-century *De claris mulieribus* [*Concerning Famous Women*], to Fernán Pérez de Guzmán's 1450 *Generaciones y semblanzas* [*Generations and Portraits*], to Juan Luis Vives's 1524 *Instrucción de la mujer cristina*, to Antonio de Guevara's 1539

---

[9] According to McKendrick: "The issues are too clear-cut, the contrast too extreme, the protagonist too blandly perfect." See *Women and Society in the Spanish Drama of the Golden Age: A Study of the* mujer varonil (Cambridge: Cambridge UP, 1974), 201. McKendrick compares it with Tirso's *La prudencia en la mujer*. As indicated in my introduction, McKendrick views these plays not as meditations on the rule of women per se, but more generally as dealing with the question of kingship. Critics who have studied *La gran Cenobia* include Frederick de Armas in *The Return of Astraea: An Astral-Imperial Myth in Calderón* (Lexington: Kentucky UP, 1986); David Hildner in *Reason and the Passions in the comedias of Calderón* (Amsterdam/Philadelphia: John Benjamins, 1982); Hildegard Hollmann in "El retrato del tirano Aureliano en *La gran Cenobia*" in *Hacia Calderón: Cuarto Coloquio Anglogermano*, ed. Hans Flasche, Karl-Hermann Körner, and Hans Mattauch (Berlin: Walter de Gruyter, 1979); and most recently, Rina Walthaus in "La fortaleza de Cenobia y la mutabilidad de Fortuna: dos emblemas femeninos en *La gran Cenobia* de Calderón*," in *Que toda la vida es sueño, y los sueños, sueños son. Homenaje a don Pedro Calderón de la Barca*, ed. Ysla Campbell (Ciudad Juárez, México: Universidad Autónoma de Ciudad Juárez, 2000), 109–28, and Walthaus in "'Representar tragedias así la Fortuna sabe': la representación de Fortuna en dos comedias tempranas de Calderón (*Saber del mal y del bien* y *La gran Cenobia*)," *Calderón 2000: Actas del Congreso Internacional IV Centenario del nacimiento de Calderón (Universidad de Navarra, 2000)*, ed. Ignacio Arellano, vol. 2 (Kassel: Reichenberger, 2002), 397–409.

[10] For a detailed account of the sources of Zenobia's story, see Richard Stoneman's *Palmyra and Its Empire: Zenobia's Revolt Against Rome* (Ann Arbor: U of Michigan P, 1992). According to Stoneman, Zenobia's appeal is not limited to distant eras: "the figure of Zenobia of Palmyra has a number of obvious resonances in our own world. Her story introduces the figure of an Arab and a woman, pitted against the Western world" (vii). In this chapter, I will use the spelling "Zenobia" to refer to the legendary queen or when citing accounts or texts that use this spelling; "Cenobia" will be used when referring to the character in Calderón's play.

Epistolas familiares [*Familiar Epistles*]. Like Dido of Carthage and Semiramis of Assyria, Zenobia belongs to a group of legendary queens with classical and/or semitic origins who held great appeal in the Medieval and early modern imaginary. Interestingly, as Rina Walthaus points out, Calderón seems to have been the only Golden Age playwright to bring her story to the stage ("La fortaleza" 113). Precisely because it is neither the most accomplished nor the most complex of Calderonian texts, *La gran Cenobia* presents a useful point of departure to study the playwright's evolving aesthetics of feminine rule and the gendering of power.

Tirso de Molina's *La república al revés* (1611)[11] also takes its inspiration from antiquity. The exemplary feminine model here is Irene, an empress of Byzantium, who, like Zenobia, was a legendary warrior queen featured in many of the same Renaissance texts cited before, including Petrarch's *Trionfi* [*The Triumphs*] and Boccaccio's *De claris mulieribus* [*Concerning Famous Women*]. In *La república al revés*, Tirso eschews the negative aspects of Irene's legend (Boccaccio, for example, called her cunning and power-hungry) and makes her a sympathetic and admirable character.[12] This play and Calderón's *Cenobia* are strikingly similar in that they both present a dialectical opposition between a clearly tyrannical male king and a much more capable—if not always unambiguous—female ruler.

Both plays offer a double performance of power—one in which simultaneous positive and negative exemplars are presented, providing an internal and gendered mirroring and performance of power. In the treatises on kingship written at the time, the dialectic dynamic implied in exemplarity is effected through the intended primary recipient of the texts: the king himself. In fact, many of the *arbitristas* and political theorists—including Saavedra Fajardo, Pedro de Rivadeneira, and

---

[11] Again, as with so many Baroque *comedias*, there is some confusion as to the date of composition. Blanca de los Ríos suggested the 1611 date, but Ruth Kennedy proposes 1615 or 1616, with some significant revisions made in 1621. Kennedy suggests that when Philip IV became king, Tirso rewrote parts of the play as part of a plan to request a position in the court of the new king; see "Tirso's *La república al revés*: Its Debt to Mira's *La rueda de la fortuna*, Its Date of Composition, and Its Importance," *Reflexión* 2.2 (1973): 39–50.

[12] *La república* has, in the past 15 years, received well-deserved attention and insightful criticism, most recently from Christopher Weimer in "A *Comedia* Re-Viewed: An Alternative Reading of Tirso's *La república al revés*," in *Looking at the* Comedia *in the Year of the Quincentennial*, Proceedings of the 1992 Symposium on Golden Age Drama at the University of Texas, El Paso, March 18–21, ed. Barbara Mujica and Sharon D. Voros (Lanham, MD: University Press of America, 1993), 219–25, and "The Oedipal Drama of Tirso's *La república al revés*," *Bulletin of the Comediantes* 47.2 (1995): 291–309. See also Ignacio Arellano's "Estrategias de inversión en *La república al revés*, comedia política y moral de Tirso de Molina," *Tirso de Molina, del siglo de oro al siglo XX*. Actas del Coloquio Internacional, Pamplona, Universidad de Navarra (Pamplona: Revista Estudios, 1995): 9–26. These two plays also reveal their authors' evolving aesthetics. Just as *La gran Cenobia* can be seen as anticipating Calderon's masterpiece *La hija del aire*, so, too, Tirso's play has been considered something of a preliminary draft for the highly regarded *La prudencia en la mujer*.

Juan de Mariana—ostentatiously dedicated their works to the monarch; and with this gesture of singling out the king as the principal reader of their tracts, they invited a comparison between the historic or legendary figures and the current circumstances of the actual monarch. The *comedias* under consideration, while partaking in the ideology of monarchy presented in these political tracts, provide a more public, immediate, and complex dialectic than the one presented by the treatises. By visually enacting simultaneously two versions of kingship, *La república al revés* and *La gran Cenobia* would have redoubled on the stage what was potentially already a dual spectacle inherent in all palace theater: the king watching versions of kingship on the stage.[13] That is, the privileged royal viewer would find himself invited to observe both negative and positive alter egos. Again, what makes *La gran Cenobia* and *La república al revés* remarkable is that in the almost Manichean opposition between wise and disastrous models of monarchy, the positive exemplars are women and the negative are feminized males. Gender informs the exemplarity of these two plays and although, as I have suggested, the king was the implied recipient of the lessons, we can also speculate on what the queens watching these plays might have taken away from such performances.

In *La gran Cenobia*, Calderón sets up an antithetical relationship from the beginning between Cenobia and the Roman emperor, Aureliano; and in this, the play replicates the typical presentation of the tyrant in Greek tragedy. As Diego Lanza in *Il tirano e il suo publico* [*The Tyrant and His Public*] points out, the Greek tyrant is always a "deuteragonist," or secondary character, paired with either the actual hero or a woman who threatens his masculinity (31). Calderón's play follows this classical model, and Cenobia will be presented as a prudent and courageous monarch who is also a formidable warrior. Aureliano, by contrast, will be the personification of tyranny, the inverted mirror of Cenobia's exemplarity. As Walthaus suggests, the queen brings to mind emblems and feminine allegorical figures that would have been familiar to seventeenth-century audiences: "Cabe considerar la presencia y actualidad—y con ello, la influencia en el imaginario colectivo—en el siglo XVII de una amplia tradición iconográfica (grabados, emblemas, pinturas, esculturas), donde la mujer fuerte aparece como personificación alegórica de una fuerza espiritual (*Justitia, Prudentia, Fortitudo, Castitas*, etc.) [It is worth considering the presence and relevance—and with that, the influence in the collective imaginary—in the seventeenth century of a vast iconographic tradition (engravings, emblems, paintings, sculpture), where

---

[13] While we have no indication that *La república al revés* was ever performed in the court, *La gran Cenobia* was presented in the palace at least four times: in 1625, presumably before Isabel of Bourbon and Philip IV; in 1676, the year after Mariana of Austria stopped being regent of Spain after Philip IV's death and her son Charles II had ascended to the throne, and there were intense negotiations as to who would become his wife (Mariana's preferred candidate, María Antonia of Austria, lost out to the French princess, Maria Luisa of Orleans); and twice in 1685, before Charles II and Maria Luisa.

the strong woman appears as the allegorical personification of a spiritual force (Justice, Prudence, Fortitude, Chastity, etc.]" ("La fortaleza" 120).

Given the compelling figure of the legendary warrior queen—one familiar to Calderón's audience—it is surprising that the play seems primarily concerned with the figure of her antagonist. Indeed, the play begins with Aureliano placed in a setting that is immediately familiar to readers of *La vida es sueño* [*Life is a Dream*].[14] He appears "en pieles [in furs]," and this is the first hint that he will represent an unnatural, uncivilized force. Treatises such as Mariana's influential and controversial *Del rey y de la institución real* [*On the King and the Royal Institution*] were specifically concerned with alerting the king to the dangers of tyranny by providing analogies such as "el tirano es una bestia fiera y cruel [the tyrant is a fierce and cruel beast]" (482). The association between the abuse of power and a bestial nature was not new, of course. In the *Republic* and the *Gorgias*, Plato had described the tyrant as a "natural" man, closer to an animal than a human because he seeks only to satisfy his own desires (Bushnell 20–23). Furthermore, and more immediate to Calderon's time, is the Machiavellian subtext that such an association uncovers, for in the infamous Italian treatise, the paradigmatic ruler is presented as half man and half beast:

> A prince must know how to use both what is proper to man and what is proper to beasts. The writers of antiquity taught rulers this lesson allegorically when they told how Achilles and many other ancient princes were sent to be nurtured by Chiron the centaur so that he would train them in his discipline. Their having a creature half-man and half-beast as tutor only means that a prince must know how to use both the one and the other nature, and that the one without the other cannot endure. (68)

Associated with nature and incivility from the beginning, Aureliano will soon find himself thrust in a leadership position for which he will prove woefully inadequate. In the introductory scene, he has just woken up from a dream in which the dead Emperor Quintilio tells him: "Ves aquí mi laurel, mi cetro toma, / que tú serás emperador de Roma [Here you see my laurel, take my scepter, for you will be emperor of Rome]" (21–2).[15] Immediately afterward, Aureliano finds a crown and scepter that have been abandoned (in an iconic representation of the absence of leadership) on a tree branch. Taking this as an omen that his fortune is about to change as announced by the dream, he dons these attributes of power and proceeds to admire himself in a pool of water. The already incongruous presentation of

---

[14] The scene is also reminiscent of the beginning of *El purgatorio de San Patricio* [St. Patrick's Purgatory], in which the ruthless king of Ireland, Egerio, also appears "vestido de pieles." See Calderón's *Obras completas*, vol. 1, ed. Angel Valbuena Briones (Madrid: Aguilar, 1959), 178*a*.

[15] I am using the version of *La gran Cenobia* edited by Ángel Valbuena Briones in the *Primera parte de comedias de don Pedro Calderón de la Barca* (Madrid: Consejo Superior de Investigaciones Científicas 1974), 1–85.

a body in a debased state—*pieles*—would have become even more complicated and potentially offensive in an actual performance when these over-determined symbols of monarchy are placed on the actor playing Aureliano.[16]

Seventeenth-century audiences were singularly skilled in reading visual codes, emblems, and symbols associated with monarchy, and they would have been aware of the oxymoronic message of this particular tableau. The scene is reminiscent of certain emblems: for example, one in Saavedra Fajardo's *Idea de un príncipe político* portrays monarchical power as a lion's skin that hangs on a peg, suggesting, as Alban Forcione has pointed out, "a disguise in a theater's dressing room" (65). Theatricality in the sense of inauthentic role-playing, another of the characteristics of tyranny, is here indirectly ascribed to Aureliano. Furthermore, the specular situation created by the character looking at his likeness in the water communicates to the audience Aureliano's inherent and all-encompassing narcissism; he sees himself, in fact, as nothing less than a reflection of the world itself:

> Pequeño mundo soy y en esto fundo
> que en ser señor de mí lo soy del mundo
> En este lisongero
> espejo fugitivo mirar quiero
> cómo el resplandeciente
> laurel assienta en mi dichosa frente.
> [I am a microcosm, a small world, and based on this, I believe that by mastering myself, I will become master of the world. In this flattering and fugitive mirror I want to see how this resplendent laurel sits on my fortunate forehead.] (65–70)

In *The Return of Astraea*, Frederick de Armas tells us that in this scene, Aureliano "is applying the Renaissance theory of man as a microcosm. Since he can rule himself, he claims, he can also rule the world, which is part of the macrocosm" (73). What predominates, however, is not self-control. Instead, megalomania, egotism, and the thirst for flattery—all characteristics associated with a tyrant and also, significantly in the case of the last two, with women—are summarized in this passage. Aureliano even goes on to ascribe sacredness to his person, associating reverence for the emperor with idolatry:

---

[16] David Hildner, who in his *Reason and the Passions* studies the Machiavellian subtext in *La gran Cenobia*, emphasizes the importance of these objects (52). For a detailed discussion of the use of props in this play, see also María Cristina Quintero, "The Things They Carried: Objects and the Female Sovereign in Calderón de la Barca's *La gran Cenobia*," in *Objects of Culture in Imperial Spain*, ed. Mary Barnard and Frederick de Armas, University of Toronto Press (forthcoming). Yolanda Novo provides a helpful reconstruction of the staging of the play in "Rasgos escenográficos y reconstrucción escénica de *La gran Cenobia* (1636)," in *Teatro calderoniano sobre el tablado: Calderón y su puesta en escena a través de los siglos*, XII Coloquio Anglogermano sobre Calderón, ed. Manfred Tietz, Archivum Calderonianum 10 (Stuttgart: Franz Steiner Verlag, 2003): 359–90.

¡Oh sagrada figura!,
haga el original a la pintura
debida reverencia,
quando llevado en mis discursos hallo
que yo doy y recibo la obediencia,
siendo mi Emperador y mi vassallo.
Narciso en una fuente,
de su misma belleza enamorado,
rindió la vida; y yo más dignamente,
dando toda la rienda a mi cuidado,
si no de mi belleza,
Narciso pienso ser de mi fiereza.
[Oh sacred figure! Let the original give due reverence to the painting, when in the midst of my eloquence I find that I both demand and receive obedience, since I am both my emperor and my vassal. Narcissus, in a fountain, in love with his own beauty, gave up his life; in a more dignified manner, giving free reign to my caution, I wish to be the Narcissus, if not of my beauty, then of my fierceness.]
(71–82)

These words allude to the limits of representation in general and his lack of authenticity, by inverting natural order and sequence: this character asks the original to give reverence to the copy, to the simulacrum. The strange sight of a "monarch" dressed in animal skins and worshiping himself would put into play and interrogate other more reverential visual representations of monarchy. Aureliano's inability to go beyond his own thirst for power and might (*fiereza*) make of this character a textbook case for despotism. In addition, Aureliano's words are of interest because they offer the antithetical opposition between two different sources of authority—"belleza" and "fiereza," beauty and force—thus preparing the audience for his enmity with Cenobia, who, in addition to possessing all the virtues associated with an ideal monarch, will be presented as the epitome of beauty.

Beauty is in fact one of the much-reiterated characteristics of queens in Calderón, one of their defining traits; and it would be worthwhile to consider briefly the concept of beauty and how it related to women and power in early modern Spain. In the literature and treatises of the time, beauty is presented in paradoxical, often contradictory modes. On the one hand, feminine *hermosura* is seen as treacherous, an inducement to sin and perdition, as Juan Luis Vives makes clear in his *Instrucción a la mujer cristiana*, for example:

> Por ende la nuestra virgen cristiana no debe estar muy ufana con su hermosura, ni engallarse con su nobleza, ni estar muy ancha, teniéndose por muy graciosa o palaciega, ni estará que no cabe en el pellejo de verse muy festejada. Porque antes debería estremecerse entre sí y llorar de todo ello, que no holgarse, pensando que la mayor joya de toda la recámara de su honra anda acosada y perseguida por tantas partes y de tantos enemigos a quien no sabe si se la podrá defender si Dios no socorre con su gran misericordia. Doliéndole en el alma que su cara sea hacha de fuego con que enciende a los hombres, a que codicien su perdición y la de ella ...

[Therefore, our Christian damsel should not feel too vainglorious with her beauty, nor let her nobleness go to her head, nor swell in self-satisfaction, considering herself so charming or so worthy of the palace, or think that she will burst out of her skin from being so celebrated. On the contrary, she should shudder and tremble inside and shed tears at all this, rather than enjoying it, remembering that the best jewel in the entire chamber of her honor is being stalked and chased from every angle and by so many enemies that if God does not succor her with his mercy she will not be able to defend it. It should hurt her very soul that her face be the fuse that will ignite men to covet their perdition and hers ...] (142)

Through the invocation of "nobleza [nobleness]" and "palacio [palace]," beauty is indirectly equated here with social status. Furthermore, there are correspondences made with chastity as mercantile value in the clichéd allusion to the woman's "mayor joya [greatest jewel]," or chastity.

The warnings on the pernicious nature of feminine beauty were most frequently directed to men. Dire indeed is the following admonition, taken from Francisco de Castro's 1585 *Reformación Christiana* [*Christian Reformation*]:

Aparta pues los ojos de la mujer ataviada y no mires la hermosura que tiene, porque de la vista nace el pensamiento, del pensamiento la delectación, de la delectación el consentimiento, del consentimiento la obra, de la obra la costumbre, de la costumbre la obstinación, y así la condenación para siempre jamás.
[Avert then your eyes from the adorned woman and do not gaze upon the beauty she possesses, because from sight is born thought, from thought pleasure, from pleasure consent, from consent the act, from the act habit, and from habit obstinacy, and then eternal damnation.] (Qtd. in Vázquez García and Moreno Mengíbar 299)

Feminine beauty, which, as these quotes attest, was conceived as a social spectacle, was dangerous, a grave threat to both men and women. And yet, paradoxically, beauty was also often viewed as the external manifestation of goodness. Neoplatonism, in particular, declared beauty to be the outward visible sign of inward and invisible virtue. In the sixteenth-century *Dialogo delle bellezze delle donne* [*On the Beauty of Women*], for example, Agnolo Firenzuola stated that

A beautiful woman is the most beautiful object one can admire, and beauty is the greatest gift God bestowed on His human creatures. And so, through her virtue we direct our souls to contemplation, and through contemplation to the desire for heavenly things. (11)

The legendary Zenobia was, in fact, often presented in literature as both the quintessence of female loveliness and an extreme exemplar of chastity, the most valued virtue—as we see in Vives, among others—in any woman. Indeed, the various literary representations of Zenobia often emphasized her disdain for the pleasures of the flesh, so much so that it was claimed that she acquiesced to lie with her husband solely for the purpose of reproduction. Vives, for example, depicts her as a "Matrona digna por su esmerada castidad, de ser adorada, que no tenia más sentimiento de las partes más mujeriles de su cuerpo que del pie o de la mano, verdaderamente que ella era merecedora de parir, o sin varón, pues nunca la consintió sino por parir: o [merecedora] de parir sin dolor, puesto que no sentía el efecto de la causa [A matron worthy of adoration because of her scrupulous chastity, for she had no more feeling in the most womanly parts or her body than she did in her foot or hand. Verily she deserved to give birth without (union) with a man, for she never agreed to the act except in order to give birth; or (deserved) to give birth without pain, since she was incapable of feeling the effect or the cause]" (268–9).[17] Zenobia, according to Vives, was so removed from the sensations of the body—both pleasure and pain—that she should have been granted the possibility, accorded only to the Virgin Mary, of procreating without any actual sexual contact with a man.

While chastity was lauded as the most important characteristic in a woman, physical attractiveness was not inconsequential to those who would wield power. Indeed, beauty was not solely a feminine attribute and was, in fact, conjoined in some cases with monarchical power, again clearly conceived of as masculine. For example, Juan Huarte de San Juan, in his *Examen de ingenios* [*The Examination of Men's Wits*], states:

> Ser el Rey hermoso y agraciado es una de las cosas que más convidan a los súbditos a quererle y amarle. Porque el objeto del amor, dice Platón que es la hermosura y buena proporción; y si el Rey es feo y mal tallado, es imposible que los suyos le tengan afición, antes se afrentan de que un hombre imperfecto y falto de los bienes de naturaleza los venga a regir y mandar.
> [For the King to be beautiful and graceful is something that will most inspire his subjects to love and admire him because the object of love, according to Plato, is beauty and good proportion; and if the King is ugly or badly formed, it will be impossible for his people to have affection for him. On the contrary, they will be offended that an imperfect man, lacking all the natural gifts of nature, should presume to rule and command them.] (347)

This ideal conjoining of power and beauty would become particularly problematic during the reign of the unsightly Charles II (1661–1700), the last of the Habsburg kings and the product of generations of inbreeding (see Figure 2.1).[18]

---

[17] Walthaus reproduces a different Spanish translation of the same quote, from the original Latin, that renders the last sentence somewhat more clearly: "Mujer merecedora de parir, y sin unión, pues nunca la consintió sino por parir, o de parir sin dolor, puesto que no sentía placer [A woman worthy of giving birth without copulation, for she never agreed to the act except in order to give birth, or {worthy} of giving birth without pain, since she was incapable of feeling pleasure]." See "La fortaleza de Cenobia y la mutabilidad de Fortuna: dos emblemas femeninos en *La gran Cenobia* de Calderón," in … *Que toda la vida es sueño, y los sueños, sueños son: homenaje a don Pedro Calderón de la Barca*, ed. Ysla Campbell (Ciudad Juárez, México: Universidad Autónoma de Ciudad Juárez, 2000), 118.

[18] As stated in the introduction, there have been several recent attempts to rehabilitate the image of Charles II. For years, historians both in Spain and abroad portrayed him as imbecilic, retarded, pathetic, almost a freak of nature. A more even-handed approach can be

Fig. 2.1   Juan Carreño de Miranda. *King Charles II*, 1673.

Perhaps with this unfortunate monarch in mind, the late seventeenth-century playwright and *tratadista* Juan de Zabaleta specifically raised the issue of the relationship between authority and the physical appearance of the king in his *El Emperador Cómodo: Historia discursiva según el texto de Herodiano* [*The Emperor Commodus: A Discursive History According to the Text by Herodotus*] (1672). Here, he provides a description of the physical attributes of the ideal monarch:

> Para la primera vista muy buena recomendación es la hermosura. En los Príncipes siempre es muy buena, porque es autoridad siempre. El Príncipe de persona mal formada con la presencia da que notar, y en quitándose el peligro, da que reír. Todos piensan que pueden burlarse, de quien creen que se burla la naturaleza.

---

found in Christopher Storr's *The Resilience of the Spanish Monarchy 1665–1700* (Oxford: Oxford UP, 2006), and especially in Luis Ribot García's *Carlos II: El rey y su entorno cortesano* (Madrid: Centro de Estudios Europa Hispánica, 2009). Nevertheless, even they would not argue that Charles had the regal bearing expected of a monarch.

[At first glance, beauty offers a good endorsement. In a prince, it is always a good thing, because it always represents authority. The prince, whose person is malformed, calls attention to his appearance, and once the threat is removed, inspires laughter. For everyone believes they can laugh at him whom natured mocked.] (24)

Beauty, then, is authority; it is power ascribed in these two quotes from Huarte de San Juan and Zabaleta to the male monarch. The question of beauty with relationship to queens was problematic. Queens were, of course, expected to be physically appealing in order to please their royal spouses and thereby ensure dynastic continuity. At times, however, beauty seems to have been indistinguishable from the attributes of power, regardless of the sex of the monarch. That is, if beauty conferred power, so too did power confer beauty. One illustration of this interchangeability between beauty and authority can be found in descriptions of royal portraits. In an article on Antonis Mor's portrait of Mary Tudor, Philip II's wife and sister of the future Elizabeth I (see Figure 2.2), Joanna Woodall tells us that the iconography in the portraits of queens "attributed personal qualities to the sitters which were considered appropriate to their role and gender" ("An Exemplary Consort" 206). Beauty and chastity were prominent among these personal qualities; and for this reason even a realistic portrait of the unhappy and plain Mary, like the one executed by Mor, elicited the following description from the contemporary painter, Karl Van Mander: "He copied the head of this Queen, who was a very beautiful woman." Van Mander also reports that Cardinal Granvelle, a Burgundian statesman and minister of the Spanish king, "praised the portrait highly, and the beauty of this princess" (Woodall, "An Exemplary Consort" 206). Woodall believes that the painter's and prelate's words were sincere, despite the demonstrable homeliness of the English queen on the canvas. Not only was there "an assumption that queens and princesses are by definition beautiful" (207), but the painter had followed certain conventions in composition and representation that aligned the image of Mary with the elaborate iconography of queenship in general and specifically with Raphael's celebrated portrait of Joanna of Aragon (Figure 2.3), who was considered the paradigm of female beauty and virtue at the time.[19]

---

[19] According to Woodall, "Van Mander's rather unexpected emphasis on Mary Tudor's beauty in his account of Mor's portrait is explicable as recognizing visual conventions ultimately derived from [Raphael's] *Joanna of Aragon*"; see "An Exemplary Consort: Antonis Mor's Portrait of Mary Tudor," *Art History* 14.2 (1991): 208. The Mor portrait had complicated political connotations. Basing himself on the work of Karen Hearn, Louis Montrose tells us that "[t]he Mor portrait of Queen Mary circumscribes her within the interests and agendas of the Emperor Charles V and Prince Philip [the future Philip II of Spain]; the control of the English Queen's image by her new Spanish husband was a synecdoche for the Habsburg dynasty's intended control of her body and her state." See "Elizabeth through the Looking Glass: Picturing the Queen's Two Bodies," in *The Body of the Queen: Gender and Rule in the Courtly World, 1500–2000*, ed. Regina Schulte (New York: Berghahn Books, 2006), 68.

Fig. 2.2   Antonis Mor. *Queen Mary of England*, 1554.

Cenobia's beauty in Calderón's play is clearly overly determined, influenced by dramatic convention, iconographic tradition, and the legend of the Byzantine queen herself, whose famed beauty and military prowess captured the "orientalizing" imagination of historians and poets alike. The first description that we have of Cenobia in the *comedia* is provided by Decio, a Roman general who has been defeated by the powerful warrior queen, both literally and metaphorically (he has fallen in love with her). He informs us that hers is a supernatural beauty, and here the typical hyperbole deployed in depicting female beauty is combined with a strategy that emphasizes sensuality and exoticism that is extended even to her place of birth in the Orient:

> Donde en braços del Alva nace el día,
> que en dilubios de fuego se desata,
> y al Fénix celestial la playa fría
> es cuna de çafir, tumba de plata

Fig. 2.3   Raphael (Raffaello Sanzio). *Joanna of Aragón, Queen of Naples*, 1518.

[Where in the arms of Dawn, the day is born, and in floods of fire becomes undone, and the cold shore is a cradle of sapphire and a silver tomb to the celestial Phoenix.] (1291–4)

The sensual imagery, reminiscent of Góngora's poetry, engages the reader and viewer's eye and prepares him or her for the almost ekphrastic description of the queen herself. Cenobia is described as an Amazon, a warrior, and even a goddess ("aquella deidad") of unsurpassed beauty:

De un esquadrón de damas coronada,
que a no estar a su lado fueran bellas,
su divina hermosura acompañada
salió; pero aviniéndose con ellas
como la Primavera celebrada
con las flores, el Sol con las estrellas,
con las fuentes el mar; que más hermosa
de aquel coro de Ninfas fue la Diosa.

[She came out acclaimed by a company of ladies, who would have been beautiful had they not been at her side; but since she did arrive with them like the celebrated Primavera with flowers, like the Sun with the stars, and the sea with fountains; more beautiful than the chorus of nymphs was the goddess herself.] (339–46)

Walthaus convincingly argues that here Calderón may be conflating the description of the queen with Botticelli's "Primavera" ("La fortaleza" 116). Cenobia is thus verbally reified, simultaneously turned into an allegorical figure and an object (a painting or an icon) to be surveyed—a spectacle to be enjoyed. It has been said that in the literature of the Early Modern period, beauty was what made women visible,[20] and in the end, this visibility was always mediated through what has come to be known in modern critical parlance as the "male gaze." Implicit in Decio's initial and subsequent descriptions of Cenobia is precisely such a gendering of the look. Although Cenobia in this play is a body of authority, she is repeatedly subjected to the dynamic of the gaze and an articulation of male desire of which the public is invited to partake.

Elaborate metaphoric detail is used to describe her garb as well, adding more plasticity to the sensual description of the queen's beautiful form:

Encarnado el vestido—que a los ojos
de su rigor le dieron la librea—
corto, porque incitasse más enojos
al que passar por sus límites desea;
pequeño pie, por muestra o por despojos
de más beldad, la vista lisongea
—bien como el mercader que, para seña
de las joyas que guarda, alguna enseña.
[The dress was scarlet, so that her rigor became the livery granted to the eyes. Short in length, so that it would incite even more turmoil in he who would desire to go beyond the dress's confines. A small foot delights the gaze, as a sample or the spoil of even greater beauty, in the same way that the merchant shows one jewel as a foretaste of the others he conceals.] (347–54)

The similarity of this description to ekphrastic descriptions of portraiture, the overt allusion to desire, and the fragmentation of the woman's beauty privileging certain parts of the body—all constitute the repertoire and rhetoric of the gaze.

There is, in passages such as this, an implicit invitation to visual delectation—what Freud called "scopophilia," or the pleasure of looking at another as an erotic object—of this paradigmatic, chaste, royal body. The emphasis on her garb, the teasing promise of her foot, and the association of her body with precious merchandise make this an eroticized specular moment that would

---

[20] See, for example, Veronique Nahoum-Grappe's essay entitled "The Beautiful Woman," in *A History of Women in the West: Renaissance and Enlightenment Paradoxes*, ed. Natalie Davis and Arlette Farge, vol. 3 (Cambridge, MA: Harvard UP, 1993), 85–100.

become literalized in a performance when the actress playing Cenobia made her appearance. Other early modern texts that deal with the figure of Zenobia also offer descriptions of the queen that fragment her body and offer it as an object of desire, even while emphasizing her virtues, as we see, for example, in Antonio de Guevara's *Epístolas familiares*:

> De su propio natural, era Cenobia, de cuerpo, alta; la cara, aguileña; los ojos, grandes; la frente, ancha, los pechos, altos; el rostro blanco; las mexillas, coloradas; la boca, pequeña; los dientes menudos; de manera que todos la temían por ser recia y la amaban por ser hermosa.[21]
> [Cenobia was physically tall of stature; her face, aquiline; her eyes, big; the forehead, broad; her breasts high, her face white; her cheeks rosy; the mouth small, the teeth small; so that all feared her for her severity and loved her for her beauty.] (94)

In the last line of Guevara's quote, beauty and its effects are again conjoined with power, and beauty simultaneously establishes and tempers authority: "la temían por recia y la amaban por ser Hermosa [all feared her for her severity and loved her for her beauty]." The descriptions of Zenobia that we find in Guevara and in Calderón's play are reminiscent of the descriptive strategies found in amatory poetry. One of the characteristics of the lyric produced in the early modern period is that the idealization of women's beauty goes hand in hand with a process of fragmentation: that is, a woman's presence is made manifest primarily through allusions to parts of her body. Lawrence Kritzman has called this "a phenomenology of desire that entails a dismemberment of the female body, one that conjures up detached body parts or fetishized objects" (99). Even the body of a queen could be simultaneously idealized and fetishized. Lest we believe that this descriptive strategy is unique to early modern Spain, we can consider the description of Zenobia by the famed eighteenth-century historian Edward Gibbons:

> Zenobia is perhaps the only female whose superior genius broke through the servile indolence imposed on her sex by the climate and manners of Asia. She claimed her descent from the Macedonian kings of Egypt, equalled in beauty her ancestor Cleopatra, and far surpassed that princess in chastity and valour. Zenobia was esteemed the most lovely as well as the most heroic of her sex. She was of dark complexion (for in speaking of a lady these trifles become important). Her teeth were of a pearly whiteness, and her large black eyes sparkled with uncommon fire, tempered by the most attractive sweetness. (Qtd. in Stoneman 5–6)

---

[21] This quote from Guevara is taken from the edition by William Rosenthal (Zaragoza: Editorial Ebro, 1938), 94. Interestingly, the 1850 edition of the *Epístolas* by Eugenio de Ochoa in *Epistolario español: Colección de Cartas de Ilustres y Antiguos y Modernos* (Madrid: Rivadeneyra, 1850) seems to have omitted all the letters addressed to women.

In Calderón's play Cenobia's loveliness is equally idealized and compartmentalized, but is also often equated with masculine attributes, especially military ones:

> No te pinto del rostro las facciones,
> y no porque el amor no las advierte,
> sino porque muger, cuyos blasones
> dan temor al temor, muerte a la muerte,
> assuntos a la fama, admiraciones
> a los cielos, muger altiva y fuerte,
> gallarda en paz, en guerra belicosa,
> parece que la sobra el ser hermosa.
> [I won't describe the features of her face, and not because my love did not make note of them, but because in a woman whose insignia frightens fear itself and gives death to death, and novelty to fame, awe to the heavens; in such a proud and strong woman, noble in peace, and bellicose in war, beauty would seem to be superfluous.] (379–86)

Decio goes on to describe her prowess in battle and how she defeated him, for not only is she a goddess of beauty, she is also a *mujer guerrero* [woman warrior], worthy of comparison with Pallas:

> Vencióme al fin; y si al rigor del hado
> he de sentir la culpa que no tuve,
> considera, ¿qué vida avrá segura
> Donde vence la fuerça y la hermosura?
> [She defeated me at last, and if in addition to the harshness of my fate I were to feel the guilt that I did not have, consider what life is safe when force and beauty together vanquish?] (407–10)

Seen through Decio's masculine gaze, Cenobia, then, is a body that fuses beauty and might, one that entices and simultaneously represents force and authority. Curiously, however, when Cenobia finally "appears" on stage, little emphasis on her appearance is made in the stage directions or in the dialogue. In marked contrast to the hyperbolic and reifying descriptions of her beauty that have preceded her actual presence, the spectator would experience an eminently pragmatic and active queen who, freshly returned from battle, is taking charge of matters of state rather than ostentatiously celebrating her victory. She assures the soldiers who are presenting petitions that she will take care of their needs: "De todo / estoy advertida ya [I am already informed of everything]" (643–4). The overwrought description of her beauty and her apparel are primarily verbal constructs produced by the male characters. The character of Cenobia herself "performs" on stage all the virtues desirable in an ideal ruler; and her wisdom, compassion, and prudence lead the soldiers to exclaim: "¡Qué govierno! ... ¡Qué muger! ... ¡Qué valor! ¡Y qué prudencia! [What governance! ... What a woman! ... What valor! And, what prudence!]" (647–8). The parallelism of these lines establishes a synonymy between "prudencia," "valor," "gobierno," and "mujer." Prudence was one of the characteristics ascribed to the legendary queen, and this made her an exemplary model for "real" historical queens and, of course, kings.

As stated in the last chapter, Isabel of Castile was often compared to Zenobia; and Rodrigo Mendes Silva, in his biography of Empress Maria (Philip III's grandmother and the widow of Emperor Maximilian II), wrote that even heretics considered the Empress a "prudent Zenobia" (Sánchez, *Empress* 147). Later in Calderón's play, we learn that Cenobia is a *mujer erudita* as well, one who is in the process of writing the *Historia de oriente* [*History of the Orient*], a chronicle of her people. She herself announces that the much-vaunted ideal of arms and letters can just as easily be applied to women:

> la mujer que pelea,
> es la misma que escribe;
> Que a un mismo tiempo iguales,
> Espada y pluma rige.
> [The woman who fights is the same one who writes, for at the same time and equally, she wields sword and quill.] (1805–8)

The erudition ascribed to Cenobia in Calderón's play corresponds to the legend of the Queen of Palmyra, who was said to have been a respected scholar and had gathered intellectuals at her court, prominently the orator Longinus (Stoneman 2–3). Chaucer, among others, celebrated the queen's superior intellect: "And though she hunted, failed not ne'ertheless / To gain some knowledge of strange languages, / When she had leisure, and much time would lend / To learned books, and seek with eagerness, / How in virtue might her life best spend" (164). Cenobia in the Spanish play is proud of her many accomplishments—and this pride may be one of her flaws—but she quickly learns that being the embodiment of so many monarchical virtues makes her particularly vulnerable to masculine envy and society's misogyny. Libio, her nephew and a pretender to the throne, tells her—falsely—that the populace is opposed to the idea of a woman ruler, hinting that they would much prefer him as monarch:

> LIBIO: Llevan mal ver governando
>   a una muger cetro igual.
> CENOBIA: ¿Por qué el ver no llevan mal
>   a una muger peleando?
> LIBIO: Sienten el verte sentada
>   en un Tribunal; y es bien …
> CENOBIA: ¿Por qué no sienten también
>   verme en la campaña armada?
> LIBIO: No quiere sufrir sus glorias,
>   que las leyes que tuvieren
>   les dé muger.
> CENOBIA: ¿Cómo quieren
>   sufrir que les dé vitorias?

LIBIO:	No es bien que este reino esperes governar.
CENOBIA:	Bien es que vean, pues los hombres no pelean, que goviernen las mugeres.
LIBIO:	Parece que hablas conmigo.
CENOBIA:	Tus hechos te contradicen.

[LIBIO: They disapprove of a woman governing with a scepter. CENOBIA: Then, why do they not disapprove of a woman fighting? LIBIO: They are unhappy seeing you sitting on a tribunal; and it is right that ... CENOBIA: Why then aren't they also unhappy seeing me armed in the military campaign? LIBIO: They cannot bear a woman giving them laws. CENOBIA: Then how can they bear that I give them victory? LIBIO: It is not right that you hope to govern this kingdom. CENOBIA: It is right that they see that since men do not fight, then women should rule. LIBIO: It sounds as if you're talking about me. CENOBIA: Your deeds contradict you.] (686–702)

Although he is lying, Libio here is voicing the proverbial rejection of the rule of women in popular views. Cenobia's response, however, reveals that there is nothing passive or indecisive about this queen; but it also makes clear that if she has assumed the throne, it is primarily because of the weakness and incompetence of the men around her: "Bien es que vean, / Pues los hombres no pelean, / Que gobiernen las mujeres [It is right that they see that since men do not fight, then women should rule]." She is thus presented as a forceful monarch first (as in this scene) by contrast to Libio; and later, she will be the perfect foil to Aureliano. Indeed, repeatedly in this play, all the negative examples of leadership happen to be masculine. Aureliano, as stated before, will become the personification of tyranny; and Libio plots with Irene to murder his uncle Abdenato, Cenobia's husband, in order to inherit the throne. Decio is the most noble of the male characters and the one who will eventually become her second husband; and yet, his leadership at times becomes suspect as well, specifically when he is torn between his obligatory loyalty to the emperor and his love for Cenobia.

The queen's beauty, combined with her many virtues as a leader, makes her a formidable opponent to the ambitious and ruthless Aureliano, who himself recognizes the importance of defeating Cenobia early on. It is only through this defeat that he can establish his own unequivocal power, a power that is intrinsically an attribute of masculinity. Throughout the play, he grapples precisely with what it means to be a man who wields authority, and the play then becomes also a meditation on proper gender roles. For one thing, Aureliano is contemptuous of Decio because, as the Roman general in charge of the legions, he has been defeated by a woman. The tyrant proceeds to humiliate Decio, symbolically unmanning him by removing his sword:

> Tú, que cobarde has nacido,
> es bien que mudança esperes,
> viniendo de las mugeres
> infamemente vencido.
> Este azero que has ceñido
> *Quítale la espada*
> puedes dexar; que a tu lado
> está el azero afrentado,
> quando limpio; considero
> que solamente el azero
> parece mejor manchado.
>
> [You, who were born a coward, should not be surprised by your change [in fortune] since you arrive after being ignobly defeated by women. You can leave behind the steel you have borne [*removing his sword*], because the clean steel is affronted to be by your side. For I know that only when it's stained (with blood) is the steel at its best.] (481–90)

The degradation of another man with equal claim to the throne through this symbolic castration is not sufficient, however, to establish Aureliano's supremacy.[22] The real threat is the unacceptable reality of Cenobia's military prowess, her beauty, and her intrinsic monarchical virtues. Therefore, Aureliano cannot be satisfied until he quite literally sees Cenobia at his feet:

> la primera empressa mía
> ha de ser Cenobia bella.
> En Roma he de triunfar della.
> …
> Y verás, cobarde, quando
> con Cenobia, al carro atada,
> humilde a mis pies postrada,
> entre por Roma triunfando,
> si sé vencer peleando,
> a quien mirando procura
> tener defensa segura.
> Marche al Assia desde aquí;
> que voy a triunfar de mí,
> del poder y la hermosura.
>
> [My first undertaking will be beautiful Cenobia. I will triumph over her in Rome … and you will see, coward, when I return triumphantly to Rome with Cenobia tied to my chariot and prostrate at my feet, whether I can vanquish through battle the one who believes she has a secure defense. Let me march into Asia; for I mean to triumph over myself, over power, and over beauty.] (493–5, 501–10)

---

[22] Walthaus analyzes this scene, and others, as emblematically enacting "la idea de una verticalidad que puede derrumbarse, sugeriendo así la idea de la rueda de Fortuna que dará otra vuelta [the idea that a verticality can be toppled, suggesting in this manner the idea of the wheel of Fortune which will take another turn]" ("Representar" 40).

Again, Cenobia provides both a real and a symbolic foil against which the tyrant can define himself; and by including the line "triunfar de mí" in this passage, Aureliano makes this connection explicit. Cenobia is the feared "Other" without whom he cannot establish his absolute tyrannical rule. Feminist criticism has often elaborated on the psychological need for masculine dominance over a subjected feminine body, a dominance that is often rehearsed through the scopophilic dynamic of the gaze. In the play, this dynamic is dramatized through the verbal descriptions—by both Decio and Aureliano—that anticipate the appearance of Cenobia on stage. Kaja Silvermann has commented on the intrinsic importance of and dependence on the figure of an Other in the construction of subjectivity. Basing herself on Lacan the feminist critic posits the gaze as "the registration within the field of vision of the dependence of the social subject upon the Other for his or her own meaning" (134). In *La gran Cenobia*, it is clear that Aureliano needs to subjugate the disturbing and powerful female body of his enemy in order to establish his own masculinist and absolutist authority. Ironically, he is unable to do so honorably by vanquishing Cenobia in the masculine space of the battlefield. In fact, Cenobia initially soundly defeats him, leaving him in a state of unmitigated rage and indignation:

> ¡Qué una muger, que una muger resista
> a Roma, a mí, tan desigual conquista!
> Diera por cautivalla,
> por prendella y llevalla
> a Roma, y en el carro
> entrar pisando su ambición bizarro,
> diera ... Pero estoy loco:
> ¿qué tengo yo que dar, si Roma es poco?
> [That a woman, that a woman should defy Rome, defy me, in an uneven victory!
> I'd give Rome itself to be able to capture her, seize her and take her, and to enter
> in my chariot majestically trampling on her ambition, I'd give ... but I'm mad,
> what else could I offer if Rome is not enough?] (1701–8)

Aureliano's altered state of mind, conveyed through the repetition of "que a una muger" and "diera," indicates the utter intolerability of female dominance. His desire for revenge and need for the total subjugation of his enemy is thus redoubled: and, as this passage makes clear, he wants to avenge his vanquished masculinity not simply to defend Rome. He seems willing to sacrifice his own kingdom for the satisfaction of conquering this arrogant woman. The opportunity to do so presents itself when Libio, with the help of Irene, betrays his nation and the queen by helping Aureliano in the hope of assuming power. Thus, it is only through the "feminine" strategy of treachery that Aureliano is able to make good on his burning desire to humiliate the powerful queen. The scene where Cenobia is displayed as Aureliano's slave makes for a formidable spectacle, and indeed, represents the climactic moment of the play. In the same manner that her beauty is first presented as a verbal construct, so too is the elaborate performance of her subjugation anticipated through Decio's eyes and words:

> En un triunfal carro, a quien
> en vez de rústicas fieras,
> racionales brutos tiran,
> atados cautivos llevan.
> Él en lo más eminente
> del triunfal carro se assienta
> en un trono, a imitación
> hermosa de algún Planeta.
> Luego va Cenobia … ¡Ay triste!
> ¿Tendrá el espíritu la lengua
> para dezirte que va
> Cenobia a sus plantas puesta,
> ricamente aderezada,
> hermosamente compuesta,
> donde, como en centro viven
> piedras, oro, plata y perlas?
> Atadas las blancas manos
> con riquíssimas cadenas
> de oro—prisiones, en fin,
> ¿qué importa que ricas sean?—,
> va a sus pies, y él, profanando
> el respeto y la belleza,
> el sagrado bulto pisa,
> la imagen rica atropella.
> [In a triumphal chariot, which is drawn by shackled slaves and not rustic beasts, there he sits upon a throne in the most prominent position of the triumphal car, a beautiful imitation of some planet. Then comes Cenobia … ¡oh, woe is me! Can my tongue be strong enough to tell you that Cenobia—richly dressed, beautifully composed, in the center where there are precious stones, gold, silver, and pearls—lies at his feet? The white hands are tied with rich chains of gold (they are prisons, so what does it matter how rich they are?), she lies at his feet, and he, profaning both respect and beauty, treads on her sacred form, abusing her rich image.] (2051–74)

This is a powerful, sensuous description, mediated through a masculine gaze that reifies the wise, proud, and beautiful queen into a "bulto," an "imagen" physically subjugated by Aureliano. Her appearance as described here is in sharp contrast to her presence earlier on stage. For example, when she appears in Jornada II—after her husband has been murdered by Libio and Irene—the stage directions describe her as wearing austere masculine clothing: "con armas negras, vestida de luto, leyendo en un libro [with black armor, dressed in mourning, reading a book]" (34).[23] The sobriety in dress of the earlier scene contrasts significantly with the spectacle of subjugation that Decio announces. It is as a "mujer humillada [humiliated woman]" that she appears in her most ostentatious and dazzling garb,

---

[23] Because the stage directions, in this and other plays, do not have line numbers, I will provide the page of the edition I am using.

thus making Cenobia part of Aureliano's booty, a "trofeo infelice / de un traidor y un tirano [unhappy trophy for a traitor and a tyrant]" (1780–81).

The ensuing scene where the chariot with its tableau of power and domination actually appears on stage is marked by great theatricality, as Decio himself suggests when he calls it "la mayor tragedia / que en el teatro del mundo / la fortuna representa [the most notable tragedy that fortune stages on the theater of the world]" (2044–6). The stage directions state: "*Suena la música, y entran soldados delante y detrás un carro triunfal, en el qual viene Aureliano emperador y a sus pies Cenobia muy bizarra, atadas las manos, y tirando del carro cautivos y detrás gente [Music is heard, and the soldiers enter first, followed by a triumphal chariot carrying Aureliano, and at his feet is Cenobia, very dazzling, with her hands tied, and pulling the car there are captives, and behind it, people]*" (62). We have the visual representation of the verticality of power, as described by Michel Foucault; in this case, establishing an inverted reciprocity between the victorious masculinity of the conqueror and a subjugated femininity.[24] Beyond the erotic and even sadistic dimension, the victory over Cenobia is metonymic of other victories, as Aureliano suggests:

> No os parezca una muger
> poco fin a tanta empressa;
> que más su vitoria estimo,
> que si en campaña venciera,
> en defensa de los Dioses,
> braço a braço, fuerça a fuerça,
> los Gigantes de Sicilia
> o los Cíclopes de Flegra.
> [Do not think that a woman is a paltry trophy for so great an enterprise; because I value conquering her more than if I were to vanquish the Sicilian Giants or the Cyclops of Phlegra in defense of the gods.] (2119–26)

As if the pageant or the spectacle of humiliation were not enough, Aureliano insists on reiterating verbally Cenobia's debased condition once more, insistently emphasizing the contrast between her glorious past and her current abased state:

> miradla agora, ¡que humilde!
> mirad la ambición depuesta,
> rendida la vanidad
> y la presunción sujeta;
> y para mirarlo todo,
> mirad a Cenobia presa;

---

[24] Michel Foucault has taught us that in early modern Europe, public executions (and, by extension, I would argue, all displays of a sovereign's dominance over a subjected body) had a "juridico-political function" in that it became "a ceremonial by which a momentarily injured sovereignty is reconstituted. It restores that sovereignty by manifesting it at its most spectacular." *Discipline and Punish: The Birth of the Prison*, trans. Alan Sheridan (New York: Vintage, 1995), 48. This is an apt description of what we witness in these scenes.

veréis arrogancias, enbidia,
ambición, poder y fuerça
puesto a mis plantas, si está
Cenobia a mis plantas puesta.
[Look at her now: how humble! Look at deposed ambition, vanity vanquished, and presumption subjugated; and to see all of this, just look at Cenobia imprisoned. You will see arrogance, envy, power, and might at my feet, since at my feet lies Cenobia.] (2135-44)

Aureliano has carefully staged this tableau, and in his penchant for theatricality—in the sense of both spectacle and inauthenticity—he displays another mark of a tyrant. In classical texts by Tacitus and Suetonius, for example, the corrupt Roman emperors Nero and Caligula were portrayed as assuming a multiplicity of theatrical functions, from playwrights to directors to actors, often performing many roles including those "crossing the boundaries dividing woman from man, man from beast, and mortal from god" (Bushnell 31). In the first scene of the play, we already saw Aureliano blurring these distinctions by simultaneously wearing animal skins and a crown and scepter. Here, his theatricality manifests itself in the elaborate spectacle that establishes his political authority as inseparable from visually vanquishing the feminine other. In the passage just cited, all of the vices he ascribes to her are, in fact, only applicable to him: arrogance, envy, and might. The demeaned body of a woman is presented, then, as the inverted mirror of the body of authority represented by the emperor—its debasement is in direct proportion to the power it bestows on him. The humiliation of Cenobia, experienced by the audience at three different moments in the play, corresponds to a need to circumscribe and even negate the power and authority attributed to this woman. The ekphrastic passages, with their emphasis on her beauty and her provocative dress, become a rehearsal for Aureliano's possession and this need to reassert authority and domination. Furthermore, Cenobia appears at the climax of the play in a cart being drawn by her enslaved people, human beasts of burden, and thus she becomes literally linked with slavery. As stated in the last chapter, there was an obsessive concern in early modern Spain with containing women's dangerous sexuality through watchful control and subjugation. While Cenobia represents the ideals of kingship, her sex and its relationship to power are problematic. Calderón may not have been overtly opposed to feminine rule, but it is significant that (possibly unconsciously) he needed to enact the construction of a masculine subjectivity as intrinsically dependent on the representation and control of the simultaneously desired and feared body of a woman.

In the climactic scene just described, Aureliano also establishes an exact correspondence between Cenobia and the allegorical figure of Fortuna:

Esta que veis a mis pies
muger humillada, esta
que, a ser mortal la fortuna,
la misma fortuna fuera.

[This humiliated woman that you see at my feet, who if Fortune were mortal would be Fortune herself.] (2127–30)

The play is rife with allusions to the vagaries of fortune, and the correlation between Cenobia and the allegorical figure Fortuna has been exhaustively studied by Walthaus, among others. One aspect that has not been commented on is the Machiavellian subtext implicit in this comparison. In *The Prince*, Machiavelli repeatedly depicted Fortuna as a woman who needed to be vanquished:

> fortune is a woman, and in order to be mastered she must be jogged and beaten. And it may be noted that she submits more readily to boldness than to cold calculation. Therefore, like a woman, she always favors young men because they are not so much inclined to caution as to aggressiveness and daring in mastering her. (94)

This scene from Calderon's play would seem to be an accurate reenactment of Machiavelli's advice to the ruler. In Aureliano, Calderón presents us the Machiavellian prince as tyrant, who subjugates not only the allegorical Fortuna but also the "real" body of a woman who had assumed authority. Like Machiavelli's prince, Aureliano is a tyrant who believes he can defy Fortuna and opportunistically control his own destiny.[25]

---

[25] By contrast, the two most sympathetic characters—Cenobia and Decio—share a stoic attitude toward the vagaries of fate. It is Decio who, early on, introduces the topic when he addresses Aureliano after being symbolically unmanned:

Tú has subido, y yo baxado;
y pues yo baxo, advirtiendo
sube, Aureliano, y temiendo
el día que ha de venir,
pues has topado al subir
otro que viene cayendo.
Los dos, estremos seremos
de la fortuna y la suerte;
más ya en la mía se advierte
el mayor de los estremos;
que si en la fortuna vemos
que no es oy lo que era ayer,
yo no tengo que temer,
y tú tienes que sentir;
pues baxo para subir,
pues subes para caer.

[You have risen, and I have fallen; and since I fall, be careful as you ascend, Aureliano, and be fearful of the day that will come, because in your ascension you have come across someone who is descending. The two of us are extremes of fortune and luck; but in mine one can see the greater of the extremes; because if in fortune we see that today is not the same as yesterday, I have nothing to fear and you have everything to regret, for I fall in order to rise and you rise in order to fall.]

Aureliano's hubris will be punished ultimately, but not before Cenobia is forced to resort to "typical" feminine wiles, once again setting up an opposition between masculine force and feminine beauty:

CENOBIA. [*Ap.*] En este passo procura
mi pecho, de amor desnudo,
pues con la fuerça no pudo,
vencer oy con la hermosura.
Yo dixe que su grandeza
avía de ver a mis pies;
ayuden mi intento, pues,
amor, ingenio y belleza:
provaré si puedo ver
humillado este rigor,
fingiendo gusto y amor.
¡Aora sí que soy mujer;
aora sí lo he parecido;
pues con mis armas ofendo,
quando a un bárbaro pretendo
vencer con amor fingido!
[In this scene, my breast, stripped of love, will attempt to conquer with beauty what it could not with force. I have said that I wanted to see his majesty at my feet; well then, let my intent be aided by love, ingenuity, and beauty. I will see if I can humiliate his severity by feigning pleasure and love. Now I really am a woman; now I really seem so, for I offend with my weapons when I pretend to vanquish with false love.] (2377–92)

In an attempt to regain her lost political authority, she is forced to abandon her former sovereignty and perform, instead, a conventional charade of femininity based on her beauty, sensuality, and feigned love and pleasure. The theatricality she embraces—she refers to "este paso [this scene]," "ahora si lo he parecido [now I really do seem (to be a woman)]," and "fingiendo gusto y amor [feigning pleasure and love]"—reinforces the lack of authenticity associated with a tyrant and women in general. When she presents herself before Aureliano, her beauty provides both a contrast and a mirror to his monstrosity (she exclaims when she sees him, "¡O, qué bárbara fiereza! / ¡Qué semblante! [Oh, what barbaric fierceness! What a visage!]" and "¡Qué fealdad! [What ugliness!]" (2400–401).[26]

There are, as critics have commented, repeated allusions throughout the play to the ups and downs of the wheel of Fortune. According to Walthaus, the use of the repetitious allusions to Fortune helps to mask the criticism of the monarchy embedded in the play. Walthaus relates the concern with Fortuna to the circumstances surrounding the fall of Rodrigo Calderón, Philip III's minister and a favorite of the Duke of Lerma. Rodrigo Calderón (no relation to the dramatist) was executed only four years before the play was performed ("La Fortaleza" 109).

[26] One can only speculate how these lines might have been received when the play was staged in 1676 and 1685 before an audience that may well have included the unprepossessing presence of King Charles II.

Further debasing herself, she announces to Aureliano that she will willingly accept the role of slave that he had previously assigned to her:

> A los pies tenéis, señor,
> esta humilde esclava vuestra
> que segunda vez se muestra
> rendida a vuestro valor.
> [At your feet, my lord, you have this your humble slave, who for a second time finds herself prostrate before your valor.] (2403–6)

Thus, Cenobia—the victorious woman warrior, the wise ruler and erudite historian—is forced to revert to conventional feminine stratagems. Her humiliation is complete when this final performance of seduction fails and Aureliano rejects her. Hildner interestingly points out "the one advantage afforded to Aureliano by his brute nature is that it makes him relatively insensitive to beauty and enables him to successfully resist Cenobia's charms and womanly imploring" (55).

In the end, the tyrant will be roundly vanquished by Decio's forces, but audiences and readers are robbed of the satisfaction of seeing Cenobia resume her wise rule. The play achieves its resolution only when Cenobia recognizes that she is in love with Decio and agrees to marry him, thus completing the transformation from exemplary woman warrior-queen into a more suitable feminine paragon. No longer queen regnant but rather the more acceptable queen consort, she has been repeatedly subjugated and finally contained when legitimate masculine rule is reestablished. In the final scene, when Decio is proclaimed "César" and he offers her his hand, Cenobia speaks only once more, and then only to magnanimously offer her life in exchange for those of the traitors Libio and Irene:

> Si yo merezco, señor,
> que a Libio y a Irene den
> tus manos la vida, esta
> pongo rendida a tus pies.
> [If I am worthy, my lord, that your hands give Libio and Irene their lives, then I put mine prostrate at your feet.] (2855–8)

It is no coincidence that here Cenobia reprises her subjugation—"rendida a tus pies [prostrate at your feet]"—before the previous Caesar, Aureliano; and, although she may once more be referred to as the epitome of prudence and strength, the fact is that from then on she will be silent. There is no longer any need, in the fiction of the play, for her to speak or to assume monarchical authority.

The ultimate political message of *La gran Cenobia* is not complicated: the monarch must behave according to the principles exemplified by Cenobia and learn to accept the unpredictable forces that affect man's fate. Nevertheless, the harsh lessons of the unpredictable turn of Fortune's wheel have been illustrated on the body of a remarkable woman whose fate turns out to be, in fact, perfectly predictable. Calderón, even when depicting an idealized monarch taken from the classical tradition, cannot but reveal an underlying anxiety about the possibility of a woman assuming a position of true power and authority. Utilizing the rhetorical strategies typical of amatory poetry (hyperbole and fragmentation) and the dramatic convention that prescribes the restoration of order, the playwright has reproduced the cultural gaze that surveys and contains feminine beauty and agency.

In this *speculum principis*, the implied male monarchs in the audience—Philip IV, who was in his early twenties when the play was first produced, and Charles II when it was revived in 1676 and in 1685—are invited to absorb lessons in statecraft through the alluring presence of a beautiful woman who embodies the desirable kingly virtues of military strength, wisdom, and compassion. To the queens who presumably also watched the play, the portrayal of a mostly sympathetic female monarch would have been mostly flattering. At the same time, the young Isabel of Bourbon, Philip IV's first wife, who would prove to be a singularly capable queen, may have also taken away the lesson of ultimate docility in Cenobia's contentment as a queen consort. It is particularly interesting to speculate how the later 1685 staging at the palace, for example, may have been received. By this time, Calderón had died, and the repeat performances took place at a time when the Spanish court was immersed in an intense power play between two queens, as described by M.J. Rubio:

> En la corona española están presentes las dos facciones: una reina francesa y una reina madre austriaca, junto a un rey débil y manejable. La pugna gira en torno a cuál de las dos soberanas será capaz de influir sobre las decisiones de Carlos II y por tanto del gobierno español. De ahí la presión de Luis XIV sobre su sobrina Maria Luisa de Orleáns y del emperador Leopoldo I sobre su hermana Mariana de Austria para que intriguen y medren en política.
> [In the Spanish crown, there are two factions at work: a French queen (Maria Luisa of Orleans, wife of Charles II) and an Austrian queen mother (Mariana of Austria), by the side of a weak and easily manipulated king. The fight revolves around which of the two queens will be able to influence Charles II's decisions and therefore, the Spanish government. This explains the pressure that Louis XIV exerts on his niece Maria Luisa of Orleans, and Leopold I on his sister Mariana of Austria, to plot and participate in politics.] (364)

Given the tensions at the palace during this fraught period, the message of Cenobia's rise and fall as monarch in this play—as in other Baroque palace *comedias*—may have been an affirmation that a stable monarchy depended on the ultimate control and exclusion of feminine authority. This is the law of the theater asserting itself in the play. At the same time, the positive depiction of Cenobia as a gifted and just ruler in the early scenes of the play would not have been negated by this ideologically conservative conclusion. Calderón and other Baroque playwrights repeatedly enact what Judith Butler has called in another context "performative contradictions." The patriarchal masculinist bias may triumph through the denouement, but the internal performance of feminine power is never completely eradicated.

Tirso de Molina's *La república al revés*

There are many striking similarities between *La gran Cenobia* and an earlier play composed by Tirso de Molina, *La república al revés*, but the differences are equally telling in elucidating the Baroque *comedia*'s presentation of gender and power.[27] In *La república al revés*, Tirso presents one of the most original manifestations of feminine power in a seventeenth-century play. Thought for a long time to be a "rough draft" of the better known and much admired *La prudencia en la mujer* or even "an instance of self-plagiarism,"[28] the play is loosely based on the history of Constantino IV, the Byzantine emperor who spearheaded a revolt against his own mother, Empress Irene, during the late eighth century. Christopher B. Weimer and other critics have demonstrated that despite its similarities to *La prudencia*, *La república* is a play that merits attention in its own right. As announced in the title, Tirso's play is notable for its multi-layered staging of the familiar medieval and Renaissance topos of the *mundus inversus*.[29] Indeed, the very title of the play invites the modern reader or spectator to anticipate carnivalesque inversions of gender as defined by Mikhail Bakhtin and studied by critics such as Natalie Davis and Peter Stallybrass, among others.[30] Within this familiar topic, we find in Tirso's text a remarkable convergence of politics and gender in the elaboration of characters and plot that provides a telling contrast to the play by Calderón just analyzed.

Tirso's play begins with the following stage direction: "Salen marchando soldados, y detrás de ellos, Irene, armada con bastón y corona de emperatriz [Enter marching soldiers, followed by Irene, armed with the staff and crown of an empress]" (57).[31] The spectator or reader would be forgiven for making an immediate mental association between the title and the appearance of this feminine

---

[27] As stated in note 11, not all critics agree on the date of composition and none of them, to my knowledge, provide any information on whether *La república* was ever staged. Dawn Smith has studied the play from a feminist perspective and Christopher Weimer has gone even further, calling the play itself "feminist" in "A *Comedia* Re-Viewed," 224. See also the essays by Ignacio Arellano. My own analysis is indebted to the work of these scholars.

[28] See the early article by E.H. Templin, "Another Instance of Tirso's Self-Plagiarism," *Hispanic Review* 5.2 (1937): 176–80.

[29] Arellano's "Estrategias de inversión" specifically studies the elaboration of the *mundus inversus* topic in the play.

[30] See Bakhtin's *Rabelais and His World*, trans. Helen Iswolsky (Cambridge, MA: MIT Press, 1968); Natalie Davis's "Women on Top: Symbolic Sexual Inversion and Political Disorder in Early Modern Europe," in *The Reversible World: Symbolic Inversion in Art and Society*, ed. Barbara A. Babcock (Ithaca/London: Cornell UP, 1978), 147–89; and Stallybrass, "The World Turned Upside Down: Inversion, Gender and the State," in *The Matter of Difference: Materialist Feminist Criticism of Shakespeare*, ed. Valerie Wayne (Ithaca: Cornell UP, 1991).

[31] I am using the version edited by María del Pilar Palomo in Biblioteca de Autores Españoles, *Obras de Tirso de Molina* (Madrid: 1971), 57–112.

character in full imperial and military regalia, suggesting that the topsy-turvy world will be illustrated first and foremost by the presence of a woman who is a warrior and the ruler of an empire. As Walthaus puts it: "El topos del poder femenino, que al invertir la jerarquía sexual tradicional se relaciona claramente con el topos del mundo al revés, ha apelado siempre la imaginación, por su carácter carnavalesco y por ser una anomalía fascinante [The theme of feminine power, which by inverting the traditional sexual hierarchy is clearly associated with the theme of the world turned upside down, has always appealed to the imagination due to its carnivalesque characteristic and because it is a fascinating anomaly]" ("*Femme forte*" 1361). Likewise, Weissberger tells us that "in Spain as elsewhere in the medieval period, a woman sovereign remained fundamentally disruptive, a sign of a world upside down in which the lower body triumphs over the upper" (124). What is remarkable about the play, however, is that the audience/reader's expectations are subverted as Tirso stages a world that is topsy-turvy precisely because a woman does *not* rule. That is, it is not the anomaly of Empress Irene's rule that creates a "república al revés," but rather her ouster by her ruthless son, Constantino, that leads to a world of inverted political, social, and gendered practices. Irene is, in fact, very much like Cenobia, a wise and courageous monarch, a mirror of queens. And like Cenobia, she is set up as the alternative to an unprincipled and brutal despot who represents all the excesses of the tyrant that political theorists such as Saavedra Fajardo and Mariana railed against.

As in Calderón's play, there is a dramatic and thematic interdependence between these two opposing monarchs who represent inverted mirror images of each other. Irene's exemplarity is set off against Constantino's unprincipled and unhinged behavior. As stated earlier, her character is based on the story and legend of an empress of Byzantium (707–802 CE) who was, like Zenobia, a warrior queen.[32] In Tirso's portrayal, Irene is wise and courageous, virtuous in the accepted meaning of the term and also in its etymological connotations, that is, manlike in her reason and leadership. In one scene, she even dresses like a man in order to escape her imprisonment.[33] At the beginning of the play, she confronts the expected dilemma faced by female rulers, fictional and real. Despite her many triumphs on the battlefield, her people are unwilling to accept her as a ruler, their rejection based entirely on her sex. When the play begins, she has discovered the senate's intention of removing her from the throne and replacing her with Constantino. Echoing other female monarchs in the *comedia*, Irene bemoans the prejudice against the rule of women:

---

[32] Tirso's play follows some of the recorded events of the real Empress Irene, but it attenuates or completely omits the more negative accounts of her ambition, treachery, and cruelty toward her son. For the historical background of the empresses' reign, see Lynda Garland, *Byzantine Empresses: Women and Power in Byzantium, A.D. 527–1204* (London and New York: Routledge, 1999), 73–94.

[33] Interestingly, Garland tells us that the historical Irene at times used the title "basileus" or "emperor" rather than "basilissa" or "empress" (87).

¿Así mis hazañas pagas,
cuando entrar en ti pensé
sobre el victorioso carro
entre el bélico tropel?
...
¿Ahora, cuando aguardaba
recibir el parabién
de tantos reinos ganados,
tantos cetros a mis pies;
ahora, Senado ingrato;
ahora, griego sin ley,
el Imperio me quitáis
porque mi hijo goce de él?
[Is this the way you repay my exploits, when I thought I'd enter in a victorious chariot amid the bellicose hordes? ... Now when I expected to receive praise for the many kingdoms I have won, the many scepters that lie at my feet; now, ungrateful Senate, now, lawless Greek, you deprive me of my empire so that my son may enjoy it instead?] (13–22, 25–32)

Constantino's arrogant response reveals a clearly gendered and conventional conception of authority. While he has been apparently content to let his mother fight the military battles, he now expects her to abandon any ambition to rule and reminds her of the proper roles of the sexes. Indeed, he ironically offers maternal pride as a consolation for her loss of power, telling her that she needs no other reward than to see her son crowned emperor.

¿Tan mal, madre, galardona
el Imperio tu persona,
si el día que entras triunfando
a tu hijo le está dando
el Imperio la corona?
...
Semíramis querrás ser
y hacerme a mí infame Nino.
Porque mientras que atropellas
bárbaros, y cuerpos huellas
con guerra que el mundo abrasa
me quede encerrado en casa
hilando con tus doncellas.
Hijo tienes que ya alcanza
en la milicia alabanza;
holandas, madre, dibuja;
que a la mujer el aguja
le está bien, mas no la lanza.
[Is it so awful, Mother, that on the day that you enter triumphant (from battle), the empire rewards your person by giving your son the imperial crown? ... You must want to be Semiramis and make of me the infamous Nino. For while you crush the barbarians and leave the traces of a raging war on bodies, you expect

me to remain confined at home, sewing with your handmaids. You have a son who is already achieving fame in battle; Mother, apply yourself to adorning brocade, for a needle suits a woman and not the lance.] (51–5, 59–70)

It is significant that Constantino alludes to Nino and Semíramis; the legend of the formidable Assyrian queen tells us that she dressed herself as her own son, Nino, and clothed him in female garb.[34] By rejecting this model of transgression and reiterating the clear separation of roles for men and women, Constantino reveals an underlying anxiety over the possible feminization of the monarchy. Furthermore, his words are reminiscent of statements by writers such as Guevara, who, in his *Epístolas*, exclaims (echoing Pedro de Luján) that no matter how noble or "estimada que sea en riqueza una gran señora, tan bien le parece en la cinta una rueca como parece al caballero una lanza y al sacerdote la estola [esteemed in her wealth a noble woman may be, the distaff at her waist is as becoming as a lance is to a knight and to the priest the stole]" (165).

At the beginning of the play, Constantino and the senate wish to reestablish proper gender roles and put to right the purportedly topsy-turvy world in which a woman rules. Irene is forced to hand over the throne; and when she expresses serious reservations about Constantino's readiness to lead, notably his ability to master his emotions, he responds emphatically in words that again reveal a gendered conception of authority:

Cesa, madre, de agorarme.
si no quieres enojarme,
que yo me sabré tener,
y cuando venga a caer
será para levantarme.
Constantino soy, mi nombre
dice constancia; resiste
tu temor y no te asombre,
que pues que tú te tuviste,
yo me tendré, que soy hombre.
Vamos, amigos, que presto
veréis a mis plantas puesto,
sin temor de enojos vanos,
el mundo que está en mis manos.
[Stop prophesying, Mother, unless you want to make me angry. I can handle myself; and if I were to fall, it would be only to pick myself up again. I am Constantino, and my name means constancy. Control your fears and don't be surprised; after all, you were able to control yourself; I too will be able to control myself, for I am a man. Let's go, friends, because soon, without fearing any useless hindrances, you will see at my feet the world (orb) that I now hold in my hands.] (151–65)

---

[34] Calderón's *La hija del aire* deals with the figure of Semíramis and will be the subject of the following chapter.

Immediately afterward, he drops three objects that are recognized symbols of the monarchy: the royal orb, a rapier, and the crown. This represents the first ominous sign that something will be terribly amiss in his rule. Indeed, masculine rule in this case will lead to a perversion of social hierarchy, political authority, and monarchical values. Throughout the play, we see that Constantino will stop at nothing to satisfy his desires, systematically rejecting the institutions that make up civilized society: he violates his filial duties by imprisoning his own mother and even conspiring to murder her; he attempts to abolish marriage, and even displays contempt for his royal lineage.[35] Again, we remember that Plato describes the tyrant in the *Republic* and the *Gorgias* as a "natural" man, closer to an animal than a human because he seeks only to gratify his every whim.[36] Although Constantino does not appear "en pieles" like Aureliano at the beginning of *La gran Cenobia*, there is no doubt as to his identification with baser instincts. As discussed previously, the inability to control emotions and the identification with the natural world (as opposed to civilization) were overtly linked in the classical and early modern world to feminine weakness. In allowing himself to be ruled by his passions and the pursuit of pleasure, Constantino evinces behavior that is more proper to women.

In attempting to justify her rule, Irene (like Cenobia) alludes to models of feminine exemplarity and also clearly states that what has made her power and leadership possible is a crisis of the monarchy, specifically the absence of a strong masculine leader. She goes so far as to suggest that had circumstances not required it, she would have embraced more acceptable models of behavior:

> Si hombre en el Imperio hubiera,
> Constantino, que hasta ahora
> le amparara, Irene fuera
> Penélope tejedora,
> no Semíramis guerrera.
> [If the empire, Constantino, had a man to protect it up until now, Irene would have been Penelope the weaver, not Semiramis the warrior.] (71–5)

It is this lack that has permitted her to gain authority. The topsy-turvy world announced in the title manifests itself specifically throughout the play through instances of gender dissonance. Irene accuses the men of her kingdom of being effeminate:

---

[35] For a perceptive interpretation of the relationship between Irene and Constantino, see Weimer's "The Oedipal Drama of Tirso's *La república al revés*," 291–309.

[36] Rebecca Bushnell describes Plato's position thus: "In giving in to the unlawful desires that most of us satisfy only in our dreams, the tyrant does, waking, what we all secretly want to do: in Plato's terms, eat forbidden foods; sleep with mother, man, god, or beast; and murder indiscriminately. These desires, says Socrates, constitute the 'bestial and savage'... part of the soul" (13).

> Mas cuando el Persa vino,
> las telas del raso y lino
> con oro y perlas bordara,
> quién sus escuadras echara
> del Imperio, Constantino?
> Los hombres no, que en regalos
> y femeniles placeres,
> por huir sus intervalos
> hilaran como mujeres
> y fueran Sardanapalos.
> [But when the Persian enemy arrived, with his silk and linen embroidered with gold and pearls, who was ready to eject his armies from the empire, Constantino? Not the men, for amidst luxury and feminine pleasure, in order to escape their responsibilities, they would weave like women and become like Sardanapalus.[37]] (76–85)

The intrinsic connection between tyranny and femininity is, at one point, overtly enacted when Constantino displaces his own feminizing tendencies onto the body of the senate and forces the entire august and patriarchal body to dress in female garb as punishment for asking for Irene's release:

> y prende luego
> todo este Senado ciego
> autor de tal desatino;
> y con basquiñas y tocas
> para que el vulgo provoques,
> ponles ruecas por estoques
> que sus pretensiones locas
> declaren ...
> porque soy de parecer
> que como mujeres vean
> los que el Imperio desean
> que gobierne una mujer.
> [Arrest those blind senators, authors of that misguided idea, and incite the populace by dressing them (the senate) in skirts and veils and have them exchange their rapiers for distaffs so that they confess their mad presumption ... It is my will that the realm see that those who want a woman to reign are like women themselves.] (242–9, 253–6)

In this and other scenes dealing with gender trangressions, Tirso seems to be echoing the preoccupations on the part of *arbitristas* with the decline of masculine behavior at the court. As stated before, Lehfeldt has linked this concern with Spain's experience of decline; and she cites, among other texts, a 1635 sermon

---

[37] Sardanapalus was supposedly the last king of Assyria and a symbol of decadence and self-indulgence, and was rumored to have enjoyed dressing up as a woman. *Wikipedia*, March 29, 2011, <http://en.wikipedia.org/wiki/Sardanapalus>.

by Francisco de León attesting: "Aora no veo capitanes, ni soldados, ni dinero, ni ocupaciones honorosas en los de mayores obligaciones, sino una perpetua ociosidad, gustos, entretenimientos, comer, y beber, vestir preciosos, y costoso [These days I do not see captains, nor soldiers, nor money, nor honorable occupations in the most important duties, but rather perpetual idleness, pleasures, entertainments, eating and drinking, and dressing exquisitely and expensively]."[38] The aristocratic idleness and self-indulgence that León's words critique is dramatized in *La república* by the cross-dressing senators, with the added twist that the emperor himself is the immediate cause of their transgression.

Constantino thus becomes the agent for a whole series of dangerous political and gender reversals; and he relishes every opportunity to subvert order and challenge social and political certainties in order to pursue absolute dominance over everyone else. In *La república*, the emperor's behavior proves contagious and it generates transgressive sexual behavior in his courtiers as well: Andrenio plans to rape Irene, and Leoncio impersonates Constantino in order to sleep with Lidora. That these transgressions are effected on the bodies of women is significant; and yet, simultaneously, we see in this behavior an enactment of the pernicious impact feminine beauty was said to have on the body politic. Constantino is particularly susceptible to feminine charms, ultimately rejecting his legitimate consort, Princess Carola, in favor of her beautiful slave, Lidora. Exploiting the accepted association between beauty and authority mentioned before—according to Zabaleta, "En los Principes [la hermosura] siempre es muy Buena porque es autoridad [in a prince (beauty) is always a good thing, because it represents authority always]"— Constantino claims that Lidora's extraordinary beauty makes her better suited to be empress than Carola: "¿No es Lidora / mejor para imperar que su señora? [Is Lidora not better suited to rule than her mistress?]" (325–6). Constantino's burning desire for a woman with no social standing is such that he vows to rape her if she resists his attentions, although this action may result in the loss of his kingdom: "Y tengo de ser, si llego a ellos, / Tarquino de Lidora, si es Lucrecia, / aunque se pierda, como Roma, Grecia [And I will be, if necessary, Lidora's Tarquin if she acts like Lucretia, even though Greece, like Rome, is lost]" (308–10). He need not have worried; Lidora gladly becomes his concubine and then plots to become his wife. Constantino, for his part, has no qualms in rejecting and humiliating Carola, the daughter of the emperor, and insisting that the unworthy Lidora become his queen instead. The blind pursuit of pleasure and his indifference to personal honor and social hierarchy—not to mention the rejection of the sacrament of marriage— prove to be deeply destabilizing to the realm.

Although Empress Irene is the central feminine character, Lidora and Carola are of interest as well, for they represent a classic binary opposition between models of womanhood inherited from the Middle Ages and still prevalent in Spain at the time the play was written. On the one hand, the ideal woman was expected

---

[38] Translation is provided by Lehfeldt in "Ideal Men: Masculinity and Decline in Seventeenth-Century Spain," *Renaissance Quarterly* 61 (2008), 463.

to be virtuous and passive, always deferential to the patriarchal structure; the ultimate models within this position were the Virgin Mary and the female saints. On the other, we have the association of women with nature, the instincts, and sin, the corresponding model being Eve. The famous Ave/Eva binary division is dramatized in *La república al revés* in the contrasts between Carola and Lidora.[39] The Infanta Carola (whose name strongly suggests legitimate authority through its association with the origins of the Habsburg dynasty in Charles V)[40] displays in *La república* all the desirable traits of the ideal royal consort. She exhibits submissive feminine behavior as she patiently suffers all type of indignities, even permitting Lidora to strike her and then to lie about it. In contrast to Carola's martyr-like behavior, Lidora is a theatrical and showy temptress who seems to personify the pernicious influence ascribed to female beauty at the time. Her relationship with Constantino is based on his sexual desire and her greed, in addition to the flouting of hierarchies (she is a slave, after all) and the violation of the sacrament of marriage.

One of the subtexts of the play, similar to what we have in *La gran Cenobia*, is a critique of Machiavellianism; and interestingly, the Italian strategist himself provided a new perspective on the binary view of femininity during the Renaissance. In his political writings, Machiavelli explored the dichotomy between two ultimate models of feminine exemplarity—Eve and the Virgin Mary. According to Arlene Saxonhouse:

> Machiavelli was to take these two portraits of women, transfer them to the men about and for whom he wrote, and transform them by turning the model of the active Eve, exploiting all of her capacity to control others through their passions, sexual or otherwise, into a positive portrait while the passive Mary, subordinate to others, is the symbolic cause of the enslavement of Italy. (154)

It is possible to identify in *La república al revés* a similar representation of the opposing models of femininity and their attributes in the characterization of Carola and Lidora. Calculating and manipulative, Lidora proves to be a profoundly Machiavellian character in her own way as she confronts the vagaries of fortune and manipulates them through her willfulness and theatricality (she dresses ostentatiously, for example) in order to achieve power. There are hints at even more transgressive behavior when she attempts to hide her sexual relationship with Clodio by having him impersonate her brother, thus incidentally suggesting the unspeakable sin of incest. There is no doubt that she is meant to be a negative exemplar, but there is also no doubt that she is a more intriguing dramatic character than the submissive Carola.

---

[39] Dawn L. Smith discusses how the Medieval anagram "Ave/Eva" is dramatized, not only in Tirso's *La república al revés*, but also in *La prudencia en la mujer* and *La mujer que manda en casa*. See "Women and Men in a World Turned Upside Down: an Approach to Three Plays by Tirso," *Revista canadiense de estudios hispanicos* 10.2 (1986): 247–60.

[40] Interestingly, we have historical accounts that the historic Constantino was at one point betrothed to one of Charlemagne's daughters, adding another imperial connotation to Carola's name.

As stated before, the carnality that Lidora inspires in Constantino leads the country to the brink of war when he makes the extraordinary decision to send Carola back to her father, the emperor. Carola herself summarizes the intolerable inversions that Constantino's behavior has brought about:

> ¡Que bueno anda el mundo ahora!
> Despreciada la señora;
> antepuesta la criada;
> presa la que está injuriada,
> con honra la que es traidora.
> La que descalzó mis pies,
> entronizada en el puesto
> del Imperio. Mas poco es
> en la República aquesto,
> que es República al revés.
> [How fine the world is now! The mistress is disdained, the servant is elevated, the wronged one is imprisoned, and the traitor is honored. The one who removed my shoes is now enthroned in the empire. But this is nothing in this republic, for after all it is an inverted republic.] (905–14)

Of all the feminine characters of the play, Irene is naturally the most complex and certainly much more layered as a character than Calderón's Cenobia; and this is perhaps one of the reasons *La república* is, in general, a more satisfying play. For one thing, Irene has renounced maternal behavior in order to assume power and a leadership position, thus echoing Huarte de San Juan's position that motherhood and political authority were incompatible (*Examen de ingenios* 374).

Indeed, she is capable of ruthlessness in the interest of the republic. Unlike the compassionate, ultimately silenced and powerless Cenobia, Irene will not be easily subsumed into the patriarchy at the denouement of the play. In the last scenes, when she resumes the regency, she orders the blinding and imprisonment of Constantino—certainly not the acts of a compassionate ruler and also a violation of the mandates of maternal love.[41] Blinding, a mutilation usually inflicted on slaves to signify total dominance, acquires in this play the character of a symbolic castration, a visible manner of establishing authority over the already weak masculine figure. Likewise, imprisonment is the ultimate enclosure, a subdued feminine state where his unruly passions may be contained. Ignacio Arellano has stated that Constantino is "exactamente la inversión del modelo del príncipe cristiano [exactly the inversion of the model of the Christian prince]" ("Estrategias" 15); by contrast, Irene is paradigmatic of this ideal of kingship promoted by Saavedra Fajardo, among others. Her speech early in the play summarizes, in Arellano's view, all the attributes and necessary virtues for the good prince. At the same time, she is an example of what we might today call "Realpolitik."

---

[41] The blinding of Constantino seems to have some historical basis in fact. Constantino VI was blinded by Irene's supporters after he attempted to overthrow her. He was 26 years old at the time and died shortly afterward in exile, in 792 (Garland 86).

In his study of Machiavellianism in Spain, Maravall tells us that attitudes toward Machiavelli in early modern Spain could be divided into three categories: 1) those who reject Machiavellianism from a traditional religious perspective; 2) those who accept it but disguise this acceptance—that is, those who accept the secularism and pragmatism as separate from the moral/religious sphere; and 3) those who try to assimilate some of the tenets of Machiavellianism into Christian morality.[42] Saavedra Fajardo would seem to fall within the last category, and Maravall tells us that the *tratadista*'s use of the two attributes—"político and cristiano"—to describe a ruler was innovative for its attempts to reconcile morality with political pragmatism: "En ese título, los dos adjetivos que califican el concepto de príncipe hacen referencia a esferas distintos, pero correlativos y armonizados. El príncipe debe ser y puede ser ambas cosas a la vez [In that title, the two adjectives that modify the concept of prince make reference to two distinct but interrelated and harmonious spheres]" (67). In the portrayal of Irene in Tirso's play, one may find an echo of this "balanced" view: an able and compassionate ruler, she is also pragmatic, recognizing the need to neutralize Constantino's toxic rule by depriving him of his sight, symbol of his sovereignty. Throughout the play, he has been metaphorically blind to the responsibilities of a monarch; now he is literally blind and politically powerless.

Another analogy that can be made between Machiavelli's famous treatise and *La república al revés* can be found precisely in the dismantling of social structures and the enactment of reversals. In her discussion of *The Prince*, Arlene Saxonhouse states that "In the process of breaking down the old hierarchies, [Machiavelli] reassesses the sources of political order and turns good into bad, bad into good, virtue into vice, men into women and women into men—or, more precisely, he makes the differences between what had been opposites so ambiguous that we can no longer tell good from bad or women from men" (151). The Italian thinker also presents an acceptance of the baser instincts in man in the process of consolidating power:

> ... it will be well for [the prince] to seem and, actually, to be merciful, faithful, humane, frank, and religious. But he should preserve a disposition which will make a reversal of conduct possible in case the need arises. It must be understood, however, that a prince ... cannot observe all those virtues for which men are reputed good, because it is often necessary to act against mercy, against faith, against humanity, against frankness, against religion in order to preserve the state. (69)

---

[42] Often these treatises tend not to mention Machiavelli overtly, but rather turn to more ancient authorities in order to promote views not unlike those of the author of *The Prince*. See Maravall, "Maquiavelo y el maquiavelismo en España," *Estudios de historia del pensamiento español*, vol. 3 (Madrid: Ediciones Cultura Hispánica, 1975), 41–76. For general discussions of Machiavelli in Spain, see Dian Fox; Stephen Rupp; and J.A. Fernández Santamaría's *Reason of State and Statecraft in Spanish Political Thought, 1595–1640* (Lanham, MD: UP of America, 1975).

Clearly, many of these Machiavellian inversions are reenacted in Tirso's play. In *La república*, Constantino's baser instincts endanger the realm and reduce him to a self-indulgent, anti-civilizing force, leading to the ultimate destruction of monarchical power—precisely the opposite of a Machiavellian prince's aims. Maravall contends that the anti-Machiavelli treatises of early modern Spain "se orientan finalmente a presentar el maquiavelismo como una destrucción del poder; por tanto como tiranía [are inclined ultimately to portray Machiavellian thought as the destruction of power; in other words, as tyranny]" (73). *La república* dramatizes this loss of power, and the presentation of Irene's triumph is a corrective to the ruthlessness of the Machiavellian prince represented by Aureliano. The twist is that in the play, the old hierarchies are restored only when a woman—who displays a pragmatic strain of "razón de estado"—once again takes control of the kingdom. Irene is triumphant at the end, and the audience and readers are meant to see this as a "happy ending."

We return again to the paradox at the center of the play. The title of the play clearly alludes to the medieval topos of the *mundus inversus*, in which reversals of gender and status were intertwined. Such carnivalesque inversions, however, were meant to be temporary conditions; and it has often been argued that these inversions are not, in fact, subversive but rather a source of order and stability in a hierarchical society. As David Underwood states in another context, "on the stage, as in carnival, gender inversion temporarily turns the world upside down—but to reinforce, not subvert, the traditional order" (qtd. in Stallybrass 204). Tirso's play represents a disorder of the body politic manifested through the language of gender and femininity; but the difference here is that, unlike Calderón, Tirso saw no need to stage a scopophilic spectacle of feminine humiliation, nor did he silence the queen or have her revert to her feminine wiles at the end. We know that, unlike Calderón, Tirso never achieved lasting favor at the court; indeed, quite the contrary was true, and he seems to have had many enemies, most prominently Philip IV's minister, the Count-Duke of Olivares, whose powerful influence may have contributed to ending Tirso's dramatic career (McKendrick, *Women and Society* 115). Several critics have seen in *La república* and other Tirso plays such as *La prudencia en la mujer* a very specific political subtext. Kennedy tells us that "Tirso, a warm admirer of Philip III, saw in the reign of Philip IV and his favorite Olivares, a topsy-turvy world" ("*La prudencia*" 50). Indeed, Kennedy believes that the play was probably revised in 1621 to include certain allusions to Philip IV, who that very year had ascended to the throne. The play, in addition to the warnings against power-hungry, self-indulgent male monarchs, would have also included an admonition to the young king to honor his marriage vows and abandon his pursuit of unworthy sexual partners. Interestingly, in the process, Tirso created a heroine who is never subdued or silenced, and this may be one reason that Tirso—an outstanding playwright—may be considered an unsuccessful "homo strategicus," as described at the beginning of this chapter. His overt performance of a weak, feminized (and feminizing) king, without a final restoration of the law of the theater and the symbolic order, may have left him vulnerable to political antagonism.

Like *La república al revés*, *La gran Cenobia* addresses the very real crisis of a monarchy put in the hands of an inexperienced young king known to be indifferent to matters of state and susceptible to pleasure and feminine beauty. That is, Calderón and Tirso chose to influence Philip by creating topsy-turvy worlds in which women assume power. Unlike Tirso, however, Calderón was able to master, in his later and more uneven *comedia*, the strategy of "decir sin decir," of trying to shape political judgment in a non-threatening manner through "play." In the character of Cenobia, a thoroughly exemplary monarch, he presents valuable lessons in statecraft, but ultimately reinforces the prevailing preference for traditional masculinist rule by staging his heroine's downfall and, ultimately, by silencing her. Tirso was much less tactical, much less diplomatic in his representation of female rule.

The differences between the two plays demonstrate the multiple challenges faced by playwrights interested in providing a *speculum principis* mediated through the exemplary figures of women in power. Together, the plays uncover the layers of contradictions that the fantasy of female rule implied. In the process of portraying two women who represent—through their strength and wisdom—an ideal of monarchy, these plays also reveal the underlying anxieties and fears toward women. Perhaps one of the underlying purposes was, as both main characters attest, to dramatize that in the absence of strong male leadership, the rule of women becomes a necessity, or perhaps a necessary evil. In other words, the apparent promotion of a woman's ability to rule may be part of a theatrical game that only serves to ultimately strengthen masculinist domination. At the same time, Tirso's play—as Christopher Weimer claims—does not display a "patriarchal bias,"[43] and, as such, is more immediately rewarding to modern feminist sensibilities. It is not surprising that *La gran Cenobia* was still being staged some 30 years after it was originally written, whereas we have no mention of Tirso's play ever being performed at the court. *La gran Cenobia* provides a suggestive point of departure for interrogating the evolution of that patriarchal bias in Calderón and studying his complex and fascinating depiction of gender and power in later plays.

---

[43] The phrase comes from Weimer's "A *Comedia* Re-Viewed." The critic compares *La república* to Tirso's better known *La prudencia en la mujer* and tells us that whereas in *La prudencia* María de Molina "does not present any threat to royal male succession or the patriarchal premises supporting it," *La república* "shares no such patriarchal bias, and it develops the *mundo al revés* motif in a far more subversive fashion" (131).

Chapter 3
Transgendered Tyranny in *La hija del aire*[1]

Considered by Wilhelm Goethe to be Calderón de la Barca's greatest work, *La hija del aire* [*The Daughter of the Air*] (1653) takes as its source the story of queen Semiramis, whose legendary beauty, ambition, and thirst for power became both an exemplary and a cautionary tale in early modern Europe. The playwright makes use of the strategies of exclusion and revision in order to fashion a political parable related to the state of the contemporary monarchy. As he does in *La gran Cenobia*, Calderón in *La hija* turns to an Oriental and classical model to elaborate this particular version or fantasy of female rule, but this time to greater dramatic effect. Gwynne Edwards tells us that the legend of Semiramis[2] was a hybrid containing both religious and historical elements, and that it provided a fluid field of interpretation throughout the Middle Ages and Early Modern period (xxiii–xxix). The "historical" Semiramis (also known as Sammuramat) governed Assyria from 811 to 808 B.C. in the minority of her son and was, by all accounts, an exceptional woman who led her armies into battle. In myth, she came to be associated with fertility and the changing of seasons, and often appeared as an erotic symbol. Semiramis appeared frequently in Renaissance treatises dealing with female exemplarity. In *De Claris mulieribus* [*In Praise of Famous Women*], Boccaccio, for example, describes her as "so spirited that she, though a woman, dared undertake to rule with skill and intelligence" (4). In Spain, the tendency was to attenuate the more scabrous versions of her story (her lasciviousness, the accusation of incest, for example) in treatises written by Juan Rodríguez del Padrón and Martín de Córdoba. An exception was Juan de Espinosa, who saw her decidedly as emblematic of feminine perfidy and dissoluteness.[3] In *La hija del aire*, Calderón eschews the mythic associations and the sexual transgressions, although he does selectively adapt other negative elements of the story, portraying the queen as a successful but ruthless military leader who abuses her authority, usurps the reign from two legitimate rulers, and precipitates the downfall of her kingdom.[4] Of particular interest in this play is the repeated enactment

---

[1] Portions of this chapter appeared in a special volume commemorating the 400th anniversary of Calderón's birth. See Quintero, "Gender, Tyranny, and the Performance of Power in Calderón's *La hija del aire*," *Bulletin of the comediantes* 53.1 (2001): 155–78.

[2] When referring to the legendary/historical queen, as opposed to Calderón's character, I use the English version of her name without the accent.

[3] For a discussion of how the Semíramis myth is handled in several treatises, see Rina Walthaus's "Classical Myth and Legend in Late Medieval and Renaissance Ideas of Gender," *Critica Hispánica* 18.2 (1996): 361–74.

[4] One of the more immediate and important inspirations for Calderón was the play *La gran Semíramis* by Cristobal de Virués, published in 1609.

of gender dissonances, only hinted at in *La gran Cenobia*, and how these relate to the portrayal of monarchical power.

The heroine of *La hija del aire* is someone who easily traverses gender categories. At the beginning of the play, Semíramis is associated with the natural, almost primitive "feminine" world, rather than the civilized, public realm associated with men. We are told that she was born in a cave, in an undefined and quasi-mythical time, separated from the chronology of history and politics. This original mythic space is clearly gendered, for the cave is suggestive of an enclosed feminine space, rather like a womb, and associated with the earth.[5] The setting of *La hija* also brings to mind the binarism that was at the root of medieval and early modern notions of the differences between the sexes. Ian MacLean summarizes the dualistic view of the sexes, derived from Aristotle, thus: "The male principle in nature is associated with active, formative and perfected characteristics, while the female is passive, material and deprived, desiring the male in order to become complete" (8). Furthermore, woman was nature, identified with irrationality, materiality, instinct, and passivity, while men were associated with civilization, reason, order, and action. At the beginning of the play, Semíramis's only human contact is Tiresias, a priest dedicated to Venus, whose responsibility is to keep her hidden away.

When the general Menón (newly arrived from the masculine sphere of war) finds her, Semíramis is still in that enclosed primal feminine locus, dressed in skin and furs that further underscore her instinctive animal-like nature.[6] Her description is reminiscent of what anthropologist Victor Turner has called the "liminal initiand":

---

[5] Susan Fischer provides an interesting analysis of the play in "The Psychological Stages of Feminine Development in *La hija del aire*: A Jungian Point of View," *Bulletin of the comediantes* 34: 2 (1982): 137–58. According to Fischer, Semíramis is found initially in a primitive stage of feminine development "where there is no separation of inner and outer worlds, of subject and object" (138). I am not convinced by the assertion, however, that "on an intrapsychic level, this means that the individual is connected in the all-embracing maternal, and protective power of the unconscious" (138). Semíramis's is a chaotic world of darkness, lacking any manifestation of a protective maternal presence. Although Tiresias may indeed be a "symbol of the union of masculine and feminine opposites" (139), it is difficult to see him as a "surrogate mother figure."

[6] There are obvious similarities with the beginning of *La vida es sueño*, in which Segismundo is discovered also dressed in animal skins and in an enclosed space. One could argue, however, that because he is imprisoned in a tower rather than a cave, his is not a comparable "feminine" space. Also, unlike Semíramis, Segismundo will overcome his animal nature by the end of the play and become the example of a perfect Christian prince. In the introduction to his edition of *La hija del aire*, Francisco Ruiz Ramón discusses in detail the similarities and differences between these two characters. He also points out the parallels with other Calderonian characters, such as Aquiles in *El monstruo de los jardines* [The Monster in the Gardens] and Irene in *Las cadenas del demonio* [The Devil's Chains] (among others). These characters, Ruiz Ramón tells us, are "marcados desde antes de su nacimiento por los ominosos signos de un adverso destino [marked even before birth with the ominous signs of adverse fortune]" (14).

"stripped of name and clothing, smeared with the common earth, rendered indistinguishable from animals ... associated with general oppositions as life and death, male and female" (26). Furthermore, her body is associated from the start with violence and transgression. We learn that she is the product of a rape; her mother, Areuta, a nymph consecrated to Diana, was violated by a soldier, who was in turn murdered by his victim: "Desta especie de bastardo / amor, de amor mal nacido, / fui concepto [From this kind of bastard love, from an ill-begotten love, I was conceived]" (I, 831–3).[7] Furthermore, she has been consecrated to Venus, the goddess of feminine beauty and sexuality, who presided at her birth to protect her from Diana's wrath and who predicted the dire consequences of this violent conception and birth:

... he temido
que Diana ha de vengarse
de mí [Venus] en ella [Semíramis], y con prodigios
ha de alterar todo el orbe,
haciendo que sea el peligro
más general su hermosura,
que es el don que tiene mío.
Excusa, pues, los insultos,
los escándalos, los vicios,
los alborotos, las ruinas,
las muertes y los delitos
que han de suceder por ella ...
[I have feared that Diana will visit on her (Semíramis) her revenge on me (Venus), and with prodigies will alter the entire orb, making a general danger of her beauty, the gift she received from me. Forgive, then, the insults, scandals, vices, uprisings, ruins, deaths and crimes that she will inspire.] (I, 934–45)

---

[7] All quotes are taken from Edwards's edition, and Roman numerals designate which of the two parts of the play the quote is taken from. Semíramis's description of the rape of her mother and of being the product of a "bastard love" has echoes in other plays by Calderón, notably *La púrpura de la rosa* [The Blood of the Rose], in which Adonis tells of being conceived from the incestuous relationship between Myrrha and her father. Myrrha had tricked her father into having sex with her; when he discovers her treachery, he tries to kill her:

Mirra, mi madre, lo diga,
pues apenas me engendró,
cuando en odio del concepto,
hurto de amante traición,
su mismo padre mi vida
y su vida abandonó,
tanto que le dio la muerte ...
nací bastardo embrión ...
[Myrrha, my mother, can testify to it, since as soon as she conceived me, when her own father, in hatred of a union that was the result of lustful betrayal, abandoned our lives, so much so that it caused her death ... and I was born a bastard embryo ...]
(*Obras completas*, vol. 1, 1767b)

These words prefigure the crimes that will be associated with Semíramis: the murder of her husband (although it is not clear that she had a direct hand in it), the usurpation of the throne, the impersonation of her son, and the tyranny of her rule. While in the first part of *La hija* it is possible to see her as a victim of her inauspicious beginnings and of her fate, her tyrannical rule in the Second Part is nevertheless anticipated in the association with the natural and the bestial. Unlike the ruthless monarchs in *La gran Cenobia* and Tirso's *La república al revés*, however, the tyrant here is a woman, thus bringing the hints of irrational femininity associated with Constantino and Aureliano to their logical conclusion. While the hyperbolic language used by Venus, with its strong echoes of Senecan tragedy, is typical of the Calderonian stage, its vehemence is in fact not that much more emphatic than the dire warnings we find in treatises that attempted to define women's nature and to proscribe feminine behavior.

The threat to order and reason that Semíramis's "otherness" represents is intuited by Menón when he first hears her plaintive cry:

> Sin luz quedaron los míos [ojos]
> al oírlo; rayo fue
> otra vez, que mis sentidos
> frías cenizas ha hecho
> acá dentro de mí mismo.
> ¡Qué frenesí!, ¡qué locura!
> ¡Qué letargo!, ¡oh qué delirio!
> [My eyes were deprived of light upon hearing (the sound of her voice); it was like another bolt of lightning that has left my senses like cold ashes here within myself. What frenzy! What madness! What lethargy! Oh, what delirium!] (I, 724–30)

Thus, even before catching sight of her, this character equates Semíramis with loss of rationality, lethargy, death, and darkness, the latter anticipating Menón's eventual literal blindness. The general, whom Susan Fischer has called "the archetypal power of the invading masculine" (142), penetrates Semíramis's private feminine space and is immediately struck by her dual ambivalent nature, calling her a "divino monstruo":

> pues truecas las señas
> de lo rústico en lo lindo,
> de lo bárbaro en lo hermoso,
> de lo inculto en lo pulido,
> lo silvestre en lo labrado,
> lo miserable en lo rico.
> [for you transpose the attributes of the rustic into the beautiful, of the barbaric into the lovely, of the uncultured into the polished, of the wild into the crafted, of the miserable into the wealthy.] (I, 779–84)

She represents in this initial state an inversion of the normal state of the world; her body is in itself a topsy-turvy microcosm. Furthermore, this description foreshadows the distortions that will come about during Semíramis's reign. Even in the early scenes we see how deeply attracted Menon is to her, all the while being also keenly apprehensive about the pernicious nature of her beauty ("me ha disculpado / el ver cuán amenazado / de tus influjos estoy [I can be forgiven, seeing how I am threatened by your influence]" [I, 1072–4]). Menón struggles to control the threat that Semíramis represents and, not surprisingly, he begins by attempting to contain her and keep her out of sight. In the following passage, he echoes not only Venus's injunction to Tiresias to keep her hidden, but also the insistence on enclosure and surveillance that characterized societal views toward women in Spain at the time:

> Pues si ocultarte pudiera,
> tanto mi amor te ocultara,
> que ni el sol viera tu cara
> ni el aire de ti supiera;
> si hacerla pudiera, hiciera
> una torre de diamante;
> y para que más constante
> fuese, Semíramis bella,
> a todas las llaves della
> quebrara luego al instante.
> [If I could hide you, my love would hide you so well that not even the sun would see your face, nor would the wind know anything about you. If I could, I would build a tower of diamonds and so that it could be even more secure, oh beautiful Semíramis, I would immediately destroy all its keys.] (I, 1085–99)

The ideology of enclosure that determined the attitudes toward women and their pernicious beauty are eloquently verbalized in this passage. Initially Semíramis presents herself as a docile body, gratefully accepting Menón's protection and vowing to defer all decisions to him. Indeed, she pointedly embraces the "masculine" principle of rationality: "Adiós, / tenebroso centro mío; / que voy a ser *racional*, / ya que hasta aquí bruto he sido [Farewell, dismal milieu: I am to become a *rational being*, for until now I have been nothing but a beast]" (I, 1003–6, emphasis added). Furthermore, she promises to voluntarily hide from the world, even suppressing her very identity to become no more than a humble slave to Menón's male authority:

> Tan sagrado es el precepto
> tuyo, que humilde y postrada,
> vivir del sol ignorada,
> y aun de mí misma prometo.
> Yo de mí misma, a este efecto,
> no sabré; porque si a mí
> yo me pregunto quién fui,

> yo a mí me responderé
> que yo no lo sé, y iré
> a preguntártelo a ti.
>
> [Your will is so sacred, that humble and prostrate, I will live hidden from the sun and even from myself. In fact, I will not know anything about myself, for if I were to ask myself who I am, I myself will answer that I do not know and will go instead and inquire it of you.] (I, 1205–14)

Despite these eloquent protestations of humility, Semíramis soon proves to be a force that cannot be controlled, and Menón's jealous attempt to enclose her is almost immediately doomed to failure. Her inconstancy is revealed as soon as Menón leaves her for the court, where he will ask permission to marry her:

> Ya,
> grande pensamiento mío,
> que estamos solos los dos,
> hablemos claro yo y vos,
> pues sólo de vos confío;
> mi albedrío, ¿es albedrío
> libre o esclavo? ¿Qué acción,
> o que dominio, elección
> tiene sobre mi fortuna,
> que sólo me saca de una
> para darme otra prisión?
>
> [My thoughts, now that we are alone, let us speak clearly, for in you alone do I trust. My will, is it free or enslaved? What possible effect or dominance, or choice does fortune claim over me by plucking me from one prison only to place me in another?] (I, 44)

Directly contradicting what she has just told Menon, she chafes at any attempt to enclose her and limit her freedom. In the meantime, Menón himself becomes the instrument of his own downfall through his arrogant and urgent need to boast of her beauty, of which he believes himself to be master. Most dangerously, he praises her in overwrought poetic terms before the king himself, thereby precipitating a confrontation between the power of beauty and political power reminiscent of the struggle dramatized in *La gran Cenobia*. His eloquent description of Semíramis's charms will fan the flame of the king's own desires, thereby setting the course of destruction for the individual characters and for the stability of the kingdom. The language the general uses to proclaim her beauty is thoroughly conventional; and, like so much amatory poetry in the Renaissance and Baroque, his praise may be seen as the verbal rehearsal of an anticipated physical possession of the beloved's body. The description is of interest because it not only reiterates the descriptive formulas of lyric poetry partitioning a female body into a series of exquisite parts, but also prefigures the dire outcome of Semíramis's intrusion into the civilized world. She is the quintessential disorderly woman whose wild beauty and the power it exerts are early on in the play metaphorically equated with political disorder. Thus, when Menón describes Semíramis's beauty to King Nino, he begins by comparing her loose hair to a rebellious populace:

> Suelto el cabello tenía,
> que en dos bien partidas crenchas,
> golfo de rayos al cuello
> inundaba; y de manera
> con la libertad vivía
> tanta república de hebras
> ufana, que inobediente
> a la mano que las peina,
> daba a entender que el precepto
> a la hermosura no aumenta,
> pues todo aquel pueblo estaba
> hermoso sin obediencia.
> [Her hair was loose, separated into two parts, and a gulf of rays inundated her neck; and that republic of arrogant tresses lived with such freedom that, disobedient to the hand that combed them, they (the tresses) made it understood that laws do not apply to beauty; for, after all, here was an entire populace that was beautiful without being obedient.] (I, 1535–46)

In this comparison, the expected description of the beloved's loose hair is transformed—through the comparison to a rebellious populace—into a witty riff on the notion of *head* of state. Echoing the metaphoric logic particular to corporeal imagery as applied to the relationship between a prince and his realm, Menón also equates Semíramis's eyes with power, sovereignty, and the suggestion of imperial enterprise:

> Los ojos negros tenía:
> ¿quién pensara, quién creyera
> que reinasen en los Alpes
> los etíopes? Pues piensa
> que allí se vio, pues se vieron
> de tanta nevada esfera
> reyes dos negros bozales,
> y tan bozales, que apenas
> política conocían.
> [Her eyes were black. Who would have thought, who would have believed that the Ethiopians could rule the Alps? Well, consider that what we saw there was precisely this, for it was apparent that two newly arrived and voiceless black slaves were kings, so new and without speech that they hardly understood politics.] (1581–9)

As in some Quevedo poems, imperial claims such as the need to subjugate darker nations are embedded in this hyperbolic amatory imagery.[8] The term *negro bozal* has some interesting connotations. It was applied to slaves who were incapable of communicating in the master's language and often incapable of communicating with each other. Indeed, slaves from different nations were often deliberately put together so that, unable to understand each other, they could not plot mutiny or escape.[9] Calderón, who here is equating the body of this unruly woman with rebellion, was no doubt aware of the connotations the use of this term would have. Extending an overused Petrachan metaphor, the playwright goes on to say that Semíramis's eyes not only kill the men they see with their beauty, but almost enter into a fight with one another: "Para que no se abrasasen / los dos en civiles guerras, / [la nariz] su jurisdicción partía [So that the two (eyes) would not be scorched in civil wars, (the nose) separated them into different jurisdictions]" (I, 1595–7). The exaggerated (almost parodic) rhetoric applied to this woman's body anticipates what will actually happen during Semíramis's reign, demonstrating in passing that even clichéd poetic tropes are not innocent of ideological connotations. Throughout the two Parts of *La hija del aire* she will come to literalize, unwittingly or not, all the evils associated with beauty and evoked in lyric conventions: She will be the cruel lady whose beauty leads to the literal blinding of Menón; she will betray, imprison, and cause the death of her lovers and admirers. What's more, her kingdom will become engulfed in rebellion and destructive civil wars. The play provides numerous remarkable examples of the literalization of metaphor that is so typical of Calderón, as commonplace poetic conventions gain dramatic and ideological force.[10] Thus, Semíramis's beauty, initially associated with unruly nature, takes on the characteristics of a symbolic body politic, but one in which the latent violence of her former nature never disappears.

---

[8] See, for example, the humorous Quevedo poem "A una dama tuerta y muy hermosa [To A Beautiful One-Eyed Lady]," which contains the following verses:
Si en un ojo no más, que en vos es día,
Tienen cuantos le ven muerte y prisiones,
Al otro le faltara monarquía.
Aun faltan a sus rayos corazones,
Victorias a su ardiente valentía
Y al triunfo de sus luces aun naciones.
[If with only one eye, which in you is as bright as day, all who gaze upon you find death and imprisonment, the other eye could be deprived of its own dominions. Its rays are still clamoring for hearts, its glowing valor still seeks victories, and its lights still want to triumph over more nations.] (*Poemas escogidos*, 153)

[9] I am grateful to my colleague Enrique Sacerio-Garí for providing a detailed explanation of the term *negro bozal*.

[10] The best essay on the literalization of metaphor in Calderón is Bruce Wardropper's "The Dramatization of Figurative Language in the Spanish Theater," *Yale French Studies* 47 (1972): 189–98.

The dangers represented by Semíramis are exacerbated by the presence of gender dissonance and confusion in the protagonist. That is, the ambivalence embodied by Semíramis goes beyond the half-human/half-beast condition in which she is initially found. As Lipmann and others have pointed out, the duality of masculinity and femininity in Semíramis is first symbolically announced in the opening scene, where we find a description of her attraction to both the martial sound of the drum and the more sublime cadences of a song:

> ... que iguales
> me arrancan el corazón
> blandura y fiereza, agrado
> y ira, lisonja y horror;
> cuándo un estruendo a esta parte,
> cuándo a ésta una admiración;
> ésta adormece al sentido,
> ésta despierta el valor,
> repitiéndome los ecos
> del bronce y de la canción.
> [They tug at my heart equally, softness and fierceness, pleasure and ire, praise and horror, when I hear on one side the clashing noise and on the other, admiring sounds; the latter calm the senses, the former awakens my courage, both repeating in me the echoes of bronze and of song.] (I, 61–70)

The gender confusion indexed by the antitheses—*blandura y fiereza, lisonja y horror*, for example—increases as the play progresses; and quite often, the masculine side seems to predominate as the numerous allusions to her *brio* or *valor* attest. In the First Part of the play, for example, Semíramis courageously saves King Nino's life, an act which leads the servant Sirene to cry out: "¡Ay, tal marimacha! [Oh, what a manly woman!]" (I, 1820). Later she forcefully defends her honor by wielding a dagger when the king tries to rape her. Her masculine characteristics are not necessarily presented as negative, at least not at first. In the popular discourse of the time, women who exhibited exceptional virtue were described as "varonil [virile]" in recognition of their ability to transcend the negative expectations of their sex.[11] Nevertheless, Semíramis is equally adept at using her feminine attributes, her beauty, and, indeed, her virtue in order to further her ambitions. It is her beauty, after all, that propels her out of the natural feminine enclosure of the cave into a public sphere, where she will become an active transgressor. Later, she virtuously refuses Nino's advances until he makes her his queen—in essence, as Gwynne Edwards suggests, exchanging her virginity for political power (xliii).

---

[11] See Melveena McKendrick, *Women and Society in the Spanish Drama of the Golden Age: a Study of the* mujer varonil (Cambridge: Cambridge UP, 1974) and Elizabeth Perry's *Gender and Disorder in Early Modern Seville* (Princeton: Princeton UP, 1990) for discussions of "la mujer varonil."

The ambiguity of gender manifests itself at a mythic/symbolic level as well. The two presiding goddesses, as described by Tiresias, are Diana and Venus, and Semíramis will assume characteristics ascribed to both: Venus's beauty and sensuality and Diana's ability as a pitiless warrior. Although often presented as opposing deities, these two figures were both considered ambivalent in nature. Diana, the chaste goddess of the hunt associated with male pursuits, was also the goddess who presided at childbirth. Venus was, of course, the goddess of feminine beauty and sexuality; but, because she was born out of the foam that contained semen from Uranus, her castrated father, she also had phallic origins, as Everett Hesse has pointed out.[12] Furthermore, this most feminine of deities at times took on both female and male characteristics and was even at times depicted with a phallus. Another tradition associated with Venus is that of the Venus victrix, an image particularly applicable to Calderón's heroine. In some stories, Venus appears wearing Mars's armor and, according to Peter Stallybrass, seems to symbolize the "fantasy of female rule" (216). In the play, furthermore, Semíramis's human protector is Tiresias, a figure who—as a hermaphrodite—was representative of sexual ambivalence in Greek myth. In Calderón's carefully constructed metaphoric universe within *La hija del aire*, gender dissonance is everywhere.

Semíramis's sexual ambivalence becomes particularly evident in the Second Part of the play, the action of which begins years later when Semíramis has become the supreme ruler of Babylon. We learn that her husband, Nino, is dead (she is presumed to have had a hand in his murder) and that she has hidden away their son, Ninias. Jealously guarding her power, she deprives the country of the rightful heir to the throne, not unlike Basilio in *La vida es sueño*. In the remarkable first scene of the Second Part, we find the queen, again in an unequivocally feminine setting—her private chamber—in the process of combing her hair and dressing among her women servants. She is surrounded by several objects, notably a mirror and a sword: the mirror an obvious symbol of feminine vanity and the passivity of self-contemplation, the sword an equally obvious marker of military masculinity and action. The staging of this scene, with the various props and sound effects, vividly dramatizes Semíramis's ability to easily traverse back and forth from the feminine to the masculine. When her enemy King Lidoro, disguised as an ambassador, interrupts this private feminine space and accuses her of murdering Nino and not allowing her son to reign, she becomes furious and proudly recounts her numerous victories and her valorous and virile behavior:

Díganlo tantas victorias
como he ganado en el tiempo
que esposa de Nino he sido,
sus ejércitos rigiendo,
Belona suya, pues cuando
la Siria se alteró, vieron

---

[12] See "Calderón's Semíramis: Myth of the Phallic Woman," *Bulletin of the comediantes* 38.2 (1986): 209–18.

los castigados rebeldes
en mi espada su escarmiento.
[Let the many victories I won while I was Nino's wife and led his armies speak of my valor. I was his Bellona, for when Syria rebelled, the punished rebels saw their defeat in my sword.] (II, 331–8)

Even within the feminine setting of her royal chamber, Semíramis presents herself as a warrior, a "phallic woman" capable of domination and control. Shortly afterward, she herself calls attention to her surroundings and vaunts her ability to assume both feminine and masculine roles at the same time:

has entrado a hablarme a tiempo
que estaba entre mis mujeres,
consultando en ese espejo
mi hermosura, lisonjeada
de voces y de instrumentos;
y así, en esta misma acción
has de dejarme, volviendo
las espaldas; pues aqueste
peine, que en la mano tengo,
no ha de acabar de regir
el vulgo de mi cabello,
antes que en esa campaña
o quedes rendido o muerto.
Laurel de aquesta victoria
ha de ser; porque no quiero
que corone mi cabeza
hoy más acerado yelmo
que este dentado penacho,
que es femenil instrumento.
[You have come to speak to me when I was among my ladies-in-waiting, contemplating my beauty in this mirror, entertained by voices and instruments. And in this same state will you leave me, when you turn your back: because this comb that I am holding in my hand will not complete its dominion over the populace of my hair until you are either defeated or killed in this military campaign. (The comb) will serve as laurel of that victory because I shall don no helmet other than this toothed comb, which is a feminine instrument.] (II, 458–76)

Here Calderón is taking up again the motif of the rebellious "head of state" and providing his own version of a well-known episode in the legend of Semíramis, one told by Boccaccio, among others:

The story is reported as fact that one day, after she had pacified her domains and was resting at leisure, she was having her maids comb her hair with feminine care into braids, as was the custom of the country. Her hair was only half combed when the news that Babylon had rebelled was brought to her. This so angered her that she threw aside her comb and immediately abandoned her womanly pursuits. She arose in anger, took up arms, and led her forces to a siege of that powerful city. She did not finish combing her hair until she had forced that mighty city to surrender, weakened by long siege, and brought it back into her power by force of arms. A huge bronze statue of a woman with her hair braided on one side and loose on the other stood in Babylon to bear witness to this brave deed for a long period of time. (6)

Among the innovations in Calderón's version is that while Semíramis abandons the mirror (symbol of feminine vanity), she keeps the comb, another marker of femininity, but immediately transforms it into a warrior's helmet before rushing off half-dressed to take up the sword against Lidoro. Again, her hair is compared to an unruly populace, an image that manifests itself literally, first in Lidoro's army and later when her own people rebel against her reign. She will return after a decisive military victory and casually resume her interrupted toilette: "Astrea, toma este acero; Libia, el espejo; que quiero acabarme de tocar [Astrea, take this sword; Libia, the mirror; I wish to finish my toilette]" (II, 716–18). In this casual (even humorous) allusion to her ability to leave aside the sword and immediately pick up the mirror to finish her feminine toilette, Semíramis proudly proclaims a duality that permits her to inhabit both feminine and masculine realms.

Gender fluidity must be viewed in part within the context of an early modern society where, as Thomas Laqueur explains, "to be a man or a woman was to hold a social rank, to assume a cultural role, and not to *be* organically one or the other of two sexes" (142). Indeed, there was little biological differentiation between male and female, as Juan Huarte de San Juan graphically makes clear:

> Y es que el hombre, aunque no paresce de la compostura que vemos, no difiere de la mujer, según dice Galeno, mas que en tener los miembros genitales fuera del cuerpo. Porque si hacemos anatomía de una doncella, hallaremos que tiene dentro de sí dos testículos, dos vasos seminarios, y el útero con la mesma compostura que el miembro viril sin faltarle ninguna deligneación.
> [And the fact is that man, although he may not seem it, differs from a woman, according to Galen, only in that he has the genital members outside the body. Because if we were to dissect a young woman, we would find that she has within her two testicles, two seminal vessels, and a uterus with the same constitution as the virile member without lacking any detail.] (370)

La hija del aire clearly explores at one level the blurred boundaries of sexual identities in early modern times, more firmly rooted as sociological categories than ontological or even biological identifications. Juan de la Cerda, for example, insisted in *Vida política de todos los estados de mujeres* [*The Political Life of Every Class of Woman*] that a good widow had to possess both the rod of discipline of the father and the nurturing breasts of the mother (qtd. in Sanchez, *Empress*). Gender is as gender does. Teresa de Lauretis tells us that psychoanalysis recognizes "the inherent bisexuality of the subject, for whom femininity and masculinity are not qualities or attributes but positions in the symbolic processes of (self) representation" (164). Basing herself on Orgel, Teresa Soufas speaks of

"Renaissance culture's blurred boundaries of sexual identity," which "empowers a human being to occupy the social space of either gender" (*Dramas* 16). As this scene indicates, Semíramis seems singularly adept at occupying the social spaces and cultural roles of both men and women, despite her biological sex. This gender fluidity is accompanied by her capacity to assume constantly shifting identities, to re-present her self in different guises. In the following, the *gracioso* Chato comments on her prodigious mutability:

> ... a la Reina serví en tantas
> fortunas; pues la serví
> siendo monstruo en las montañas,
> siendo dama en Ascalón,
> siendo en las selvas villana,
> siendo en palacio señora,
> y en Nínive Reina. ¡Ah, cuánta
> mala condición sufrí
> en todas estas andanzas!
> [I served the queen in many capacities, for I served her when she was a monster in the mountains, when she was a lady-in-waiting in Ascalon, when she was a peasant in the forest, and a noblewoman in the palace, and a queen in Nineveh. Oh what poor treatment I suffered in all of those mutations!] (II, 2610–18)

Her many identities signal an intense theatricality presented as intrinsically connected with her growing political ambition. Again, we find the tripartite identification (originating in the classical world, as we have seen) between femininity, theatricality, and tyranny. The tyrant's nature, Bushnell tells us, "is fundamentally histrionic" since, in contrast to the proper king, the tyrant presents "a multitude of different faces ..." (7). Indeed, as discussed in the first chapter, Plato was suspicious of drama in general (likening it to desire) because with its emphasis on role-playing, it may ultimately encourage the fragmentation of the self. This inveterate theatricality is one of Semíramis's intrinsic characteristics, as she assumes whatever identity is necessary to further her ambitions.[13] Thus, her chronic role-playing and constant re-presentations and negotiations of gender result in a serious crisis of selfhood and a lack of authenticity. Indeed, throughout the play, we witness a progressive disintegration of Semíramis's identity. The most serious crisis in the Second Part is precipitated by her people's insistence that the kingdom return to proper masculine rule ("!Que rey varón queremos! [We want a male king!]" [II, 799]), and that this rule be based on dynastic lineage:

---

[13] Lipmann claims that it is a mistake to take Semíramis's ambition as a desire for power. Rather, he suggests that her ambition is, quoting St. Augustine, "an unbalanced desire for recognition" (42). I would argue that this desire is not incompatible with the thirst for power. Equally important, her need to be seen and admired is yet another manifestation of her intense theatricality. See Lipmann's "The Duality and Delusion of Calderón's Semíramis," *BHS* 59 (1982): 42–57.

> No una mujer nos gobierne,
> porque aunque el cielo la hizo
> varonil, no es de la sangre
> de nuestros Reyes antiguos.
> [We don't want a woman to rule us, for although the heavens made her masculine, she is not of the blood of our ancient kings.] (II, 781–4)

The issue, then, is not just that she is a woman, but also that she is a usurper of the throne. The question of inherited monarchy was constantly debated in Spain, with most political authors accepting its desirability without question. Semíramis, however, will not be persuaded to give up the throne voluntarily. Her ambition has led her to identify completely with the body politic, and she rails against the demand that she abandon her rule:

> Desagradecido monstruo,
> que eres compuesto vestigio
> de cabezas diferentes,
> cada una con su juicio,
> pues, cuando acabo de darte
> la victoria que has tenido,
> ¿de que soy mujer te acuerdas,
> y te olvidas de mi brío?
> [Ungrateful monster, relic composed of different heads, each with its own reasoning, since just as I finish offering you a victory, you remember that I am a woman and conveniently forget my bravery?] (II, 791–8)

I have translated the word "vestigio" here as 'relic' because it communicates the queen's outrage at what she deems an antiquated way of thinking—that only a man is fit to lead the kingdom. When she is forced by the rebellion to abdicate in favor of her son, Ninias, she cries out:

> ¿Yo sin mandar? De ira rabio.
> ¿Yo sin reinar? Pierdo el juicio.
> Etna soy, llamas aborto;
> volcán soy, rayos respiro.
> [I, without the ability to command? I will die of rage. I, without the ability to reign? I shall go mad. I am an Etna, expelling flames. I am a volcano, breathing rays.] (169)

Semíramis cannot conceive of any identity beyond that of absolute monarch, for her very essence is that of a body politic:

> Mujer soy afligida,
> pues muero sin reino y no tengo vida.
> Mi ser era mi reino;
> sin ser estoy / supuesto que no reino.

[I am a desolate woman because I die without the throne. My essence was my kingdom. I am without essence because I do not reign.] (II, 2164–7)

She extends this complete identification to that most precious possession of any woman: "Mi honor mi imperio era; / sin él honor no tengo ... [The empire was my very honor. Without it, I have no honor ...]" (II, 2168–9). Her obsession with power, and the absolute correlation she establishes between her very self and the kingdom, leads to her most serious crime: the impersonation of her own son, Ninias. Throughout the Second Part, she systematically attempts to obliterate Ninias's identity and even his sex: first, by hiding him from view (thereby assigning to him an exclusively feminine space away from the public sphere); later, by drugging him and depriving him of his consciousness; and finally, by dressing like him and literally taking over his identity:

Ninias es mi retrato;
pues con sus mismas señas robar trato
la majestad; que sin piedad alguna
ladrona me he de hacer de mi fortuna ...
A este efecto ya tengo prevenidos
adornos a los suyos parecidos,
porque aun las circunstancias más pequeñas
no puedan desmentirnos en las señas.
A este efecto, en aqueste vil retiro,
donde un suspiro alcanza otro suspiro,
del femenil adorno haciendo ultraje,
me he ensayado en el traje
varonil, porque en nada
me halle la novedad embarazada.
[Ninias is my spitting image; well then, with his selfsame features I will attempt to rob him of his majesty; without pity, I will become the thief of my own fortune. To this end, I have already prepared adornments similar to his, for even the smallest details can give us away. To this end, in this vile retreat where a sigh meets another sigh, violating my own feminine adornment, I have slipped into masculine dress, because the novelty (of this garb) will in no way impede me.]
(II, 2102–15)

This act of usurpation is the culmination of the crisis of gender and theatricality that has been announced and developed from the beginning. She herself calls it a violent act, a metaphorical violation: "haciendo ultraje." The theatricality—in the sense of duplicitous role-playing often associated with women—is both clear and ironic, for when Semíramis assumes Ninias's identity, what is being presented is an internal performance of kingship and masculinity. The impersonation of Ninias is a transgression that violates social conventions at every level. Not only is it a symbolic regicide, echoing the previous murder of Nino, but it also negates the very notion (the sanctity even) of motherhood; and, indeed, Fischer has associated Semíramis with the archetypal Terrible Mother (152). In Calderón's time, motherhood as an institution was viewed in contradictory ways from a political standpoint. On the one hand, maternity was often cited as yet one more reason why a woman could not wield political power, as the previously cited words by Huarte de San Juan suggest:

> Luego la razón de tener la primera mujer no tanto ingenio, le nasció de haberla hecho Dios fría y húmida, que es el temperamento necesario para ser fecunda y paridera, y el que contradice al saber; y si la sacara templada como Adán, fuera sapientísima, pero no pudiera parir ...
> [The reason the first woman was not born with much intelligence is that God created her cold and moist, the necessary temperature for women to be fecund and suitable for childbirth, but inimical to knowledge; for if he had made her temperate like Adam, she would have been very wise but not fecund.] (II, 374)

At the same time, the queen's body played an inestimable political role, for it guaranteed the continuity of the royal line. As mentioned in an earlier chapter, the court and the nation at large were obsessed with the queen's ability to provide an heir to the throne. In *La hija del aire*, Semíramis is not content with the reflected power that giving birth to a future king represents. On the contrary, she recognizes that maternity is in fact a stumbling block to assuming absolute power; and, in her ambition, she inverts the act of giving birth by annihilating her own son's presence and identity.[14] Interestingly, when she refers to Ninias as "mi retrato," she is invoking the commonplace equation of portraiture with genealogy, not only in that children were often described as portraits of the parents, but also in the importance of painting in promoting dynastic continuity.[15] Erasing the difference between herself and Ninias, she violates the proper political functioning of a queen's body by denying her people the heir whom they so long for. "Becoming" Ninias is the ultimate outrage, an action that has received contradictory critical interpretations. Fischer, for example, calls it a "psychosexual transformation" (137), while Hesse suggests an even worse crime: "Figuratively speaking, she commits an act of incest by penetrating Ninias's image and presenting herself as king and thus projecting the illusion of herself as a man" (214). Lipmann sees this impersonation as her masculine spirit assuming a visible shape (44), and goes so far as to suggest that in assuming Ninias's persona, Semíramis has "resolved the masculine-feminine duality of her nature" (49). Quite the contrary is the case, in my opinion, for this new role represents a final disintegration rather than a

---

[14] In her book *Juana the Mad: Sovereignty and Dynasty in Renaissance Europe* (Baltimore: Johns Hopkins UP, 2005), Bethany Aram states: "Like marriage, motherhood potentially restricted the proprietary queen. Juana's procreative success not only freed her of the obligation to rule Castile and Aragon, as Charles V argued—it deprived her of that very right" (166).

[15] On the topic of the association between portraiture and genealogy, see Laura Bass, *The Drama of the Portrait: Theater and Visual Culture in Early Modern Spain* (University Park: Penn State UP, 2008), esp. 63–6.

resolution, something that Lipmann himself recognizes later when he calls this an act of madness. Indeed, through the violent inversion of her maternal role, she not only effaces once and for all her authentic self, but in the process, becomes an overly determined transgressive body.

This assumed transgendered role precipitates a chain reaction of confusion and destabilization, both personal and political. For one thing, her language becomes duplicitous, reflecting both her current dual masculine/feminine nature and her incipient madness. When Lisías confronts the changed "Ninias," he is taken aback by "his" equivocal "discursos." Semíramis as Ninias responds to his confusion:

> Neciamente los extrañas [discursos];
> que ya no soy el que fuí;
> que el reinar da nueva alma.
> Y así, si piensas que soy
> quien piensas, Lisías, te engañas;
> porque ya no soy quien piensas,
> sino otra deidad más alta.
> [You are impertinent in finding my words so strange, for I am no longer who I was before, because the act of ruling gives one a new soul. And so, if you think that I am who you think I am, Lisías, you are wrong; for I am no longer who you think I am, but rather an even loftier deity.] (II, 2574–80)

By perpetrating a second symbolic regicide, a reiteration or new performance of the possible physical murder of Nino, she destabilizes the very idea of kingship, and furthermore, perverts certain basic social and gender roles. That is, in the staging of a false monarchy and in her self-representation as a man, she eradicates difference, presenting an unbearable doubleness of being: a man who is really a woman, a son who is really the mother, a king who is really a queen. In performing all of these contradictory roles, Semíramis personifies the convergence between femininity, theatricality, and tyranny.

Semíramis's histrionic personality is equally apparent in both parts of the play, and we have already alluded to her various metamorphoses—from half savage to lady of the court to queen, and finally to absolute ruler. Her tyranny, on the other hand, manifests itself most clearly in the Second Part, and several characters condemn her for it. Lidoro, for example, tells her in the first scene that denying her people the rightful heir is nothing short of tyrannical:

> sin el decoro y respeto
> debido a quien es, le tienes,
> donde de corona y cetro
> tiranamente le usurpas
> la majestad y el gobierno.
> [You are holding him without the decorum and respect owed to him for who he is and in a place where you tyrannically deny him crown and scepter, majesty and government.] (II, 264-8)

Her later unspeakable cruelty against Lidoro, whom she treats literally like a dog, and against anyone who crosses her makes for a vivid performance of the tyranny and capriciousness of absolute power. At one point, she exclaims:

> Ayer premié, y hoy castigo;
> que si ayer una ignorancia
> hice, hoy no he de hacerla, a todos
> diciendo una acción tan rara,
> que de lo que errare hoy,
> sabré enmendarme mañana.
> [Yesterday, I saw fit to reward; today, I punish; if yesterday I did something out of ignorance, today I won't repeat the same mistake by announcing to all my unusual behavior. For the mistakes I make today, I'll know how to amend tomorrow.] (II, 2553–8)

The blatant capriciousness of her judgments and her ruthlessness mean that she has broken the sacred bond between a prince and his vassals, as Saavedra Fajardo warns:

> Peligran tambien los reinos ... cuando el [Rey], olvidado de los institutos de sus mayores, tiene por natural la servidumbre de los vasallos; y no reconociendo dellos su grandeza, los desama y gobierna como á esclavos, atendiendo mas a sus fines propios y al cumplimiento de sus apetitos que al beneficio público, *convertida en tiranía la dominación*; de donde concibe el pueblo una desestimación del príncipe y un odio y aborrecimiento á su persona y acciones, con que se deshace aquella unión recíproca que hay entre el rey y el reino donde este obedece y aquel manda, por el beneficio que reciben, el uno en el esplendor y superioridad de gobernar, y el otro en la felicidad de ser bien gobernado.
> [Kingdoms are also at risk ... when the king, forgetting the edicts of his forebears, takes as normal the servitude of his vassals; and not recognizing their merit, he disregards them and treats them like slaves, attending more to his own goals and the satisfaction of his appetites than to the communal benefit, *transforming his domination into tyranny*; from which the populace loses respect and conceives a hatred and abhorrence of the king's person and actions, thereby undoing that reciprocal union that should exist between a king and his kingdom, where the latter obeys and the former commands, to the mutual benefit of both, one in the splendor and superiority of governing, and the other in the happiness of being well-governed.] (*Idea de un príncipe*, 167, emphasis added)

As we have seen, the dangers of tyranny were an obsessive theme among political theorists—not just Saavedra Fajardo, but also Juan de Mariana, Francisco Quevedo, and Pedro Rivadeneira, among others.

While Semíramis represents a literal embodiment of the link between femininity, theatricality, and tyranny, this tripartite link is strengthened through the characterization of both Nino and Ninias. Nino starts out as an admirable, even exemplary monarch, a triumphant imperial figure described by Menón as "Invictísimo joven cuya frente / no solo de los rayos del Oriente / inmortal se corona, /

pero de zona trascendiendo en zona, / de hemisferio pasando en hemisferio, / hasta el ocaso extenderá su imperio ... [Most invincible youth, who is not only crowned with the rays of the immortal Orient but whose empire will extend from region to region, from hemisphere to hemisphere, until the end]" (291–6). After his many victories, Nino announces a period of peace: "cese, cese / el militar acento / de estremecer al sol, herir al viento, / turbar el mar y fatigar la tierra, / y hoy a la blanda paz ceda la guerra [Let the military din cease and no longer make the sun shudder or injure the wind, or disturb the sea or fatigue the earth, and today let war cede to gentle peace]" (238–42).[16] What's more, he is a generous king who showers his general, Menón, with praise and gifts, thus displaying gratitude, a quality that was highly praised by theorists such as Saavedra Fajardo at the time: "los servicios mueren sin el premio; con él viven y dejan glorioso el reinado; porque en tiempo de un príncipe desagradecido no se acometen cosas grandes ni quedan ejemplos gloriosos a la posteridad [Good services die without recompense; with it, they thrive and bring honor to the realm. Because under an ungrateful prince, great deeds are not accomplished, nor are glorious accomplishments left to posterity]" (*Idea de un príncipe* 156). At the beginning of the play, Nino's kingdom seems to be on the cusp of prosperity, peace, and glory. All of that will change when the disturbing presence of Semíramis is introduced, and the king's passion for this unruly woman will transform him from the exemplary king of the early scenes into a tyrant and a negative example of subordinated masculinity. Ironically, it is precisely Menón's description of Semíramis's beauty that initiates the king's fall into disgrace and death. Nino intuits this when he warns Menón not to praise his beloved too graphically:

> Pero quiérote advertir
> que en tu vida no encarezcas
> hermosura a poderoso,
> si enamorado estás della;
> porque quizá no hallarás
> otro que vencerse sepa.
> [But let me warn you: you must never praise a beautiful woman before a powerful man if you love her, for perhaps you will find that he will not be able to control himself.] (I, 1667–72)

Nino's fall into disgrace (prefigured, in typical Calderonian manner, through an earlier physical fall from his horse) is also intrinsically associated with theatricality. In the type of self-conscious passage that we associate with the playwright, Menón urges Nino to reject the histrionic role that fate seems to have assigned to him:

---

[16] In this early scene, Nino appears accompanied by his sister Irene, whose name means 'peace' and who, like Tirso's Irene, is dressed "*con espada y plumas*," according to the stage directions (11).

No, señor; cansado está
el mundo de ver en farsas
la competencia de un Rey,
de un valido y de una dama.
[No, sire, the world is weary of watching farces where a king and his vassal
compete for the favor of a lady.] (I, 2107–10)

Nino, however, proves incapable of resisting the dramatic destiny that requires him to play rival to his own *privado* for Semíramis's love. He repeatedly ignores the general's warnings, many of which echo the obsessive concern in political treatises over a monarch's responsibility to conquer his passions:

Señor, vencerse a sí mismo
un hombre es tan grande hazaña,
que sólo el que es grande puede
atreverse a ejecutarla.
Tú eres Rey, vasallo soy.
[My lord, a man's ability to conquer himself is such a lofty feat that only the
great can hope to accomplish it. You are king, and I a vassal.] (I, 2243–7)

Later, when Nino invokes his "droit de seigneur" and asks whether he is not permitted as king to take Semíramis away from his general, Menón pleads his case more forcefully:

En quitármela tú, *harás*
una tiranía; en dejarla
yo, una infamia; y al contrario,
tú una grandeza en no amalla,
yo una fineza en quererla.
Mira ahora las distancias
Que hay de tiranía a grandeza,
Y que hay de fineza a infamia.
[If you take her from me, it would be tyranny, and if I abandon her, it would be
infamy. On the contrary, by not taking her you would achieve greatness, and I
courtesy by giving her my love. Just ponder the distances between tyranny and
greatness, and between graciousness and infamy.] (I, 2273–80, emphasis added)

Nino's ruthlessness and inability to "vencerse a sí mismo" ultimately lead him to despicable acts of cunning and tyranny, notably the blinding of Menón. Nino displaces onto his advisor his own figurative blindness; and Menón becomes a mutilated body, his face a visible marker for the tyranny of a king who has allowed himself to become subdued by the power of a woman's beauty. As with Constantino in *La república al revés*, we are confronted here with a despot, closer to an animal than a human precisely because he seeks only to gratify his desires. In the normative treatises of the sixteenth and seventeenth centuries, women, also associated with nature, were said to show a similar lack of restraint. Thus, as Bushnell argues, both in classical tragedy and in English Renaissance drama, the inability to control desire and to master oneself conjoins femininity and tyranny. The same identification is clearly dramatized in Calderón's play, as Nino's passion for Semíramis and his growing abuse of power make him increasingly effeminate. In the scene in which he tries to take Semíramis by force, we witness a remarkable transposition of gender characteristics and behavior. It is Semíramis who wields the sword (although, ostensibly, she turns it against herself), and Nino who cowers and begs for mercy:

>   NINO: Prodigiosa mujer, tente;
>   que ya en mi sangre bañado
>   estoy, viendo, osada y fuerte,
>   esgrimir contra mi vida
>   iras y rayos crueles.
>   ¡Mi mismo cadáver, cielos,
>   miro en el aire aparente!
>   Pálido horror, ¿qué me sigues?
>   Sombra infausta, ¿qué me quieres?
>   ¡No me mates, no me mates!
>   SEMÍRAMIS: ¿Qué te acobardas? ¿Qué temes,
>   señor, si este acero sólo
>   contra mí sus filos vuelve?

[NINO: Prodigious woman, stay back! For I see myself already bathed in my own blood while you, bold and strong, threaten my life with ire and cruel rays. I can see my own cadaver, oh heavens, in the illusory air! Pale horror, why do you pursue me? Unlucky shadow, what do you want from me? Don't kill me! Don't kill me! SEMÍRAMIS: Why are you cowering? What do you fear, sire, since this sword turns its blades only toward me?] (I, 3196–3205)

This scene of debased kingship and masculinity prefigures the regicide that will take place offstage, between the First and Second Parts of the play. Later, Semíramis will try to prove her innocence of Nino's death by saying that there was no need to kill him, since his love for her had already rendered him incapable of reigning:

> En cuanto a que di a mi esposo
> muerte, ¿no es vano argumento
> decir que, porque me dio
> antes de morir el reino
> por seis días, le maté?
> ¿No alega en mi favor eso
> más que en mi daño? Sí; pues
> si vivía tan sujeto,
> tan amante y tan rendido
> Nino a mi amor, ¿a qué efecto
> había de reinar matando,
> si me reinaba viviendo?

[As for the accusation that I killed my husband, isn't it absurd to claim that I killed him because he gave me the kingdom six days before he died? Doesn't this actually argue in my favor? Yes, if Nino was already so subject to my will, so in love, so defeated, what would have been the point of my gaining the kingdom by killing him, since I already reigned while he was still alive? (II, 389–400)

Nino's cowering and subservience to Semíramis make him a decidedly effeminate monarch, not unlike the tyrant described by the French playwright Guillaume La Perrière as "a monstrous Hermaphrodite, who was neither true man nor true woman, being in sexe a man, and in heart a woman" (qtd. in Bushnell 68).

The feminization of the body of the king is reiterated and intensified in the characterization of Ninias, the issue of Semíramis's and Nino's union. Semíramis characterizes her own son as "temeroso por extremo, / cobarde y afeminado [timorous in the extreme, cowardly and effeminate]" (II, 420–21). Indeed, other characters often describe him in terms of his beauty rather than his manly valor:

Vino a Babilonia Ninias,
y ganando su belleza
un común afecto en todos ...
[Ninias arrived in Babylon, and his beauty inspired a shared love among all his subjects.] (II, 1205–7)

When later Lidoro addresses Ninias, he does so in terms more typically reserved for a woman:

Vivas, ¡oh Príncipe augusto!,
en la verde primavera
de tu juventud lozana,
sin que el invierno se atreva
de los años a borrar
la flor más inútil della.
[Long may you live, august Prince, in the green springtime of your youth, and may winter never dare to erase even the least of its (springtime's) flowers.] (II, 1447–52)

Ninias turns out to be, like his father, an unworthy manifestation of kingship. Machiavelli thought of effeminacy as the inability or unwillingness to engage in battle, and this is certainly the case with Ninias. When he hears that Irán's army is approaching to rescue Lidoro, we have the following exchange:

NINIAS: Dices bien, mas yo quisiera
que guerra en Siria no hubiera.
LISÍAS: Pues no lo des a entender;
que aunque el natural temor
en todos obra igualmente,
no mostrarle es ser valiente,
y esto es lo que hace valor.

[NINIAS: I agree, but I wish we could avoid war with Syria. LISÍAS: Don't let anyone hear you say that because, although fear is natural in all of us, to hide it is to be courageous, and it is that which makes us brave.] (II, 1876–82)

Later, Licas exclaims: "De verle / de un ánimo tan cobarde, / no sé cómo se lo enmiende [Seeing in him such a cowardly spirit, I don't know how he can be helped]" (II, 2249–51). Ninias also lacks restraint and discretion, responding to personal desires rather than the good of the state. For one thing, he wishes to marry Astrea, who is beneath his station and thus unworthy to be a king's consort. He further displays dishonorable behavior when he feigns love for Libia in order to deflect attention away from Astrea, causing the former to be abandoned by the man she loves. Friso, one of Semíramis's supporters, believes Ninias to be incaple of accepting wise counsel:

> Esa
> razón en un pecho, Flavio,
> de sustancia y de prudencia
> militada es, pero no
> en el suyo; porque piensa
> que, afeminado, de todo
> se recata y se recela.
> [That argument, Flavio, would influence a breast filled with prudence and substance, but not his; because consider this: he is so effeminate that he fears and hides from everything.] (II, 1328–34)

Ninias's lack of readiness for the throne is vividly staged when he is shown to be asleep, thus providing the perfect opportunity for Friso and Semíramis to drug and kidnap him. Friso delivers the lesson to be gleaned from this scene, namely that a true king should always be alert: "Infeliz joven, / tu desdicha te condene / a esta prisión de mortal, / puesto que eres Rey y duermes [Unhappy youth, your unlucky fate condemns you to this mortal prison, for being a king, you sleep]" (II, 2298–301).[17] When he is thrown in a prison, he is in fact being relegated to

---

[17] The following *décima* directed at Philip IV warned of the dangers of sleeping on the job:
Felipo, que el mundo aclama
Rey del infiel tan temido,
Despierta, que, por dormido,
Nadie te teme ni te ama,
Despierta, rey, que la fama
Por todo el orbe pregona
Que es de león tu corona
Y tu dormir de lirón.
[Philip, whom the world acclaims, king feared by the infidels, wake up, because if you sleep, no one will fear you or love you. Wake up, for Fame is proclaiming throughout the world that your crown is of a lion (león) and your sleep is of a dormouse (lirón).]
The quote comes from Teófanes Egido, *Sátiras políticas de la España moderna* (Madrid: Alianza Editorial, 1973), 115.

an enclosure that is more suitable for a woman, and it is not surprising that he is wearing the queen's dress. Earlier on, in perhaps the most dramatic expression of the reversal of gender categories, Semíramis had said of her own son:

> que, yo mujer y él varón,
> yo con valor y el con miedo,
> yo animosa y él cobarde
> yo con brío, él sin esfuerzo,
> vienen a estar en los dos
> violentados ambos sexos.
> [For, I a woman and he a man, I have the valor and he the fear, I am courageous and he is cowardly, I have the bravery and he lacks the strength. In the two of us, the sexes have been violated.] (II, 429–34)

The rhetoric of violence and the suggestion of rape employed in this passage describe a lack of gender distinction that goes against nature. Interestingly, one aspect of the Semíramis legend that Calderón chose to ignore is the queen's alleged uncontrolled lust that leads her to commit incest with her own son. Boccaccio provides the following account:

> It is believed that this unhappy woman, constantly burning with carnal desire, gave herself to many men. Among these lovers, and this is something more beastly than human, was her own son Ninus, a very handsome young man. As if he had changed sex with his mother, Ninus rotted away idly in bed, while she sweated in arms against her enemies. (6)

Although the playwright avoids this scandalous episode, the feminization and abasement that Boccaccio described is evoked in the words "violentados ambos sexos [the two sexes have been violated]."

All the male monarchs are displayed as deeply flawed; and thus, in the absence of authentic masculine power, Semíramis claims that she has been forced, like Lady Macbeth, to "un-sex" herself in order to fill a void. We have seen similar claims made by Cenobia and by Tirso's Irene in *La república al revés*. As noted before, there were antecedents in Spain for the idea that a woman could, under certain circumstances, assume masculine characteristics, and there was in fact a popular tradition of the woman warrior, a figure that was often positive. As François Delpech has shown, this female warrior often formed part of the myth of nationhood, associated with a heroic past. Stories of women who are forced to become warriors in a moment of crisis in the resistance to an enemy nation were particularly prevalent in the Middle Ages. We can cite as examples the women of Numancia, or the popular stories of "la doncella guerrera [the maiden warrior]" or "La varona de Castilla [the manly woman of Castile]," the nickname given to the legendary twelfth-century female warrior María Pérez de Villanañe. What sets these figures apart from Semíramis is that when the crises that had necessitated their virile behavior are over, they reverted to their traditional feminine roles. According to Delpech:

> Ce qu'il y avait de potentiellement subversif dans cette représentation de féminité guerrière fut emblée neutralisé par son intégration dans le cadre étroit du patriotisme local ... les femmes en armes ne sont que de guerrières occasionnelles, qui reprendront après l'exploit leurs rôles fondamentaux de mère et d'épouse, qu'elles n'ont provisoirement et apparemment abandonnés que pour mieux les sauvegarder.
> [That which was potentially subversive in this representation of a warring femininity was neutralized by its integration within the narrow framework of local patriotism ... armed women were nothing more than occasional warriors who returned after their exploits to their fundamental roles of mother and wife, roles that they had provisionally and apparently abandoned only to better safeguard them.] (31)

While she exhibits some of the heroic characteristics of these legendary women, Semíramis refuses to relinquish any of the power that she has acquired and return to comportment that is more proper for women. At the same time, despite her excesses, the chaos she generates is presented as the logical result of a crisis of monarchical power. In such a vacuum of authority, Calderón seems to be warning his audience, the irrational reign of a woman may become possible. Saavedra Fajardo, among others, describes the paralyzing effect that "feminine" upbringing and treatment can have on a prince:

> El miedo, cuando el Príncipe lo teme todo, y desconfiado de sus acciones, ni se atreve á hablar ni á obrar; piensa que en nada ha de saber acertar; rehúsa el salir en público, y ama la soledad. Esto nace de la educación femenil, retirada del trato humano, y de la falta de experiencias ...
> [Fear, when the Prince is frightened by everything; and, unsure of his actions, doesn't dare to either speak or act. He believes that he cannot be successful in anything; he refuses to go out in public and he embraces solitude. This comes from a feminine education, isolated from human contact and the lack of experience ...] (*Idea de un príncipe* 25)

Semíramis's impersonation of Ninias represents a tour de force of theatricality and performance in more ways than one. In the climactic moment of the Second Part, Semíramis sheds her feminine dress, transforming herself into a man before the audience. The stage directions state, "Desnúdase y queda en jubón [She undresses and is left wearing only a bodice]," and then the character exclaims:

> Adiós, femenil modestia;
> que desta vez has de verte
> desnuda de tus adornos,
> aunque en los ajenos quedes.
> [Farewell, feminine modesty; from now on, you will appear stripped naked of your adornments, while wearing those that belong to another.] (II, 2332–5)

Daniel Rogers has convincingly argued that the same actress must have played the roles of both Semíramis and Ninias. He points out, for example, that Ninias and Semíramis never appear onstage at the same time, nor do they ever speak to each other.[18] This scene in which Semíramis sheds her feminine garb in order to "become" a man makes sense only if the parts were doubled and performed by the same person. At a superficial level, Calderón is repeating the popular *comedia* convention of presenting a "mujer vestida de hombre," or "woman dressed like a man," a practice that was so prevalent as to represent something beyond its appeal as a marketing ploy (that is, the appeal of revealing the feminine form in men's clothing).[19] Indeed, the repeated inversion of sex roles in the *comedia* is indicative of certain societal preoccupations with gender and power. For one thing, according to anthropologists, the inversion of sexual roles is often a ritualistic, magical action meant to ward off evil: "ceremonies of reversal are ultimately sources of order and stability" (N. Davis 153). Theater has always provided the setting for these usually comic inversions. Nevertheless, this was a practice that proved controversial, as mentioned in the first chapter; and was, in fact, prohibited several times in the first half of the seventeenth century. The danger of women cross-dressing on the stage was frequently addressed in the anti-theatrical tracts of the time. Ignacio de Camargo, for example, stated vehemently:

> ¿Qué cosa más torpe y provocativa que ver á una muger de esta calidad que estaba ahora en el tablado dama hermosa afeitada y afectada, salir dentro dè un instante vestida de galán airoso, ofreciendo al registro de los ojos de tantos hombres todo el cuerpo que la naturaleza mismo quiso que estuviese siempre casi todo retirado de la vista?"
> [Can anything be more vulgar and provocative than to see a woman of this type, who one moment is on stage playing the part of a beautiful, adorned, and pretentious woman, and the next appears dressed as an elegant young man, thereby offering to the gaze of so many men the entire body that nature meant to be almost entirely hidden from view?] (Cotarelo y Mori 124)

Calderón intensifies this "torpe y provocativa" practice by having the already threatening body natural of an actress appear as a deeply ambivalent body politic that gathers within it feminine and masculine components. If, as Joseph Roach suggests, the actor often acts as a "surrogate for sovereign authority" (86),

---

[18] The one exception is when Semíramis and Friso are kidnapping Ninias. In this scene, however, the young king is asleep and his face is covered, so he could have easily been played by a double who was not required to speak.

[19] In addition to McKendrick's discussion of the "mujer vestida de hombre" in *Women and Society*, Catherine Connor has an interesting discussion of the ideological implications of this *comedia* figure in "Teatralidad y resistencia: el debate sobre la mujer vestida de hombre," *Actas XI del Congreso de la Asociación Internacional de Hispanistas*, in *Encuentros y desencuentros de culturas: desde la edad media al siglo XVIII*, ed. Juan Villegas, vol. 3 (Irvine: AIH, 1992), 139–45.

we can't help but speculate how this particular performance must have been received by its intended audience. In this instance the use of the "mujer vestida de hombre" convention had an ideological and didactic purpose. The doubling of roles in Calderón's play must have provided a multi-layered spectacle of gender ambiguity and a dizzying performance of compromised kingship and illusory identity. This scene and its casting emphasize the arbitrariness of gender as well as the arbitrariness of the monarchy; in this play, both gender identification and the identity of the monarch are determined by a costume that is put on and can presumably be taken off with ease. In many ways, we can apply to monarchy what critics like Judith Butler have said about gender: that it is not a stable identity or a "locus of agency" but rather something that is instituted through a stylized repetition of acts; something that is continuously rehearsed ("Performative Acts" 519).

With his brilliant understanding of the visual theatrical codes, particularly the use of the same actress to play both Semíramis and Ninias, Calderón vividly stages in *La hija del aire* the articulation between tyranny, theatricality, and gender. Rebecca Bushnell tells us that the tyrant and woman are seen as threats to civilized order, but both are necessary for the construction of order, reason, and the masculine self. That is, they represent the necessary Other, "the antithesis and mirror of an idealized, rational, masculine self" (21). In *La gran Cenobia* and *La república al revés*, the feminization of the tyrant was merely suggested. Here, it is made quite literal as Semíramis becomes a pure manifestation of the dreaded Other. This dual construction of alterity would explain, in part, the fascination with women in power that we find in the *comedia*. And it would also explain the dire punishment that is often reserved for these feminine characters who have managed to escape all manner of social control.[20]

In *La hija del aire*, Semíramis's death is particularly violent. Earlier on, in the First Part, intoxicated with fantasies of power, she exclaims: "¿Qué importa que mi ambición / digan que ha de despeñarme / del lugar mas superior? [What does it matter if people say that my ambition will hurl me from the highest place?]" (I, 148–50). In the end, she is in fact crushed and broken after being thrown into a precipice, her body riddled with arrows. She has become the effigy of

---

[20] Cross-dressing, according to Susana Henández Araico, also suggests a tragic dimension to the characterization of Semíramis. By assuming a male disguise, the queen cannot express her love for Licias: "Vestida de hombre, ha quedado atrapada en el disfraz que le impide revelar sus verdaderos sentimientos ... La única expresión que el traje masculino le facilita es su temperamento guerrero que va a acarrarle la muerte. Su capacidad de amor queda tronchada [Dressed as a man, she has been trapped in a disguise that prevents her from revealing her true feelings ... The only expression that the masculine garb permits is that of her war-like temperament, which will lead to her death. Her capacity for love will remain thwarted]" (39). See "La Semíramis calderoniana como compendio de estereotipos femeninos," *Iberorománica* 22 (1985): 29–39.

tyranny, and her death is the literal disintegration of a dangerously dualistic body natural, one that has illegally usurped the body politic by staging an illusory and insubstantial monarchy (she is, after all, "la hija del aire").[21] Semíramis's death amounts to a public ritual execution, necessary for the public restoration of legitimate rule. Semíramis's death represents, to borrow Foucault's words, "a ceremonial by which a momentarily injured sovereignty is reconstituted. It restores that sovereignty by manifesting it at its most spectacular" (48). Through the political spectacle of punishment of this doubly transgressive body, the authentic monarchy (the real embodiment of which, the king, is witnessing the play) can be affirmed.

As with other Calderón palace plays, the interplay between the action of the play and the political circumstances within which the play was produced may lead to a more complex understanding of the plot, character, and staging of the play. Like so many of Calderón's plays, *La hija del aire* may be considered a theatrical *De regimine principum* from which the royal audience may derive various lessons in the art of ruling well.[22] At the same time, it is difficult to establish direct correspondences between the action of the play and the contemporary situation in the court and beyond. There is, for one thing, some controversy surrounding the date of composition. Gwynne Edwards dates it from around 1652 or 1653; but we now have information that both parts were presented at the Corral de la Montería as early as 1643, and that the play received

---

[21] Incidentally, the title of the *comedia* is explained in the play itself in the following lines, curiously omitted from Edwards's edition:
Nacio de una Ninfa suya,
y entregándola a las fieras,
la defendieron las aves,
de quien el nombre conserva,
pues Semíramis se llama,
que quiere en la siria lengua
decir la Hija del Aire.
[She was born to a nymph (dedicated to Diana), and given over to the beasts, she was defended by birds, from whom she receives her name, Semíramis, which means in Syrian "Daughter of the Air."] (I, 1543–9). *La hija del aire*, ed. Francisco Ruiz Ramon (Madrid: Cátedra, 1998).

[22] As cited before, Dian Fox's *Kings in Calderón: A Study in Characterization and Political Theory* (London: Tamesis, 1986) and Stephen Rupp's *Allegories of Kingship: Calderón and the Anti-Machiavellian Tradition* (Philadelphia: U of Pennsylvania P, 1996) discuss the strong anti-Machiavellian content in Calderón's plays. Although neither Fox nor Rupp discusses *La hija del aire*, an argument can be made for seeing Semíramis as a Machiavellian tyrant. See also José Antonio Maravall's "Maquiavelo y el maquiavelismo en España," in *Estudios de historia del pensamiento español* (Madrid: Ediciones Cultura Hispánica, 1975), 41–76; and J.A. Fernández Santamaría's *Reason of State and Statecraft in Spanish Political Thought, 1595–1640* (Lanham, MD: UP of America, 1975).

its first palace performance before Philip IV in 1653.[23] Other critics, notably Alan Patterson, provide compelling reasons for dating the composition of the play—if not its staging—even earlier, at around 1625 to 1630 (204). Patterson bases his opinion on the strong Senecan flavor of the play, similar to that in *La gran Cenobia* and *La cisma de Inglaterra*, for example—plays that date from around 1625–1628 (205). If Patterson is right and the play was written in the second decade of the 1600s, one of the lessons of the play may have been directed to Philip IV as a warning about his weakness for beautiful women. Indeed, in 1627, he began a scandalous and long-term affair with the actress known as La Calderona, who would give birth to the king's bastard, Juan José de Austria, a powerful political figure in his own right after his father's death. The play may be a warning against the dangers of unrestrained lust in the portrayal of the weak and ineffectual Nino. Specifically, Calderón seems to be warning his audience of the disruptive nature of feminine beauty and the manner in which a woman's body natural can intrude upon the sphere of power. In the feminization of the figure/body of the king, there is also a warning to the king against becoming soft and irrational and against putting private desires above the public good. As Saavedra Fajardo states:

> Porque si se consideran bien las caídas de los imperios, las mudanzas de los estados y las muertes violentas de los príncipes, casi todos han nacido de la inobediencia de los afectos y pasiones a la razón.
> [For if we consider carefully the demise of empires, the transformation of states, and the violent deaths of princes, all of these have had their origin in the insubordination of emotions and passions to reason.] (*Idea de un príncipe* 24)

Even if we reject the earlier date of composition, Philip's weaknesses as a ruler had permitted, according to some, the controversial supremacy of the Count Duke of Olivares in the politics of the realm; and it would not be difficult to read into the play a cautionary tale about *privanza*. For one thing, in the enactment of the king's betrayal of the general, Menón, and his ignominious end, we might be able to find echoes of the fortunes of the Count Duke of Olivares. Olivares's fall from grace came in 1642, just a decade before the play was performed at the court. Some believed that Olivares's hold on the king was such that he seemed to have possessed the monarch body and soul, and one could even interpret Semíramis's assimilation of Ninias's persona as another warning of what can happen when the monarch is too weak to sustain his authority and, by extension, the integrity of his identity.

---

[23] Thanks to the work by N.D. Shergold and J.E. Varey and especially to DICAT, the very helpful database prepared under the direction of Teresa Ferrer Valls, we have information on the various performances of *La hija del aire* at the palace. The two parts were staged in November of 1653, in November of 1683, and in November of 1692. The First Part had three additional presentations, independently of the Second Part, in February of 1675, in July of 1683, and in May of 1684.

Another embedded message may have had to do with the ever-present question of the succession. In the performance of inverted maternity, this play may contain a reminder to Philip's second wife, Mariana of Austria, that in 1653, after four years of marriage, she still had not provided a male heir.[24] Furthermore, according to Edwards, "This [play] is exactly the kind of dish to be set before a king and his young wife: not only would the danger of over-indulging her be made clear to him; the pitfalls of excessive ambition would equally impress her" (xxii). Thus, in the negative portrayal of an ambitious woman of suspicious origins who usurps power, there might even be a veiled reference to and criticism of the foreign-born queen whose relentless promotion of the Habsburg imperial cause above the more immediate needs of Spain was seen by many as disastrous.

It is indeed tempting to see in this play some reference to the formidable person of Mariana of Austria, whose will of steel and political ambition may have already become apparent when the play was first performed at the court. In fact, the action of *La hija del aire* is uncannily prescient of what would happen in the court after Philip IV's death. I have already alluded to Mariana in previous chapters, but it would be worthwhile to revisit this redoubtable figure and explore whether in the figure of Semíramis we might find traces of the historical queen. Mariana was viewed as an ambiguous figure, as indicated by a satirical riddle that circulated during her lifetime: "¿En qué se parece la Reina Nuestra Señora al huevo? R[espuesta]. En que ni es carne ni pescado. [How is the Queen like an egg? She is neither fish nor fowl.]" According to Eleanor Goodman, "the riddle underscores the difficulty of defining Mariana's identity at the Spanish court and the uncertain nature of her power" (162). There is no doubt that Mariana was (and, indeed, continues to be) a controversial figure. She was a woman with a very strong personality who wielded a tremendous amount of influence at the Habsburg court during her long life as queen consort (1649–1665), queen regent (1665–1675), and queen mother (1675–1696).

Philip IV seems to have been aware of the difficulties his second wife would encounter after his death, and decreed the creation of a powerful Junta de Gobierno to help her govern as regent until his son Charles gained majority. After Philip died, this corporate structure of governing created problems as Mariana struggled to maintain some measure of control over different aspects of the court, from who would form part of her household to how to raise her son. The evidence of Mariana's unpopularity among many members of the court after the king died has led to many negative portrayals by contemporary historians. John Lynch calls her "an unstable, ignorant, and obstinate woman, unfit to rule a vast and complex empire" (361), for example. Lynch's is an extreme view, however; and recently, there have been attempts to provide a much more

---

[24] Indeed, Mariana had suffered a miscarriage only weeks before the play was performed. In 1651, she had given birth to the Infanta Margarita María, who would become Empress of the Holy Roman Empire when she married Leopold I.

balanced assessment of Mariana's image.[25] As is often the case with women in power, the unfavorable views toward this woman may be more the result of an unquestioning acceptance of contemporary accounts written by her enemies at the court, possibly combined with lesser and greater degrees of misogyny, than an accurate account of her political role. Mariana seems to have been intimately involved in every political decision concerning her son, and was able for a considerable length of time to parry the threat to the throne represented by her husband's illegitimate son, Don Juan José.

At the same time, it seems to have been expedient at the court to blame her for Charles's deficiencies, and we do know that there was a great deal of concern in the court over the education of the prince after Philip died.[26] The pernicious effect that mothers had on their sons was a frequent topic within the misogynous discourse of the time, as we see in Saavedra Fajardo's *Idea de un príncipe*, for example: "... los padres suelen entregar a sus hijos en los primeros años al gobierno de las mujeres, las cuales con temores de sombras, les enflaquecen el ánimo y les imponen otros resabios que suelen mantener después [... Fathers have the custom of giving their children in their early years to the care of women who, with their fears of shadows, weaken their spirit and impose on them other bad habits that they retain afterwards]" (10). Ninias, the effeminate, weak, and cowardly prince of *La hija del aire*, would have made a fitting dramatic double for Charles, given all the anxiety in the court about his ability to lead. Clearly, unless information appears showing the play to have been written much later than is currently believed, these parallels are nothing more than fanciful coincidences. At the same time, it is curious that this play was revived at the Alcázar in 1675, the year that Charles achieved his majority and Mariana's regency came to an end; and one may try to read something into the fact that only the First Part was performed. Eight years later, in 1685, after Calderón's death, the First Part was again presented in July and both parts in November at the Alcázar. By this time, Charles was married to María Luisa of Orleans, and it is possible that both the queen consort and the queen mother attended the performance. As stated in the previous chapter, there was an intense power play at the court, with different factions headed by the two queens trying to influence the young king's (and the court's) support for either the French or the Austrian cause. The protean and unstable depiction of a Semíramis by turns virile and tyrannical may have proven convenient as a message to the formidable Mariana of Austria and her daughter-in-law.

---

[25] See, for example, Stradling *Spain's Struggle for Europe*, London: Hambledon Press, 1994; and the works already cited by Goodman, Storrs, and M.J. Rubio.

[26] See Josefina Castilla Soto's "Tratados para la educación del rey niño," in *Carlos II. El rey y su entorno cortesano*, ed. Luis Ribot (Madrid: Centro de Estudios Europa Hispánica, 2009), 55–79; and Galino Carrillo's *Los tratados sobre educación de príncipes (Siglos XVI y XVII)* (Madrid: CSIC, 1948) for a description of the numerous treatises that address the education of Charles.

In the introduction, I speculated about another more distant but compelling historical referent in the repeated portrayal of queens on the Calderonian stage: the reign of Elizabeth I of England, who died in 1603, some 50 years before the play is believed to have been written and performed. Would it be possible, then, to view in Semíramis echoes of the hated Elizabeth? For one thing, one of the most important sources for the play was Cristobal de Virues's *La gran Semíramis* [*The Great Semíramis*], written in 1609 when the memory of the formidable Protestant queen would have been quite fresh in the minds of Spaniards. Most interestingly, we remember that the Protestant queen actively promoted the feminine/masculine duality within her single body, often adopting the use of androgynous imagery to describe herself. Indeed, Elizabeth was frequently criticized for the same erasure of difference that we have identified in Semíramis, the uniting in one body of male/female, king/queen, mother/son dichotomies.[27] Semíramis, as a woman who has escaped all manner of social control, represents all the evils endemic to female power attributed (from the Spanish perspective) to the Protestant monarch. These are compelling parallels, although, of course, it would be impossible to prove that Calderón included them deliberately with the famed English monarch in mind.

As with *La gran Cenobia*, Calderón presents in *La hija del aire* a meditation on the dangers of absolutism; and as such, the play is a political act that condemns the abuse of power. In dramatizing disorders of the body politic incarnated in Semíramis, the play offers a mirror of tyranny, an enactment of how *not* to rule. What separates this play from the earlier one is that here the performance of improper monarchical rule is explicitly conjoined with effeminacy. Ultimately this *comedia* enacts a complex political ritual whose ultimate goal is to affirm a strong monarchy conceived as masculine. Nevertheless, this affirmation seems again fraught with anxiety, reminding us—as it must have reminded its intended audience—that all performances of kingship (and queenship) are dangerous, for they raise the possibility that all power is temporary, arbitrary, and illusory, written in "el aire," as it were.

---

[27] For this aspect of Elizabeth's reign, see Carole Levin's *"The Heart and Stomach of a King": Elizabeth I and the Politics of Sex and Power* (Philadelphia: U of Pennsylvania P, 1994) and the articles by Louis Montrose.

Chapter 4
English Queens and the Body Politic

Calderón's *La cisma de Inglaterra* and Pedro de Rivadeneira's *Historia Eclesiástica del Scisma del Reino de Inglaterra*[1]

The plays considered in the previous chapters, written several decades apart, take their inspiration from classical sources, but Calderón and his contemporaries also used historical events as the basis for their plays. I turn now to Calderón's *La cisma de Inglaterra* [*The Schism in England*][2] (1627), which had as its immediate source the first volume of Pedro de Rivadeneira's *Historia Eclesiástica del Scisma del Reino de Inglaterra* [*Ecclesiastical History of the Schism in the English Realm*][3] (1588). The play engages, then, not with a distant, quasi-historical, and quasi-mythical context, but rather—like the chronicle that preceded it—provides the modern reader with a distinctively Spanish perspective on a defining moment of

---

[1] A shorter version of this section appeared in *MLN* 113 (1998): 259–82.

[2] Although there has been considerable debate on the date of this play, Shergold and Varey have provided compelling reasons for dating it as early as 1627, when a play with this title was performed in El Pardo before Philip IV and Isabel of Bourbon (277). This date makes *La cisma* one of the earliest of Calderón's plays to display his considerable talents before the monarchs. For a detailed account of the debate on the dating of the play, see the excellent introduction by Ann L. Mackenzie to the bilingual edition to the play, translated by Mackenzie and Kenneth Muir (Warminster: Aris and Phillips, 1990). All quotes in Spanish (verse numbers) and English (page numbers) are taken from this edition, although I have occasionally changed the translation. Any changes are indicated in brackets [ ]. In some critical essays on the play, its title at times is rendered with the alternative spelling of the country as *La cisma de Ingalaterra*.

[3] Rivadeneira himself bases his *Historia Eclesiástica* on a previous chronicle written by an English Catholic "historian," Nicholas Sander. His *De origine ac Progressu Schismatis Anglicani* [Account of the Origin and Growth of the Anglican Schism] was published in 1585, three years before Rivadeneira's own chronicle. The Spanish Jesuit says that Sander's text is a "libro de ser leido de todos … con tanta verdad, llaneza y elegancia de estilo [a book that should be read by everyone … it is filled with so much truth, simplicity, and elegance of style]" (182). Alexander Parker has commented on Rivadeneira's debt to Sander in *The Mind and Art of Calderón* (Cambridge: Cambridge UP, 1988), and argues convincingly that the Spanish text is not merely a translation of Sander, since Rivadeneira adapts, elaborates, and uses other sources (396). Rivadeneira was also the author of the important treatise titled *Tratado de la religión y virtudes que debe tener el príncipe cristiano* [Treatise on the Religion and Virtues That a Christian Prince Should Have], which dealt with the art of kingship. Both *Historia Eclesiástica* and *Tratado de la religión* can be found in *Obras escogidas del Padre Pedro de Rivadeneira*, ed. D. Vicente de la Fuente (Madrid: M. Rivadeneyra, 1868).

European history, namely the calamitous series of events that led to the definitive break between England and Papal Rome. The dialectic between two genres—drama and "history"—dealing with a specific event that had painful consequences for Habsburg Spain represents a privileged example of the manipulation of historical events to forge convenient ideological narratives. Within these invented narratives, we can identify some of the same collectively accepted conceptions on the relationship between gender, sexuality, and monarchical power that we have seen in the other plays; but here, these tensions are compounded by the issue of religious orthodoxy. In both the chronicle and Calderón's play, we find a convergence of Renaissance discourses pertaining to women and the role of these discourses in promoting the ideology of monarchy and masculinist supremacy. Rivadeneira's chronicle and Calderón's *La cisma* once more reiterate the deep ambivalence and anxiety felt by seventeenth-century Spaniards toward women and their claim to a political identity.[4]

Ironically, one of the figures who helps determine the narrative—both as pre-text and subtext—in Rivadeneira's *Historia Eclesiástica*, as well as Calderón's *La cisma de Inglaterra*, is none other than Elizabeth I of England. As stated in the introductory chapter, the misogyny and paranoia surrounding the question of women in power would have found historical justification in the formidable figure of Elizabeth, especially for Spaniards. In Calderón's play, Elizabeth disappears completely as a character or even a fleeting reference. Nevertheless, this palpable absence in a play written some two decades after Elizabeth's death is a telling example of how Calderón used the *comedia* as a medium for enacting selective historical memory and for replacing disturbing recent events with a narrative that was ideologically more palatable to his audience. In addition, the choices the playwright makes in describing the English crown illustrate some of the defining characteristics of performance, as described in the introductory chapter. Specifically, this play highlights the tension between the *comedia*'s obeisance to certain ideological structures and dramatic conventions and the simultaneous questioning and perhaps even dismantling of this ideology in performance. Rivadeneira's *Historia*, on the other hand, was written while Elizabeth was still on the throne, and cannot but engage the figure of the English monarch directly. Since this purportedly historical treatise had as its goal the repudiation of the Protestant movement, it is not surprising that Rivadeneira portrays Elizabeth with indignation, and the chronicle assumes the momentum of a compelling

---

[4] The bibliography on *La cisma de Inglaterra* is extensive. In addition to Ann L. Mackenzie's introduction to her edition of the play, the following articles have been particularly helpful: John Loftis's "Henry VIII and Calderón's *La Cisma de Inglaterra*," *Comparative Literature* 34 (1982): 208–22; Alexander Parker's "Henry VIII in Shakespeare and Calderón: An Appreciation of *La cisma de Inglaterra*," *Modern Language Review* 43.3 (1948): 327–52; George Mariscal's "Calderón and Shakespeare: The Subject of Henry VIII," *Bulletin of the Comediantes* 39 (1987): 189–213; and the chapter on *La cisma* in Charles Oriel's *Writing and Inscription in Golden Age Drama* (West Lafayette, Indiana: Purdue UP, 1992).

cautionary tale. Partaking of the humanist notion that history is exemplary, the author emends and manipulates history in the service of exemplarity. Political and ideological considerations, as well as religious partisanship, override any sense of historical accuracy and the historical players are all presented as paradigmatic. Even Henry VIII, the "bestia fiera y cruel [que] destruyó todo su reino, y se engolfó en un piélago de infinitos males [the fierce and cruel beast who destroyed his entire kingdom and who engulfed himself in a profusion of infinite evils]" (182), is exemplary in that he provides a negative model of kingship.

In the Prologue to the chronicle, called "El Autor al Cristiano y Piadoso Lector," Rivadeneira claims that his national identity as a Spaniard and his religious affiliation as a Jesuit impel him to produce this *Historia*. Remarkably, each component of his double identity is explicitly associated with one or two women whom history placed at, or close to, the center of power. First of all, he attaches his Spanish national identity to the figure of Catherine of Aragon:

> ... el ser español me obliga á desear y procurar todo lo que es honra y provecho de mi nación, como lo es que se sepa y se publique en ella la vida de la esclarecida reina doña Catalina, *nuestra española*, hija de los gloriosos Reyes Católicos don Fernando y doña Isabel, que fué mujer legítima del rey Enrique VIII de Inglaterra.
> [... being a Spaniard obliges me to desire and seek everything that would bring honor and benefit to my nation, such as publicizing, so that it becomes known, the life of the noble queen Catalina, *our Spanish lady*, daughter of the glorious Catholic Monarchs Fernando and Isabel, who was the legitimate wife of king Henry VIII of England.] (184, emphasis added)

Catherine becomes the embodiment of a national identity that he affirms ("el ser español me obliga [being a Spaniard obliges me]" and "nuestra española [our Spanish lady]"). She is, furthermore, associated with that most Spanish of virtues: honor ("honra y provecho de mi nación [honor and benefit to my nation]"). Interestingly, her identity within this nationalist narrative is not primarily that of an individual historical player, but rather one based on her kinship to other powerful entities: she is the daughter of the Spanish monarchs and the rightful wife of the English king. The identification of Catherine as everything that is good, orthodox, and authentically Spanish—while emphasizing her right as the legitimate *English* queen consort—is reiterated throughout this long chronicle.

Rivadeneira's second identity, that of a Jesuit priest, is highlighted next in the introduction when he goes on to claim that the Order of Jesus was instituted by God himself, for the explicit purpose of

> defender la fe católica y oponerse a los herejes ... como por la merced tan señalada que el mismo Señor nos hace á todos los hijos della, *tomando por instrumento á la reina de Inglaterra, Isabel, hija de Enrique y de Ana Bolena (que fué la levadura desta lamentable tragedia y la fuente y raíz de tantas y tan graves calamidades)*.

> [defending the Catholic faith and opposing heretics ... through the remarkable mercy that the Lord grants all of her (the Catholic faith's) children, *taking as instrument the queen of England, Elizabeth, daughter of Henry and Anne Boleyn (who was the leavening of this lamentable tragedy and the source and root of so many grievous calamities).*] (185, emphasis added)

If Catherine is the symbol of Spanish nationalist pride and the true faith, Elizabeth and her mother, Anne Boleyn, are the personifications of foreign Protestant heresy and, as such, the rallying point for all defenders of the true faith. This treatise, Rivadeneira claims, is part of a concerted Jesuit defense of Catholic orthodoxy against its enemies, the most powerful of whom was the English queen. He equates the exemplarity of the history he is about to recount with the need to establish precise ideological differences between Spain and England, the latter a country headed by a heretical female ruler:

> Pues ¿qué diré de otra utilidad maravillosa que podemos todos sacar desta *Historia*? Ella es la compasión por una parte, y por otra la santa envidia que debemos tener á nuestros hermanos los que en Inglaterra, por no querer adorar la estatua de Nabucodonosor y reconocer á la Reina por cabeza de la Iglesia, cada día son perseguidos.
> [Well, what could I say of the other sublime benefit that can be had from this History? It is the compassion on the one hand and the holy envy on the other that we should feel on behalf of our brethren in England, who, because they do not wish to adore the statute of Nebuchadnezzar and recognize the Queen as head of the church, are persecuted on a daily basis.] (184)

The historical figures of Catherine of Aragon, Anne Boleyn, and Elizabeth I thus become central players who determine the first part of Rivadeneira's *Historia Eclesiástica*, the impetus for its writing. Some 40 years later, Calderón de la Barca was in turn inspired by Rivadeneira's account to dramatize the same historical event and its players. For the playwright, even more than for his Jesuit forebear, historical accuracy was of little importance. Indeed, Calderón's *La cisma* takes such astonishing liberties that Alexander Parker was moved to call the play a "travesty of history" (*Mind and Art* 251). In addition to a flexible definition of "history," *La cisma* and Rivadeneira's chronicle share a concern with the representation of monarchical power and the reenactment of positive and negative models for feminine behavior.

As stated before, Calderón eliminates from his play any mention of the figure of Elizabeth I, while Rivadeneira presents in detail the dire consequences that result when a woman (morally and socially inferior by nature) defies the gender hierarchy. First of all, the Jesuit describes the hierarchical politico/mystical body with its various patriarchal heads (God, Christ, man) and how it determines women's silence and submission, the latter symbolized by the requirement that women cover their heads when in prayer:

Cuando se trata de la gobernación de la Iglesia, toda la naturaleza de las mujeres se ha de excluir y apartar de la grandeza y peso de tan alta administración; porque como Dios crió al principio la mujer del varón y para el varón, naturalmente quedó sujeta, de manera que *el varón es cabeza de la mujer, así como Cristo es cabeza del varón, y de Cristo Dios*, como dice san Pablo. Y para declarar esta sujecion de la mujer manda el mismo apóstol que no ore ni profete la mujer sino cubierta la cabeza.
[When it comes to the governance of the Church, all of women's nature has to be excluded and separated from the greatness and responsibility of such a lofty administration; since God created woman from a man and for the man, she was naturally made subservient to him, so that *the man is the head, in the same way that Christ is the head of the man, and God of Christ*, as St. Paul states. And to illustrate the subservience of woman, the selfsame apostle ordered that woman should pray and profess only with her head covered.] (258, emphasis added)

Earlier in the Prologue ("Al príncipe don Felipe nuestro señor [To Prince Philip, our lord]"), the Jesuit had reiterated the accepted identification of the state with the king's body: "como el Rey es la cabeza del reino y como la vida y ánima dél, al paso que anda el Rey, anda el reino, que depende del mismo Rey [Since the King is the head of the realm and as its life and soul, the King sets the pace by which the kingdom marches, since it depends on the King]" (181). Rivadeneira decries the alteration of divinely ordained hierarchy that had taken place in England:

Mas la malicia humana todo lo estraga y pervierte, y hace que la que no puede ser cabeza del hombre se llame y se tenga por suprema y soberana cabeza de la Iglesia, inmediata a Cristo; y confunde las cosas civiles con las eclesiásticas, y las corporales con las espirituales, y á César con Dios; y quita toda la órden y distincion que hay entre el gobierno de las ánimas y de los cuerpos, entre el político, que mira la paz y tranquilidad de la república, y el espiritual y divino que se endereza á conocer, amar y servir á Dios verdadero.
[But human malice perverts and corrupts everything, and permitted that she who cannot be the head of man name herself and take herself for the supreme and sovereign head of the Church, next only to Christ; and this confuses secular with ecclesiastic matters, and corporal and spiritual matters, and Caesar with God; and removes all order and distinction that exists between the government of souls and that of bodies, between the political which is concerned with peace and tranquility in the republic, and the spiritual and divine which is directed toward knowing, loving and serving the true God.] (258)

Rivadeneira here echoes the Papal Bull of 1570 that had denounced the Protestant queen as "usurping (monster-like) the place of the chiefe Sovereigne of the Church" (qtd. in Findlay 187). Elizabeth represented the inversion, and indeed the perversion, of masculine supremacy and the accepted binomial view of the differences between male and female: form versus matter, completion versus incompletion, active versus passive, spirit versus the body. The result of this perversion occasioned by a woman's unregulated agency is "desvaríos prodigiosos y monstruosos, espantosos y horribles, y un cáos de confusión y un piélago y abismo sin suelo de infinitos desatinos y maldades [prodigious, monstrous, frightening, and horrible madness, and a chaos of confusion and a profusion and bottomless abyss of stupidity and evil]" (258). The unspeakable had happened in England, for not only had a woman, who because of her sex possessed an inferior and limited nature, become the head of state, but she had also been proclaimed the head of the church. Rivadeneira feels compelled in his narrative to provide an antidote to this dangerous femininity.

The perfect foil for Elizabeth's pernicious presence is, not surprisingly, Catherine of Aragon. In the *Historia*'s presentation of Catherine, we find echoes of the humanist discourse on the proper role of women combined with Marianist imagery and hagiography. Rivadeneira tells us that Catherine was mistreated by Henry VIII "con los mayores agravios que se pueden imaginar, los cuales ella sufrió con increíble constancia y paciencia, y dió tan admirable ejemplo de santidad, que con muy justo título se puede y debe llamar espejo de princesas y reinas cristianas [with the greatest affronts that can be imagined, which she suffered with incredible constancy and patience, and provided so admirable an example of sanctity that she can justly be called the mirror of Christian princesses and queens]" (184). Catherine, the queen consort of an English monarch, is the embodiment of Christian Spanish virtues, a *speculum reginae*. She is presented not as a political player, however, but rather as "la perfecta casada," the dutiful wife who provided an heir to the throne (albeit not a male one) and who embodied and performed the gender-specific virtues of patience, constancy, and, most important, chastity. She is repeatedly depicted as a saint in Rivadeneira's text and, finally, a martyr for the Catholic cause: "¡Oh mujer santa, digna de mejor marido! Pero quiso nuestro Señor, con esta cruz y nuevo linaje de persecución, afinarla y perfeccionarla, para que recibiese más ilustre corona de gloria [Oh blessed woman, worthy of a better husband! But our Lord willed that she be tested and perfected with this cross and unheard-of persecution, so that she might receive a more illustrious crown of glory]" (200).

Calderón's play reproduces much of the hagiographic tone and idealizing presentation of Catherine that we find in Rivadeneira's chronicle. For example, when Enrique decides to sacrifice his wife to satisfy his lust for Ana Bolena, he says: "Padezca Catalina / por cristiana, por santa, por divina (1657–1668) [So Catherine must suffer as Christian saint, angelic being]" (128).[5] Much later, toward the end of the play, a repentant Enrique announces her apotheosis as a Catholic martyr: "¡Ángel hermoso / que en trono de luz asistes / y en tu venturosa muerte / mártir generosa fuiste (2698–701) [Beautiful angel, now an attendant at the throne of light, / A noble martyr by your blessed death]" (183). As in Rivadeneira, Catherine embodies and enacts in *La cisma* the virtues of "la perfecta casada" and the self-abnegation of martyrs, who were often exalted as the optimal models of feminine behavior.

---

[5] Throughout this chapter, I will provide the verse numbers for the Spanish text and the page number for the English, both taken from MacKenzie's edition.

In their exaltation of Catherine's virtue, Calderón and Rivadeneira unwittingly expose the complexity and precarious nature of a queen's body and status in the political arena of early modern Europe. The historical Catherine exemplifies in a particularly vivid manner the exchange of women among men for political and territorial purposes. Both Rivadeneira and Calderón dramatize indirectly the fact that Catherine had been a pawn in a power play that involved the commerce of women and the trafficking of their chastity for political purposes. Catherine had married Arthur, Henry's older brother, in 1501; but when Arthur died, special papal dispensation was sought from Julian II permitting Catherine to marry Henry in order to maintain a delicate diplomatic relationship between England and Spain.[6] The extraordinary machinations were necessary since the prevailing view in England was that once a man and a woman married, they became one flesh, an indivisible corporate entity. Thus, for a man to marry his brother's widow would be akin to committing incest, a situation that Shakespeare slyly presents as a subtext in *Hamlet* when he has Claudius refer to Gertrude as "my sometime sister," or later, when Hamlet calls Claudius "mother," again emphasizing the indivisibility between man and wife. Furthermore, a Biblical prohibition of such a union would be found in a passage in Leviticus that specifically prohibited a man from marrying his brother's widow. To deflate criticism of Henry VIII's marriage to Catherine, it became necessary to claim publicly, and in all the appropriate official documents, that the queen was a *virgo intacta*, despite the fact that she had been married to Arthur for a year. The political importance of the queenly body could not be better demonstrated than by this public insistence on Catherine's purity.[7] The question of her virginity, as the historian Mattingly reminds us, was one that would be debated for 400 years, "the disputants being divided less by variations in their common sense and credulity than by their religious antecedents" (55). In his *Historia Eclesiástica*, Rivadeneira concedes that the marriage to a brother's wife might be offensive to some, but he quickly asserts unequivocally that it is nevertheless perfectly permissible in the eyes of God. Furthermore, he reiterates the Pope's right to provide a dispensation for such a union:

> no se debe poner duda sino que el matrimonio que se hace entre el hermano y la mujer que fué de otro hermano, principalmente difunto, sin hijos, no es contrario ni repugna á la ley divina, eterna ó natural, sino solamente á la humana y eclesiástica, y en la cual puede y debe el Pontífice romano dispensar cuando hay justas causas para ello, como en este negocio las hubo.

---

[6] For the historical background, see—among many other books—James A. Williamson's *The Tudor Age* (London: Longman, 1979); Garrett Mattingly's *Catherine of Aragon* (Boston: Little, Brown and Company, 1941); Karen Linsey, *Divorced, Beheaded, Survived: A Feminist Reinterpretation of the Wives of Henry VIII* (Cambridge, MA: Da Capo Press, 1996); and Retha Warnicke's *The Rise and Fall of Anne Boleyn* (Cambridge: Cambridge UP, 1989).

[7] Years later, as Carole Levin and others have demonstrated, Elizabeth I would famously manipulate the political dimension of her virginity in order to strengthen her authority.

[It should not be doubted that the matrimony of a man to a woman who was previously the wife of the man's brother—especially when the latter is dead and there were no children—does not go against nor is it repugnant to divine law, whether eternal or natural, but rather goes against human ecclesiastic law, over which the Pontiff may and should dispense when there are just causes, as in this case there were.] (188)

Calderón, in turn, also dramatizes emphatically the validity of the marriage in the very first act by having Enrique himself affirm Catalina's virginity at the time of their nuptials and, at the same time, acknowledge the political importance of this union:

porque Doña Catalina,
hija la más santa y bella
de los Católicos Reyes,
nuevos soles de la tierra,
casó con mi hermano Arturo,
el cual, por su edad tan tierna,
o por su poca salud,
o por causas más secretas,
no consumó el matrimonio;
quedando entonces la Reina,
muerto el Príncipe de Walia,
a un tiempo viuda y doncella.
Los ingleses y españoles,
viendo las paces deshechas,
los deseos malogrados,
y las esperanzas muertas,
para conservar la paz
de los dos reinos, conciertan,
con parecer de hombres doctos,
que yo me case con ella;
y atento a la utilidad,
Julio Segundo dispensa,
que todo es posible a quien
es Vice-Dios en su Iglesia. (33–56, emphasis added)

[For lovely Catherine, most saintly offspring of the Catholic Monarchs—new suns upon this earth—married my brother Arthur who, because of his tender years, poor health, or else some other more private reason, *did not consummate the marriage. When the Prince of Wales expired, his wife, the Princess Catherine, found herself a virgin widow*. The English and the Spaniards, seeing their treaty void, their desires frustrated, and their hopes dead, *in order to preserve the peace between their kingdoms, they agreed that, following the opinion of the wise consulted by them, I should marry her*. And, conscious of the usefulness of this, Julius the Second granted the dispensation, for all is possible to one who is no less than viceroy in the Church of God.] (51, emphasis added)

Calderón puts this explicit view in Enrique's mouth to later demonstrate his hypocrisy and opportunism in declaring the marriage to Catalina an unclean union. Even after he repudiates the queen publicly, Enrique admits in an aside:

> Bien sé que no repugna (caso es llano)
> el casamiento que hace el un hermano
> con mujer del hermano
> ...
> Todo es ley natural también lo fundo,
> y en Escritura, pues que fue forzoso
> que la mujer, después de muerto esposo,
> y más cuando sin hijos se quedase,
> con el hermano suyo se casase. (1635–7, 1642–6)
> [For as I know full well—the case is plain—to wed one's brother's widow is not unlawful, nor even repugnant ... All this is based on both a natural law and Holy Scripture, for it was obligatory for a wife on her husband's death—especially when childless—to marry with his brother.] (127)

In both the play and the chronicle, allusion is made to a queen consort's duty to provide an heir to the throne. The sexual performance of the king's and queen's bodies natural was, as mentioned in the introduction, the object of constant vigilance, since it would determine the stability of the body politic through the continuity of the royal line. Rivadeneira reminds his readers that Catherine, as the dutiful consort, put her body to "appropriate" use by providing an heir to the throne, the princess Mary. He mentions only in passing Catherine's miscarriages and still-born children, and vigorously bemoans the fact that Henry used her failure to produce a male heir as the overriding pretext to divorce her. Calderón, for his part, has Enrique forcefully proclaim their daughter María as the celebrated fruit of a joyful union:

> De cuya felice unión
> salió para dicha nuestra,
> un rayo de aquella luz,
> y de aquel cielo una estrella:
> la Infanta doña María,
> que habéis de jurar Princesa
> de Walia, con que la nombro
> mi legítima heredera. (57–64)
> [Then from that happy union was born, to increase our happiness, a ray, a star from that light, that heaven of womanhood, the Princess Mary, to whom you are to swear allegiance as Princess of Wales, for thus I name her as my heir.] (51)

Later in the play, the king will banish María, only to ultimately restore her as his legitimate heir to the throne in the last act.

Not surprisingly, the considerable political role of the historical Catherine in Henry VIII's monarchy is essentially ignored by both Rivadeneira and Calderón. The real Catherine was a remarkable woman of great learning (Erasmus admired her erudition, even praising it above Henry's) who had served as Spain's ambassador to England and was probably a willing political agent for her Machiavellian father, Fernando of Aragon. Before her fall from favor, she had been Henry's political confidante, and had been trusted enough by him to be made Governor of the Realm and captain-general of the forces for home defense when Henry was away at war (Mattingly 155). Indeed, she had been commander of the English troops when Scotland attacked during Henry's absence, and her troops won a decisive victory at Flodden Field in 1513. An accurate historical account of her role would not relegate this complex woman, who was by all accounts well liked and respected by the court and populace alike, to that of victim and saint as Rivadeneira and Calderón (to a lesser extent) do.

While the playwright neglects the complex political dimension and implications of her role as queen consort, he does present us with a more nuanced and fleshed-out Catalina. For one thing, she is depicted as an accomplished poet, capable of witty improvisation in a remarkable scene that showcases feminine talent at the court. In this key scene, Catalina presides over a group of noblewomen engaged in a variety of creative activities: singing, composing verse, displaying conversational wit, and dancing. Despite this scene that dramatizes the cleverness of the queen and her ladies, there is a blatant discrepancy between the real Catherine's accomplishments, as evidenced by historical documents, and her much more limited role in both the chronicle and the play. At the same time, and unlike Rivadeneira, Calderón does not shy away from showing some negative characteristics in the queen. His Catalina is a proud woman who is quick to anger, as demonstrated in the early scene in which she lashes out at the scheming Tomas Volseo (Cardinal Woolsey) when he attempts to keep her from entering the king's chambers:

Reina:	Pues, ¿cómo tan atrevido,
	Volseo, habéis detenido
	mis pasos?
Volseo:	Guardo el preceto
	a que me tiene sujeto
	el Rey.
Reina:	¡Loco, necio, vano!
	Por Príncipe soberano
	de la Iglesia hoy os respeto;
	aquesa púrpura santa,
	que, por falso y lisonjero,
	de hijo de carnicero
	a los cielos os levanta,
	me turba, admira y espanta,
	para que deje de hacer ...
	Pero bastará saber,
	ya que Amán os considero,
	que los preceptos de Asuero
	no se entienden con Ester. (656–72)

[Queen: Well, Woolsey, How do you dare obstruct my path? Woolsey: I keep The King's commandment. Queen: Madman, fool, vain fellow! I respect you for the present as Prince of the Church. This saintly purple which exalts you to the heavens, flatterer, from being a butcher's son, confounds me now, astonishes and shocks me; I refrain from doing ... but it will suffice for you to know that, since I look on you as Haman, Ahasuerus's laws do not apply to Esther.][8] (79)

In the portrayal of the explosive relationship between Catalina and Volseo, Calderón may have had in mind Margarita de Austria's disastrous relationship with Philip III's favorite, the Duke of Lerma.[9] When Calderón de la Barca was 11, the young Margarita died; and, not unlike what happened when Catherine of Aragon died in England, it was rumored that Margarita had been poisoned by Lerma's agents. Furthermore, in 1621, a few years before the play was composed, Rodrigo Calderón (no relationship to the playwright) was tried, in part for his alleged role in the death of Margarita. He was acquitted of this charge, although he was convicted of (and later executed for) other crimes. Another parallel is that, like Catherine before her, Margarita of Austria was often depicted as a saint during her lifetime and as a martyr after her untimely death.[10] In the conflictive relationship between favorite and queen, however, there may have been an even more immediate model for Catalina: Felipe IV's wife, Isabel of Bourbon, whose increasing antipathy to the Count Duke of Olivares was already rumored when the play was written. Like so many other Calderón plays, *La cisma de Inglaterra* falls within the *speculum principes* tradition, and it wouldn't be surprising if, through a complex layering of historical "texts"—Enrique, Catalina, and Volseo evoking Felipe III, Margarita de Austria, and the Duke of Lerma, in addition to the current king, his wife, and the favorite Olivares—the play would have presented a complex commentary on the dangers of overdependence on a *privado*. All of these levels of allusion could have been easily apprehended by his audience; and it is perhaps significant that the play was not presented at the palace again after its debut in March of 1627.

If Elizabeth is the pretext or subtext for Rivadeneira and Calderón and Catherine is the symbolic foil, Anne Boleyn becomes the catalyst and immediate target of repudiation in both. After describing Catherine's exemplary life and death, Rivadeneira states: "Pasemos adelante, y veamos el fin de Ana Bolena, que le sucedió en el reino [a Catalina], cotejemos linaje con linaje, vida con vida

---

[8] Here, the Queen is referring to the story of Haman, the chief minister to King Ahasuerus, who tried to prevent Esther from seeing the king. For a more detailed account of the Biblical story, see Mackenzie's commentary (207).

[9] As Raymond MacCurdy has shown, there were many so-called *comedias de privanza* written in the early part of the seventeenth century as a response to the increasing influence of court favorites such as the Duke of Lerma and the Count Duke of Olivares. See *The Tragic Fall: Don Alvaro de Luna and Other Favorites in Spanish Golden Age Drama* (Chapel Hill: North Carolina Studies in the Romance Languages and Literatures, 1978).

[10] See Magdalena Sánchez, *The Empress, the Queen, and the Nun: Women and Power at the Court of Philip III of Spain* (Baltimore: Johns Hopkins UP, 1998).

y muerte con muerte [Let us go forward and consider Anne Boleyn's demise who succeeded Catherine as queen, let's compare lineage with lineage, life with life, and death with death]" (218). This *cotejar* results in lurid accounts of Anne Boleyn's sexual depravity. Rivadeneira delights in presenting the antithetical inverted relationship between the virtuous and chaste Catherine and the lascivious Anne, enacting the typical dichotomization of feminine characters into representations of good and evil. As in other misogynist treatises, the feminine body is suspect in both Rivadeneira and Calderón, linked not only with unruly sexuality but, more seriously, with heresy. Both the chronicler and the playwright betray a fascination with the way Anne Boleyn employs her "body natural"—her physical attributes and talents—to pursue political ambitions. In Rivadeneira, she is a woman whose uncontrollable sexuality suggests an instinctive animal-like nature, as the following passage demonstrates:

> Siendo muchacha de quince años, se revolvió con dos criados de su mismo padre putativo Tomas Boleno. Despues fué enviada á Francia, y habiendo entrado en el palacio real, vivió con tan grande liviandad, que públicamente era llamada de los franceses *la haca ó yegua inglesa*, y después la llamaban *mula régia*, por haber tenido con el Rey de Francia amistad. Y para que la fe y creencia desta mujer fuese semejante á su vida y costumbres, seguía la secta luterana, aunque no dejaba de oir misa como si fuera católica.
> [When she was a girl of 15, she fornicated with two servants of her presumed father, Thomas Boleyn. Afterward, she was sent to France, and after entering the palace, she lived so wantonly that she was publicly known by the French as the English *mount or mare*, and afterwards they called her the *royal mule* because she'd had a relationship with the King of France. And so that the faith and beliefs of this woman matched her life and customs, she was a follower of the Lutheran sect, although she never missed mass as if she were Catholic.] (193, emphasis original)

After she becomes queen consort of England, she is depicted as a wanton adulteress whose sexual appetites transgress class divisions:

> con las malas mañas que había aprendido en su mocedad, fácilmente se inclinó y determinó con otros; de manera que no solamente se aficionó á algunos hombres nobles, y tuvo acceso con ellos, mas tambien con un músico ó maestro de danzar, que se llamaba Marcos, hijo, como algunos dicen, de un carpintero.
> [with the bad habits that she had learned in her youth, she was easily attracted to and had dealings with other men; so much so that she not only desired some noble men and had relations with them, but also with a musician or dance instructor whose name was Marcos, the son (some say) of a carpenter.] (218–19)

Rivadeneira goes beyond the accusation of adultery and attributes to Anne a second and more serious crime, that of incest. The chronicler thus repeats and elaborates on the salacious rumor that Anne was actually Henry's daughter, the more to repudiate the "monstrous" union that led to England's spiritual fall:

Estas son las bodas que todos los herejes de Inglaterra, luteranos, zuinglianos, calvinistas, puritanos, y todos los otros monstruos que arruinan é inficionan aquel reino, reverencian y adoran como fuente de su evangelio, fundamento de su iglesia, orígen y principio de su fe. Arrebató la furia infernal de la carnalidad y torpeza al rey Enrique, y despeñóle en el abismo de tantas maldades y abominaciones como habemos visto y adelante se verá más.
[This is a union that all the heretics in England—Lutherans, Zwinglians, Calvinists, Puritans, and all the other monsters who ruin and infect that kingdom—revere and adore as the fount of their gospel, the foundation of their church, the origin and source of their faith. The infernal furor of carnality and stupidity took hold of King Henry and plunged him in the abyss of so many evils and abominations, as we have seen and will see later.] (206)

The Jesuit describes with great zeal other alleged debaucheries, including further accusations of incest: "convidó con su cuerpo a Jorge Boleno, su hermano, y tuvo abominable ayuntamiento con él [she enticed her brother George Boleyn with her body and had abominable coupling with him]" (218). Incest is one of the most damning accusations that can be leveled against any woman, for with that act, she violates the sacred integrity of the family and the basis of a civilized community. To accuse a queen of such a heinous act was a powerful political tool to turn public opinion against a monarchy, as Marie Antoinette would discover when she was accused of having sexual relations with her eight-year old son (Hunt 108–30). Anne is thus presented in Rivadeneira's text as a sexual social outlaw, the disorderly woman whose fate is a warning of what happens when female carnality escapes the limits of patriarchal control. In the depiction of Catherine, the emphasis was on her chastity, the total denial of sexuality. By contrast, Rivadeneira's lurid portrayal of Anne underscores a surfeit of corporeality and sexuality.

Although there are indications that the real Anne Boleyn was an intelligent, charming, and witty woman, contemporary accounts suggest that she was not a great beauty (Figure 4.1). Her own father's chaplain states that she was only "compétemment belle," and the Venetian ambassador to England (who was sympathetic to Catherine) claims that: "Madame Anne is not one of the handsomest women in the world; she is of middling stature, swarthy complexion, long neck, wide mouth, bosom not much raised, and in fact has nothing but the English king's great appetite and her eyes, which are black and beautiful" (qtd. in Warnicke 58).

Taking his lead from Nicholas Sander, whose chronicle inspired his own, Rivadeneira exaggerates Anne's lack of beauty with enthusiasm: "Era Ana alta de cuerpo, el cabello negro, la cara larga, el color algo amarillo, como atiriciado, entre los dientes de arriba le salía uno que la afeaba; tenía seis dedos en la mano derecha, y una hinchazón como papera ... [Anne was tall of stature, with black hair, a long face, her complexion somewhat yellow as if jaundiced, among her upper teeth there was one that stuck out and made her look ugly, she had six fingers on her right hand, and a growth like a goiter]" (193). As we saw in the discussion of beauty in the chapter on *La gran Cenobia*, deformities were believed to be reflections of a corrupt inner moral nature. Furthermore, the six fingers and the "hinchazón [growth]"—

Fig. 4.1   Anonymous. *Anne Boleyn*, late 16th century.

in addition to being physical attributes ascribed to witches (Warnicke 58) —suggest the exuberant carnality associated with transgressive women.

The Jesuit's attention to Anne's appearance extends to her clothing. He tells us that she had "extremada curiosidad en el vestido, con nuevas invenciones y trajes y galas [she was extremely concerned with her wardrobe and the latest fashions in clothing and adornments]" (193), suggesting her vanity and frivolity. The obsession with the newest styles is equated with her inclination toward the new heretical doctrines as well. Later, the chronicler describes in great detail the costume and jewels that Anne displays on the day of her wedding to Henry, alluding to the inherent connection between ostentation, luxury, and power in the European courts during the sixteenth and seventeenth centuries. Monarchies in early modern Europe vied with each other to dazzle with pomp and spectacle as a way of demonstrating and enacting power. Clothing played an important part in this court pageantry, and Rivadeneira recognizes the symbolic and rhetorical importance of Anne's dress. Thus, in the following passage from the *Historia*, Anne Boleyn's dress and jewelry are meant to be emblematic of her political triumph through a performance of showy feminine splendor:

> Ana iba vestida de una ropa de brocado carmesí, sembrada de infinita pedrería; al cuello llevaba un hilo de perlas mayores que grandes garbanzos, y un joyel de diamantes de inestimable valor, y sobre los cabellos una guirnalda á manera de corona riquísima, y en la mano unas flores, y volvíase de una parte á otra, como quien saludaba al pueblo, y del cual apénas hubo diez personas que la saludasen y dijesen: "Dios te guarde", como solian decir á la reina doña Catalina. Este fue el triunfo de Ana Bolena, bien diferente del triste y lastimoso espectáculo y fin que tuvo cuando, poco despues, le fué cortada la cabeza, como adelante se verá. [Anne was dressed in clothing made of crimson brocade sprinkled with an infinite number of gems. She wore around her neck a string of pearls bigger than chickpeas and a diamond ornament of inestimable value, and in her hair a garland shaped like an elaborate crown, and in her hand she carried flowers; she turned from side to side, like someone greeting the public, of which there were fewer than ten people who greeted her back or blessed her in the way they all used to bless the Queen, lady Catherine. This was Anne Boleyn's triumphant moment, very different from the sad and pitiful spectacle and end that befell her when, not long afterwards, she was beheaded as we shall see.] (208)

The ostentation of her dress and her gestures are played out in the court, where power, like honor, depends on being seen and admired. Rivadeneira claims, however, that despite the elaborate finery, Anne Boleyn's bejeweled performance of femininity and power fails. He describes the absence of the admiring public gaze and recognition ("apenas hubo diez personas que la saludasen") so necessary to the establishment of authority, and casts this absence as a prefiguration of her death. In his *De Regis et Regis Institutione* (1599), Juan de Mariana warned that "El poder de los príncipes se destruye y se debilita desde el momento en que les falta el apoyo del respeto y del amor en los súbditos [The power of Princes is destroyed and weakened at the moment when they lack the respect and love of their subjects]" (qtd. in McKendrick, *Playing the King* 38). The ostentatious rejection by the English subjects, Rivadeneira suggests, directly anticipates Anne Boleyn's "lastimoso espectáculo y fin [pitiful spectacle and end]." Later in the chronicle, Rivadeneira provides a further sign of Anne's perfidy when he recounts that she dressed in showy colors on the day Catherine died: "… sola Ana Bolena dió muestras de su alegría y regocijo, y se vistió de colores y muy galana ella y sus damas [… the only one who showed any happiness and rejoicing was Anne Boleyn who with her maidens dressed ostentatiously in bright colors]" (218). Earlier, he had suggested that she may have poisoned Catherine who "de mal aire y continuo dolor y tristeza del corazón murió … (no sin sospechas de veneno) [died of an ill wind and a broken heart … (although not without suspicions of having been poisoned)]" (217). Finally, the account of Anne's beheading resumes the motif of ostentatious clothing and adornment, but with an ironic twist. On the day of her execution, according to Rivadeneira, it is Henry whose showy apparel signifies publicly his repudiation of Anne:

> Tambien dicen que el dia que se hizo justicia della, el Rey se vistió de color, permitiéndolo así nuestro Señor, para pagarle en la misma moneda la desvergüenza y libertad con que ella se habia vestido de colores el dia que se hicieron las honras de la santa reina doña Catalina, como queda referido.
> [They say also that on the day when justice was exacted against her, it was the king who dressed in bright colors, the Lord thereby allowing him to repay in the same coin the brazenness and wantonness with which she wore bright colors on the day of the funeral of the saintly queen, lady Catherine, as we have already related.] (219)

Like an exemplary narrative, this neat sartorial parallel—which has no historical basis—gives readers a satisfying dénouement suggesting both poetic and divine justice.

Calderón, for his part, shows much more restraint and decorum in the portrayal of Anne Boleyn, but her body is still repeatedly (if indirectly) made the site of seduction, temptation, and heresy in the play. The sexual transgressions overtly expressed in Rivadeneira are implied rather than shown in *La cisma de Inglaterra*. In the title, Calderón announces that the main preoccupation of the play will be the event that had momentous religious implications; and the play becomes, as George P. Andrachuk suggests, an anti-Protestant treatise related in ideology to the *autos sacramentales*.[11] In this context, the figure of Anne Boleyn becomes the theatrical vehicle in displacing blame for the schism away from Henry VIII, and for facilitating a sympathetic depiction of the monarch.[12] Overt heretical acts could not have been directly depicted in this type of drama, as it would have meant courting trouble with the censors and enemies of the theater. Nevertheless, although Ana is not quite an allegorical figure in *La cisma*, heresy is in a sense embodied in the figure of Ana. As with Catherine, we discover in the character of Ana Bolena a multiplicity of discourses applied to women in early modern Europe. Unlike Rivadeneira's negative portrayal of a woman whose sinful nature

---

[11] See "Calderón's View of the English Schism," in *Parallel Lives: Spanish and English National Drama 1580–1680*, ed. Louise and Peter Fothergill-Payne (Lewisburg, PA: Bucknell UP, 1991).

[12] Given the historic and immediate hostilities between the two countries, seventeenth-century spectators could not but have been surprised (as modern readers are) at the sympathetic treatment accorded Henry VIII. He is called "un hombre tan celebrado, / tan prudente y advertido, / tan docto y sabio, que bien / leer en escuelas podia / cánones, filosofía, / y teología también (267–72) [A man so much admired, so keen and prudent, / So learned and so wise that he might well / Have followed a career in Canon Law, / Philosophy, or Theology]" (60). Furthermore, the English monarch is portrayed as a tragic figure worthy of compassion. In this, Calderón differs radically from Rivadeneira's *Historia* but follows contemporary theories of decorum in drama that would have proscribed the portrayal of any monarch as a villainous and hateful apostate, satisfying though such a depiction might have been to contemporary audiences.

is made manifest in her physical deformities, excessive carnality, and ostentatious dress, Calderón bows to theatrical convention and presents his Ana initially as "corona / de cuantas bellezas dio / al mundo Naturaleza, / pues a su rara belleza / otra ninguna igualó (280–84) [the nonpareil of beauty / Nature has given the world. There is no other / to match her wondrous loveliness]" (61). Her beauty is nevertheless indicative of a dangerous sexuality: "aquella deidad hermosa y pura, / de los hombres bellísima sirena, / pues aduerme en su encanto los sentidos, / ciega los ojos y abre los oídos (345–8) [that immaculate and lovely goddess, that siren who enchants men's quietened senses]" (65). This conventional praise of beauty juxtaposed with its devastating effect corresponds to the era's views of feminine attractiveness as morally pernicious. When Ana is invoked in terms borrowed from the repertoire of amatory poetry (she is an "enemiga [enemy]," "sol [sun]," the "llama [flame]" that fatally attracts the moth), these images are recontextualized and associated with the dark forces of sexuality, sin, and eternal damnation. Thus, Enrique acknowledges his passion for her by exclaiming: "¡Ay de mí, que me abraso! / ¡Ay Cielos que me quemo (1517–1518) [Alas! I am on fire, Oh Heavens! I'm consumed in raging flames!]" (123). Ana's French suitor, Carlos, describes her arrival in his native country: "No sé de los carámbanos del norte, / cómo en fuego llevó tanto veneno (337–8) [I do not know how from the northern icicles he (Ana's father) brought such poison, wrapped in fire]" (65). Mackenzie suggests that this play may contain a specific warning to the young Philip IV, who—at the time the play was performed—may have already started his affair with the actress La Calderona (Introduction, *The Schism* 5). In Ana's performance of femininity, beauty is suspect not only because it seems an invitation to unruly sexuality but, more seriously, because it threatens the stability of the throne and is, ultimately, an invitation to heresy.

In the famous opening scene, we discover Enrique asleep at his desk, where he has been writing a defense of the seven sacraments, a treatise that won for the historical Henry the title of *fidei defendor* or "Defender of the Faith." Ana Bolena's phantasmagoric yet alluring shape appears and announces that she will erase what he is writing: "Yo tengo que borrar cuanto tú escribes (6) [I am going to erase / All you write down]" (49). Shortly afterward, we are told that the "sombra" [shadow] appeared at the very moment when the king was writing an affirmation of holy matrimony, and it is this sacrament that she threatens to erase.[13] In the first scene, then, Calderón anticipates the divorce that will bring about the schism, as he symbolically telescopes complex historical circumstances into a visually stunning allegorical spectacle that is instantly understandable to his Catholic audience. In the scene that follows, Volseo (Woolsey) appears with two letters, one from Pope Leo X and the other from Luther. Enrique wants to physically enact his allegiance to the church by throwing Luther's letter to his feet while raising the Pope's over his head like a crown. Still flustered from his encounter with the chimera of Ana Bolena, however, he confuses the two papers; and the Pope's letter ends up on the ground

---

[13] Charles Oriel provides a detailed and persuasive analysis of this scene, 138–45.

while the "heretic's" missive is elevated. This scene will be echoed kinetically shortly afterward when Ana dances seductively before the king and feigns to fall at his feet.[14] Calderón masterfully establishes a visual correspondence between the rejection of the Pope's authority and Ana's feigned fall. In this scene, Ana is performing a *gallarda*, one of the dances that church authorities had designated as lewd and repeatedly tried to prohibit. As discussed in the introduction, the female body in movement was deemed particularly dangerous. The following quote from Alfonso de Andrade's 1648 *Itinerario historial que debe guardar el hombre para caminar al cielo* [*Detailed Itinerary that a Man Should Follow in Order to Attain Heaven*] vividly describes the perils of music and dance:

> Los despertadores de este vicio [sensualidad] y como los fuelles que encienden el fuego de los apetitos sensuales son las músicas y bailes lascivos y las representaciones deshonestas con que las mugeres afeitadas y libres incitan à los hombres y despiertan los apetitos, y juntamente enseñan las trazas y marañas de la escuela de Cupido ....
>
> [The instigators of this vice, like the bellows that stoke the fire of sensual appetites, are music and lascivious dances and the unchaste performances with which painted and libertine women incite men and awaken the appetites, and at the same time teach them the ways and tricks of Cupid's academy.] (Cotarelo y Mori 58)

Ana's dancing is part of her sensuality, her theatricality in the sense of showiness and ultimate lack of authenticity. As mentioned earlier, Philip may have already embarked on a scandalous affair with La Calderona at around the time the play was composed. It was rumored that Olivares had served as go-between in this relationship, which clearly threatened the dignity of the king and, by extension, the kingdom in multiple ways. For one thing, Philip at one point became quite ill and it was believed that the illness was a result of his affair with La Calderona. The actress later gave birth to the future Juan José de Austria, thereby complicating the succession. Furthermore, sometime around 1623, Olivares had also engineered an affair between Philip and one of Isabel's ladies-in-waiting, *Ana* Maria Manrique. In the portrayal of Ana Bolena, Calderón may be trying to layer historical figures condensed into a character that represents the excesses of the body and the threat to the stability of the realm.

Through music, movement, and dance, Calderón deploys multiple theatrical codes in order to further eroticize Ana's body before the spectators' gaze. Her dance, suggestive of her physical excess, is anticipated by Carlos's account of the first time he met Ana at a ball in France: "Danzó, dancé con ella. No quisiera / decirte cómo allí mis confianzas / resucitaron, conociendo que era / mujer quien supo hacer tantas mudanzas (373–6) [She danced and I danced with her. / I will

---

[14] This scene has some basis in historical fact. Warnicke tells us that the king and Anne danced for the first time in Catherine's chambers (59). In "Henry VIII in Shakespeare and Calderón," Parker discusses the importance of what he calls "up-and-down imagery" in this and other scenes in the play.

not tell you how it was that then / my confidence revived, because I knew / it was a woman who had showed herself / capable many times of changing step]" (65, 67). The seductive movements of her body visually signify the inconstancy of her soul. Thus, her *mudanzas* in the dance signal both her easy virtue—Carlos says: "gocé, tuve, alcancé dulces favores (385) [I enjoyed, possessed, yes, I achieved sweet favors]" (67)—and her religious duplicity: "y aunque en público la ves / católica, pienso que es / en secreto luterana (454–6) [And though she seems a Catholic in public, I have a strong suspicion that in private she is a Lutheran]" (69). Even Carlos, who claims to love Ana, places her beyond social respectability by refusing to marry her, thereby designating her a sexualized body whose primary purpose is to give pleasure: "Yo, enamorado y dudoso / de condición semejante, / quisiera gozarla amante, / antes que llorarla esposo (457–60) [I am in love, / But doubtful of her nature, and I'd rather / Enjoy her as a lover than lament / To have her as a wife]" (69).

Ana, who is called by one of the characters a "pavón de Juno [Juno's peacock]" is also associated from the start with pride: "Su vanidad, su ambición, / su arrogancia y presunción / la hacen, a veces, esquiva, / arrogante, loca y vana (450–53) [Her vanity, ambition, and presumption / Makes her at times disdainful, arrogant, / And wild, as well as being frivolous]" (69). Ambition and arrogance in a woman are not only signs of a desperate ("loca") and vain nature but, in this case, also provide evidence of religious apostasy. The accusations against Protestants made by church officials at the time included the sin of pride, the pursuit of free agency, and what we would call subjectivity. George Mariscal, in his article on the depiction of Henry VIII in Shakespeare and Calderón, reminds us that subjectivity—unmediated selfhood—and individual agency were considered inimical to Christian absolutist ideology. Mariscal quotes a sixteenth-century cleric, Alonso de Cabrera: "La singularidad es esta de los herejes: aquel no pasar por lo que pasan los otros, aquel sacar novedades a las plazas, nuevas doctrinas, opiniones de su propio cerebro nunca por nadie hasta ellos inventadas [This is the singular characteristic of the heretics: the refusal to go through what others have gone through, the desire to bring novelties to the public squares, new doctrines, opinions from their own brain never invented by anyone before them]" (195). During the dance scene, Ana's rage at having to bow and kneel before Catalina— "Llegar a verme / a los pies de una mujer, / ¿qué gloria, qué triunfo es éste? / ¡Yo la rodilla en la tierra (724–7) [To see myself at a woman's feet, what glory or what triumph could be in that? I am down upon my knees!]" (83)—is only one indication of her exaggerated pride, Cabrera's "aquel no pasar por lo que pasan los otros [the refusal to go through what others have gone through]." Her arrogance is associated with heresy and the thirst for power, a characteristic also deemed unnatural in a woman. Ana is thus an overly determined, transgressive woman: arrogant, willful, duplicitous, sexual, adulterous, and heretical; wholly unsuited to be queen. Identified with the perverse power of beauty, she and her body natural intrude upon the sphere of power; and as such, she must be contained.

The need to contain dangerous sexuality as represented by women so that masculine monarchical power can be maintained is dramatized in other Calderonian plays. As studied by Ruth El Saffar and Dian Fox, political expediency necessitates—in plays like *La vida es sueño* and *El médico de su honra*—the eradication of the dangers that a female body represents. Like the murdered Mencía in *El médico* and the absent mothers (Violante, Recisunda, and the two Clorilenes) in *La vida es sueño*, Ana represents the erotic body that disrupts the secular order. In those plays, Calderón is clearly not promoting the negation of the feminine, but rather dramatizing the psychic costs borne by a society that attempts to banish the feminine. The situation is different in *La cisma*, but the repudiation of Ana ends up being complete: she is banished from the symbolic order first by the suitor who will not marry her, then by her husband, who is also her king; and ultimately even by her father, Tomás Boleno, who not only rejects her but also carries out the execution. Women, even queens, derived their identity from kinship relationships with the male members of the family, and this repudiation by husband and father is, in essence, the public destruction of her social identity.[15]

The scenes with Ana as the focus of Enrique's and the spectator's gaze make for powerful theater, particularly the remarkable closing scene, when Enrique crowns María Tudor on the throne while Ana Bolena's lifeless and headless body lies at the base of the throne, wrapped in a silken cloth. The repeated verbal allusions to the crown and the new *head* of state are punctuated in a most macabre and ironic manner through the presence of Ana's decapitated body at the two monarchs' feet. María states: "¡Qué bien Vuestra Majestad / satisfizo mis ofensas, / pues que me ha puesto a los pies / quien pensó ser mi cabeza (2766–9) [How well Your Majesty has satisfied / The wrongs I suffered, by placing at my feet / The woman who had thought to be my head!]" (185). The health of the body politic—within the play's ability to emend history—is possible only through the destruction of Ana's body natural: the character that began as an insubstantial phantasm ends up as a headless "bulto" [form] absolutely devoid of agency. The debased reification of Ana has been anticipated from the opening scene of the play and is announced throughout. For example, when Enrique repudiates Ana after discovering that she had an affair with Carlos before her marriage, he cries out: "¿A la Reina? ¡Qué mal dije! / A esa mujer, a esa fiera, / ciego encanto, falsa esfinge, / a ese basilisco, a ese / áspid, a ese airado tigre, / a esa Bolena prended … (2561–6) [The Queen! / How badly I express myself! That woman, / That fierce animal, that blind enchantment, / False sphinx, that basilisk, that poisonous serpent / that enraged tigress, [that] Anne Boleyn, arrest her]" (175). Through this accumulation of labels, Ana is first stripped of her royal status, then reduced from "mujer" to mythical monster, then to beast, and finally to a mere name that is equated with ignominy. The play begins and ends with a woman iconographically represented as a non-being.

---

[15] Magdalena Sánchez tells us, for example, that the Empress María was usually described in terms of her relationship to the male members of the Habsburg dynasty (*The Empress* 65).

Anne's sexuality in both Calderón and Rivadeneira makes of Henry VIII an example of subordinated masculinity, with dire consequences for England and Christendom. As stated in the first chapter, the body politic had as its center the actual body of the monarch; or as Álamos de Barrientos puts it: "Ay tanta trauazón y dependencia entre el Príncipe y su República que no le puede acontecer a vno dellos cosa, que el daño, o prouecho della, no toque al otro; siendo el Príncipe el alma, y la República el cuerpo [There is so much interconnectedness and dependence between the Prince and his republic that nothing of harm or benefit can happen to one without affecting the other, the Prince being the Soul and the Republic the body]" (qtd. in Charles Davis 34). Enrique, although he is depicted in a relatively sympathetic manner, is ultimately a Machiavellian monarch who has allowed his lust for a woman and his own desires to determine any "razón de estado."[16] At the end of *La cisma de Inglaterra*, the body of the condemned woman appears as the symmetrical inverted figure of the monarch. Ana's dismembered body becomes the site for affirming and exercising monarchical and religious dominance. It is a symbolic restitution for what Calderón and his countrymen considered a historical tragedy. The ideological linkage between Crown and male subject that informs so many Golden Age *comedias* could not be more powerfully depicted.

There is surprisingly little detailed description in Rivadeneira's chronicle of Anne Boleyn's execution, but he does indulge in an impassioned epigraph to her brief but extravagant reign. He reminds his audience that Anne's body was the site of yet one more transgression: she gave birth to the monstrous virago who would become the scourge of Catholicism:

> ¡Triste mujer, que nació y se crió, y se casó y murió con tal oprobio é infamia! Malaventurada, porque destruyo á su padre y á su hermana, y á muchos otros consigo, y más por la arrogancia y presuncion que tuvo en querer competir con una reina, en sangre y virtud clarísima, de la cual en todas las cosas ella era tan desemejante. Pero sobre todas las cosas infelicísima y abominable, por haber sido

---

[16] Ingrid Vindel Pérez has gone so far as to claim that "el propósito inicial de *La cisma de Ingalaterra* no es otro que el de exponer las premisas políticas que los autores anti-maquiavélicos (concretamente, aquellos escritores cristianos) se esforzaban por impugnar de manera incansable; y que, más allá de hacerse eco y de quedarse en un nivel meramente expositiva, *La cisma* debe comprenderse desde una clave de denuncia política que muy pocos han visto en la letra de la obra [the initial purpose of *The English Schism* is none other than the exposition of political premises that anti-Machiavellian thinkers (specifically, Christian writers) endeavored to refute tirelessly; and which, beyond echoing and remaining at a solely expository level, *La cisma* has to be understood in the register of a political denunciation, something that few have seen in the letter (reading?) of the work]." See "Política y teodicea: una disertación de *La cisma de Ingalaterra*," *Calderón 2000* (Kassel: Edition Reichenberger, 2002), 385. In my opinion, while this work does in fact engage with the anti-Machiavellian arguments that were disseminated at the time, the play remains a *dramatic* work meant to be staged and enjoyed—not as a political treatise but as a play, with the conflict of power and ideology acquiring a performative rather than a theoretical significance.

el orígen y fuente manantial del cisma y destruicion de su patria, y por habernos dejado una hija que así la imita, é hinche y colma la medida de su madre.
[Pitiful woman, who was born, raised, married and died with such great ignominy and infamy! Cursed woman, because she destroyed her father and her sister, and many more, and even more, because of the arrogance and presumption she displayed in wanting to compete with a queen who was most pure in blood and virtue, and who in all things was completely different from her. But above all she was wretched and abominable, because she was the origin and source of the schism and destruction of her country, and because she left us with a daughter who imitates her in everything and indeed, enlarges and overflows her mother's evil example.] (219)

It is an interesting exercise in historical partisanship to compare Rivadeneira's description of Anne Boleyn to the description of the same queen by the English chronicler John Foxe (Levin, "John Foxe" 113–33). In his *Acts and Monuments* (better known as *The Book of Martyrs*), Foxe comes to Anne Boleyn's defense, asserting Anne's moral superiority also on the evidence of her body's reproductive function:

Furthermore, to all other sinister judgments and opinions, whatsoever can be conceived of man against that virtuous queen, I object and oppose again (as instead of answer) the evident demonstration of God's favour, in maintaining, preserving, and advancing the offspring of her body, the lady Elizabeth, now queen. (qtd. in Levin, "John Foxe" 124)

Written in England during the reign of Elizabeth, the most powerful monarch of the Renaissance, Foxe emphasizes Anne's modesty, piety, and gentleness, the very attributes Rivadeneira assigned to Catherine of Aragon. Foxe was among the Protestant historians who countered the Catholic view of Anne as the destroyer of the sacrament of marriage, and who based their rehabilitation of her historical role on the fact that she was mother to Elizabeth (Warnicke 57). We see how elastic the constructs of the feminine body and its relationship to political power really were, determined always by ideology and nationalistic or religious partisanship.

The impetus to control and subjugate feminine power in Calderón's play is not limited to the portrayal of Ana, and the repression of the feminine is complex in this play. Indeed, it occurs at various, simultaneous levels and is applied to all the female characters, even the idealized Catalina. Catalina is, after all, banished from the patriarchal/monarchical order so that Enrique can give himself over to his passions. By giving up Catalina, moreover, the king is rejecting wife and mother, the maternal order. The enthronement of María at the end of the play is also deeply problematic, for it falsifies what happened historically (Henry never abdicated the throne), and it presents María's authority as a reflection of, and deflection of, her father's authority. Historically, the English Crown was inherited by the nine-year-old Edward VI after Henry's death; and only after he died six years later did Mary Tudor ascend to the throne. She became the champion of Tridentine Roman Catholicism, and as such, we are not surprised by her apotheosis at the end of Calderón's play. There is, nevertheless, an ironic exchange between Enrique and María in which the repentant and desperate king advises his daughter to restrain, at least temporarily, her religious zeal. María is presented as a somewhat duplicitous fanatic, and there are allusions to the reign of terror over which she would preside.[17] When both Enrique and Tomás Boleno advise María to moderate her religious ardor in order to unify the country and secure popular allegiance to the crown, she responds:

> ... crea [el reino]
> que al que me jure y faltare
> a lo que mi Ley profesa,
> si no le quemare vivo,
> será porque se arrepienta. (2867–71)
> [... it (the kingdom) ought to know / That he who swears allegiance, and then fails / To obey what my law teaches, if I do not / Burn him alive, it then will only be / Because he has repented.] (191)

To which the king responds: "Callad y disimulad, / que tiempo vendrá en que pueda / ese celo ejecutarse, / ser incendio esa centella (2880–83) [Be silent and dissimulate; the time / Will come when you can carry out your zeal, / and what is now a spark become a bonfire]" (191). Earlier, he had also anticipated her marriage to Philip II: "Tú serás de Inglaterra / Reina ... Y casaréte en España / con el segundo Felipe ... (2706–7, 2712–13) [You shall be Queen of England ... And I'll wed you in Spain to (the second) Philip]" (183). "Real" historical events surrounding the reign of "Bloody Mary" and her ultimate demise, events well known to Calderón's audience, expose the staged victory of Catholicism over the heretics as an illusory exercise in wish-fulfillment, as illusory as Enrique's dream at the beginning of the play. There is a deep pessimism at the root of this play, as if the playwright himself recognized the futility of his appropriation and rewriting of history. Enrique's tragic words, "es ya / restitución imposible (2692–3) [Restitution is impossible]" (181) and "Pero es muy tarde (2704) [But it's too late]" (183), are quite likely representative of the playwright's own views.

---

[17] Interestingly, Rivadeneira's portrayal of Mary is also somewhat reticent. He praises her extreme piety and emphasizes her extreme suffering, which, he says, made her "dechado de reinas y por ejemplo de toda virtud y santidad [paradigm of queens and exemplar of every virtue and sanctity]" (255). At the same time, he comments on her lack of beauty: "Cuando moza, dicen que fue hermosa, y que después con el mal tratamiento, perdió la hermosura, aunque no era fea ... la voz gruesa y más de hombre que de mujer [When she was young, they say she was beautiful, but afterwards, with the ill treatment she received, she lost her beauty, although she was not ugly ... her voice was deep, more like a man's than a woman's]" (253). See Figure 2.2 in Chapter 2. He also tells us that after her painful death, her autopsy revealed "el corazón como seco y consumido, y no es maravilla, habiendo pasado tantas y tan extrañas fatigas y quebrantos de corazón [her heart was dried up and spent, and it is no wonder, after the copious and extraordinary travails and heartbreaks that she suffered]" (255).

Parker and Mackenzie separately suggest that, in addition to the schism that had taken place some one hundred years before the play was written, Calderón may have had in mind more recent historical events. Specifically, a few years before the play was written, there had been much excitement in the court surrounding the so-called "Spanish match" between the Prince of Wales—the future Charles I—and the Infanta Maria, sister of Philip IV.[18] In March 1623, Charles Stuart and George Villiers, the Duke of Buckingham, had shown up incognito in Madrid, an event called by the historian Thomas Cogswell "one of the most mysterious episodes in early modern English history" (qtd. in Redwood 2). Apparently anxious for the engagement with Maria to go forward with some haste, the English prince had sidestepped diplomatic channels, taken matters into his own hands, and arrived uninvited at the Spanish court. The visit turned out to be a personal, political, and international fiasco. Nevertheless, for many in Madrid, the joining of this pair of royal bodies represented the last chance to achieve a historical restitution for the schism. The pessimism that is palpable at the end of Calderón's play, again written only two years after the episode with Charles Stuart, may be due in part to the consciousness that the last opportunity for an acceptable resolution had been irrevocably lost.

The last scene of *La cisma*, with its horrifying spectacle of public punishment—Enrique calls it "el más funesto teatro y espectáculo más triste (2748–9) [the most tragic scene, / The gloomiest spectacle]" (185)—is deeply disturbing, particularly because the iconic repudiation and negation of Ana Bolena point to an even more conspicuous erasure in Calderón's play.[19] While María—Catalina and Enrique's daughter—is celebrated in the last scene as the true heir to the English throne, no mention is made of Elizabeth, the issue from Henry's union with Anne Boleyn. Thus, the exemplary and allegorical victory over heresy as represented by the dismembered body of Ana Bolena goes hand in hand with the exclusion from the play of the most successful Protestant monarch. It could be said that Calderón is promoting a temporary collective amnesia on his audience in order to amend, through an elaborate spectacle of penance and restitution, the painful lessons of history. From the Spanish perspective, as suggested before, Elizabeth

---

[18] See Mackenzie's introduction to *La cisma* (1–5) and Parker's *The Mind and Art of Calderón* (283–7). For a detailed and fascinating account of this visit and its political repercussions, see Glyn Redworth's *The Prince and the Infanta: the Cultural Politics of the Spanish Match* (New Haven: Yale UP, 2003). Redworth states wryly that "Charles's foolish miscalculation in presenting himself in person at the Spanish court casts doubt on his judgment rather earlier in his career than is normally the case" (3). A quarter of a century later, as King Charles I, he would be beheaded. Andrachuk suggests a connection between the denouement of the play, with its beheading of Anne, and the execution of Charles I in England, whose body would be buried next to Henry's (224). This suggestion nevertheless is not supported by the evidence we have on the staging of the play. Charles I was executed on January 30, 1649, over 20 years after *La cisma* was performed at the court.

[19] In his excellent study of the play, the chapter "The Ethics of Erasure" in *Writing and Inscription*, Oriel makes no mention of this particular omission in *La cisma*.

was the historical embodiment of all the evils endemic to female power—a heretical woman who had escaped all manner of repression, social control, and enclosure. In *La cisma de Inglaterra*, Calderón's response to this transgressive real historical woman is to deny her even a fleeting presence on the stage. He may have felt that to make even the briefest mention of Elizabeth would have dissolved the tightly wrought allegory of good triumphing over evil. It would have provided too uneasy a reminder and awareness on the part of his audience of the tragic vagaries of lived history. And yet, though never shown or even mentioned, Elizabeth seems to be inscribed throughout the play. Many of Ana's negative attributes—pride, vanity, sexual profligacy—were the same accusations made against Elizabeth I by her enemies. It is quite possible that throughout *La cisma*, Ana is meant to prefigure her daughter, and the audience cannot but have had Elizabeth in mind when viewing the play. One of the clearest instances of the identification between Ana and "Isabel" comes at the end of the play when Enrique calls Ana a "Jezebel." As Mackenzie reminds us, during Calderón's time, "Jezebel" (which rhymes conveniently with "Isabel") was a frequently used moniker to refer to the hated Protestant queen (Introduction, *The Schism* 26). Certainly, Ana's decapitated and covered body at the end is also meant to suggest the symbolic removal of Elizabeth as a "suprema y soberana cabeza" on the real political stage.

Rivadeneira's *Historia Eclesiástica del Scisma del Reino de Inglaterra* rewrites and transforms history in order to present historical events as a narrative with a coherent moral message. Calderón's play is more ambivalent and more rewarding in its ironies, but again, we witness the process of rewriting and re-presenting history. Historiography and drama become part of the collective imagination, the construction of gender, and the production of empire and monarchy. The ideological strategies used in both texts in the depiction of the schism remind us of Edward Said's assertion that all nations are narrations and that "the power to narrate, or to block other narratives from forming and emerging, is very important to culture and imperialism" (xiii). Calderón, as discussed earlier, wrote at a time when the monarchy seemed particularly vulnerable; and in *La cisma*, he would seem to be constructing a more exemplary and advantageous past by eliding the painful narrative of Elizabeth's reign. In the process of drastically transforming historical facts to suit the purpose of the authors, both the play and the Jesuit chronicle also reveal the early modern male anxiety and paranoia toward the female body, sexuality, and feminine power. Calderón's play, in particular, can be interpreted as a tightly constructed political ritual that attempts to affirm a Counter-Reformist, Spanish, and masculinist dominance even when this dominance has been repeatedly challenged by historical circumstance, as recently experienced by the play's audience. Theater has often been considered an act of collective remembrance. *La cisma de Inglaterra* shows how spectacle can also be a melancholy and ironic exercise in collective forgetfulness and erasure.

Taming the Shrew in Antonio Coello's *El conde de Sex*[20]

Elizabeth was not entirely absent from the *comedia*; and as a companion piece to *La cisma de Inglaterra*, it would be instructive to consider a play believed to be by Antonio Coello, a dramatist of the Calderonian school from the first half of the seventeenth century (1610?–1652). Titled *El conde de Sex* [*The Earl of Essex*] and featuring Elizabeth I as the female protagonist, the play remains, with some exceptions—notably Ann Mackenzie and Raymond MacCurdy—generally ignored by *comedia* critics.[21] Coello has been considered a playwright "de segundo rango [second rank]" and there have been questions surrounding its authorship. In addition to Antonio Coello, the play has been attributed to his brother Luis Coello, to Juan de Matos Fragoso, and even to "un ingenio de esta corte" [A Wit of this Court], an attribution that many believed to be an allusion to King Philip IV himself. In fact, some have even considered this particular play as a collaborative effort between Coello and the Habsburg monarch. In his *Catálogo Bibliográfico y biográfico del teatro antiguo español*,[22] Cayetano de la Barrera includes the following entry on Coello:

> Por los años de 1630 á 1640, parece indudable que residió Coello en Madrid, favorecido con el aprecio de S.M. el rey Felipe IV, á cuyos trabajos y desenfados literarios, coadyuvaba y concurria con otros señalados ingenios. *Hubo de ayudarle muy especialmente en la composicion del célebre drama*: El conde de Essex, *que se publicó por primera vez, en 1638*, como obra de nuestro autor, y siguió atribuido al mismo en muchas de sus posteriores reimpresiones.[23]

---

[20] A shorter version of this section appeared as "'The Body of A Weak and Feeble Woman': Courting Elizabeth in Antonio Coello's *El Conde de Sex*," in *Crossing the Channel: Symbolic and Material Circulations Between Spain and England*, ed. Anne J. Cruz (Aldershot, UK: Ashgate, 2008), 71–87.

[21] See Ann Mackenzie, "Antonio Coello como discípulo y colaborador de Calderón," in *Calderón desde el 2000*, ed. José María Díez Borque (Madrid: Ollero & Ramos, 2001), 37–59; and Raymond MacCurdy's "The Earl of Essex: Antonio Coello, 'El conde de Sex,'" in *The Tragic Fall*, 220–29. I have taken all quotes from the edition prepared by Donald Schmiedel: *El conde de Sex, Estudio y edición crítica* (Madrid: Colección Plaza Mayor Scholar, Playor, 1973). I have also consulted two nineteenth-century editions: the first by Eugenio de Ochoa, *La tragedia mas lastimosa: El conde de Sex, Tesoro del teatro español desde su orígen hasta nuestros días*, vol. 5 (Paris: Librería Europea de Baudry, 1838), 98–127; and the second by Carolina Michaëlis, *La tragedia mas lastimosa de amor, Dar la vida por su dama ó El conde de Sex, Tres Flores del teatro antiguo español* (Leipzig: F.A. Brockhaus, 1870). Schmiedel provides a useful and detailed preliminary study of the play.

[22] Michaëlis believes it was published in 1653, 15 years later than the publication date suggested by Cayetano de la Barrera (168). We do know, however, that the play was performed at least twice in the court: in 1633 and in 1637 when Isabel of Bourbon was queen consort.

[23] In his early nineteenth-century edition, Eugenio de Ochoa continues to attribute the play to Felipe IV, although he states in the introduction: "Atribuyendo esta tragedia à Felipe IV, no hemos hecho más que seguir la opinión general, si bien no fundada en documentos

[During the years between 1630 and 1640, it is certain that Coello lived in Madrid, favored with the high regard of His Majesty King Philip IV, whose works and literary diversions he aided and shared with other well-known playwrights. *He must have helped him especially with the composition of the celebrated play*, El Conde de Essex, *which was published for the first time in 1638* as the work of our author (Coello) and which was attributed to him in many of the subsequent editions.] (95, emphasis added)

Intriguing though the attribution to Philip may be, it has all but been discredited since the eighteenth century. In the introduction to her 1870 edition of the play, Carolina Michaëlis states that "la opinión general la atribuye, pero sin fundamento al rey, FELIPE IV, y á esta suposición más que á sus méritos poéticos debe su fama [general opinion attributes this play, without any basis, to King Philip IV, and it is to this supposition more than to its poetic merits that it owes its fame]" (167). Nevertheless, as Mackenzie has shown, collaboration among the playwrights belonging to the "escuela de Calderón" was quite common;[24] and some critics have attributed the play's relative dramatic value to the helping hand of others, including Calderón himself. To add further to the confusion, the play is known under three different titles: *La tragedia más lastimosa de amor* [*The Most Pitiful Tragedy of Love*], *Dar la vida por su dama* [*To Give One's Life for One's Lady*] and, more frequently, *El conde de Sex* [*The Earl of Essex*]. The play, first performed in 1633 and published in 1653, dramatizes the relationship between Elizabeth I and one of her favorites, Robert Deveraux, the Earl of Essex. The alleged courtship between the aging queen and the much younger Essex was a matter of speculation during Elizabeth's reign and remained of interest for centuries to come in England and abroad. It became the subject of dramatizations in France and England during the eighteenth and nineteenth centuries[25] and, more recently, in the 1939 Hollywood movie with Bette Davis and Errol Flynn titled *The Private Lives of Elizabeth and Essex*. Coello's play is reputed to be the first play ever to deal with the death of Essex, and may well be the first play to present Elizabeth I as a protagonist in the *comedia*. Why this play would appear at this particular time, ending the silence on the English queen on the seventeenth-century Spanish stage, is open to speculation and may never be definitively resolved. It may simply be that enough time had

---

seguros [By attributing this tragedy to Philip IV, we are merely following general opinion, although it is not founded on solid documentation]" (99).

[24] For a detailed study of such collaborations, see Ann L. Mackenzie's *La escuela de Calderón: Estudio e investigación* (Liverpool: Liverpool UP, 1993), particularly chapter 3, 31–67.

[25] Other versions of the story are *Comte d'Essex* by the French dramatist Gautier de Costes de la Calprenède in 1638; another play with the same name by Thomas Corneille (brother of the great French tragedist) in 1678; and John Banks's *The Unhappy Favourite* in 1682, among others. For more titles related to the same topic, see the introductions to the play in the editions by Michaëlis (168) and Schmiedel (42–4).

passed since the queen's death to make the fictionalization of a romantic episode in the queen's life an attractive topic for the stage. In addition, the playwrights belonging to the School of Calderon seemed to have been particularly keen to mine relatively recent historic events as inspiration for their work.[26]

Although the *comedia* under consideration deals with identifiable historical figures and has as its background the religious tensions between Protestants and Catholics (specifically, the conflict with Scotland) during the second half of the sixteenth century, it would be difficult to categorize this strictly as a historical play. It contains many factual inaccuracies, prominently the telescoping of several incidents that took place at widely different times during Elizabeth's reign: for example, the visits to England of Francis, Duke of Alençon, as a potential suitor for Elizabeth in 1579 and 1581, the execution of Mary, Queen of Scots in 1587, and the Essex rebellion in 1601. In addition to these chronological anomalies, modern readers would be particularly struck with the liberties the playwright takes in the presentation of the English queen.

Most of the *comedia* critics and historians who have dealt even cursorily with the play comment on what they perceive as the play's sympathetic portrayal of the English queen. Despite the title by which it is most commonly known, the dramatic and emotional center of the play is Elizabeth herself, explaining, perhaps, why the play became known by alternative titles. Francisco Bances Candamo, in his *Theatro de los Theatros*, tells us that although "ninguna reina ha sido más torpe que Isabela de Inglaterra [no queen has been more obtuse than Elizabeth of England]" (35), Coello's play portrays her love for Essex "tan retirado en la Majestad y tan oculto en la entereza, que el Conde muere sin sauer el Amor de la Reina [so discreet in its majesty and so secret in its integrity that the Earl dies without learning of the queen's love]" (35). Indeed, in his defense of the *comedia* against daunting detractors such as the Jesuit Ignacio de Camargo, Bances Candamo uses Coello's tragedy as an example of the decorum that playwrights maintained even when dealing with negative figures such as Elizabeth I. Centuries later, Cotarelo y Mori comments in an article on Coello:

> Mucho valor, mucha audacia eran, en efecto, necesarios para ofrecer al pueblo español con circunstancias nobles y simpáticas a aquella Reina tan odiada, causante principal de nuestras desdichas políticas ... En la obra de Coello [la reina] aparece dulce, sensible, honesta, digna, altiva, pero no cruel cuando ve menospreciado su amor y hasta ofendida su cualidad de Reina, y que, en lugar de gozarse en su venganza, perdona como mujer sus agravios más íntimos, los del corazón, y trata de salvar al causante de ellos.
> [Much courage, much audaciousness, were in effect, necessary to present to the Spanish public in a noble and sympathetic manner that hated Queen who was the principal cause of our political disasters ... In Coello's work, (the queen) appears sweet, sensitive, chaste, dignified, proud, but not cruel when she sees

---

[26] See Mackenzie's *La escuela de Calderón*, especially chapter 6 on "El drama serio-seglar" (103–29).

her love rejected and even when her dignity as a queen is offended; and instead of enjoying taking vengeance, like a woman, she forgives even the most intimate affronts, those of the heart, and she tries to save the one who has caused them.] ("Dramáticos" 582–3)

While it is true that the English queen is not portrayed as a Jezebel (a name, as mentioned before, that was frequently applied to Elizabeth for its homophonic echo and rhyme with "Isabel") or as the "incestuoso parto de la arpía [incestuous spawn of the harpy]" that Lope called her in his epic poem *Corona trágica*,[27] a careful reading of the play demonstrates that the portrayal of this Isabel is not as entirely sympathetic and complimentary as Bances Candamo and other more recent critics would have us believe. The play in fact partakes of many of the prejudices toward the English queen and toward the rule of women in general that were characteristic of seventeenth-century Spain and that we have seen in previous chapters.[28]

The action begins, dramatically enough, with the words "Muere, tirana [Die, tyrant]!"—words that frame the audience's and the reader's expectations and announce the serious treatment of potentially explosive topics such as sedition and tyrannicide. While these themes are deftly woven into the plot, the contrivances of the play will mostly resemble the action of the popular *comedias de enredo* [comedy of errors] or *comedias de capa y espada* [cloak and dagger plays]. That is, we find in *El conde de Sex* the same formulas and conventions endlessly repeated in these comic plays: mistaken identities, hidden suitors, chance encounters, letters that fall into the wrong hands, and so on. The incendiary words "Muere, tirana" are overheard by el conde de Sex, that is, the Earl of Essex,[29] who is visiting his lover, Blanca, a lady-in-waiting to the queen, in a country home outside London. In the opening scene, the Conde rushes to the rescue of a woman who is being attacked

---

[27] The full name of Lope's poem is *Corona trágica: vida y muerte de la serenísima reina de Escocia María Estuarda*. See the modern edition by C. Gianffreda (Firenze: Alinea, 2009), 109.

[28] In an interesting study on how the English were presented on the Spanish stage and vice versa, Don W. Cruickshank tells us that although there was a great deal of animosity among the English toward the Spaniards, the same seems to not have been true of the Spaniards toward the English. English characters in general were not common in the *comedia*, but when they do appear they are sympathetically portrayed, according to the British critic. The relative lack of antipathy toward England felt by the average Spaniard was probably due to a "generalized belief that most of the English were good Catholics living under a heresy imposed on them by a tyrannical monarchy" (206). Cruickshank deals briefly with *El conde de Sex* and tells us that what is interesting about the play is that "the play doesn't take sides" (202). See "Lisping and Wearing Strange Suits: English Characters on the Spanish Stage and Spanish Characters on the English Stage, 1580–1680," in *Parallel Lives: Spanish and English National Drama 1580–1680*, ed. Louise and Peter Fothergill-Payne (Lewisburg: Bucknell UP, 1991), 195–210.

[29] Throughout the chapter, I will use the names of the characters as they appear in the Spanish play to distinguish them from their historical counterparts.

by masked men. An able swordsman, he scares off the attackers, although he is slightly wounded in the process. In typical *comedia de capa y espada* fashion, the damsel in distress, although grateful, refuses to reveal her identity, giving him instead a green "banda" or sash to wrap around his wound and telling him that by this token, she will recognize him later and repay his kindness:

> Aquesa banda
> señal para hacer buscaros
> será, y adiós, que estoy
> en grande riesgo, si acaso
> sabe la Reina este exceso;
> y así, el secreto os encargo
> de todo.
> [By this sash I will find you, and now farewell, for I am at great risk if the Queen happens to learn of this predicament. Thus I beg you to keep all this completely secret.] (53–9)

We learn in a subsequent scene that this mysterious woman is none other than Elizabeth (here called Isabel), who had been bathing in the river when the would-be assassins attacked her. In another instance of dramatic license and historical inaccuracy, Elizabeth is presented as both beautiful and young, although we know that, historically, Elizabeth was decades older than the Earl.

There are several elements that make this opening scene remarkable. For one thing, according to the stage directions, the queen appears "en enaguas y cotilla, a medio vestir y con mascarilla [in a slip and corset, half-dressed, and wearing a mask] (79)." Her garb would seem singularly inappropriate in the representation of a royal body on stage. These undergarments no doubt made the body of the actress playing the English queen visible and accessible to the spectator. Thus, a royal person is provocatively put on display in a sexualized and vulnerable state. This represents an ironic visual counterpart to the many portraits of the Protestant queen—the famous "Armada Portrait" (see Figure 4.2) comes to mind, for example—where Elizabeth's body remains well hidden under heavy, elaborate gowns and ostentatious jewelry. The materiality of the elaborate costumes in the portraits was meant to convey power and, in the process, announce the queen's virginal self-containment.[30]

The reverse process is enacted in Coello's play, as the impregnable body politic is made into an available body natural. Here, the queen who was famous for controlled self-display is seen making a sensual spectacle of herself, as the character herself admits: "Mas ¿quién dirá que yo estoy / en hábito tan humano [But who would believe that I find myself in such a human disguise?]" (61–2).

---

[30] For an analysis of this portrait and others, see Andrew and Catherine Belsey's "Icons of Divinity: Portraits of Elizabeth I," in *Renaissance Bodies: The Human Figure in English Culture, c. 1540–1660*, ed. Lucy Gent and Nigel Llewellyn (London: Reaktion Books, 1990), 11–35.

Fig. 4.2   George Gower. *The Armada Portrait of Elizabeth I*, 1588.

In *Majesty and Humanity: Kings and Their Doubles in the Political Drama of the Spanish Golden Age*, Alban Forcione has written eloquently on the *comedia*'s concern for disrobing and humanizing the king.[31] When a play deals with a female monarch, however, the dynamic is different; and it is not the queen's humanity, but rather her sensual "body natural" that is emphasized. Played by a real actress on the stage, this scene would have presented a singularly equivocal performance of monarchy. Actresses, as we have seen, were considered by the guardians of morality to be women who, as Rivadeneira put it, "han vendido su honestidad [have sold their chastity]" (Cotarelo y Mori 525). They were, quite literally, public women who starkly defied the reigning ideology of enclosure that forbade women to see or to be seen.

---

[31]   Forcione discusses in great detail two plays by Lope de Vega—*El villano en su rincón* and *El rey don Pedro en Madrid*—where "kings are depicted who choose or are compelled to remove their masks, to depart from the space of absolutism and its political agendas in search of something that is missing" (21). That which is missing is the humanity of the king. According to Forcione, these plays incorporate "different conceptions of individual dignity in the face of the rising statism, among other things" (21). The depiction of a queen's body in its unrobed state would have been a different matter altogether.

The "mascarilla" that Elizabeth is wearing is also iconographically significant, and much is made in the dialogue of the fact that her face is half hidden by the mask:

> Yo, que al principio vi, ciego y turbado,
> a una parte nevado,
> y en otra negro el rostro,
> juzgué, mirando tan divino monstruo,
> que la naturaleza cuidadosa,
> desigualdad uniendo tan hermosa
> quiso hacer por asombro o por ultraje
> de azabache y marfil un maridaje.
> [Blinded and perturbed, I first saw her countenance, one part snowy and the other blackened, and, as I looked on this divine monster, I came to believe that, by joining such beautiful disparity, cautious nature—out of either wonder or outrage—wanted of jet and marble a marriage make.] (183–90)

The queen is presented, then, as an ambiguous creature, a combination of light and darkness, a monster whose presence inspires awe ("asombro") but also suggests violence ("ultraje"). More than once, the Earl will characterize her as "un enigma."

The mask as a dramatic prop is itself an overly determined marker of theatricality. It is well known that the historical Elizabeth was singularly concerned with her own self-dramatization and, as stated before, she was given to assuming different roles and identities. Indeed, according to Carole Levin, "her success came from how fluid and multifaceted her representations of self were" (*The Heart and Stomach* 2). For Elizabeth, theatricality and role-playing were a means of manipulating and wielding political power. Nevertheless, as we have seen in previous chapters, in the political ideology of early modern Europe inherited from a classical tradition, excessive theatricality was also often seen as an indication of the abuse of power; in other words, a manifestation of tyranny. The tyrant's nature "is fundamentally histrionic (therefore feminine). In contrast to the proper king, the tyrant presents a multitude of different faces," as Bushnell reminds us (7). In Coello's play, the *gracioso* Cosme humorously reflects on the protean nature of the queen, announced by the mask, when he states:

> Detrás de una mascarilla
> pudo estar Arias Gonzalo
> la monja Alférez, el cura,
> Y la moza de Pilatos.
> [Behind the mask, there could have been Arias Gonzalo, the Lieutenant Nun, a priest, and Pilate's whore.] (261–4)

Isabel, who has already been called a "tirana" in the opening lines, is presented as an ambiguous body that can take on different identities, thereby suggesting duplicity and a lack of authenticity. Combined with the eroticized display of her body, the character of Isabel—a simulacrum of the historical queen—becomes a personification of the tripartite link between inauthentic femininity, theatricality, and tyranny, a link we saw indirectly dramatized in the character of Constantino in *La república al revés* and blatantly developed in *La hija del aire*.

In a later scene, the Conde will describe to his servant how he came across the vision of the mysterious woman as she bathed in the river before being attacked. As he describes her physical attributes at length, he presents himself as a new Actaeon espying the forbidden and exposed body of a chaste goddess:

>—escucha lo que vi, que aun no lo creo—
>una mujer divina,
>reclinada en la margen cristalina,
>quitarse, descuidada,
>azul cendal y media nacarada,
>negros después coturnos al pié breve,
>que, primavera errante, floras llueve;
>las dos colunas bellas
>metió dentro del río y como al vellas
>vi cristal en el río desatado,
>y vi cristal en ellas condensado,
>no supe si las aguas que se vían
>eran sus pies, que líquidos corrían,
>o si sus dos colunas se formaban
>De las aguas que allí se congelaban.
>[Listen to what I saw, although I still can scarcely believe it: a divine woman who, reclining on the crystalline shore, took off unawares the blue silk and pearly stocking; next, she removed the black buskins on her small feet. Like an errant spring that showers flowers, she then put the two beautiful columns (of her legs) in the river ... And because, as I saw them, I saw crystal unleashed in the river and I saw crystal in the columns condensed, I could not tell whether the water that could be seen were her feet which were flowing like liquid or if her columns were composed of the water that there froze.] (147–61)

He proceeds to describe her hair ("suelto al viento / en quien ... el céfiro lascivo se abrigaba [untied to the wind, the lascivious Zephyr sought refuge in her hair]"), her hands ("fueron cristalino vaso sus manos [her hands were crystalline vessels]"), and her face in equally overwrought poetic terms. No Petrarchan cliché or Gongorine hyperbole is spared in this poetic *blazon*, which, like countless amatory poems, catalogues the lady's parts: her hair, her hands and her half-hidden face, her legs and feet. Thus, Elizabeth—the scourge of Catholicism, the destroyer of the Armada, the virgin queen—is here presented as an erotized object inadvertently performing a striptease for the count's scopophilic delectation. The Conde describes her stepping out of the waters in the following lines:

>Llegó la noche en fin, salió del río,
>y delgado cambray chupó el rocío
>De las dos azucenas ...
>Y luego en acabando de enjugarlas,

A cubrir empezó sus dos colunas,
Con dos nubes de nácar importunas:
Adorno suele ser; pero ¿quién duda
Que era mayor adorno estar desnuda?
[Night arrived at last, she stepped out of the river and a thin chambray sucked up the dew on the two lilies and then, when she finished drying them, she began to cover her two columns with two inopportune clouds of mother of pearl. Stockings are normally thought of as adornment, but who would deny that her nakedness would be a greater adornment still?] (205–14)

As in the depiction of Cenobia's humiliation in Calderón's play, there is an overt erotization of the gaze, both verbally and visually. The half-naked body natural of the historical queen is simultaneously exposed but also appropriated and contained through the use of familiar poetic conventions. This is a remarkable portrayal of Isabel, and we could say that Coello, in the process of describing an idealized beauty, is in fact dehumanizing the historical figure, fragmenting her, and making her familiar by incorporating her body into the clichéd conventions of poetry and theater. In addition, she is further demystified in this scene as Cosme counters the Conde's idealizing description with vulgar terms such as "dueña," "tranga," and "vil mondonga" [matron, whore, and dirty scullery maid]. The juxtaposition of two descriptive registers, consciously or not, tidily reproduces the contradictory language used to allude to the historical Elizabeth during her lifetime and beyond. Levin tells us that throughout her reign, the Protestant queen was the object of veneration and also constant speculation about her sexuality, and was even accused of being a "lewde woman" and an "arrant whore" (*The Heart and Stomach* 76, 83).

The central plot of Coello's play, as stated before, concerns the relationship between the queen and her favorite or *privado*, el conde de Sex. Historically, we know that the real Essex was a man of great charm whose meteoric rise in royal favor inspired envy and intrigue on the part of his rivals.[32] He was also, by all accounts, an impetuous and even dangerous courtier who can be viewed, in Levin's words, "as a touchstone for the problems and fears over Elizabeth's reign as it was nearing its close" (*The Heart and Stomach* 150). On the one hand, he represented for the London populace the ideals of honor and chivalry and, indeed, assiduously courted Elizabeth with the mannered language of courtly love. On the other, he was recklessly ambitious and often disdainful of Elizabeth as monarch. The latter attitude ultimately led him to instigate what is known as the "Essex rebellion," a poorly planned and desperate attempt—most likely inspired, according to historians, by the prospect of financial ruin

---

[32] For a discussion of Essex, see the last chapter of Carole Levin's *The Heart and Stomach of a King: Elizabeth I and the Politics of Sex and Power* (Philadelphia: U of Pennsylvania P, 1994), 149–72; and Paul E.J. Hammer's "'Absolute and Sovereign Mistress of Her Grace'? Queen Elizabeth I and Her Favourites, 1581–1592," in *The World of the Favourite*, ed. J.H. Elliott and L.W.B. Brockliss (New Haven: Yale UP, 1999), 38–53.

than any real political conviction—to force the queen to change her policies and reinstate him as a favorite. Nevertheless, in Coello's play, the Conde is presented as an honorable, if at times misguided, *privado*. Unlike the real Earl, whose lack of discretion seems to have left him unprepared for the responsibilities placed on his shoulders, the corresponding character in the play is deeply aware of his responsibility to his monarch: "los que a reyes asistimos / nunca ... descansamos [those of us who counsel kings can never rest] (1079–80). Coello has clearly taken liberties with the historical record in the portrayal of Essex, and, significantly, exonerates him of the charge of sedition for which the real Deveraux lost his life. In the play, the Conde chooses loyalty to the queen over religious partisanship and his affection for Blanca. To protect Isabel, he pretends—rather too convincingly—to back the Scottish conspirators against the queen and is overheard saying to Blanca: "¡muera esta tirana! ¡Muera [death to the tyrant! Death]!" (685). When, in a misguided attempt to foil the Catholic plot, he writes to the rebels expressing support for their rebellion, he further seals his fate.

El conde de Sex, then, displays a preoccupation with *privanza* or *valimiento*, an issue that would be the focus of endless commentaries and critiques, beginning with the rise of the Duke of Lerma under Philip III. At some point in the play, the *gracioso* Cosme exclaims:

> Gran desdicha es el privar
> pues hace a los más amigos
> ser hacia dentro enemigos.
> [It is a great misfortune to be the king's favorite because it makes even the greatest of friends become secret enemies.] (1089–91)

The Conde responds by saying: "la privanza ocasiona envidias [Being a favorite inspires envy]" (1102–3).

As we have seen, exemplarity is at the core of many of the plays written in the seventeenth century, and certainly lessons on the advantages and dangers of *privanza* are embedded in the play. The play seems to have been performed twice before King Philip IV and his first wife, Isabel of Bourbon, in November of 1633 and in February of 1637. The play may be in part intended as a cautionary tale for the actual monarch, whose dependence on the most famous *privado* in Spanish history was a source of conjecture and concern to many of his subjects. The Count Duke of Olivares was, at the time, enjoying the height of his influence over the king, but there were already complaints about the *valido*'s immense power. We know, for example, that Calderón de la Barca's court spectacle, *El mayor encanto amor* [*The Greatest Enchantment, Love*], performed in 1635, contained a not-so-veiled attack on Olivares's undue influence on the king.[33] In the case of *El conde de Sex*,

---

[33] J.H. Elliott tells us that "allegations of sorcery and enchantment were common currency among those who aspired to bring about the overthrow of favourites. In Madrid, where they provided a continuous accompaniment to the twenty-two years of Olivares's

given the fact that the protagonist of the play is a queen (perhaps not coincidentally named Isabel), it may be likely that there was a hidden subtext involving Isabel of Bourbon, whose relationship with the count duke was increasingly fraught. In 1640, a satirical dialogue titled "La cueva de Meliso" (attributed to Francisco de Quevedo) appeared, depicting Philip's *valido* as having made a pact with the devil. Among the advice the devil offers to the count duke we find the following, which gives us a sense of the difficult situation the queen was said to be experiencing vis á vis Olivares:

> Se humillará la Reina a cuanto mandes,
> y entenderá rendida
> que de tu voluntad depende su vida
> y la de su Marido ...
> [The queen must bend in humiliation to whatever you command, and she will surrender and understand that her life and that of her husband depend on your good will.] (Qtd. in Rubio 302–3)

While in Coello's play the *valido* is far from being a treacherous man, he does make one fatal mistake, and that is that he allows his personal feelings toward Isabel the woman to supercede his duty to the Isabel the queen, and beyond that, to the realm itself, despite his own earlier recognition that he must not confuse the personal with the political: "No hagamos razón de estado / del gusto, ni del deseo [Let us not concoct a reason of state out of our pleasure and desire]" (1271–2). His ultimate inability to separate his "gusto" and "deseo" from his responsibilities as a counselor to the queen will precipitate his demise.

While the Conde's mistake is grave, the tensions between private passion and responsibility to the state are most prominently embodied in the figure of Isabel. There are several scenes of intense flirtation in which we see both characters wage battle against their passions. In the following exchange, the characters are supposedly addressing their own thoughts in simultaneous asides, but through the use of stichomythia, the rapid exchange of short lines of "dialogue," they are in fact sparring with each other:

CONDE:	El mayor premio es serviros
	(¿Si es tanto favor acaso?)[34]
REINA:	(Amor loco ...)
CONDE:	(Necio imposible ...)

---

rule, they surfaced in an unusually sophisticated form in 1635 when Calderón presented his court spectacle, *El mayor encanto, amor* ... It was widely alleged at the time that the king was being prevented by Olivares from leading his armies on campaign against the French, and the audience, beginning with Philip himself, would have had no difficulty in equating Circe with Olivares and Ulysses with the king held in thrall by his favourite." See "Staying in Power: The Count-Duke Olivares," *The World of the Favourite*, ed. J.H. Elliott and L.W.B. Brockliss (New Haven: Yale UP), 112.

[34] Following Schmiedel's edition, parentheses designate the asides.

REINA:	(que ciego ...)
CONDE:	(que temerario ...)
REINA:	(me abates a tal bajeza ...)
CONDE:	(me quieres subir tan alto ...)
REINA:	(advierte que soy la Reina.)
CONDE:	(advierte que soy vasallo.)
REINA:	(Pues me humillas al abismo ...)
CONDE:	(Pues me acercas á los rayos ...)
REINA:	(sin reparar mi grandeza ... ,)
CONDE:	(sin mirar mi humilde estado ...,)
REINA:	(ya que te admito acá dentro ...,)
CONDE:	(ya que en mí vas entrando ...,)
REINA:	(muere entre el pecho y la voz.)
CONDE:	(muere entre el alma y los labios.)
REINA:	¿Oísme, conde?
CONDE:	¿Señora?
REINA:	Vedme después.
CONDE:	Soy tu esclavo.
	(¡Necio engaño, no me subas
	para caer de más alto!)

[EARL: The best reward is to serve you. (Could the favor be even greater?) QUEEN: (Mad love ...) EARL: (Impertinent love ...) QUEEN: (how blind ...) EARL: (how audacious ...) QUEEN: (you [love] fling me into such depths ...) EARL: (you raise me to such heights ...) QUEEN: (remember that I am the queen.) EARL: (remember that I am but a vassal.) QUEEN: (Since you shame me into the abyss ...,) EARL: (Since you lift me to the sun ...,) QUEEN: (without taking into account my majesty ...,) EARL: (without repairing on my humble state ...,) QUEEN: (Since I have admitted you [love] here within me ...,) EARL: (since you are entering inside me ...,) QUEEN: (die then between my breast and my voice.) EARL: (die then between my soul and my lips.) QUEEN: Do you hear me count? EARL: Yes, my lady. QUEEN: Come to see me later. COUNT: I am your slave. (Impertinent thought, do not raise me only to drop me from the highest point.)] (973–92)

In this and other scenes between the queen and her vassal, the playwright captures a verbal chafing that is erotically charged and that emphasizes the impossible and dangerous situation these characters find themselves in.[35] After receiving repeated, if veiled, encouragement from the queen, the Conde openly declares his affection for her. Isabel, suddenly realizing the inappropriateness of the situation and the affront to her royal person (as opposed to her private womanly self), reacts with ire:

---

[35] In the chapter "Fiction and Friction," from his book *Shakespearean Negotiations: The Circulation of Social Energy in Renaissance England* (Berkeley: U of California P, 1988), 86–93, Stephen Greenblatt studies instances of this erotically charged dialogue in Shakespeare.

> ¿Qué decís?
> ¿A mí? ¿Cómo? loco, necio
> ¿Conoceisme? ¿Quién soy yo?
> Decid quién soy; que sospecho
> que se os huyó la memoria.
> [What are you saying? To me? How dare you! Madman, fool! Don't you recognize me? Don't you know who I am? Tell me who I am, because I fear that it has escaped your memory.] (1507–11)

Isabel's words, while directed at the Conde, ironically point to the almost ontological dilemma she finds herself in. By encouraging the count's affections, it is she who has forgotten her own identity. Indeed, time and time again, this drama queen is shown to be an imprudent and all too human ruler who lets her passions get the better of her. At another point, she exclaims:

> Pero yo no soy quien soy:
> la Reina soy; no lo creo
> como Reina que no tiene
> sobre una pasión imperio.
> Yo, ¿vasallaje a un cuidado?
> Yo, ¿sujección? ¿Qué es aquesto?
> ¿No soy Isabela [yo]:
> Isabela, la que tengo
> pendiente de mis motivos
> a todo el mundo suspenso?
> [But I am not who I am: the Queen; I don't believe I am like a queen who cannot control a passion. I, a vassal to emotions? I, subjected in this manner? What can this be? Am I not Elizabeth, she who has the entire world in suspense, waiting on my every motive?] (1031–40)

Like countless other male monarchs in the *comedia*—Constantino in *La república*, Nino in *La hija del aire*, Enrique in *La cisma de Inglaterra*—Isabel has succumbed to a love that controls her body and soul; and it is here (perhaps more than in the reliance on a favorite) that the most important lesson on kingship is imparted. A monarch's responsibility to put the kingdom and *razón de estado* above any personal desires is an obsessive theme in the theater, as well as in the many political commentaries written in the sixteenth and seventeenth centuries. In texts such as Pedro de Rivadeneira's *Tratado de un príncipe cristiano* or Pablo Martín Rizo's *Norte de Príncipes*, the inability to control the passions is often presented as a defining characteristic of a tyrant. In *Idea de un príncipe político-cristiano*, Saavedra Fajardo includes the following warning:

> No tiene el bien público mayor enemigo que á ellas [las pasiones] y a los fines particulares ... El daño está en el abuso y desórden de ellos [los afectos], que es lo que se ha de corregir en el príncipe procurando que en sus acciones no se gobierne por sus afectos sino por la razón de estado.

[The common good has no greater enemy than these (passions) and selfish goals ... The danger is in the abuse and disorder of the passions, which have to be corrected in the prince, always endeavoring that his actions be governed not by his emotions but rather by the reason of state.] (24)

Isabel in this play will prove herself incapable of controlling her *afectos*, or passions. She flies into a fury when she sees Blanca wearing the green sash she had given Essex, and when Blanca suggests that perhaps she is jealous, she exclaims:

No son celos esta ofensa
que me estáis haciendo vos.
Supongamos que quiera
al Conde en esta ocasión;
y alguna atrevida, loca,
presumida, descompuesta,
le quisiera—¿qué es querer?—
le mirara, que le viera,
—¿Qué es verle?—no sé qué diga:
no hay cosa que menos sea;
con las manos, con los dientes,
con la vista, con las quejas,
con la intención, con el ceño,
o con las palabras mesmas,
¿no le quitara la vida,
la sangre no la bebiera,
los ojos no la sacara,
y el corazón hecho piezas,
no le abrasara? (Mas ¿cómo
hablo yo tan descompuesta?
Los celos, aunque fingidos
me arrebataron la lengua,
y despertaron mi enojo.
¡Jesús! ¿yo tan sin modestia?
¡Qué necedad! ¡Qué locura!)

[This offense that you are committing is not jealousy. Let's suppose that I did love the Earl; well then, if I loved him and some impudent, brazen and presumptuous little fool loved him too—no, not love, for what is love?—if she were to look upon him or even see him?—what does that mean, to see him?—I don't know what I'm saying. There is nothing more innocent than looking, but even so, with my hands, with my teeth, with my sight and with my sighs, with my intention and my scowl and with my very words, wouldn't I take her life, drink her blood, take out her eyes, and burn her heart in pieces? (But, how is it that I am talking in such an unseemly manner? Jealousy, though feigned, took hold of my tongue. Jesus! How can I behave with such lack of discretion? What foolishness! What madness!)] (1782–1807)

The exaggerated reaction to what is a hypothetical situation reveals a monarch unmoored by her personal feelings.[36] Stories about the sexual jealousy of the historical Elizabeth had circulated in her lifetime and afterwards. It was reported, for example, that when another favorite of hers, Robert Dudley, the Earl of Leicester, secretly married the Dowager Countess of Essex (Deveraux's mother, no less), Elizabeth never forgave him and always referred to the wife as a "she-wolf."[37] Although Coello's Isabel struggles with her emotions and is aware of her inappropriate behavior, passages such as the one above show her to be incapable of governing her passions with prudence.

In Coello's play, Blanca is Isabel's rival for the affections of the Conde; and in her character, broader historical circumstances are interwoven with dramatic contrivance. Blanca recounts that her father and brother were executed by the queen for being partisans of Mary, Queen of Scots. She describes in vivid and moving terms the death of Mary, calling her "noble víctima, inocente, / fue de injusto sacrificio [a noble, innocent victim of an unjust sacrifice]" (499–500). The tragic story of Blanca's family may be a dramatic echo of the fate of Lady Arbella Stuart, a pretender to the throne who was disinherited by Elizabeth. We know, for example, that in a letter written in 1603, Lady Arbella drew many parallels between herself and the Earl of Essex, who had supported her claim to the English throne against Elizabeth (Findlay 187). In *El conde de Sex*, Blanca repeatedly tries to gain the Conde's sympathy. In the following passage, she explains the many reasons for pretending to be a devoted lady-in-waiting in order to ultimately avenge Isabel's treachery:

La Reina ofendió mi sangre,
La Reina, tirana y fiera,
hermano y padre me quita
y sin estados me deja;
La Reina manchó el cuchillo
de María en la inocencia;
la Reina me quita al Conde,
y me amenaza soberbia

---

[36] Some critics have noted the similarities between this speech by Isabel and that of Manrique in Calderón's *El médico de su honra*. Daniel Rogers believes that Coello was probably influenced by Calderón, who was his mentor and collaborator; while MacCurdy suggests that it was the other way around. See Rogers's "Los monólogos femeninos en *El conde de Sex* de Antonio Coello," in *Hacia Calderón: Séptimo Coloquio Anglogermano* (Stuttgart: Verlag, 1985), 175–82; and MacCurdy's *The Tragic Fall*, 19.

[37] Spaniards were aware of her affection for Dudley. Theodora Jankowski quotes a letter from the Spanish envoy, Gómez Suárez de Figueroa: "During the last few days ... Lord Robert has come so much into favour that he does whatever he likes with affairs and it is even said that her Majesty visits him in his chambers day and night. People talk of this so freely that they go so far as to say that his wife has a malady in one of her breasts and the Queen is only waiting for her to die to marry Lord Robert." See *Women in Power in the Early Modern Drama* (Urbana: U of Illinois P, 1992), 142, note 13.

> con equívocas palabras
> que no le mire ni quiera;
> la Reina al Conde le obliga,
> ya amorosa o ya severa,
> a que él me niegue, perjuro,
> mi honor; pues la Reina muera.
> [The Queen offended my own blood, the Queen—tyrant and beast—deprived me of my father and brother and left me without my estate; the Queen stained the blade with Mary's innocence; the Queen robs me of the Earl, and with veiled threats forbids me to look at him or love him. The Queen, both loving and severe, forces the Earl to dishonor me: well then, let the Queen die.] (1847–60)

In addition to juxtaposing the historical background with the allusion to Mary Stuart with her own predicament in the play, Blanca's words show the queen in the most negative light possible. They remind the audience of the English queen's tyranny toward the Catholic cause Spaniards supported, and they serve as an effective way of preparing for the climax of the play—the earl's execution.

In the final scenes of the play, Isabel is shown as a deeply divided and tragic entity. In perhaps the most moving soliloquy of the play, she admits to herself her love for the earl and realizes that what hurts her even more than his alleged treason is that he seems to be in love with Blanca:

> El Conde, mi dulce dueño,
> que ya en mi pecho amoroso
> ídolo fue, a quien el alma
> consagró en culto devoto
> …
> ¿con otra mujer me ofende?
> ¿Con otra mujer? Pues ¿cómo?
> ¿Es Blanca mejor que yo?
> ¿Tiene valor más heroico?
> ¿Tiene más ambles partes?
> …
> ¿Quiérete más? Mas ¿qué es esto?
> ¿Yo ternuras? ¿Yo sollozos?
> ¿Yo, a pesar de mi grandeza,
> con infame llanto mojo
> la púrpura real que viste
> la majestad por adorno?
> [The Earl, my sweet love, the idol I fervently adore in my heart … can he be offending me with another woman? But, pray, how can this be? Is Blanca better than I? Is her valor more heroic? Does she have more courteous ways? … Does she love you more? But, what is this? Can this be me lost in tender sighs? Can I be sobbing? Ignoring my grandeur, am I really soaking with shameful tears the royal purple that majesty dons as its insignia?] (2361–4, 2369–73, 2381–6)

In a later scene, torn between her love for the dashing Essex, who had earlier saved her life, and her hatred for his alleged treachery, she seeks a solution by splitting herself in two. In one of the last scenes, the queen goes to Essex's prison cell, and the stage directions tell us that she appears "de la suerte que salió al principio de la comedia, con máscara y enaguas [In the same garb as she appeared at the beginning of the play, with a mask and in her slip]" (162). That is, Isabel has once again abandoned her public identity and royal decorum in order to resume the role of the mysterious *dama* of the opening scene. She expresses her improbable situation in the following:

> El Conde me dio la vida,
> y así, obligada me veo:
> El Conde me daba la muerte,
> y así, ofendida me quejo.
> Pues ya que con la sentencia
> esta parte he satisfecho,
> pues cumplí con la justicia,
> con el amor cumplir quiero.
> [The Earl gave me life, and thus I am indebted to him; the Earl tried to kill me and thus, offended, I accuse him. Since with the death sentence I have satisfied the affront and complied with the law, now I want to comply with my love.]
> (2597–604)

On the one hand, as the representative of justice and order in the body politic, it is her duty to punish the crime of treason and sedition. On the other, she will literally divest herself of her royal robes and other markers of monarchy and appear as a mere woman in love, her body natural again on display, in order to help the Conde escape. Indeed, as she resumes the identity of the mysterious half-clad woman, she begins to refer to her royal self in the third person. It is almost as if Coello were wittily staging the real Elizabeth's famous exploitation of the medieval concept of the king's two bodies. When the earl asks to see the queen's face one last time before dying, she responds: "Nada con la Reina puedo; / que aunque estoy muy cerca della, / también della estoy muy lejos [I have nothing to do with the Queen; although I am very close to her, she is very far from me]" (2690–92).

Later, when she agrees to take off the mask, she describes her paradoxical situation:

> Aunque siempre es uno mismo [el rostro],
> éste que ahora estáis viendo,
> Conde, es solamente mío;
> y aqueste que agora os muestro
> es de la Reina, no ya
> de quien os habló primero.
> (*Descúbrese*)

[Although my countenance is always the same, Count, the one you see right now is mine alone; and this other one that I am now going to show you is that of the Queen, and not of the person who first spoke to you.] (*She takes off the mask.*) (2757–62)

We are reminded in this passage of the historical queen's contention that the eternal body politic (understood to be male) was only temporarily embodied in the weak vessel of a woman, Elizabeth herself. For the English queen, the importance of this controversial theory was determined by the question of gender: she and her supporters frequently used the language of the king's two bodies to justify the undesirable rule of a woman.[38] For example, Nicholas Heathe, the Archbishop of York, stated once that by the "appointment of God she [is] our sovarainge lord and ladie, our kinge and quene, our emperor and empresse" (qtd. in Levin, *The Heart and Stomach* 121). We remember that Elizabeth herself is famously thought to have claimed at the Battle of Tilbury to have "the body of a weak and feeble woman" and "the heart and stomach of a king."[39]

Beyond gender, the doctrine also emphasizes the duality in terms of the private, natural body of the monarch versus the public or politic body. Although, as stated in the introduction, political treatises in Spain tended to avoid a legalistic separation of the two bodies, we do encounter frequent allusions to a binary conception of kingship in the reference to two types of majesty. Álamos de Barrientos states, for example, that "El Príncipe tiene dos personas, de particular y de Rey [the Prince has two persons, that of a private individual and that of the King]" (qtd. in Civil 22). The struggle between the body politic and the body natural could not be more vividly staged in *El conde de Sex*. Earlier in the play, the Queen had exclaimed:

Creame deidad el Conde,
Que lo que tienen de humanos
No han de revelar los Reyes
A los ojos del vasallo.
[Let the Earl believe me to be a deity, for kings must never reveal their human aspect to the eyes of vassals.] (935–8)

Despite her protestations, Isabel is unable to reconcile her passions with her duty to the state as monarch. When she learns that el conde de Sex was, in fact, innocent of plotting against her and had only confessed to protect Blanca, the real traitor, she tries to undo the damage by reversing her sentence. It is too late, however, and she and the audience are subjected to the horrific *descubrimiento* of the earl's beheaded body, reminiscent of the last scene in *La cisma de Inglaterra*.

---

[38] By the same token, it has been argued that the theory of the two bodies was a double-edged sword: on the one hand, it made the reign of Elizabeth more acceptable; on the other, it was used by lawyers and theologians at the time as a way of restricting and controlling the headstrong queen (Levin, *The Heart and Stomach* 122).

[39] As stated earlier, there is disagreement among historians as to whether Elizabeth actually uttered these words. See note 34 of Chapter 1.

Furthermore, the play's denouement offers the spectacle of a distraught and repentant queen:

> ¡Qué perezosa que estuvo
> Mi piedad y mi clemencia;
> qué diligente el rigor,
> Y la crueldad, que ligera!
> ¡Qué tarde llegó el remedio!
> ...
> ¿Yo castigué a la lealtad?
> ¿Yo di muerte a la inocencia?
> ¿Yo a la esperanza de Europa;
> yo al amparo de mi tierra?
> [How sluggish was my pity and clemency but how diligent my rigor and how swift my cruelty! How late the remedy has arrived! ... Did I punish loyalty? Did I give death to innocence? Did I kill the hope of Europe? Did I kill the protector of my land?] (3041–5, 3049–52)

Her words echo Enrique's deep regret at the end of *La cisma*, but unlike the melancholy and despair of Enrique in Calderón's play, Isabel vows to unleash her implacable fury on Blanca and the other Catholic conspirators. There is, then, a lack of self-knowledge and control; and compassion, a characteristic deemed indispensable for the good Christian prince, is absent.

Like Ana's *bulto* in *La cisma*, the Conde's beheaded body becomes the inversion of the monarch's body; but unlike Calderón's play, this denouement doesn't remotely or ironically suggest a resolution. Unlike Maria Tudor in *La cisma*, who exulted over the cadaver of Ana Bolena, Isabel cannot bring herself to look at the count's mutilated body:

> cubrid aqueste cadaver;
> no mire yo tal tragedia
> hasta que, matando a Blanca
> y vengado el Conde, tenga
> fin su traición con su muerte ...
> [Cover that corpse; I don't want to look at this tragic scene until Blanca is dead and the Count is avenged and her death puts an end to her treason.] (3085–9)

The punishment of the innocent Essex and the promise to avenge his wrongful execution becomes, in the play, the metonymical dramatization of Elizabeth's persecution of Catholic martyrs, as perceived by Spaniards. After presenting Isabel as a conventional, if tragic *dama*, the final image of the queen is made to correspond to one that was still current in Spain's political imagination. That is, despite the pathos of her character—she is a pitiable figure forced to outlive the consequences of her action—the character embodies many of the evils endemic to female power. She is a duplicitous and ultimately unstable woman. As mentioned in the beginning of the chapter, critics have interpreted the presentation of Elizabeth in Coello's play as a sympathetic version of the dreaded queen. A close analysis of the play, however, reveals tensions and contradictions that expose deeper ideological issues about what it means to be an effective monarch, the unease surrounding the question of female rule, and the ambivalent attitudes toward Elizabeth herself.

In her parliamentary accession speech in 1558, Elizabeth declared that although she was "ordeyned ... one bodye naturallye considered," she was now also, by God's "permission, a Bodye politique to governe" (qtd. in Frye 13). Almost 100 years later, Coello attempts to reverse the equation by emphasizing the natural, fallible, and mortal body of the queen. We may never fully answer the question of why Elizabeth was absent for such a long time from the Spanish stage, or why, in *El conde de Sex*, Coello chose to break with the perhaps subconscious but significant silence and invisibility that had surrounded the figure of the Protestant monarch. Nevertheless, it is significant that when she does appear, she is divested of any true, lasting majesty. In the end, the play affirms the convenient nationalist fiction that constructed the English queen as an inauthentic, theatricalized, and thoroughly feminized tyrant. The body of a weak and feeble woman, indeed!

Chapter 5
Christina of Sweden and Queenly Garb(o)

... las damas de Calderón tienen siempre algo de hombrunas
—Marcelino Menéndez y Pelayo[1]

Calderón's *Afectos de odio y amor*

Art historians have, for the most part, ignored the equestrian portraits of two Habsburg queens: Margarita of Austria, Philip III's consort, and Isabel of Bourbon, Philip IV's first wife (Figures 5.1 and 5.2). Attributed to Velázquez's studio and revealing the hand of the Spanish master himself in some of the details, these portraits provide some iconographic insights about seventeenth-century attitudes toward women in power. Jonathan Brown suggests that they were displayed in the Hall of Realms alongside the portraits of the kings (*Velázquez* 112) and were, no doubt, meant to be the companion pieces to the better known and studied equestrian portraits of Philip III and Philip IV (Figures 5.3 and 5.4).[2] Walter Liedtke and John Moffitt tell us that the equestrian portraits represented a common form of court art with origins in antiquity and the early Renaissance (529).[3]

---

[1] "Calderón's ladies always have something mannish about them" in *Calderón y su teatro* (Madrid: Pérez Dubrull, 1881), 343.

[2] It is not clear what Velázquez's role may have been in the production of these equestrian portraits. Walter A. Liedke and John F. Moffitt believe the portraits of Philip III and the queens were painted by other artists and then revised by Velázquez around 1634. See "Velázquez, Olivares, and the Baroque Equestrian Portrait," in *The Burlington Magazine* 123.942 (1981): 531. According to Jonathan Brown: "While virtually no one has doubted that the equestrian portraits of Baltasar Carlos and Philip II were painted without assistance, it is apparent that the portraits of Philip III, Margarita of Austria, and Isabella of Bourbon involved the participation of another artist or artists;" in *Velázquez: Painter and Courtier* (New Haven: Yale UP, 1986), 111.

[3] I am grateful to Gridley McKim-Smith for her generous help in providing bibliography and suggestions for my reading of the equestrian portraits and royal portraiture. The literature on the latter is vast. Among the most useful works related to Spanish royalty are Jonathan Brown, *Velázquez: Painter and Courtier*; Miguel Falomir Faus, "Sobre los orígenes del retrato y la aparición del 'pintor de corte en la España bajomedieval," in *Boletín del arte* XVII (Universidad de Málaga, 1996): 177–96; and Pierre Civil, "Le Corps du roi et son image: une symbolique de l'état dans quelques représentations de Philippe II," in Augustin Redondo, *Le corps comme métaphore dans L'Espagne des XVIe et XVIIe siècles. Du corps métaphorique aux métaphores corporelles, Colloque International, Sorbonne et Collège d'Espagne, 1–4 octobre 1990* (Paris: Sorbonne, 1992). Laura Bass's book *The Drama of the Portrait: Theater and Visual Culture in Early Modern Spain*

Fig. 5.1   Diego Velázquez and others. *Margarita of Austria, Wife of Philip III, on Horseback*, ca. 1631.

Nevertheless, while the portraits of the kings can be inscribed within a visual genealogy of power (Velázquez was working in the shadow of Titian and Rubens, who had also executed equestrian portraits), portraits of queens on horseback were relatively rare. A comparison of these two sets of portraits—the queens on the one hand and those of the kings and of other men in power, such as the Count Duke of Olivares (Figure 5.5), on the other—is revealing. The portraits of Margarita and

---

(University Park: Penn State UP, 2008) contains a comprehensive bibliography on the topic of portraiture in Spain. Beyond the Spanish context, see also Roy Strong's *Gloriana: The Portraits of Queen Elizabeth I* (London: Pimlico, 1987); Jodi Cranston's *The Poetics of Portraiture in the Italian Renaissance* (Cambridge: Cambridge UP, 2000); and Joanna Woodall's article "An Exemplary Consort: Antonis Mor's Portrait of Mary Tudor," in *Art History* 14.2 (1991): 192–224, in addition to her edition of collected essays, *Portraiture: Facing the Subject* (Manchester: Manchester UP, 1997).

Fig. 5.2   Diego Velázquez and others. *Equestrian Portrait of Queen Isabel of Bourbon, Wife of Philip IV*, 1635–1636.

Isabel are large canvases (approximately 3 x 3 meters), and what first draws the viewer's attention are not the faces of the queens themselves but the meticulously detailed gowns they are wearing.

The textures, colors, and patterns of the dresses dominate the canvas, vying for preeminence only with the enlarged and somewhat disproportionate horses. Jonathan Brown has characterized the technique employed in rendering the gowns as "dull [and] mechanical"; and this, in his opinion, suggests that someone other than Velázquez was the primary painter (*Velázquez* 111). Nevertheless, it is precisely the intricacy of that mechanical rendition of the royal robes that initially captures the viewer's eye. As Carmen Bernis has stated in her history of fashion during the reign of Philip II, "Los retratistas de la Corte pintaban con especial cuidado el traje de sus modelos; algunos ponían tal énfasis en la interpretación

Fig. 5.3   Diego Velázquez and others. *Philip III on Horseback*, ca. 1631.

de sus más pequeños detalles que casi llegaban a convertirlo en el verdadero protagonista del cuadro [The portraitists of the court took special care in painting the attire of their models; some put so much emphasis on the smallest details that they almost made it the real protagonist of the painting]" ("La moda" 66). In the portraits under consideration, the ostentatious and heavy texture of the cloth contributes to the impression of strangeness and stylized splendor. Although the overall effect is fetching, the queens' bodies are kept well hidden, erasing all hint of sensuality (unless we count the delicate white hands gracefully holding the reins of the horses). Thus, the gowns, which dominate the canvas, encase the women's "natural" bodies in a type of body armor or, better yet, a kind of body mask, since there is no allusion to military prowess. The effect mitigates the body's display and thereby denies erotic access, reminding us of the emphasis on a woman's chastity and of the ideology of enclosure that dominated the "official" attitude toward women in general. In the tradition of portraiture of royal personages, representation

Fig. 5.4   Diego Velázquez. *Philip IV on Horseback*, 1631–1636.

of the physical features of the queens is complemented almost always—often even surpassed—by the detailed, meticulous rendering of gems and other emblems of rank, power, and wealth. In these particular images, there is less emphasis on the jewelry, although the diamond and pearl necklace that adorns both queens is the famous "el Joyel," obsessively used as a dynastic marker by the Hapsburg monarchy in royal portraiture. Nevertheless, it is primarily the gowns here that connote value and royal authority. The elaborate materiality of the queens' dress contrasts with the relative sobriety of the costumes in the male portraits.

In the portrait of Philip IV, the monarch is shown in profile and his stance commands our attention through the nobility of his look. The queens are staring directly out of the canvas at the spectator—like the portrait of Philip III—but they seem distant and unapproachable. Theirs is a static, idealized beauty that attracts but keeps the viewer at a safe distance. Perhaps one of the most interesting comparisons between these equestrian portraits lies in the depiction of the horses. The horse was seen as a timeless and universal symbol of authority and power, as the historian R.A. Stradling tells us (*Spain's Struggle* 235); and in the Spanish court, the horses and their relationship to the royal body held particular importance. For example, once the king had ridden a horse, it could not be ridden by anyone else (*Spain's Struggle* 293). In addition, horses were of paramount importance in the endless dynastic and religious wars that Spain was waging, and that were impoverishing the country during these years. It is no coincidence that Velázquez executed, in a relatively short period of time, a total of seven equestrian portraits of the royal family and of King Philip IV's chief minister, the Count Duke of Olivares (*Spain's Struggle* 235–6). In fact, Olivares counted as one of his many duties in the court that of being Master of the Horse. In comparing the queens and kings atop their mounts, we note one important difference that may be analyzed in terms of gender. The horses of the kings and of Olivares (Figure 5.5) are performing what in equestrian terms is called a *levade*. Liedtke and Moffitt tell us that this was an air of *haute ecole*

> in which the horse bends its haunches deeply (in a manner more similar to sitting or squatting than to the standing movement or rearing), holds the body at no more than a forty-five degree angle, tucks in the forelegs, holds the head straight and close to the body, and maintains this position for as long as his strength and skill allow (usually about five seconds). (536)

The depiction of the *levade* required a metaphorical and ideological dimension, for it provided a visual way of showcasing a king's ability to lead the military and the kingdom. If we look at Philip IV's equestrian portrait, we observe the monarch in his captain-general garb—red sash, armor, and baton—calmly executing this difficult exercise using only one hand. By contrast, the queens' horses seem majestic but subdued and are shown prancing with only one leg lifted from the ground. The women are riding sidesaddle and although they seem very dignified and controlled in posture and look, they do not communicate the same sense of authority and control that we see in the king's portraits. The richly textured blankets on the horses seem to be a continuation of the queen's gowns, suggesting that these women—like the noble animals—are primarily accoutrements in the visual display of monarchical power. That is, they are objects to be gazed at and admired, but they do not seem to possess real authority. Through the ostentatious materiality and wealth of their dress, these queens become components of the body politic and part of a complex tableau of power within the Habsburg court. At the same time, like all women in the popular opinion of the time, they do not display the ability to lead. Certainly, the paintings seem to suggest they could never be "heads of state"; and, indeed, the heads (the corporeal site of reason and authority) depicted here are rather miniscule and rest upon narrow shoulders.

A consideration of these portraits highlights the broader problem of what it means to represent the queen's body visually. There is an intrinsic contradiction between the rank of the subjects in these paintings and the social status of women in general. As critics such as Louis Montrose have suggested, the female body

Fig. 5.5   Diego Velázquez. *Gaspar de Guzmán, Count-Duke of Olivares, on Horseback*, 1635.

was always a subjected body, regardless of rank. Treatises in Spain regarding the role of women make this abundantly clear. We remember that Luján had claimed in his *Coloquios matrimoniales* that regardless of the woman's rank, the spinning distaff was the best attribute, just as the lance was to the knight or the habit to a priest (80). When portraying a queen, either on canvas or on the stage, particular strategies of representation are brought into play in order to display a body that, because of its rank, was meant to be a public and visible component of the power structure, but because of its sex was by definition submissive and meant to be relegated to the private sphere. Rose Marie San Juan, in a different context, calls this paradox the "juxtaposition of the queen's unindulged private body with the greatness of her political body" (25).

A gendered analysis of the equestrian portraits is complicated by the existence of still another contemporaneous portrait of a queen on horseback. In 1653, Philip IV requested an equestrian portrait of Queen Christina of Sweden (Figure 5.6), the monarch whose life (1626–1689) spanned almost three-quarters of the seventeenth century and who was to fire the imagination of Europe in the seventeenth century and for centuries to come.[4] The request for the portrait in question was made when the Spanish king learned of Christina's decision to renounce Protestantism and embrace Catholicism.[5] It was not unusual for equestrian portraits to be painted either to commemorate some special event or to show royal favor, and both of these excuses can be applied to the genesis of this particular painting, executed by the French artist Sébastien Bourdon (1616–1671). Christina's renunciation of the Protestant faith was a circumstance that was celebrated in Spain as a triumph over heresy; and it was clear that Philip wanted to align her name and her image to the Habsburg dynasty and the Catholic cause.

---

[4] Indeed, she commanded a fascination that, as Ruth Lundelius reminds us, far outstrips her actual political importance and legacy. See "Queen Christina of Sweden and Calderón's *Afectos de odio y amor*," *Bulletin of the comediantes* 38.2 (1986): 231.

[5] Historians are not in agreement on the fortunes of this painting during the seventeenth century. In *Christina, Queen of Sweden: the Restless Life of a European Eccentric* (New York: Harper Collins, 2004), Veronica Buckley states that the portrait was the queen's own favorite and that it hung in her bedroom to the end of her life (180). Arne Danielsson, on the other hand, offers detailed accounts (based on contemporaneous documents) on the efforts to send this large canvas to Madrid. He tells us that once it arrived, none other than Velázquez oversaw the positioning of Christina's portrait in the Alcázar, where "in 1666 it graced the king's dining room." See "Sébastien Bourdon's Equestrian Portrait of Queen Christina of Sweden—Addressed to 'His Catholic Majesty' Philip IV," in *Konsthistorisk Tidskrift* 58 (1989): 95–106; quote is on page 106. The portrait is currently part of El Prado's collection. For a detailed consideration of how Queen Christina was visually portrayed during her lifetime, see Rose Marie San Juan's "The Queen's Body and Its Slipping Mask: Contesting Portraits of Queen Christina of Sweden," in *ReImagining Women: Representations of Women in Culture*, ed. Shirley Neuman and Glennis Stephenson (Toronto: U of Toronto P, 1993), 19–44.

Fig. 5.6   Sébastien Bourdon. *Queen Christina of Sweden on Horseback*, 1653–1654.

Commenting on the equestrian portraiture dated from around 1550 to 1650, Liedke and Moffitt have convincingly suggested that imperial, Christian, and rulership concerns are the three dominant themes (532). All of these, I believe, come into play in the consideration of the equestrian portrait of Christina. What sets the portrait of the Swedish queen on a horse dramatically apart from the two equestrian portraits of Margaret of Austria and Isabel of Bourbon is that it does not fit neatly into the gendered differences as described above. Christina's pose, curiously, has more in common with masculine equestrian portraits, such as the one of Philip III and, especially, Velázquez's equestrian rendering of the Count Duke of Olivares. The portrait thus displays a different technique in representing the queen's body. Unlike the demure and miniscule presentation of the queen's head in the other two portraits, we are treated to the strong masculine features of Christina's face. Her hair is loose and she is wearing a riding costume that is quite austere and drab of color, especially compared to the figure of the falconer standing behind the horse. In its severity, her garb is more reminiscent of the "virile" costumes worn by Philip and the Count Duke of Olivares. Unlike the bodies of the Habsburg queens, which remain entirely inaccessible to the viewer through the meticulous depiction of their gowns, Christina's costume allows her limbs to be discernible and therefore accessible to the viewer's gaze. Although she is clearly sitting sidesaddle as befits a woman, the horse is not ceremonially prancing like Margarita's and Isabel's horses. According to contemporary accounts, Christina was an accomplished rider and hunter, a woman of "extraordinary physical endurance" who "could stay ten hours in the saddle in the hunting field and shoot a hare with a single shot better than any man in Sweden ..." (qtd. in San Juan 24). The horse in the painting is prominent, but the queen is in no way dwarfed by the powerful creature. Indeed, her body seems slightly larger than might seem natural. It is clear in this portrait that the queen is fully in control; and not insignificantly, her horse is performing a *levade*, the move most frequently associated with male equestrian portraits. Bourdon's rendering of this monarch is hardly that of a subjected or enclosed feminine body. As San Juan states in her brief consideration of the portrait: "The queen, as skillful hunter unimpeded by physical boundaries, injects the image with the authority to challenge the viewer's consuming gaze" (26). In the seventeenth century, Jerónimo de Barrionuevo commented on her remarkable talent as an equestrian and, in passing, raised questions about her sexual identity: "Dícese hace mal a un caballo, como si fuera hombre, y que por esto le envía el Rey estos caballos, y aun se dice que es más que mujer [It is said that she is hard on her horses, as if she were a man, and that is why the king sends her these horses, and it is even rumored that she is more than a woman]" (*Avisos* I. 58).

Queen Christina was indeed "more than a woman"—she was a conspicuous and ambiguous royal body during her lifetime, who inspired numerous representations beyond painting. Legend had it that she had been brought up as a prince and, throughout her life, she expressed an aversion to wearing women's clothes. The French ambassador in Sweden, Pierre Chanut, stated: "... if any stranger saw her out hunting, wearing a masculine type of coat with a small man's collar, he would never have imagined that she was the Queen" (qtd. in Masson 115). She would become the subject of many literary works, particularly poetry and theater, during her lifetime and afterwards.[6] Christina abdicated in 1654 and publicly converted and professed at Innsbruck in 1655. There is strong evidence that her conversion was influenced by the Spanish crown, particularly through its ambassador in Sweden, don Antonio de Pimentel. Contemporary accounts tell us that Christina had been impressed with the ambassador's diplomatic skills and dashing military bearing (Lundelius 232). Incidentally, Hollywood would exploit this account in the 1933 Rouben Mamoulian film *Queen Christina*, in which Pimentel (played by John Gilbert) and Christina (Greta Garbo) are depicted as lovers.[7] It is not likely that there was a sentimental relationship between these two personages, but what is clear, as stated before, is that Christina's sympathies toward the Catholic cause and her eventual conversion made her a singularly compelling figure in Spain's political imaginary.

All the political players in Europe were interested in controlling her image as well. The papacy, for example, actively promoted her as the most powerful Protestant monarch who had nonetheless recognized the superior authority of the Catholic Church (San Juan 35). It is no wonder that shortly after commissioning Bourdon's portrait, Philip IV also asked Calderón de la Barca to write an *auto sacramental, La protestación de la fe* [The Declaration of Faith] (1656) celebrating her conversion. As the critic Henk Oostendorp states: "la transición de Cristina del luteranismo hacia el catolicismo se convierte en el prototipo de la victoria definitiva de lo bueno sobre lo malo al final del mundo [Christina's transition from Lutheranism to Catholicism would become a prototype for the definitive victory of good over evil at the end of the world]" (249). It was a story, then, tailor-made for the proselytizing, allegorical aesthetic of the *auto*; and indeed, in *La protestación*, Calderón presents the queen first as the representative of heresy who, nevertheless, embraces the true religion and accepts the Eucharist at the end. It is a testament to the volatile religious and political climate of the time that Calderón's *auto* was never actually staged. Indeed, Philip IV himself prohibited the *auto* from being performed, apparently angry and frustrated by Christina, who, allying herself with

---

[6] In Spain, Bances Candamo's play *¿Quién es quien premia al amor?* was written and performed at the end of the sixteenth century. I will consider this play briefly at the end of this chapter, but for a more detailed comparison between Bances Candamo and Calderón de la Barca, see Ann L. Mackenzie, "Dos comedias tratando de la reina Cristina de Suecia: *Afectos de odio y amor* por Calderón y *Quien es quien premia al amor* por Bances Candamo," in *Hacia Calderón*, IV Coloquio Anglogermano (Berlin: Walter de Gruyter, 1979), 56–70. Almost two centuries later, the English poet Robert Browning wrote the poem "Cristina and Monaldeschi" (1883) about a purported love affair in France between the queen and the Marquis of Monaldeschi.

[7] According to her biographers, Christina was indeed very attached to Pimentel. Buckley tells us, for example, that "Christina's ... conspicuous inclusion of Pimentel at every last court occasion, and her myriad attempts to arrange personal meetings with him, led many people to believe that the two were lovers" (147).

France, scorned his attempt to manipulate her situation in order to garner greater political power in Europe. Within two years after writing the auto sacramental, however, Calderón wrote a *comedia* entitled *Afectos de odio y amor* [The Emotions of Hate and Love], also clearly inspired by the Swedish queen.[8] One has to wonder whether the title of the play isn't Calderón's ironic commentary on the fluctuating affections of Philip toward Christina.

Afectos de odio y amor is a difficult play to categorize and a challenge to summarize. It has been called a *comedia novelesca*, but it might also just as easily be considered a quasi-historical play, since it was clearly inspired by the story of a contemporary monarch. Through the slightly masked names of Cristerna for Cristina and Süevia for Suecia (Sweden), Calderón announces the historical source and simultaneously fictionalizes it. There are also several elements in the play that are historically accurate: for example, Cristerna takes over the throne after the death in battle of her father, Adolfo. This parallels Christina's historical succession to the Swedish throne upon Gustavus Adolphus's death in the Battle of Lützen in 1632 against Spanish forces. Also, the rivalry between the fictional Süevia and Rusia that is the background to the action of the play parallels the real tensions between Sweden and the surrounding kingdoms in the second half of the seventeenth century. Throughout the play, there are other historically accurate references, but it is in the differences that the real interest of the play lies, particularly in the transformation effected on the figure of the Swedish queen.

Before proceeding with a detailed consideration of *Afectos de odio y amor*, it would be useful to briefly compare Calderón's *comedias palaciegas* with royal portraiture in general. Both are visual forms that share a deliberate concern with producing a public image of royal power. According to Roy Strong, in early modern Europe, "Portraiture was one aspect of [the] massive expansion of the Idea of Monarchy, involving the dissemination of the ruler's image in paint, stone, print, and metal throughout the realm on a scale unheard of since Classical antiquity."[9] Louis Montrose has said that in early modern Europe, "the monarchical state was given iconic form in the royal portrait" ("Elizabeth through the Looking Glass" 61). Theater, too, as we have seen, often had the function of making a ruler and his power visible to his subjects. Although the *comedia* is not merely a tool of propaganda, in the hands of a court playwright and *homo strategicus*, it necessarily contributed to the promotion of the monarchy as the optimal—indeed,

---

[8] *Afectos* was clearly a popular play at the court during the second half of the seventeenth century. It was staged for the first time at the Palacio del Buen Retiro in March 1658, and it was subsequently shown in the court—either at the Alcázar or the Buen Retiro Palace—on the following dates: May 1675, January 1680, April 1684, 1687, March and December of 1693, October 1695, and, finally, April 1696.

[9] Strong is, of course, specifically referring to Elizabeth I, who, as we know, repeatedly manipulated her image through commissioned portraits. See Strong's *Gloriana. The Portraits of Queen Elizabeth I* (London: Pimlico, 1987), 12.

the only viable—form of government. Both portraits and plays—many directly commissioned by the Habsburg Court—are responsible for duplicating power and for providing versions of monarchy and, in passing, also versions of appropriate gender roles.

At the same time, the presentation of the queenly body in the *comedia* is, for the most part, radically different from what we find in portraiture. The portraits tended to present a double spectacle—one that was meant to convey both awe and inaccessibility—and we discover in them highly conventional and stylized poses and gestures: the subjects are frozen in time and there is little emotion displayed. In the performances of the *comedias*, on the other hand, there was constant movement, fluidity, and even accessibility. There is nothing static in the presentation of Semíramis in *La hija del aire*, for example, as we saw in a previous chapter. The protagonist seems to be in perpetual motion, changing identities and costumes. In terms of emotions, another very clear difference is suggested by the very title of the play under consideration: *Afectos de odio y amor*. Passions, movement, agency— all in theory proscribed to women and to real queens, for that matter—are mediated in performance through the bodies of real actresses, considered by the enemies of the theater as public women in all the negative connotations of the term. We remember that Juan Bautista Fragoso, for example, stated that:

> En las comedias escritas en nuestra vulgar se mezclan muchas cosa impúdicas y obscenas, porque se introducen mujeres de no mucha edad á danzar y cantar, las cuales con su garbo y movimiento y con la desenvoltura de su semblante introducen en los que las ven y oyen el amor torpe."
> [In the plays written in our vernacular many shameful and obscene things are mixed together, for very young women are introduced dancing and singing and they, through their lively movements and with the shamelessness of their faces, introduce impure love in all who see them and hear them. (Cotarelo y Mori 320)

The emphasis in Fragoso's words is on movement and appearance ("garbo"). Unlike the heavy, ostentatious gowns that hide the Habsburg queens' bodies in the paintings discussed at the beginning of the chapter, the costumes worn by actresses playing monarchs were at times meant precisely to emphasize their body natural. Theatrical costumes in general would provide a visual code that signified status and gender, but both status and gender would have been fluid constructs, constantly problematized in the *comedia*.

Queens on the seventeenth-century Spanish stage are often given a remarkable range of disguises. Semíramis in *La hija del aire*, Cenobia, and Cristerna in *Afectos de odio y amor* appear in costumes ranging from animal skins, to manly dress, to full military armor. Their masculine costumes are not unlike what we see in Bourdon's portrait of Queen Christina, in that they make the queen's womanly body, her limbs, and so on, visible to the audience. Critics of the *comedia* often cited these "mujeres vestidas de hombre" as particularly offensive to respectability. Ironically, the manly garb emphasized their status as objects of desire by revealing the contours of their feminine bodies to the admiring public. Furthermore, these fictional characters are often described as participating in manly activities, duels, battles, and of course, riding on or being thrown from wild horses (the appearance of horses on the stage would have been difficult but was not unheard of). The most famous example of the latter is, of course, Rosaura, who in the opening lines of *La vida es sueño* curses the "hipogrifo violento" that has thrown her (off stage) from the saddle. In *La hija del aire*, as we saw in Chapter 3, Semíramis displays her courage by saving King Nino from a horse that has gone out of control. This action leads another character to call her a "marimacha," underscoring the hybrid of masculine and feminine characteristics that she embodies. No wonder Marcelino Menéndez Pelayo, as indicated in the quote that begins this chapter, once claimed that "Calderón's ladies always have something mannish about them."

In *Afectos de odio y amor*, we first learn about Cristerna from Casimiro, the Duke of Russia, who is in a state of deep melancholy because he has fallen in love with his enemy, the queen herself. He tells us that the first time he saw Cristerna was during a battle, when another rider and his horse fell dead before her. Although it is not made explicit in the text, the implication is that she, too, was on a horse when the dead rider collapsed. In a later scene another raging battle is described, with Cristerna in the thick of the action and in mortal danger. Casimiro saves her and urges her to ride a horse to safety. Unlike the unmoving queens of the equestrian portraits, enclosed in their elaborate gowns and riding decorously on their elegantly prancing horses, Semíramis in *La hija* and Cristerna in *Afectos* are shown as warriors, symbolically subduing a horse in one instance and about to mount another one in a later scene.

Cristerna would seem to be the embodiment of the *mujer varonil*, a type Calderón had used many times before but had never based on a real person. As Melveena McKendrick suggests, it is almost as if the real Queen Christina had been born to prove that the popular *mujer varonil* and its multiple manifestation in the *comedia* was not merely a figment of theatrical imagination (*Woman and Society* 294–5). In addition, Cristerna also represents another feminine *comedia* type: the *mujer esquiva*. Indeed, the play follows the same sequence of events that we find in so many *comedias de enredo*: it begins with a chaotic *mujer esquiva* who refuses all suitors but gradually learns to love and ultimately accepts marriage. Lundelius notes that there are also elements taken from the ballad tradition, notably the story of the Cid and Jimena, in Casimiro's duel with and eventual slaying of Cristerna's father. Cristerna, like Jimena, is a woman put in the thorny if familiar situation of having to choose between family honor and true love (Lundelius 235). It is not surprising that immediately after the Swedish queen's conversion, and in keeping with Philip's original political designs, Calderón would have wanted to associate her with the story of El Cid, one of the founding myths of the Spanish nation.

In *Afectos de odio y amor*, Calderón reprises the association between women and chaotic nature that we encountered before in *La hija del aire*, for example, but with a twist. Early in the play, she is portrayed as a fierce huntress, at home even in the most inhospitable forest. Her prowess in the hunt contributes to her arrogance, as Casimiro declares:

Es Cristerna tan altiva
que la sobra la belleza.
¡Mira si la sobra poco
para ser vana y soberbia!
Desde su primera infancia,
no hubo en la inculta maleza
de los montes, en la vaga
región de los aires, fiera
ni ave que su piel redima
ni que su pluma defienda,
sin registrar unas y otras
en el dintel de sus puertas,
ya desplumadas las alas
ya destroncadas las testas.
[Cristerna is so lofty that she doesn't really need her beauty. Indeed, she needs very little to be vain and proud! Since her early infancy, there was no beast in the wildest thicket of the hills nor bird in the highest regions of the skies, able to safeguard its skin or plumage, ultimately ending up as trophies over her doors once feathers had been removed from wings and the heads from the trunks.] (1755b–1756a)[10]

Thus, Cristerna is someone initially associated with unruly nature but, at the same time, someone who can dominate this unruliness. As a *mujer varonil*, she appears specifically as a warrior ("nueva Tomiris" and "Floripes nueva") described in military garb (1757a). Like Semíramis in *La hija del aire*, the duality of her nature is further expressed by comparing her to "Palas y Venus / ... tomando de una la ira / y de otra la belleza [Pallas Athena and Venus ... taking from one the fury and from the other the beauty]" (1757b). These are all allusions to a genealogy of powerful women taken from classical sources. Cristerna herself compares her military prowess to that of classical models:

¿No vió Roma en sus estrados,
no vió Grecia en sus campañas
mujeres alegar leyes,
mujeres vencer batallas?
[Did not Rome see in its tribunals, and did not Greece see in its battlefields, women practicing law and women conquering in battles?] (1760a)

Like the real Queen Christina, who was a great admirer of Alexander the Great and Julius Caesar—indeed, Bourdon's portrait may well have been inspired by paintings and statues of Alexander[11]—Cristerna in the play specifically compares herself to the Roman emperor (as both leader and chronicler of his exploits):

---

[10] I am using Ángel Valbuena Briones's edition in *Obras completas: Comedias*, vol. 2 (Madrid: Aguilar, 1956), 1747–1794. Because this version does not contain verse numbers, I am providing the page and the column (a or b) in which the quotes appear.

[11] See Danielsson's "Sébastien Bourdon's Equestrian Portrait of Queen Christina of Sweden" for a detailed discussion of the sources and symbolic implications of the portrait.

> Que si de noche escribía
> César lo que de día obraba
> Yo, mientras el día no acaba,
> Aun no he de perder el día.
> [For if Caesar wrote at night about his daytime deeds, why shouldn't I take advantage of the day as well since it is still light?] (1759b)

Cristerna's military prowess is established several times in the play through elaborate detailed descriptions, as we see early on when Casimiro describes her in full military gear:

> traía
> sobre las doradas trenzas
> sola una media celada,
> a la borgoñota puesta;
> una hungarina casaca
> en dos mitades abierta,
> de acero el pecho vestido
> mostraba, de cuya tela
> un tonelete,
> que pasaba de media pierna,
> dejaba libre el batido
> de la bota y de la espuela.
> [Atop her golden braids, she wore only a sallet (a half helmet) worn in the Burgundian style (a bourgonet), a Hungarian cape or cassock, opened in two halves, showing a breast covered in steel and an overskirt whose cloth did not fall below mid-leg, leaving unencumbered the boot and the spur.] (1757a)

The description is preceded by the words "Oh, quien supiera pintarla [Oh, who could have the talent to paint her]" (1757a), and it is possible, as Lundelius suggests, that here Calderón may in fact have been ekphrastically describing yet another portrait of Christina. For one thing, Casimiro's verbal portrayal corresponds to a painting in the king's possession, described by Barrionuevo: "Al Rey [Cristina] le ha enviado su retrato: está armada, de medio cuerpo arriba, gallardísimo el talle, hermosa cara, ojos vivos y rasgados ... Sabe le arte militar tan bien como el general más experto [(Christina) has sent the king her portrait; she is armed on the upper half of her body, her bearing is gallant, beautiful face, bright almond-shaped eyes ... Her knowledge of military arts is as good as that of the most experienced of generals]" (*Avisos* I. 237). When Cristerna first appears in the play, she is still in full military regalia and is accompanied by a detachment of warrior women, as the stage directions make clear: "*Cajas y trompetas, y salgan las mujeres que puedan, todas con plumas y espadas, y detrás CRISTERNA, con bengala* [Drums and trumpets; as many women as possible appear, all wearing plumes and swords, and behind them CRISTERNA with a military baton]" (1759a).

In addition to her legendary military prowess, Queen Christina was considered an able legislator and ruler, and also a woman who possessed a remarkable intellect.

Indeed, she became a protector of Descartes and gathered in her court some of the best minds in Europe.[12] Later, when she found herself in Rome, in self-imposed exile, she presided over famous literary academies. Barrionuevo tells us that she not only speaks 11 languages but is also "estudiosísima en todas ciencias, y tan viva y presta, que con ser un azogue, es todo un oro [very erudite in all the sciences; and so sharp and quick, that being quicksilver, she is all gold]" (I. 237). While Cristerna in the play is most prominently associated with the warrior queen figure, she also embodies the characteristics of two other feminine *comedia* types: *la erudita* and *la esquiva*, as Henk Oostendorp has pointed out (249). Calderón had alluded to the historical queen's love of learning in the *auto La protestación de la fe*, when the allegorical character Sabiduría calls her "docta, / desde su niñez, se emplea / en los sutiles estudios / de la gran religión nuestra [learned since childhood, she is dedicated to studying the subtleties of our great religion]" (*Obras completas* 3, 734a). In *Afectos de odio y amor*, the fictional Cristerna equates the ability to lead with the ability to learn, and certainly the education of women is one of the subtexts of the play:

> Quiero empezar a mostrar
> si tiene o no la mujer
> ingenio para aprender,
> juicio para gobernar
> y valor para lidiar.
> [I want to begin to demonstrate whether or not a woman has the intelligence to learn, the wisdom to govern and the courage to do battle.] (1750b)

In this passage, learning is placed on equal terms with military strength and political savvy. She requires her ladies-in-waiting to don "plumas y espadas"[13] and is herself, like Semíramis, able to traverse easily back and forth from the sword to the pen: "me ha de ver tomando, ahora / la espada, y ahora la pluma [they will see me using now the sword and now the quill]" (1759b). In this fashion, the Renaissance masculine ideal of "las armas y las letras" would seem to be ostentatiously applied to a woman. Both the historical Christina and the fictional Cristerna represent women who lay vigorous claim to the purportedly masculine attribute of *ingenio*. Huarte de San Juan had stated categorically that:

> las hembras, por razón de frialdad y humidad de su sexo, no pueden alcanzar ingenio profundo. Sólo vemos que hablan con alguna apariencia de habilidad en materias livianas y fáciles, con términos comunes y muy estudiados; pero

---

[12] Alas, she would also come to be known as the queen who inadvertently caused the death of the French philosopher by insisting that he meet with her for tutoring sessions in the early morning in the palace's unheated chambers. The author of *Discourse on the Method* died in Sweden in 1650 of complications from pneumonia.

[13] While "plumas" here can mean "feathers" in addition to "pens," the verses just quoted appear immediately afterward, and it would be equally valid to imagine these ladies carrying quills as well as plumes.

metidas en letras, no pueden aprender más que un poco latín, y esto por ser obra de la memoria.
[Women for reason of their cold humor and the humidity of their sex, cannot achieve any profound wisdom or ingenuity. We see that they can speak with some appearance of ability on trifling and easy matters, with simple and much used terms; but when they delve in letters, they can only learn a little Latin, and this only through memorization.] (388)

The fictional women of the *comedia*, particularly the ones considered in this study—Cenobia, Catalina de Aragón, Semíramis, Irene, and Cristerna—all theatrically prove this assertion wrong.

The scenes where Cristerna presents herself as a robust defender of the rights of women must have been striking to seventeenth-century audiences, and are gratifying to modern readers as well. In a memorable scene, she has Lesbia, one of her ladies-in-waiting, read the new laws she is instituting from a book titled "Nuevas leyes, que Cristerna, / reina de Süevia, manda / promulgar en sus Estados [The new laws, that Cristerna, Queen of Suevia, commands be promulgated in her realms] (1759b). To begin with, the queen repudiates the Salic laws that denied women access to power and invokes in the process some powerful maternal imagery:[14]

> Se dé por traidor a toda
> la naturaleza humana
> el primer legislador
> que aborreció las entrañas
> tanto en que anduvo, que quiso
> del mayor amor privarlas.
> [Traitor to humanity is the label that shall be given to the first legislator who loathed the womb that bore him so strongly that he tried to deprive women of the greatest honors.] (1759b)

Furthermore, she insists that women have equal access to the public sphere beyond that of military action, and again forcefully blames men for keeping women in subservient positions:

> Y porque vean
> los hombres que si se atrasan
> las mujeres en valor
> e ingenio ellos son las causa,
> pues ellos son quien las quitan
> de miedo libros y espadas,

---

[14] It is not clear why Calderón makes a point about the Salic laws, since they were not in effect in most of Europe. According to Henry Kamen, "[t]he only western state that insisted on applying principles of male dynastic power (the so-called Salic law) was France, where ironically, women dominated the political scene for the best part of the century." See *Early Modern European Society* (London: Routledge, 2000), 172.

dispone que la mujer
que se aplicare, inclinada
al estudio de las letras
o al manejo de las armas
sea admitida a los puestos
públicos, siendo en su patria
capaz del honor que en guerra
y paz mas al hombre ensalza.
[And so that men may understand that they themselves are to blame if women fall behind in courage and wit, for they are the ones who, out of fear, deny them books and swords, (the law) proclaims that any woman who wishes to pursue the study of letters or the deployment of arms, be admitted to public office, so that she may prove herself capable of earning the honors that in war and peace are granted to man.] (1760a)

This speech is strongly reminiscent of other proto-feminist manifestos, notably the ones written by women authors such as Sor Juana Inés de la Cruz in *La Respuesta* and Maria de Zayas. In the prologue "Al que leyere" to the *Novelas amorosas y ejemplares*, Zayas uses similar language in blaming men for holding back women's intellectual achievements:

¿qué razón hay para que ellos sean sabios y presuman que nosotras no podemos serlo? Esto no tiene a mi parecer más respuesta que su impiedad o tiranía en encerrarnos, y no darnos maestros; y así, la verdadera causa de no ser las mujeres doctas no es defecto del caudal, sino falta de aplicación, porque si en nuestra crianza ... nos dieran libros y preceptores, fuéramos tan aptas para los puestos y para las cátedras como los hombres, y quizá más agudas por ser de natural más frío, por consistir en humedad el entendimiento ...
[What other reason can there be for (men) to be wise and to presume that we cannot be so? This has only one answer, in my opinion, and that is their cruelty or tyranny in keeping us enclosed and not giving us teachers; and so, the real reason why woman are not learned is not a defect in our intellect but the lack of opportunity to use it. If in our upbringing ... they gave us tutors and books, we would be as adept in any profession or academic position as any man, and perhaps even sharper since we are naturally of a colder temperament, and intelligence is of a damp humor ...] (48)

Zayas also states that "las almas ni son hombres ni mujeres [souls are neither men nor women]" (48); and in the play, Cristerna echoes this emphasis on the fundamental equality of the sexes: "ser valientes y ser sabias / es acción del alma, y no es / hombre ni mujer el alma [being brave and wise is an action that belongs to the soul and the soul is neither a man nor a woman]" (1760a).

Lundelius rightly asserts that in the portrayal of Cristerna, and especially in the scene where she enacts her new legislation, Calderón seems to be proposing a feminist utopia (239). There is nothing to suggest that this depiction is a parody, despite the fact that such an idealized feminist scenario would have been unthinkable in Calderón's time. One has to wonder what the audience's reaction—

particularly among the ladies of the court—might have been to this staging of women's emancipation. A clue may be found in the following assessment of the play in a catalogue that appeared in Madrid in the early eighteenth century: "Aunque [*Afectos de odio y amor*] ... es bastante irregular en lugar y tiempo, agrada mucho a las mujeres por la defensa que hace de ellas y las leyes que dicta a su favor [Although (the play) is quite irregular in its use of place and time, it is very pleasing to women for the defense of them that is presented and for the laws in their favor that are dictated]."[15] Another of the laws that Cristerna institutes merits particular attention, for it addresses the concern with honor that is said to characterize Spanish society at the time: "que se borren / duelos, que notan de infamia / al marido que sin culpa / desdichado es por desgracia [Let duels be abolished, for they mark with infamy the blameless husband who is unfortunate (to have an unfaithful wife)]." Cristerna's prohibition of duels is a remarkable proposition, since dueling was one of the preferred and more blatant performances of masculine honor presented in the *comedia*. Male characters, particularly in the type of play designated as "de capa y espada [cloak and dagger]," repeatedly enacted these rehearsals of masculine preeminence and honor. Through the prohibition of this act, Lundelius suggests, Cristerna challenges the code of behavior that assumed that all women had to be watched and protected in order to sustain family honor.[16] Alas, the enlightened views attributed to Christina's dramatic double by Calderón unfortunately had no basis in history. The Swedish queen herself claimed to despise women and, surprisingly, had very little interest in promoting their rights.

---

[15] This is cited by María Remedios Prieto in "Reaparición en el siglo XVIII del auto sacramental de Calderón *La protestación de la fe* y polémica que originó," *II Simposio sobre el P. Feijoo y su siglo*, vol. 2 (Oviedo: Centros de Estudios del S. XVIII), 559. According to Prieto, the play continued to enjoy popularity more than 100 years after it was written: "De sus puestas en escena tenemos noticias. La famosísima María Ladvenant, al frente de su compañía, la representó el 29 de abril de 1763 y el 5 de diciembre de 1764, ambas en el teatro de la Cruz ... Seguramente que gustaría al vulgo bullicioso, aunque no a los ilustrados ni a los neoclásicos ... [We have information on its staging. The very famous (actress) María Ladvenant, leading her company, staged it on April 29, 1763, and on December 5, 1764, both in the Cruz Theater ... it no doubt pleased the raucous crowd, although not the learned and neoclassical members of the audience]" (558).

[16] While I agree in principle with Lundelius that the play represents a challenge to the code of honor, her portrayal of the obsession with honor in Spanish society at the time is somewhat overstated: "The entire honor complex worked to the disadvantage of women. For having over-sheltered their women, men had no alternative but to exercise a repressive supervision over their women folk. In an obsessively macho society of don Juans, where prestige was garnered by "scoring" on another man's honor, this sequestering of women simply turned every woman into a temptation, every stranger into a threat, and every husband into a paranoid judge. The merest happenstance of suspicion could turn deadly ..." (242). The work of historians and critics has helped us understand that the honor code was not as inflexible as previously thought. Two recent books are particularly helpful in this regard: Renato Barahona's *Sex Crimes, Honour, and the Law in Early Modern Spain* (U of Toronto P, 2003) and Scott Taylor's *Honor and Violence in Golden Age Spain* (New Haven: Yale UP, 2008).

Robert ter Horst, in his astute interpretation of the play, states that if Cristerna's laws—the establishing of total equality between the sexes, the ban on duels and love matches between a man and a woman of unequal social stature, the lessening of society's obsession with women's honor—were to be implemented, "the whole subject matter of [Calderón's] art [would be] in danger of disappearing" (40). Indeed, duels, honor, and what ter Horst calls the "romantic intrigue that is an essential narrative part of most of Calderón's non-allegorical plays" (42) would be rendered meaningless, and the play itself seems to promote its own obsolescence. Calderón was perhaps the most self-conscious and self-referential of early modern Spanish playwrights—often his characters make comments such as "¿Es comedia de don Pedro / Calderón, donde ha de haber / por fuerza amante escondido / o rebozada mujer [Is this a play by don Pedro Calderón where there is to be perforce a hidden suitor and a veiled woman]?"[17]—and the metadramatic ironic twist implied in Cristerna's legislation would be in keeping with an aesthetic that self-consciously comments on social and dramatic conventions.

Above all, *Afectos de odio y amor*, like the plays already considered, is a complex and even paradoxical meditation on power and monarchy. Calderón, as I have argued, was a *homo strategicus* who accepted the institution of monarchy without question, but who at the same time felt compelled to offer repeated representations of failed kingship. *Afectos de odio y amor* is no exception, and Calderón provides us with a double performance of leadership, a binary spectacle of good and failed kingship ultimately intertwined with considerations of gender. While there is no doubt that Cristerna is the most compelling character of the play, there is much to suggest that Casimiro, the Russian prince, is also the embodiment of an important political message of the play. He is the first important character we encounter and it is through him that we first learn of Cristerna. That he, and not Cristerna, is meant to be the bearer of the play's message is illustrated by the following summary of the plot that appeared in the journal *El Censor* in 1763: "Comedia de las más acreditadas ... en la que *se presenta como modelo a un príncipe*, que enamorado de una princesa, con quien se halla en guerra, no como quiera, abandona sus vasallos ... haciendo lo que sería un delito capital en el más ínfimo soldado [one of the most celebrated *comedias* ... in which as an example, we see a prince who, in love with a princess against whom he is warring, without much thought, abandons his vassals ... committing what would be a capital crime in the most humble of soldiers]" (qtd. in Prieto 559, emphasis added). As in *La gran Cenobia*, with its foregrounding of Aureliano at the beginning of the play, and as in the title of Ana Caro y Mallén's *El conde Partinuplés*,[18] there is often

---

[17] This quote is from the second act of *No hay burlas con el amor*, in *Obras completas*, ed. Angel Valbuena Briones, vol. 2 (Madrid: Aguilar, 1959), 512b.

[18] According to Teresa Soufas, "Considering Ana Caro's play *El conde Partinuplés* ... one notes that even though the playwright imagines for her cast of characters a realm presided over by a female monarch, the drama is not named for her but carries instead the title of the male protagonist." See *Dramas of Distinction: a Study of Plays by Golden Age Women* (Lexington: UP of Kentucky, 1997), 46. I will comment briefly on this play in the Epilogue.

in the *comedia* a shifting of interest toward the male protagonists despite the centrality of the female sovereign.

Casimiro is presented from the very beginning as a flawed prince, who—like other Calderonian kings, such as Enrique VIII in *La cisma de Inglaterra*, Aureliano in *La gran Cenobia*, and Nino in *La hija del aire*—has succumbed to a passion that controls him body and soul. It is tempting to see in this monarch, as Valbuena Briones suggests, a double for Philip IV,[19] and the play as the dramatization of a theme obsessively repeated in treatises from Pedro de Rivadeneyra's *Tratado del príncipe cristiano* (1595), to Juan de Mariana's *De Rege et Regis Institutione* (1599), Quevedo's *Política de Dios y gobierno de Cristo* (1625), and Pablo Martir Rizo's *Norte de principes* (1626), among others. We turn again to *Idea de un príncipe político-cristiano*, where Saavedra Fajardo includes the following warning, a variation on a theme seen before:

> En lo que mas ha menester el príncipe este cuidado es en la moderación de los afectos, gobernándolos con tal prudencia, que nada desee, espere, ame ó aborrezca con demasiado ardor y violencia llevado de la voluntad y no de la razón. Los deseos de los particulares fácilmente se pueden llenar, los de los príncipes no.
> [The prince must take particular care in moderating his passions, governing them with prudence ... let him not desire, hope, love, or hate anything with too much ardor or violence, allowing himself to be guided by will rather than reason. The desires of individuals can easily be fulfilled, not so those of princes.] (104)

The very title of the play announces its preoccupations with the passions. In the portrayal of Casimiro, Calderón stages an extreme case of a monarch whose inability to govern his *afectos* or passions has put his nation in dire peril. Unlike Aureliano in *La gran Cenobia* or Constantino in Tirso's *La república al revés*, Casimiro is not a tyrannical figure, but he is like Constantino and Enrique VIII in that he is too weak to resist his passions. He starts out as a melancholy ruler, depicted in the very first scene with his eyes hidden as a visual representation of his metaphorical blindness: "*Corre una cortina y vese CASIMIRO sentado, con un pañuelo en los ojos* [a curtain opens and Casimiro is seen with a handkerchief over his eyes]" (1753a). One of his courtiers describes him as "siempre encerrado, ni habla, / ni ve, ni escucha, ni alienta [always behind closed doors, he neither speaks, nor looks, nor listens, nor breathes]" (1753a). Recent literary criticism has turned its attention to the question of the emotions in early modern literature.[20] The *comedia* and moral treatises share very similar rhetoric on the question of emotions and the deleterious effects they have on those who are in power.

---

[19] See Valbuena Briones's introduction to the play in *Obras completas*, vol. 2, 1751.

[20] See, for example, the recent collection of essays, *Reading the Early Modern Passions: Essays in the Cultural History of Emotions*, ed. Gail Kern Paster, Katherine Rowe, and Mary Floyd-Wilson (Philadelphia: U of Pennsylvania P, 2004).

Casimiro describes his feelings for Cristerna in typically overwrought language, for example, when he refers to "el volcán del pecho [the volcano in my breast]" and "del alma el Etna [the Etna of my soul]" to describe his desire for Cristerna. His melancholy has rendered him passive and almost feminine in his behavior; and his sister Auristela is forced to remind Casimiro repeatedly of his princely responsibilities. She alludes to bellic myths and symbols of masculinity; and in passing, she also invokes equestrian terminology to refer to the control of his kingdom:

> … Siendo en tu primera
> cuna, tus gorjeos las cajas,
> tus arrullos las trompetas
> creciste tan invencible
> hijo de Marte, que apenas
> pudiste, ocupando el fuste
> tomar el tiento a la rienda,
> ni la noticia al estribo,
> cuando, calzada la espuela,
> trenzado el arnés, el asta
> blandida, empezaste, en muestra
> de que eras rayo oprimido
> a herir con mayor violencia …
> [In your cradle, your gurgles were drums, your lullabies were trumpets, and so you grew to be the invincible son of Mars. And, as soon as you were able to grip the staff, get a feel for the reins, reach the stirrup, wear the spur, ready the harness, and brandish the lance, you began like muted thunder to show that you could unleash the most violent damage (in war)]. (1754b)

Casimiro has dropped the reins of leadership and this irresponsible behavior eventually leads him to do the unthinkable and abandon his kingdom. Disguising himself (significantly) as a *Spanish* "soldado de fortuna"—basically a mercenary soldier—he travels to Süevia and offers his services to Cristerna in the fight against his own country. This is a scandalous depiction of a prince who has forsaken all responsibility and betrayed his sacred duty to his people. Furthermore, assuming a lowly identity is a serious betrayal of the royal persona. Although one *arbitrista* once suggested metaphorically that the monarch "en verdad mercenario de sus vasallos es [is in reality a mercenary to his vassals]" (qtd. in Lisón Tolosana 68), treatises in the sixteenth and seventeenth centuries repeatedly emphasized the importance of maintaining dignity and majesty. The king must never be mistaken for a vassal, as Saavedra Fajardo, among others, advises: "Si no se conserva lo augusto de la Majestad, no habrá diferencia entre el príncipe y el vasallo [If he does not conserve what is august in his majesty, there will be no difference between him and a vassal]" (*Idea* 99). Casimiro is deliberately erasing any difference between himself and any ordinary suitor. In fact, he has renounced his identity and his authority to such an extent that he does not even bother to assume a new name and asks to be known only as "soldado," leading the *gracioso* to address him at one point as "Don Soldado." This is an instance of extreme abjection, completely unbecoming in a monarch. Once again, as we saw in the discussion of *La hija del aire*, theatricality in the sense of excessive role-playing is associated with inauthenticity and the inability to rule effectively.

To compensate for the vacuum of power once Casimiro rejects his responsibility as prince, his sister Auristela is forced to assume the leadership of a military expedition against Cristerna (and, indirectly, against her own brother). There is, then, more than one *mujer varonil* in this play to compensate for the failures of masculine leadership. As he does in *La gran Cenobia* and *La hija del aire*, Calderón implies that in the absence of strong masculine power, the rule of women becomes a necessity. Both Auristela and Cristerna seem to provide, by contrast to Casimiro, examples of wise and decisive leadership; and it is tempting to think that Calderón is here suggesting that women are better rulers. Auristela is brave and resolute, a worthy opponent to the equally heroic Cristerna. However, the final message of the play is, not surprisingly, more complex and ambivalent toward the rule of women than might at first seem apparent. As stated before, Cristerna embodies simultaneously several dramatic types, and one of them is that of the *mujer esquiva*. This was a popular feminine character in the *comedia*, the woman who adamantly refuses love and marriage. This defining quirk of Cristerna's character is described in the following passage:

> No solo, pues, de Diana
> en la venatoria escuela
> discípula creció; pero
> aun en la altivez severa
> con que de Venus y Amor
> el blando yugo desprecia.
> No tiene príncipe el Norte
> que no la idolatre bella,
> ni príncipe tiene que
> sus esquiveces no sienta,
> diciendo que ha de quitar,
> sin que a sujetarse venga,
> del mundo el infame abuso
> de que las mujeres sean
> acostumbradas vasallas
> del hombre, y que ha de ponerlas
> en el absoluto imperio
> de las armas y las letras. (1756a)

[Not only did she grow to be Diana's disciple in the art of hunting, but even more in the unyielding arrogance with which she disdains Venus's and Cupid's soft yoke. There is no Northern prince who does not idolize her beauty nor feel her scorn, since she claims that, by never marrying, she will avenge and disabuse the world of the notion that women are the common vassals of men; and furthermore, she will place women in absolute command of arms and letters both.] (1756a)

Her association throughout the play with the goddess Diana underscores symbolically her chastity and refusal of men, in addition to emphasizing her skills as a huntress. Cristerna's *esquivez* is also dramatized through the enactment of a law forbidding marriages between people belonging to different social classes, even when based on love. Cristerna's refusal to be confined within the convention of marriage—"nunca al matrimonio di plática [I never gave matrimony much credence]" (1758a)—is presented as unnatural, and her *esquivez* has dire consequences for her kingdom. Thus, in the ideology of the play, she too, like Casimiro, starts out to be a failed monarch. The rule of a woman who refuses to marry not only makes the country more vulnerable to attacks from foreign powers; but also, by denying her function as a reproductive body, she is endangering the stabilizing principle of inherited monarchy. The queen's body, as discussed previously, had a primary importance as the vessel that could guarantee an heir to the throne and a continuation of the dynasty. Cristerna ultimately relents in her *esquivez* only because her desire to avenge her father's death becomes more powerful than her aversion to matrimony. She announces that she will marry the person who either kills or captures Casimiro. Ultimately, in a typical Calderonian twist, her disdain of men is punished when she falls in love with a man—the disguised Casimiro himself—who not only seems to be a lowly soldier but who will turn out to be the man responsible for Adolfo's death.

The depiction of Cristerna's *esquivez* was, no doubt, directly inspired by Christina, the "living" queen who was notorious for spurning powerful suitors. Indeed, when she abdicated the throne, the Swedish court cited her unwillingness to marry and to provide a legitimate heir to the throne as a reason.[21] The real-life drama of Christina would become a cautionary example of the dangers of independence and notoriety for women, even when they are powerful. For one thing, she began to be seen as an uncontrolled entity whose currency as a possible conjugal and reproductive body became politically explosive. At one point, she was considered a potential wife for Philip IV, setting off waves of alarm among Spain's enemies. The frequent exchange of portraits—equestrian or otherwise—between the Swedish and Spanish monarchs was quite likely an indication that there was indeed a courtship, since this type of exchange was often a mechanism for promoting unions between the royal houses of Europe.[22] The French were particularly afraid of a potential marital alliance with Spain and decided to wage a propaganda war against her by distributing pamphlets accusing Christina of promiscuity, lesbianism, hermaphroditism, and atheism (San Juan 20). Across the channel in England, Oliver Cromwell was so fearful that Christina would marry yet another monarch, the exiled Charles II, that he had her put under surveillance

---

[21] Queen Christina's reasons for abdicating have been a source of controversy. She herself claimed, perhaps disingenuously, that it was the mark of a good ruler to abdicate.

[22] Portraits played an important role in marriage negotiations in medieval and early modern Spain, as studied by—among others—Laura Bass in *Drama of the Portrait* and Miguel Falomir Faus's "Sobre los orígenes del retrato."

(San Juan 35). Cromwell's foreign secretary went so far as to state: "We hear stories of the Queen of Sweden and her Amazonian behavior, it being believed that nature was mistaken in her, and that she was intended for a man, for in her discourse, they say she talks loud and swears notable" (Masson 220–21). Christina's penchant for self-display became a double-edged sword and she was ultimately unable to control her image. The virile behavior that made her a fascinating and even admirable figure ultimately would lead her to be perceived as a transgressive, uncontained, and therefore dangerous body.

The instability presented by this ambiguously gendered woman is the underlying text in Calderon's *Afectos de odio y amor*. It is almost as if Calderón felt compelled to rewrite and correct the real-life drama of the Swedish queen that was still unfolding. For one thing, he attenuates the sexual ambiguity attributed to the historical queen, although perhaps we may see some slight hints of this in Cristerna's refusal to marry, the establishment of a proto-feminist utopia, and the fact that one of her ladies-in-waiting is called Lesbia. Slowly and meticulously, Cristerna's proud, rebellious nature is cut down to size in the play. First of all, as we have seen, she promises to marry the person who avenges her father's death. Later, she finds herself in the humiliating situation of falling in love with the mysterious soldier of fortune who not only is intolerably inferior in status, but also turns out to be the very man against whom she has sought revenge. Not surprisingly, her ultimate downfall is prefigured in Act I by a fall from a horse; Casimiro's servant announces her entrance as "Que, herido el caballo, viene / de aquel ribazo, cayendo / una mujer [Because the horse is wounded, from that embankment, a woman is falling]" (1763b). Calderón's audience would have been trained to anticipate, in the literal fall of a character on stage, a manifestation or anticipation of a symbolic fall from grace (for example, Rosaura in *La vida es sueño* and Enrique in *El médico de su honra*). In *Afectos*, the ultimate revelation of the mercenary's true identity leads to a crisis of anguish and despair, and Cristerna—even more than Casimiro—becomes the personification of the antithesis announced in the title: odio y amor.

In a situation similar to what we saw with Isabel in Coello's *El conde de sex*, Cristerna finds herself torn between her love for the dashing soldier who had earlier saved her life and her hate for the prince who killed her father. When another prince challenges him to a duel, she is determined to pursue Casimiro as her enemy, but also, curiously, to protect him from the harm that may come from the duel:

> Que a mí me des un caballo;
> pues hallándome presente
> yo al empeño de seguirle
> y al duelo de defenderle,
> probaré entre dos afectos
> tan poderosos, tan fuertes
> como odio y amor, cuál es
> el vencido o el que vence.

[Get me a horse; because finding myself in the situation of having to both pursue him and defend him in a duel, I will be able to determine, between the powerful passions of hatred and love, which is the victor and which the vanquished.] (1791b)

As this quote suggests, hers—like Isabel's in *El conde de Sex*—is a divided self, as she pursues Casimiro as her enemy but simultaneously wishes to rescue him as the man she loves. In the last scenes of the play, the internal and external confusion reach a feverish pitch. Auristela, who has led Russia's army against Cristerna in Casimiro's absence, takes it upon herself to capture her own brother. She then appears before Cristerna, demanding that the queen honor her promise to marry the person who captures Adolfo's killer. Cristerna, perhaps realizing that Auristela's stratagem may resolve her own dilemma, agrees to give her hand in marriage to Auristela, thereby momentarily presenting the astonishing possibility of a same-sex marriage and perhaps even subtly suggesting the lesbianism attributed to the real Cristina. At this point, the gracioso exclaims mischievously:

Mas ¿qué fuera que se viese
acabar una comedia
casándose dos mujeres?
[Now, how would it be if the *comedia* ended with the marriage of two women?] (1793b)

Calderón, however, immediately diffuses this potentially scandalous situation by having Auristela claim that, now that Cristerna's hand is her possession, she is free to give it to someone else, and immediately makes a gift of Cristerna's hand to Casimiro.

... que en tanto es mía una joya,
en cuanto, si bien lo adviertes,
tengo el uso della, y puedo
dársela a quien yo quisiere.
[Because, when you think about it, as soon as a jewel belongs to me and as soon as I have use of it, I can give it to whomever I please.] (1793b)

Thus, the proud, competent, and independent queen who had refused to be enclosed in marriage becomes another woman's property—an object or *joya*—to be promptly transferred to a new, this time male, owner. The total subjugation of the transgressive body is finalized when Cristerna herself asks Lesbia to rescind the progressive laws favoring women that she had previously enacted:

... Estése
el mundo como se estaba
y sepan que las mujeres
vasallos del hombre nacen;
pues en sus afectos, siempre
que el odio y amor compiten
es el amor que vence.

[Let the world remain as it was, and let everyone understand that women are the born vassals of men because in their passions, whenever hate and love compete, love will always conquer.] (1794a)

These are Cristerna's last words, and the denouement turns out to be entirely conventional within the *comedia* tradition. The recalcitrant female body is yet again subjugated and order is, at least nominally, restored: Cristerna will marry Casimiro, and he will assume the throne. Nevertheless, this ending, while entirely predictable in dramatic terms, represents a bold ideological revision of the historical record. Calderón seems intent on providing a more palatable ending to the real-life drama of Queen Christina. As stated before, although the attitude in Spain toward the Swedish queen was initially quite positive, her image suffered an abrupt transformation when it became clear that she would not be manipulated by Philip, nor would she press her own countrymen to convert to Catholicism. Nowhere is this change of opinion more glaring than in the writings of Barrionuevo, who, as we have seen, had initially praised Christina's wisdom and prudence when she had abjured Protestantism, only to document later how her reputation had suffered among Spaniards:

Pusieron a la reina de Suecia un pasquín muy bellaco, tratándola de hipócrita, vana, loca y deshonesta con don Antonio Pimentel, su querido del alma, y otros ... Y se dice ha mandado Su Majestad se aparten de ella los españoles que la asisten. [A vulgar satire has come out about the Swedish queen, calling her hypocritical, arrogant, unbalanced, immoral in her dealings with don Antonio Pimentel, the love of her life, and with others ... And it is reported that His Majesty has ordered that the Spaniards who were part of her retinue should leave her side.] (I, 227)

In the queen's lifetime, as mentioned earlier, Christina was clearly viewed as a transgressive body.[23] Calderón's play becomes a symbolic vehicle for regulating the uncontained feminine body that Christina represented. For one thing, by emphasizing Cristerna's love for Casimiro, Calderón attenuates the sexual ambiguity that has until recently been attributed to the historical queen. Furthermore, Cristerna's marriage and acceptance of the role of obedient wife and queen consort enacts a wish-fulfillment political fantasy in which the disturbing performance of feminine power that the real Christina represented is transformed. The play follows the same sequence of events that we find in so many comic plays: the masquerades and mistaken identities all lead inexorably to the restitution of order through multiple weddings at the end. Inspired by a real figure characterized by her theatricality, it is not surprising that Calderón would choose the exaggerated conventions of the *comedia de enredo* to dramatize Cristerna's fictional story.

---

[23] Even in the twentieth century, Queen Christina's sexuality continued to be a matter of speculation. In 1965, anthropologists, historians, and anatomists had her body exhumed from its sarcophagus in St. Peter's to be examined. They measured and examined the body meticulously in an attempt to find male characteristics in her skeletal formation. Nevertheless, as San Juan puts it: "after almost three hundred years the body refused yet another attempt to fix its 'true' sexuality" (20).

Like Queen Elizabeth I, Christina of Sweden was fully aware of the importance of controlling her own image. She clearly enjoyed dramatizing herself and promoted herself through several portraits and coins, often appearing as Diana or Minerva. Her most compelling and consistent role or disguise, however, was that of a man, as Ruth Lundelius tells us: "it was as a man in language, dress, and behavior that Christina, with time, increasingly presented herself before the European world" (231). This extreme theatricality, this inauthenticity, while making her a curiosity also ultimately suggests that she was unfit to rule.

Although the *comedia* character herself would simultaneously embody different dramatic types—*mujer guerrero, mujer erudita, mujer esquiva*—the real Christina's multiple personas and unfettered theatricality is diffused and dispersed among other characters in *Afectos*. As a response to the cross-dressing, manly woman who refused marriage, Calderón offers a drama that is driven, like so many of Shakespeare's plays, for example, by a marriage plot and an affirmation of heterosexuality and subjugated femininity. By deploying the typical novelesque circumstances presented by a *comedia de enredo*, the real, recalcitrant "living" political body is made into a malleable fictive body.

We return briefly to Bourdon's equestrian portrait and a brief consideration of Calderón's earlier work, the *auto* titled *La protestación de la fe*. As stated earlier, before writing *Afectos de odio y amor*, Calderón had already appropriated the historical Christina in the *auto sacramental* by allegorizing her, in essence dehumanizing her and transforming her into a metaphor. Although in the *auto* she appears as the Queen of Sweden, she is also made to share dramatic space with "Herejía [Heresy]," "Religión [Religion]," and "Sabiduría [Wisdom]." *La protestación* dramatizes the unique and intimate relation between history, time, and allegory as elaborated by Calderón in so many of his other allegorical pieces. This is a relation grounded, according to Barbara Kurtz, in "homology, in the essential christocentrism of both history and time" (122). The historical Christina, who provided a real-life, breathing referent for the *mujer varonil*, also provided a real-life referent for this Christocentric view of history. The *auto*, for example, exploits her very name, and twice it is said that she lacks only the "a," the Alpha representing God, in order to go from "Cristina" to a true "cristiana":

> ... Cristina, que el nombre
> hoy imperfecto el nombre conserva
> de Cristiano, mal viciado
> por la falta de una letra
> (siendo la A la que falta,
> que es la Alfa en frase griega
> significación de Dios) ...
> [... Christina, who now possesses the imperfect name of a Christian, spoiled by the lack of a single letter (the A is missing and this is the Greek Alpha, which means God) ...] (*Obras completas* III, 734)

In the *auto*, Christina, the Protestant queen, whose father had been considered the enemy of Catholic Spain, is made into the embodiment of Catholic orthodoxy.

Interestingly, the equestrian portrait of Christina executed by Bourdon turns out to be strongly allegorical as well. According to Arne Danielsson, when Philip IV requested her portrait, the queen used the painting to send an embedded message signaling her intention to convert. She had already been involved in secret negotiations with the Spanish monarch, requesting help in arranging her conversion and departure from Sweden for a Catholic country, perhaps Spain. The painting is replete with symbolism. The falconer at the right was a historical figure, Mathias Palbitzki, who had been sent by Christina on diplomatic missions to Spain and France and who was privy to the queen's plans to convert. The falcon itself was a widely recognized symbol of hope for the future. The depiction of the rider steering her horse toward the sun and away from the threatening clouds represents, according to Danielsson, "Christina's path from darkness to light" (105). Most fascinating is Danielsson's interpretation of the two hunting dogs and of the unseen viewer to whom both the queen's and the falconer's gazes are directed. One of the dogs displays a large collar with the letters *L+CRS+DA*, which stands for "Legatus Christina Regina Sueciae Dominus Antonius [Envoy to Queen Christina of Sweden don Antonio]," indicating that this dog belonged to none other than Antonio Pimentel, the Spanish ambassador. According to Danielsson, Pimentel is standing just outside the frame, presumably waiting to assist Christina in her negotiations with Spain; and yet the respectful gaze and salutations of both the queen and the falconer are not ultimately directed to Pimentel or to the painter, but to someone else:

> This someone who is the object of the salutations of Christina and her falconer is not Bourdon, painting the picture, nor is it any ordinary viewer. Philip IV, and he alone, is being honored with this greeting—the Philip IV who commissioned the painting and to whom its message is directed.

Thus, Christina reverses the gaze and looks upon the monarch whom she hopes will guide her as she moves away from Protestantism and takes up the Catholic cause. Three years after the equestrian portrait was painted, Philip commissioned Calderón to write his *auto sacramental*.

As luck would have it and as already indicated, Christina ended up resisting Philip IV's efforts to align her with the Spanish cause, and it is, no doubt, for this reason that the king himself kept the *auto* from being performed. According to Barrionuevo:

> Habiendo hecho don Pedro Calderón de la Barca un Auto sacramental de la reducción a la fe de la Reina de Suecia, bajó decreto del Rey al Presidente no se hiciese, porque las cosas de esta señora no estaban en aquel primer estado que tuvieron al principio, cuya casa y servicio de criados se compone ahora de solos franceses. Y decía el decreto del Rey una cosa particular: "No dejaréis que se represente el Auto de la Reina de Suecia; y aunque está tan adelantado el tiempo, yo fío del ingenio de don Pedro Calderón que hará otro luego para que no haya falta en el festejo de tan gran día."

[Having had Calderón de la Barca compose an *auto sacramental* about the change in faith of the Swedish queen, the king decreed to the president that it not be performed, because the state of affairs with this lady was not what it was at the beginning, since now her household and servants are composed entirely of the French. And the King's decree stated something specific: "You shall not allow that the *auto* pertaining to the Swedish queen be represented; and although there is little time left, I so trust don Pedro Calderón's genius that I am certain that he will be able to write another so that the great feast day will not be lacking."] (I, 284)

Frustrated in this initial attempt to represent in drama this formidable monarch, Calderón attempts to take control of her image in *Afectos de odio y amor*. He provides a much more satisfactory ending to a real-life drama that was still unfolding. As he does in other plays, notably in *La cisma de Inglaterra*, Calderón rewrites history in order to present a more acceptable version of female rule. Like the equestrian paintings of Isabel and Margarita, Calderón encases this unruly body in the elaborate, highly stylized, and mechanical armor of dramatic convention.

Christina Postscripts

Some 30 years after Calderón wrote *Afectos de odio y amor*, his disciple and admirer Francisco Bances Candamo wrote a very different play about Christina of Sweden called *¿Quién es quien premia al amor* [*Who is Who Rewards Love?*]. The few critics who have written about this play disagree on the date of composition and, surprisingly for a play that was specifically written for and staged at the palace, we have no conclusive information on when it was performed. A *loa* attached to the play—but perhaps written by someone other than Bances Candamo— states that the play was represented by "las señoras damas de su Magestad en el gran salón de su Real Palacio con ocasión de la mejoría de la señora viuda [Her Majesty's ladies in the great hall of her Royal Palace, on the occasion of the lady widow's recovery]." This short statement gives us a brief and evocative glimpse of feminine involvement in the *comedia* at various levels: this is a play about a remarkable historical queen being performed before another queen, and acted out by the queen's own ladies-in-waiting.[24] Women are thus acknowledged as inspiration, theme, targeted audience, and performers. The interest in Christina,

---

[24] According to Belén Álvarez García: "Tanto la loa como la comedia fueron representadas por las señoras damas de su Majestad … y el hecho de que no lo hayan sido por ninguna compañía teatral puede ser la causa de que no se encuentren datos sobre la representación en documentos teatrales de la época [Both the *loa* and the *comedia* were acted out by Queen's ladies … and the fact that it was not done by a theater company may be the reason why we don't have information on its staging in the theatrical documents of the time]" (189). See "Loa para la comedia de *¿Quién es quien premia al amor?*" in *Loas completas de Bances Candamo*, ed. Ignacio Arellano, Kurt Span, and M. Carmen Pinillos (Kassel: Edition Reichenberger, 1994): 189–211.

as demonstrated by the number of times Calderón's *Afectos de odio y amor* was staged at the palace (at least seven times between 1659 and 1696), apparently continued even after the Swedish queen was no longer an important player in European politics.

One problem with the description attached to the *loa* is that it is not clear which "Magestad" is being invoked. F. Cuervo-Arengo suggests that the play was written in 1701 and that the *viuda* mentioned in the *loa* is Charles II's second wife, Maria Anna of Neuburg, widowed when Charles died in 1700. Other critics, however, believe that the play was written some 15 years earlier, and thus the *viuda* being honored was actually Charles's mother, Mariana of Austria. Oostendorp and Bertil Maler state that the play was written at around 1686 or 1687, while Mackenzie thinks that the play was written in 1689, shortly after Christina died ("Dos comedias" 60).[25] Sixteen eighty-nine was also the year Charles's first wife, Maria Luisa, died; and in a recent article on the *loa*, Álvarez García suggests that the play was probably staged in the short period between Maria Luisa's death and Charles's second marriage to Maria Anna of Neuburg. The 1689 date would mean that the widow being invoked was indeed the queen mother Mariana. At the same time, Álvarez García convincingly argues that the primary target of the play's message was the king himself, who is being urged, like the heroine of the play, to choose a successor and ensure the stability of the realm.

At one level, Bances's play adheres more closely to the historical record; that is, he presents Christina qua Christina, and there is greater historical and geographical accuracy incorporated into the action of the play.[26] While Calderón had written his play at a time when the Swedish queen's actions were still of immediate political interest at the court of Philip IV, enough time had elapsed by the time Bances wrote his version that it was no longer necessary to disguise the identity of the queen or change the fate of her fictional counterpart to fit *comedia* conventions or the wish-fulfillment fantasies of the royal audience. Nevertheless, Bances also takes clear liberties in his portrayal of the monarch. For one thing, the *varonil* aspect of the real Christina's character is greatly attenuated—even more

---

[25] Mackenzie rightly notes that by 1701, Bances had already left the court under some mysterious circumstances, and it is unlikely that he would have overseen the performance ("Dos comedias" 60). At the same time, his absence would not have prevented the play from being presented after Charles's death, with a *loa* written by someone else in order to make it more topical.

[26] According to MacKenzie, "a la reina [Bances] le situó en su propio ambiente con toda exactitud. Colocó a su alrededor a los personajes históricos que le influyeron: el príncipe Carlos Gustavo de Suecia, el Conde de Dona, el embajador español, Antonio Pimentel [Bances situated the queen in her own context with precision. He surrounded her with the historical characters who influenced her: the Prince Charles Gustavus of Sweden, the Count of Dohna, the Spanish ambassador Antonio Pimentel]" (60). While there was a historical Count of Dohna, this was also an identity that Queen Christina assumed at times when she traveled in disguise.

so than in *Afectos*—and her behavior is much more conventionally "feminine." Paradoxically, this makes Bances's Christina a *less* conventional *dama de comedia* in that, unlike so many of the Amazonian figures that we find in the plays of Calderón and his contemporaries, there is little gender dissonance. When Madama (as the queen is called in *¿Quién es quien?*) first appears, she does so dishabille, in a clearly feminized space, surrounded by her female attendants:

> [S]e descubre un gabinete de espejos con aparatos reales, y en él un tocador con todos sus adornos. Van saliendo al son de la música la reina Christina, en brial y con un peinador puesto, todas las damas en traje de Suecia van sacando en azafates los vestidos y haciendo cortesías al pasar la reina.
> [(A) gallery with mirrors decorated with royal regalia is revealed and in it, a dressing table with all its adornments. Processing to the music, Queen Christina will appear wearing an over-tunic and a protective wrap, followed by her ladies, all dressed in the Swedish style, carrying gowns in long baskets and curtsying as they pass the queen.] (80)[27]

This staging of feminine rituals (robing the queen and, later, arranging her hair) makes the Christina of *¿Quién es quien?* a much less ambiguous figure than Calderón's Cristerna. We remember that in *Afectos de odio y amor*, when Cristerna appears with her *damas*, they are carrying swords and *plumas* and the queen shows little concern about her appearance. What's more, while Calderón's play has a conventional ending in which Cristerna is married off and domesticated, it still manages to create a vibrant dramatic figure who champions women's rights in the earlier scenes. Although closer to the historical record (as stated previously, the real queen did not much care for women or their status), Bances's Christina lacks the ambiguities and suppleness found in the heroine of Calderón's play. According to Mackenzie, she "nos da la impresión de persona bastante femenina y decorosa. No se viste de hombre, ni monta caballo, ni toma parte en batallas [gives the impression of being feminine and decorous. She doesn't dress as a man, nor does she ride a horse, nor does she take part in a battle]" (64).

Indeed, the queen of *¿Quién es quien?* seems initially much more concerned with "feminine" questions of love and beauty than with matters of state. In an early scene, the *gracioso* teases her for being vain and for spending time on her attire and appearance when she should be celebrating the military victories of her cousin, Carlos Gustavo:

> Beltrán: ¿Es bueno, cuando tenemos
> victorias que celebrar,
> huéspedes que recebir,

---

[27] I have used the 1977 edition of the play prepared by the Swedish Hispanist, Bertel Maler (Stockholm: Almqvist & Wiksell International). Unfortunately, the edition is difficult to obtain in the U.S. and its long introduction is in Swedish (with one brief summary in French). I have also consulted the facsimile of the play available through the Biblioteca Virtual Miguel de Cervantes.

> gastar el tiempo en pulir,
> en prender y matizar
> belleza de tal primor
> que, como se deje ver,
> nunca menor ha de ser,
> nuca puede ser mayor?
> ¿Hay tiempo más mal gastado?
> ...
> Madama: ¡Ay Beltrán,
> déjame gustar de mí,
> y no en el prolijo aseo
> sino en que, si bien se apura,
> no gozo yo mi hermosura
> si no el rato que la veo.
> [Beltrán: Is it right that when we have victories to celebrate and guests to receive, you are wasting time polishing, adorning, and enhancing your beauty, one that is already so great, that as long as it is seen, it could never be less or greater than it already is? Can there be a greater waste of time? ... Christina: Oh, Beltran! Let me delight in myself; and not in the careful grooming itself but rather in the fact that, if you think about it, I can only relish my beauty during those moments when I actually get to see it.] (I, 490–99; 505–10)[28]

This is a psychologically plausible enactment of feminine vanity, but it would be difficult to imagine the real Christina or Calderón's fictional Cristerna expressing similar sentiments.

In *Theatro de los theatros*, Bances categorized the different types of *comedias* that were written at the time. Although one might expect this play to fall under the rubric of *comedia historica*, it resembles more the type he called *comedia de fábrica*:

> El Argumento de aquellas Comedias que llamamos de Fábrica suele ser vna competencia por vna Princesa entre personas Reales, con aquel Magestuoso decoro que conuiene a los Personaes que se introducen, maiormente si son Reies o Reinas, o Damas de Palacio ...
> [The plot of those plays that we call "de Fábrica" is normally a competition for a Princess's hand among royal personages, maintaining that majestic decorum that is proper to the characters introduced, especially when they are kings or queens or ladies of the court ...] (*Theatro de los theatros* 34–5)

And indeed, an important subplot of this *comedia*—as in so many other plays at the time—is the courtship of the queen by various princes and the need for her to marry in order to ensure the stability of her kingdom. An all-consuming concern when Bances wrote the play, the question of dynastic succession is directly addressed in the play. The anxiety in Spain over the increasing threat that

---

[28] Because Maler in his edition doesn't number the verses of the plays continuously, but rather begins with the number 1 in each act, I am designating the acts with a Roman numeral followed by the verse numbers.

a foreign power would assume the throne, through peaceful or hostile means, finds expression in the words of the character Enrique, the Duke of Holstein. In one scene, he assures Othon, another courtier, that Christina will responsibly adhere to the principle of an inherited monarchy:

> Nada temas, que Christina,
> reina en Europa aclamada,
> de muchos solicitada
> es por su beldad divina
> y por su corona. Pero
> del reino es fundamental
> ley que sea natural
> el rey, y todo extranjero
> queda por esto excluido.
> [Don't be afraid (of Christina's anger) for Christina is acclaimed by many throughout Europe for her divine beauty and for her crown. But, it is a fundamental law of the realm that the king has to be a native of the country, and therefore, all foreigners are excluded.] (I, 857–65)

As he would do later in another play, *La piedra filosofal*, Bances opportunistically uses the staging of a *comedia* to remind the king of the importance of choosing a successor.[29]

By the time he wrote the play, there was serious concern that Charles and his consort would prove incapable of providing an heir. If the play was completed around 1686 or 1687, Charles II and Maria Luisa of Orleans would have been married for almost 10 years and were still, despite occasional rumors of a royal pregnancy, without progeny. As stated before, Maria Luisa would die in 1689 and almost immediately afterwards, Charles would take a new bride, Maria Anna of Neuburg, who would also remain childless.

Although in Bances's play Christina is not as imposing a figure compared to the other *comedia* queens considered here, she does display many of the characteristics of the good prince, as delineated in the treatises cited in previous chapters. Indeed, she is concerned with attending to even the minutest details of governing her people, as the fictionalized Antonio de Pimentel tells us:

---

[29] According to Maler, the reason for writing it was to urge Charles to choose one particular prince: "La comedia *¿Quién es quien premia al amor?* est donc une pièce écrite par Bances Candamo dans le but de recommander le vainqueur de Buda, l'Electeur Maximilien II, le beau-frère de Charles II [the comedia *¿Quién es quien premia al amor?* is therefore a play written by Bances Candamo with the goal of recommending the victor of Buda, Maximilien II, Charles II's brother-in-law (as successor)]" (67). In reality, it would be his son Joseph Ferdinand who would be chosen to inherit the throne in 1692, although he would die seven years later, an event that helped usher in the War of Spanish Succession after Charles II's death. Philip of Anjou eventually became king, beginning the Bourbon dynasty in Spain.

> ... lo que me confunde es ver
> un reino tan extendido,
> de vos también gobernado,
> y que tienen el camino
> las quejas de los vasallos
> tan franco a vuestros oídos.
> Después de eso, ¿quién dirá,
> que cuando tratáis conmigo
> unas materias tan altas,
> y de tan graves motivos,
> que la Europa, aun sin saberlos,
> se pasmara al discurrirlos,
> tan hallada en estas fiestas
> estéis, y con tan tranquilo
> semblante ...
>
> [What confuses me is seeing that, in such an extensive realm so well governed by you as it is, the concerns of your vassals still have such easy access to your ears. Who would have thought that (at the very moment when you are consulting with me on such lofty matters and serious purposes that Europe without knowing them would be astonished to learn of them) you still find the time to get involved in the preparation of these festivities, and all with such calm.] (II, 685–98)

She responds with a clear allusion to the notion of the body politic, echoing the language of the treatises discussed in the first chapter:

> Alma de un reino es un rey,
> y así, como la alma, asisto
> toda yo en todas las partes,
> en ninguna me divido,
> y aun a la menor acción
> entera me participo.
>
> [The king is the soul of the kingdom and so, as the soul, I am wholly present in everything and no part do I divide myself, for I participate even in the least of my people's activities.] (II, 706–11)

She goes on to add:

> ... divertir necesito
> con fiestas mi reino, pues
> con el agrado benigno,
> dejándome ver gustosa,
> en los ánimos domino,
> y obedecen mas alegres
> vasallos mas divertidos.
>
> [I have to entertain my realm with festivities, because if I seem to take delight in benign pleasures, I can thus better control my vassals' wills, for they are happy to obey when they are entertained.] (II, 717–23)

There is here a Machiavellian subtext, as the queen seems to be promoting a "bread and circus" strategy for governing the populace; and we can also identify a metadramatic dimension, for what is Bances doing here but providing "benign" entertainment and at the same practicing what he called, in his treatise *Theatro de los theatros*, "arte áulica [courtly art]"?

Perhaps the most successful aspect of the play is the portrayal of the conflicted queen. She discusses with her attendants the dilemma of never knowing if she is loved for herself or because of her royal status. Indeed, we frequently find Madama agonizing over her two identities, her body natural and her body politic. At one point, we have the following exchange with one of her ladies-in-waiting:

> Madama: ¡Ay si supieras por eso
> cuánto el ser Reina me cansa!
> Enriqueta: ¿Pues qué quisieras ser?
> Madama: Una de vosotras.
> [Christina: If you only knew how tired I am of being queen! Enriqueta: Well, what do you want to be? Christina: One of you.] (I, 353–6)

Cristina is deeply concerned that her suitors and her people are insincere in their loyalty to and admiration for her:

> No sólo los que pretenden
> mi mano, mas los que alaban
> mi discreción o hermosura
> y las perfecciones varias
> que en mí pintan, ya de ser
> en todas ciencias versada,
> de poseer once idiomas,
> y en fin lo que más estrañan,
> que es hacer versos en todos,
> juzgo que tanto lo ensalzan
> por ser reina de Süecia;
>
> ...
>
> ¿No me basta a mí ser yo?
> ¿Ha menester mi arrogancia
> más estado, más fortuna,
> que ser Christina Alexandra?
> [Not only those who aspire to my hand in marriage, but also those who praise my discretion, or beauty, or the various perfections that they ascribe to me— from being adept in all the sciences to knowing eleven languages and that which surprises them the most, which is that I write poetry—all of them praise me only because I am Queen of Sweden. ... It is not enough for me to be me? Does my ambition need more status, more riches, than just being Christina Alexandra?] (I, 361–71; 375–8)

When she discovers that Carlos Gustavo has been courting her only because he aspires to the Crown and that, in fact, he is really in love with the princess Leonor, her feminine vanity suffers from this rejection even though she feels no emotional attachment to him:

> ¿Quedamos bien, vanidad?
> Estamos bien, corazón?
> ¿Que toda mi perfección
> se esconde en mi majestad?
> ¿Ella es más que mi beldad?
> ¿Pues cómo no la procura
> aborrecer mi cordura?
> [Are we in agreement, vanity? Are we understood, heart? Can it be that all my endowments are wrapped up in my majesty? Is it more powerful than my beauty? Then, why doesn't my wisdom despise it (majesty) more?] (III, 658–64)

She ultimately decides to abdicate and leave Sweden attended only by her favorite lady-in-waiting, Laura, and her loyal vassal Federico, who, as it happens, is genuinely in love with her. Christina admits to Laura that, although it might seem unseemly in a queen, Federico's love for her appeals to her womanly side:

> Madama: No es quien lo dice
> la reina, sino Christina,
> que es lo que ama Federico.
> Laura: ¿Y te precias de querida?
> Madama: Sí, Laura, que no sé que haya
> otro contento en ser linda,
> y la hermosura para algo
> se pule, prende y matiza,
> pues no se esmera en ser bella
> para ser aborrecida.
> [Christina: It is not the queen, but Christina who is saying (that this love does not offend) for that is whom Federico loves. Laura: And are you pleased to be loved in this manner? Christina: Yes, Laura, because there is no other pleasure in being beautiful, and there's a reason why beauty is polished, adorned, and enhanced. One doesn't make such great efforts to be beautiful in order to be hated.] (III, 802–11)

This is, again, a nuanced presentation of an all-too-human woman—similar to Isabel in Coello's *El conde de Sex*—who battles her private self in order to meet responsibly the demands of governance. Bances goes on to provide a psychologically plausible reason—albeit one with no historical basis in fact—for the queen's abdication: the need to be accepted for who she truly is:

> Yo estoy, Laura, yo estoy, conde,
> en resolución muy fija
> de peregrinar la Europa,

por si mi orgullo averigua,
cuanto más que por mi reino
me veneran por mí misma.
De lo que me amáis los dos
me he dado por entendida,
...
a quien me quiera por mí
mis secretos se confían,
no a quien me quiera por reina
y de ser leal desista
en no siéndolo.

[I am determined, Laura; I have come to the firm resolution, Count, to take a pilgrimage through Europe to see if my pride can discover whether I am venerated for who I am or for my kingdom. I realize that the two of you truly love me and ... I will entrust my secrets only to those who appreciate me for myself, and not to those who would stop being loyal if I were not queen.]
(III, 832–9, 844–8)

These words are moving, and one can imagine that they would have had some resonance with the queen mother, Mariana of Austria, a woman who had been married off at the age of 15, become a widow at 35, acted as regent for 10 years, and (by the time the play was likely performed) had survived some 40 years of virulent court politics at the Habsburg court.

The Christina in *¿Quién es quien?* is ultimately a melancholy queen who, unlike other *comedia* monarchs—from the ideal Christian prince Segismundo in *La vida es sueño* to the Machiavellian virago Semíramis—ends up choosing the personal over the political *razón de estado*. Following Duncan Moir, Mackenzie has characterized the denouement of the play as a *tragedia di lieto fine*, that is, one in which there is a technically happy denouement but inherent tragedy as well ("Dos comedias" 69–70). The queen, who has shown an innate talent and aptitude for governing, according to Mackenzie, never gets the chance to use her talents and instead has to bow to pressure and abandon the throne. Another important component that makes this a *lieto fine*, in my opinion, especially for the immediate audience at the court, is the fact that the queen, at the end, has decisively chosen a successor to the throne, something that many courtiers were pressuring Charles II to do.

Bances wrote another play, *La piedra filosofal*, which would again take up the question of succession with even more urgency, and in an almost reckless manner. It is an interesting play to consider (albeit briefly) because, in many ways, it is emblematic of the demise of the performance of queenly power in the *comedia*. Like *¿Quién es quien?*, *La piedra filosofal* may be categorized as a *comedia de fábrica* but with a strong allegorical component. The play was performed at the Alcázar in 1693, and as such it is the last of the plays discussed in this book to have been performed at the court while Mariana of Austria was still alive. Charles, by this time, had married his second wife, Maria Anna of Neuburg, and it was becoming clear (after four years of marriage) that she would be no more successful than her predecessor in providing an heir to the throne. The concern over a successor had reached such a fevered pitch that some courtiers were advocating extreme measures, such as regularly feeding the king bull's testicles and performing exorcisms in order to "restore" his potency. The exorcisms would earn Charles the moniker of "El Hechizado [the Bewitched]." This study has repeatedly alluded to the modern theoretical idea that performance is a type of surrogation; in other words, that it takes the place of something that it is not and therefore supplements an absence. The absence that Bances and the rest of the court had to confront in the last decades of the seventeenth century was not just the current absence of a strong monarch, but also the potential absence of a suitable successor to the crown. In the context of this present and future crisis, Bances turns to a mythic past of Spain, one that had its sources in historiographical texts produced during the Middle Ages and the Renaissance, such as the thirteenth-century chronicle by Rodrigo Ximénez de Rada or the *Crónica General de España* by the sixteenth-century Florián de Ocampo. In the latter, for example, we find an account of a myth that none other than Hercules was the originator of the Spanish monarchy through his nephew, called Hispanus or Hispalus.[30] In *La piedra filosofal*, Bances enacts this myth, thus intensifying the surrogation possibilities of the *comedia* by presenting three personifications of the political body: King Hispán, his daughter Iberia, and the suitor Hispalo—characters whose names all designate the geographical and historical entity of Spain.

Through the characterization of the female protagonist, Iberia (who, as far as I can tell, was not mentioned in other versions of the myth found in the texts cited earlier), Bances makes the ultimate association between a feminine body and the realm itself. The character is, in fact, an allegorical figure who behaves like the ultimate *mujer esquiva*, devoid of passions except for a profound concern for her reputation, one that she identifies as inseparable from the reputation of her kingdom. The plot centers on the attempts by her father, Hispán, to marry her off to one of a number of suitors. Perhaps the most daring dimension of the play is the negative portrayal of an indecisive king. Hispán's reluctance to give up power and choose a successor places his daughter and the realm in a precarious situation. In a remarkable scene, the playwright reenacts visually and kinetically the political predicament in which Spain found itself during the last decade of the seventeenth century. At the beginning of Act II, we find the following stage directions: "*Salen con IBERIA todas las damas y la Música, y van atravesando el teatro; y los tres príncipes están por diferentes paños, como acechando* [IBERIA and her ladies appear, with the musicians, and they traverse the stage; (meanwhile) the three princes are behind different wall panels, as if laying in wait]." Departing from a passive surveillance of the princess, the suitors then begin to accost her, each pressing his suit. Iberia angrily denounces their temerity and, when Hispán arrives, she forcefully criticizes him for putting her and the realm in such a precarious situation:

---

[30] See Robert B. Tate for an account of these historiographical texts in "Mythology in Spanish Historiography of the Middle Ages and the Renaissance," *Hispanic Review* 22.1 (1954): 1–18.

> Esto es, señor, haber puesto
> (quizá inadvertidamente)
> a competencias mi mano
> en afectos que, indecentes,
> quieren con sus arrogancias
> disuadir mis altiveces,
> siendo tu razón de estado
> quien me obliga a que sujete
> con dos lazos al laurel
> y a la coyunda las sienes.
> Bien fuera que tu razón
> allá la elección hiciese,
> sin dar lugar a que quieran
> atrevimientos infieles
> con los rendimientos suyos
> malquistarme lo rebelde ... .
>
> [This comes, my lord, from promoting (perhaps inadvertently) a competition for my hand among subjects who are rudely trying to conquer my pride with their arrogance, when all the time it is your reason of state that requires me to tie the knot (subject the laurel with two ribbons and my temple to the yoke). It would be better if your own reason made the election to prevent their faithless impudence from trying to wear down my resistance with their obsequiousness.]
> (1391–406)[31]

The realm is thus feminized and made into a desirable but elusive body politic who is pursued by suitors anxious to possess her (and perhaps violate her); and the machinations surrounding Iberia's courtship mirror the machinations surrounding the various pretenders to the throne in Spain at the time.[32] Despite her haughtiness, Iberia ultimately will prove to be a much wiser ruler than her father, someone who diplomatically channels the rivalry for her hand into a series of civic projects that will strengthen her kingdom. In the end, she will choose Hispalo, who conveniently happens to be Hispán's nephew (replicating the uncle-nephew relationship between Hercules and Hispanus/Hispalus in the myth), thus uniting two allegorical manifestations of Spain.

---

[31] I am using the edition prepared by Carmen Díaz Castañón, *El esclavo en grillos de oro y La piedra filosofal* (Oviedo: Caja de Ahorros de Asturias, 1983). For more detailed analyses of the play, see Quintero, "Monarchy and the Limits of Exemplarity in Francisco Bances Candamo's *La piedra filosofal*," *Hispanic Review* 66 (1998): 1–21; and the previously cited articles by Arellano, García Castañón, and Sánchez Belén in note 5 to Chapter 2.

[32] Among the princes who had some claim to the Spanish throne during Charles's reign were Victor Amadeus II of Savoy, Maximilian II Emanuel (Elector of Bavaria) and his son, Joseph Ferdinand of Bavaria, the Archduke Charles, Pedro II of Portugal, and Philip of Anjou. As stated earlier, Charles would ultimately—after much delay—choose Philip of Anjou as successor, a choice that would lead to the War of Succession.

Staged just seven years before the Habsburg dynasty would come to an end with the death of Charles, the figure of Iberia in the play may be seen as the final symbolic containment of feminine authority. In Bances's play, there are no manly women on horseback or fantasies of utopian gynocracies. Instead, the woman here is an abstraction, an allegory, who is throughout conflated with the territory of Spain. *La piedra filosofal*, as suggested before, may be said to represent the end of the performance of active queenly power in the *comedia*. After the various iterations of feminine authority that have been studied in this book, what remains is a feminized personification of the realm, a culmination of the association of power and gender, and the ultimate transformation of a body natural into a body politic.

* * *

I want to end this chapter as I began, with a reading of a visual representation of Christina of Sweden, although not in the context of the *comedia*. One of the most enjoyable artistic doublings of this remarkable body of authority can be found in the 1933 Rouben Mamoulian film *Queen Christina*. Although temporally distant from the world of Calderón and Bances Candamo, the film interestingly (and, no doubt, coincidentally) shares many of the same conventions and aesthetics of the *comedia*. In fact, it provides a privileged opportunity to experience in a multi-dimensional manner the performative dimension of what it means to represent a royal body. The plot of the film is filled with characters and situations familiar to anyone acquainted with the *comedia*. For one thing, through the elaborate costumes and spectacular sets, the movie gives modern viewers some idea of the pageantry that a court performance might have implied. In addition, the film reproduces many of the plot devices familiar to *comedia* readers: mistaken identities, chance encounters, star-crossed lovers, and the competition for a desirable woman by various suitors.

Most importantly, in the beautiful and androgynous Greta Garbo as Queen Christina, the movie replicates many of the feminine types found in the *comedia*: she is the *mujer vestida de hombre* (she spends much of the movie dressed as a man); the *mujer esquiva* (at one point she declares, "I shall die a bachelor"); and also the *mujer erudita* (she discusses Descartes and gets up at the crack of dawn to read Molière before her official duties begin). In addition, the film stages the gender ambiguity associated with the real Swedish queen and only hinted at in Calderón (and not at all in Bances). Greta Garbo was described as being "big-boned, square-shouldered, mannish,"[33] and there was early speculation about her sexual orientation, making her the perfect actress to play a latter-day *mujer varonil*. The movie exploits gender dissonance in surprising ways.

---

[33] See the informative article by Marcia Landy and Amy Villarejo, "Queen Christina," *British Film Institute Film Classics*, ed. Edward Buscombe and Rob White, vol. 1 (London: Taylor and Francis, 1997), 223.

Garbo is shown furiously riding a horse across the snowy countryside and wielding a sword and a firearm. In one famous scene, Greta Garbo kisses Elizabeth Young, the actress playing a young lady-in-waiting, fully on the mouth (Figure 5.7). This character is based on the real Ebba Sparre, one of the historical Christina's protégés, who was rumored to have been the queen's lover.[34]

Most scandalous (this is a pre-code Hollywood film) is the scene when, while still pretending to be a man, Christina finds herself having to share a bedroom at a snow-bound inn with none other than Antonio Pimentel, the Spanish ambassador, played by John Gilbert (rumored to be Garbo's one-time lover).[35] There is a discernible intimation of homoeroticism in that scene as Gilbert/Pimentel registers his attraction for the young "man" before him and asks him—in what we have to believe is a double-entendre—which side of the bed he prefers: "Which side of the bed do you sleep on, your right or your left? ... They say a man should always sleep on his side to keep his sword arm free. It's hereditary. It's instinct. [Pause]. Aren't you going to undress?" He soon discovers the true sex of his roommate, and the audience is left to understand that they spend three days in the bed enjoying each other's company.

We also discover many of the same political issues that have occupied these pages, related to the gendering of the royal body. The movie elucidates how visual codes can help establish or reinforce the thematic preoccupations of a text. For example, in a study of the Mamoulian film, Jane Gaines tells us that the movie's costume designer, Adrian, created outfits for Garbo that constitute "a sartorial essay on sexuality and power" (qtd. in Landy and Villarejo 223). The actress's frequent changes of costume in the movie, along with other effects, such as Garbo's husky voice, give us a sense of how *comedia* actresses might have used the versatility of performative and visual codes to transcend the normative limitations of gender and theatrical convention. At the end of the movie, as Christina is about to run off with Pimentel, she is shown wearing a "feminized" version of the male costume she had worn earlier. The effect that this scene has on the viewer gives us an inkling of the effect on a *comedia* audience of, for example, Irene's first appearance in *La república al revés* in full armor, or Semíramis half dressed, wearing a woman's comb as a helmet; and, most famously, Rosaura's appearance before Segismundo in the third act of *La vida es sueño*. As Marcia Landy and Amy Villarejo put it: "The in-between nature of [Garbo's garment in the last scene] seems to situate her in a place between masculine and feminine, homosexuality and heterosexuality, symbol and mortal, public and private person." It would not be unreasonable to assume that this gender in-betweenness is what Calderón and his contemporaries often achieve in their representation of fictional virile queens.

---

[34] See Buckley for a description of this relationship, 71–3.

[35] There were, apparently, some objections to the scene, and it had to be reviewed by a panel that ultimately decided that the film was acceptable as it was (Landy and Villarejo 226).

Fig. 5.7   Greta Garbo and Elizabeth Young in *Queen Christina*, 2005.

In *Queen Christina*, the director replicates the dilemma between reasons of state and reasons of the heart, although, in typical Hollywood fashion, the heart wins out and Christina abdicates because she intends to run off with the dashing Spanish ambassador. Unfortunately, he is killed by envious courtiers, led by the prime minister who had been Christina's lover. Like Bances's Christina, Garbo's character voices the binary conflict of the private vs. the public in elegant terms. In a scene where she appears in the throne room at night, dressed in a loose gown, she exclaims: "I have been a symbol of eternal changelessness, an abstraction. A human being is mortal and changeable with desires and impurities, hopes and despairs. I am tired of being a symbol, Chancellor, I long to be a human being, a longing I cannot suppress." Furthermore, the film picks up on the importance of portraits in monarchical marriage arrangements during the seventeenth century. Specifically, it dramatizes the negotiations that may have taken place to arrange a union between Philip IV and Christina. Halfway through the movie, Pimentel presents Christina with a portrait of a young Philip IV (Figure 5.8). The portrait shown is, in fact, very similar to one executed by Velazquez in 1628—making this an anachronistic touch, since Philip would have been in his early forties when there was talk of a possible marriage with Christina. When she sees the portrait, Garbo's Christina does a double-take, asks "Does he really look like that?" and then exclaims with a sigh: "All my suitors come in oil."

One notable aspect of Garbo's performance is that there is never any doubt that her character is anything but a woman, despite the androgynous body, her low, throaty voice, and her swaggering, "manly" gait. The scenes with Garbo

Fig. 5.8   Greta Garbo and John Gilbert with Painting of Philip IV in *Queen Christina*, 2005.

dressed and "acting" as a man—riding furiously on a horse, rescuing the Spaniards when their carriage gets stuck, drinking and cursing in the tavern—gives us some sense of how the performance of a *mujer vestida de hombre* might have been perceived by the *comedia* audience in the seventeenth century. No one would have been duped into thinking that a mujer varonil was a man, and the pleasure of viewing would be achieved in the willing suspension of disbelief, in the knowledge that there is a feminine body only barely hidden under the clothing of a man. As Roland Barthes puts it in his brief essay on Garbo's face:

> her face is almost sexually undefined, without however leaving one in doubt. It is true that this film (in which Queen Christina is by turns a woman and a young cavalier) lends itself to this lack of differentiation; but Garbo does not perform in it any feat of transvestism; she is always herself, and carries without pretense, under her crown or her wide-brimmed hats the same snowy solitary face. (56)

In the same manner, no one would have been fooled when Semíramis impersonated Ninias in *La hija del aire* or when *comedia* women appeared in breeches. The attraction, then and now, is precisely in the transparent masquerade of masculinity displaying for the spectator the uncanniness of gender.

One last comment about the movie: there is a remarkable scene in which Greta Garbo, still pretending to be a man, shares a drink with Pimentel (Figure 5.9). Garbo/Christina demands, in her throaty voice, news from Spain.

Specifically, she asks after Velázquez and adds, "and what of Calderón? He writes plays so quickly, there must be new ones since last I heard." At this point, the cinematic Pimentel might well have answered, "Well, your majesty, he happens to be writing a play about you." What the real Christina might have made of *Afectos de odio y amor*, we will never know; but she no doubt would have been pleased to know that her gender-bending performance would continue to fascinate long after her death. The impetus to stage the flexibility of gender and the precarious nature of power, not to mention the tensions between the personal and the political, would continue to be played out through the representation of the Swedish queen in visual texts spanning more than 300 years.

Fig. 5.9   Greta Garbo and John Gilbert in *Queen Christina*, 2005.

Epilogue

This book has dealt primarily with fantasies of female rule created by men, and it is perhaps appropriate to conclude with a glancing consideration of a fictional gynocracy fashioned by a woman. Ana Caro Mallén de Soto's *El conde Partinuplés* (probably written in the 1630s or 1640s and published in 1653) invites us to consider how a woman playwright addressed the multiple contradictions implied in the rule of women. The play has endured changeable critical fortunes and was, in fact, ignored or dismissed for a long time, in no small measure because of the sex of its writer. In the last decades, the play has gained steady attention, beginning with the excellent editions prepared by Lola Luna and Teresa Scott Soufas. *El conde Partinuplés* has gone from being described by none other than Melveena McKendrick as "extremely bad" (*Women and Society* 172) to being considered a paradigm of feminist writing and contestation. It has benefited from multiple intelligent and provocative readings from critics as diverse as Luna, Soufas, María Mercedes Carrión, Rina Walthaus, J.L. Montoussé Vega, and Jonathan Ellis.[1]

A playwright who flourished in seventeenth-century Seville and one of the few women of her time to make a living from the theater, Ana Caro may have found herself at some remove from the center of monarchical power. In fact, we have no record that her *comedias* were ever performed at the court.[2] At the same time, *El conde Partinuplés* reiterates many of the same situations and thematic preoccupations surrounding gender and power that we find in other plays examined in this study. Based on a twelfth-century French romance, *Partonopeus de Blois* and containing echoes of the Apuleius myth of Cupid and Psyche, the

---

[1] See María Mercedes Carrión's "Portrait of a Lady: Marriage, Postponement, and Representation in Ana Caro's *El Conde Partinuplés*," *MLN* 114.2 (1999): 241–68; Jonathan Ellis's "Royal Obligation and the 'Uncontrolled Female' in Ana Caro's *El conde Partinuplés*," *Bulletin of the Comediantes* 62.1 (2010): 15–30; Lola Luna's "Ana Caro, una escritora 'de oficio' del Siglo de Oro," *BHS* 72 (1995): 11–26; José Luis Montoussé Vega's "'Si me buscas, me hallarás': la configuración del discurso femenino en la comedia de Ana Caro *El Conde de Partinuples*," *Archivium* 44–5, Web PDF, n.d; Teresa Soufas's *Dramas of Distinction: a Study of Plays by Golden Age Women* (Lexington: UP of Kentucky, 1997); and Rina Walthaus's "La comedia de Doña Ana Caro Mallén de Soto," *Estudios sobre escritoras hispánicas en honor de Georgina Sabat-Rivers*, ed. Lou Charnon-Deutsch (Madrid: Castalia, 1992), 326–41.

[2] According to Alicia R. Zuese, however, Caro may well have spent some time in Madrid and even participated in the literary academies there. See "Ana Caro and the Literary Academies of Seventeenth-Century Spain," *Women's Literacy in Early Modern Spain and the New World*, ed. Anne J. Cruz and Rosilie Hernández (Farnham, UK: Ashgate, 2011): 191–208.

play begins with a familiar situation: Empress Rosaura[3] of Constantinople finds herself confronted by her subjects who demand that she choose a husband in order to ensure dynastic succession. The first words of the play are "Sucesor pide el imperio; / dénosle luego, que importa [The empire demands a successor; / let her give him to us soon because it is an urgent matter]," followed a few lines later by "Cásese o pierda estos reinos [Let her marry or lose her kingdom]" (1–2, 5).[4] Like Tirso's Irene and Calderón's Cenobia and Semíramis, Rosaura reacts with anger at a demand that ignores her virtues and dedication as a monarch and concentrates only on her sex and reproductive potential. Nevertheless, with the help of her cousin Aldora (who serves the function of a female counselor or *valido*), she ably deflects the populace's demands by requesting a year's grace period to identify a suitable husband. Much has been written about the implications of this deferral, with Mercedes Carrión suggesting, for example, that it is "both a catalyst for dramatic action and a strategy for the performance of female representation" and that the postponement finds a "historical intertext in the figure of Elizabeth I of England" (250).

Scholars who have studied the play have been quick to establish connections between the fictional empress, Rosaura, and the two historical "Isabels" invoked repeatedly in my study: Isabel of Castile and Elizabeth I of England. Luna, Soufas, and Ellis have seen in Caro's Rosaura echoes of the Catholic monarch who successfully negotiated a joint "corporate" rule with her husband, Fernando. Carrión, on the other hand, deems Rosaura's situation "radically different" from that of Isabel, claiming that the more fruitful comparison is, in fact, with the Virgin Queen's manipulation of marriage: "Elizabeth and Rosaura, performers and empresses, meet in the construction of postponement as a rhetorical strategy that displays a clear feminist agenda to resist matrimony as a strategy of containment" (251). At the same time, Rosaura is not an entirely ideal body of authority, and the comparisons to Elizabeth I—while suggestive—overlook the fact that Caro's heroine (unlike the English monarch and many of the fictional queens considered in previous chapters) does not exhibit on stage the actions and characteristics of a truly remarkable ruler. Although at the beginning she does express her willingness to take arms to defend her realm, the viewer is not regaled with scenes where Rosaura actually displays military prowess or political wisdom; nor is she a *mujer erudita* or someone who shows any interest in promoting women's equality.

---

[3] In the original French romance, the empress is called Melior. Critics such as Christopher Weimer and Montoussé Vega have considered the importance of the change of name to Rosaura and the suggestive intertextual relationship between Caro's play and Calderón de la Barca's *La vida es sueño*. See Montoussé Vega's "Si me buscas me hallarás" and Weimer's "Ana Caro's *El conde Partinuplés* and Calderón's *La vida es sueño*: Protofeminism and Heuristic Imitation," *Bulletin of the Comediantes* 52.1 (2000): 123–46.

[4] I am citing (by lines) the edition of the play prepared by Teresa Soufas in *Women's Acts: Plays by Women Dramatists of Spain's Golden Age* (Lexington: U of Kentucky P, 1997): 133–62.

In reality, Rosaura indulges early on in behavior that seems less than admirable. For one thing, she chooses the eponymous Conde Partinuplés as a likely consort when she discovers him admiring the portrait of another woman, Lisbella. When she learns, furthermore, that he is engaged to Lisbella, her interest is roused more by feminine caprice and a desire to compete with another woman than by the count's merits:

> ¿Con Lisbella?
> Por eso, Aldora, por eso
> me lleva la inclinación
> aquel hombre
> ... si le miro ajeno,
> ¿cómo es posible dejar,
> por envidia o por deseo,
> de intentar un imposible,
> aun siendo sus gracias menos?
> [With Lisbella? For that reason (that he is engaged to her), for that very reason, I am inclined to choose this man.... If I see that he belongs to someone else, how can I—out of envy or desire—pass up the chance of obtaining something forbidden, even if his personal charms were not as great?] (371–4; 380–84)

By choosing Partinuplés out of vanity and rivalry, she indulges in the very capricious behavior that is stereotypically ascribed to women and, incidentally, to the tyrants who appear so often in the *comedia*.

The play's denouement—with its multiple marriages, including Rosaura's to Partinuplés—is something of a disappointment to contemporary readers who might expect a different, more daring outcome from a female playwright. At the same time, there are instances in the play where it becomes clear that Caro is ironically playing with the conventions of theater as law—in Joseph Roach's sense of being the repository of social performances past and present (55)—and intends, instead, to maximize the possibilities of performance so as to release what Féral has called "the flow of desire" ("Performance" 178). I have alluded throughout this study to the repeated performance of women's bodies before a masculinized gaze and the manner in which women are incorporated into the conventions of the theater and society through punishment, marriage, or other forms of containment. One question that this study has implicitly examined is whether there is a coercive identification on the part of the audience with the subordination and fetishization of the feminine. Barbara Freedman has said that in the theater in general,

> ... not only pleasure but plot is derived from male fantasies, which depend on the scopic and narrative exploitation of woman; she is the linchpin in the system whose losses propel the relay of looks and whose sins move the plot forward. In question, then, is the reliance of theatrical desire on the fetishized spectacle of woman and the narrative of her domination and punishment. ("Frame-Up" 59)

In her study of the play, Soufas has pointed out that when her vassals demand that she marry while still young and beautiful, Rosaura "becomes the objectified courtly *dama*, gazed upon by the entire court and scrutinized as to her physical attractiveness from the male perspective" (*Dramas of Distinction* 47). What is most remarkable about the play, however, is that Caro presents a clear reversal of this initial dominating male gaze that fetishizes the female character. *El conde Partinuplés* is a play written by a woman which dramatizes women looking and holding the look, women desiring, women manipulating courtship and marriage in their own terms. Caro's play allows its female characters to meditate on how they have been perceived, but also to perceive themselves and to look back. As Freedman has claimed: "To return the look ... is to break up performance space, deconstruct the gaze, subvert the classical organization of showing and seeing, revision spectatorship, and restructure traditional canons, genres, and personal-political identities" ("Frame-Up" 69).

In the play, the enchantress Aldora creates an elaborate illusion in which Rosaura's suitors are shown acting out their defining characteristics and desirability as potential husbands. By resorting to magic, an activity not coincidentally associated with the nefarious potential of women's power, Aldora sets up an intricate and composite *mise en scene*:

> ¡Espíritus infelices,
> que en el espantoso reino
> habitáis por esas negras
> llamas, sin luz y con fuego,
> os conjuro, apremio y mando
> que junto mostréis a un tiempo
> de la suerte que estuvieren
> a los príncipes excelsos,
> de Polonia a Federico,
> de Transilvania a Roberto,
> de Escocia a Eduardo, de Francia
> Partinuplés ... ¿Bastan estos?
> [Ill-fated spirits, who inhabit the fearsome realm amid dark flames, without light but with fire, I conjure, entreat, and command you to reveal all at once the exalted princes in whatever form they currently are: Federico from Poland, Roberto from Transylvania, Edward from Scotland, and from France, Partinuplés ... will these suffice?] (324–34)

The last line addressed to Rosaura—with its pointed contrast to the menacing lines that begin the incantation—reads like a sly inside joke on Caro's part, suggesting that Aldora (the playwright's fictional double) can conjure up any number of potential suitors, thus endlessly duplicating performances of masculinity. As these two women sit and exercise the look, and ponder each performance of purported manliness—Federico admiring himself in a mirror (itself a reversal of a typical feminine scopic situation in both art and literature), Eduardo buried in his books, Roberto posturing heroically with a sword, and Partinuplés staring at the aforementioned portrait—the two women look, comment, and pass judgment on the merits of each male subject. In a metatheatrical *tour de force*, Aldora's interior *mise en scene* literally breaks up the performance space into four additional sites in which the male gaze is wittily reversed, thus subverting—to use Freedman's words—"the classical organization of showing and seeing."

The gendered reorganization of the look continues in the following scene, where Aldora orchestrates the appearance of Rosaura's portrait before Partinuplés. Thus, here, it is the woman who generates or "commissions" the portrait in a reversal of the use of the portrait as fetish and rehearsal of possession that we find in numerous *comedias*, such as Lope's *Peribáñez*, Tirso de Molina's *El vergonzoso en palacio*, or Calderón's *El pintor de su deshonra*.[5] That is, Aldora controls the production of Rosaura's image, and the appearance of the portrait for Partinuplés's delectation instigates curiosity (yet another characteristic routinely ascribed to women) and desire on the part of the unsuspecting count. As if that were not enough, Aldora cleverly dramatizes the timeworn cliché of the man as hunter and the woman as prey, except that here it is the prey who controls the chase. Rosaura's brief transformation into a *fiera* is an ingenious enactment or literalization of the association of woman with savage nature, although—again—the transformation is brought about by Aldora's intelligence and knowledge of arcane science. Later, as several critics have noted, Caro rewrites the myth of Cupid and Psyche by reversing the gender roles of the original; that is, it is Rosaura who appears as a potentially monstrous woman and who here denies Partinuplés permission to gaze on her countenance and body.[6] Caro's audience and today's readers can delight in the multiple ironies, the reversals of poetic and dramatic clichés, the transformation of power dynamics between the sexes, and the rewriting of myths such as Apollo and Daphne and Actaeon and Diana, in addition to the more immediately identifiable story of Psyche and Cupid.

And yet, *El conde Partinuplés* may still frustrate the contemporary reader from the perspective of the rule of women, not because it is a bad play (it isn't); but because, as implied before, Rosaura does not display the wisdom of an Irene or a Cenobia, the ruthlessness and might of a Semíramis, the feminist passion of a Cristerna, or the allegorical significance of an Iberia. Her one act of responsible queenship seems to be recognizing the need for an heir and ultimately submitting to tradition (admittedly on her own terms) by marrying Partinuplés. The last words she speaks in the play are "yo soy tuya [I am yours]," demonstrating her surrender to the traditional role of consort to the male prince. Equally questionable is her choice of husband: Partinuplés—like Casimiro in *Afectos de odio y amor*—has

---

[5] See Laura Bass, *The Drama of the Portrait: Theater and Visual Culture in Early Modern Spain* (University Park: Penn State UP, 2008), especially chapters 2 and 3, for discussions of the use of portraits in the plays by Tirso and Calderón.

[6] Carrión playfully comments on the cross-gendering of the myth: "If ... Partinuplés were a male version of Apuleius's Psyche, Rosaura might become the wife of a man who in a previous literary life was a beautiful confused woman ..." ("Portrait" 249).

been shown throughout most of the play to be more interested in amorous pursuits (first Lisbella and then the empress), leading him to abandon his responsibilities to his country, France. Ellis tells us that Partinuplés's situation "belongs to [the] long tradition in which the hero arrives at the kingdom or island of a beautiful queen or sorceress and forgets about his other duties" (22). Ultimately, at Rosaura's instigation, the count accepts his duty and leaves Rosaura to defend his realm against the English forces. This transformation of Partinuplés into a conscientious prince is perhaps meant to show Rosaura's ultimate wisdom in choosing the right man, as Ellis suggests.

We do not see a similar performative transformation in Rosaura herself: despite the reversal of dramatic conditions of seeing and generating desire, she is never seen wielding real political or martial authority. What's more, neither Rosaura nor Aldora ever assume male garb or behave in a truly "varonil" manner. Caro seems to be displacing onto the secondary character of Lisbella the attributes of the virile woman associated with the *comedia*. At the end, it is Lisbella who not only assumes a military role but is set to become the new ruler of France in Partinuplés's stead. The playwright reserves for her two protagonists, however, a different type of authority. Instead of a performance of political power, the emphasis is on the power of performance and theatrical activity. Rosaura may not be the most majestic or unforgettable of queens, but she is very much a creature of theater and theatricality. She and Aldora re-write the courtship plot set out by her vassals at the beginning of the play (interestingly, Partinuplés is not one of the suitors they mention as a potential consort). Aldora is also an *autora de comedias* (stage manager) in her orchestration and casting of the characters in the internal *mise-en-scene*, for which Rosaura will be the privileged spectator. Finally, Rosaura is the *actriz principal* or leading actress who assumes multiple roles. While it is fair to say that the queens created by male playwrights studied here seem more compelling as proto-feminist icons than Rosaura, Caro is in fact manipulating the masculinist law of the theater, maximizing the possibilities of performance, and making them her own.

Concluding Remarks

The baroque *comedia*, as fashioned by Caro and the other playwrights studied here, is replete with performative contradictions. With its conventional denouements of order reestablished, the *comedia* often seemed to re-present the symbolic realm, the law; that is, the reproduction of values and precepts of the dominant patriarchal and masculinist social system. And yet, in the performance of these plays, repressed gender-inflected tensions are repeatedly made visible, revealing an axis where body, gender, politics, and performance come together and where attitudes and ideologies can be interrogated. Within the limited *comedia* space, the mere act of dramatizing a commanding female presence and making feminine authority visible ultimately undermines the final restoration of order.

According to Ruth Anthony "the order restored at the level of the plot is an order that, in Calderón, always bears the mark of its own fragility" (168). The plays analyzed here, I believe, exhibit that fragility.

Louis Marin once stated that a king is not really king "that is monarch—except through the images that confer upon him a reputedly real presence."[7] If this is the case, what does it mean that one of the images conferred on the monarch within the Spanish Baroque *comedia* was so repeatedly a woman? A consideration of a limited number of plays cannot provide a conclusive account of the complex gendered representations of monarchy that we find everywhere on the seventeenth-century stage. Nevertheless, there are insistent parallels in the different texts examined that point to a shared ambivalence over the agency and rule of women that went hand in hand with an anxiety toward the state of the monarchy and the nature of power in general.

The plays analyzed in this book aspire, as I suggested in the introduction, to embody and replace certain monarchical values and virtues that were perceived to be absent or had been perhaps forgotten. Those virtues had to do with certain masculine ideals of strength, self-control, efficacy, and stability based on (among other beliefs) the importance of dynastic continuity. These ideals were being tested in the perceived weaknesses of the reigns of Philip IV and Charles II; and underlying all these plays, there is unease over the crisis of authority and an awareness of national decline. Calderón and his contemporaries seem to have found in the staging of fictional gynocracies a powerful vehicle for enacting those concerns. The remarkable bodies of authority represented by the legendary queens Cenobia, Irene, and Semíramis are juxtaposed to the weaknesses of feminized kings (Aureliano, Constantino, Nino, and Ninias). These princes—along with Enrique in *La cisma*, Casimiro in *Afectos*, Hispán in *La piedra filosofal*, and Partinuplés—all display stereotypical behavior ascribed to women: vanity, hedonism, and an excess of passion. In addition, historical queens such as Elizabeth I and Christina of Sweden—women who in real life displayed disturbing virile behavior—are domesticated in the *comedia*, thus re-writing history in a more "gender appropriate" manner. These plays are an attempt—not unlike the treatises of *arbitristas* and political theorists—to reinvigorate what Ledhfelt has called "proper standards of manhood" in the monarchy ("Ideal Men" 491).[8]

At the same time, the very reiterability of dramatic situations—repetition, after all, is another intrinsic characteristic of performance—offers the opportunity to not just revive but also supplement, negotiate, and perhaps reinvent alternatives to those values. The repeated display of feminine bodies of authority would have had multiple contradictory functions. Yes, these performances reveal a

---

[7] Qtd. in Paul Ricoeur, *Memory, History, Forgetting* (Chicago: U of Chicago P, 2004), 264.

[8] The crisis of masculinity Lehdfeldt studies is limited to the aristocracy. She does not deal with the monarchy at all, but I believe that many of her conclusions can be applied to the monarchy as well.

deep apprehension about weakened monarchical authority and the dangers of women's rule; but at the same time, these *comedias* also reflect the reality of feminine power that was negated in public opinion and in political tracts, with their gender-inflected lexicon that presumed the body politic to be male. The *comedia*, then, was in one sense supplementing the real incidence of female power at the court and elsewhere in early modern Europe. These plays, whether in the *corrales* or the *teatro palaciego*, restore the rule of women and make it quite literally corporate. Of course, the representation of the queen's body was always a fluid and often-contradictory process, as fictional and historical queens were simultaneously celebrated and undermined, legitimated and criticized.

One is reminded of Judith Butler's description of performativity as "this relation of being implicated in that which one opposes, this turning of power against itself to produce alternative modalities of power, to establish a kind of political contestation that is not a 'pure' opposition, a 'transcendence' of contemporary relations of power, but a difficult labor of forging a future from resources inevitably impure" (*Bodies that Matter* 241). The repeated enactment of both good and bad models of monarchy in Calderón and other Baroque playwrights figuratively turns power against itself; and the *comedia* became a compelling medium to produce, if not actual opposition, then an alternative if temporary modality of power. The *comedia*, with its dialectic between the conservative ideology of theater and the fluidity of performance, ultimately subverts the ideological rigidity and patriarchal imperative associated with theater. Just as the feminine and masculine prove to be mutable categories in these plays, so do the notions of the body politic reveal themselves to be unstable in their performativity. *Comedia* women may never have been able to escape the tyranny of roles, and neither could Calderón and his contemporaries fully escape the tyranny of theatrical convention and the expectations of the audience and thus fully transcend the established dynamics of power. Throughout their plays, however, they created astonishing dramatic heroines who can still take our breath away with their valor, erudition, and eloquent performance of women wielding authority, however ephemeral.

Works Cited

Allen, John. *The Reconstruction of a Spanish Golden-Age Playhouse: El Corral del Príncipe 1583–1744*. Gainesville: UP of Florida, 1983.

Álvarez García, Belén. "Loa para la comedia de ¿*Quién es quien premia al amor?*" *Loas completas de Bances Candamo*. Ed. Ignacio Arellano, Kurt Span, and M. Carmen Pinillos. Kassel: Edition Reichenberger, 1994. 189–211.

Andrachuk, Gregory Peter. "Calderón's View of the English Schism." *Parallel Lives: Spanish and English National Drama 1580–1680*. Ed. Louise and Peter Fothergill-Payne. Lewisburg, PA: Bucknell UP, 1991. 224–38.

Anthony, Ruth (El Saffar). "Violante: The Place of Rejection." *The Prince in the Tower: Perceptions of* La vida es sueño. Ed. Frederick de Armas. Cranbury, NJ: Associated UP, 1993. 165–82.

Aparicio Maydeu, Javier. "The Sinful Scene: Transgression in Seventeenth-Century Spanish Drama (1625–1685)." *Bodies and Biases: Sexualities in Hispanic Cultures and Literature*. Ed. David William Foster and Roberto Reis. Minneapolis: U of Minnesota P, 1996. 24–36.

Aram, Bethany. *Juana the Mad: Sovereignty and Dynasty in Renaissance Europe*. Baltimore: Johns Hopkins UP, 2005.

Arellano, Ignacio. "Estrategias de inversión en *La república al revés*, comedia política y moral de Tirso de Molina." *Tirso de Molina, del siglo de oro al siglo XX*. Actas del Coloquio Internacional, Pamplona, Universidad de Navarra. Pamplona: Revista "Estudios" (1995): 9–26.

———. "Teoría dramática y práctica teatral. Sobre el teatro áulico y político de Bances Candamo." *Criticón* 42 (1988): 169–93.

Bakhtin, Mikhail. *Rabelais and His World*. Trans. Helene Iswolsky. Cambridge, MA: MIT Press, 1968.

Bances Candamo, Francisco. *Como se curan los celos y Orlando Furioso*. Ed. Ignacio Arellano. Ottawa: Dovehouse, 1991.

———. *El esclavo en grillos de oro y La piedra filosofal*. Ed. Carmen Díaz Castañón. Oviedo: Caja de Ahorros de Asturias, 1983.

———. *¿Quién es quien premia al amor?* Ed. Bertil Maler. *Ett Gammalt Spanskt Skädespel om Drottning Kristina och Karl X Gustav: Francisco Bances Candamo: Kärlekens belöning (Quién es Quien premia al amor)*. Stockholm: Almqvist & Wiksell International, 1977.

———. *¿Quién es quien premia al amor?* Electronic facsimile in Biblioteca Virtual Miguel de Cervantes: <www.cervantesvirtual.com>.

———. *Theatro de los Theatros de los passados y presentes siglos*. Ed. Duncan Moir. London: Tamesis Books, 1970.

Barahona, Renato. *Sex Crimes, Honour, and the Law in Early Modern Spain*. Toronto: U of Toronto P, 2003.

Barrera y Leirado, Cayetano Alberto de la. *Catálogo Bibliográfico y biográfico del teatro antiguo español desde sus orígenes hasta mediados del siglo XVIII (Madrid 1860)*. London: Tamesis, 1968.

Barrionuevo, Jerónimo de. *Avisos*. Ed. A. Paz y Melia. Biblioteca de Autores Españoles. 2 vols. Madrid: Ediciones Atlas, 1968.

Barthes, Roland. *Mythologies*. Trans. Annette Lavers. New York: Hill and Wang, 1957.

Bass, Laura. *The Drama of the Portrait: Theater and Visual Culture in Early Modern Spain*. University Park: Penn State UP, 2008.

Belsey, Andrew and Catherine. "Icons of Divinity: Portraits of Elizabeth I." *Renaissance Bodies: The Human Figure in English Culture, c. 1540–1660*. Ed. Lucy Gent and Nigel Llewellyn. London: Reaktion Books, 1990. 11–35.

Bennassar, Bartolomé. *La España del siglo de oro*. Barcelona: Editorial Crítica, 1983.

Bernis, Carmen. "La moda en la España de Felipe II a través del retrato de corte." *Alonso Sánchez Coello y el retrato en la corte de Felipe II*. Madrid: Museo del Prado, 1990. 66–111.

Boccaccio, Giovanni. *Concerning Famous Women*. Trans. Guido A. Guarino. New Brunswick, NJ: Rutgers UP, 1963.

Brown, Jonathan. *Velázquez: Painter and Courtier*. New Haven: Yale UP, 1986.

Brown, Jonathan and John Elliott. *A Palace for a King: The Buen Retiro and the Court of Philip IV*. New Haven: Yale UP, 1980.

Buckley, Veronica. *Christina, Queen of Sweden: The Restless Life of a European Eccentric*. New York: Harper Collins, 2004.

Bushnell, Rebecca. *Tragedies of Tyrants: Political Thought and Theater in the English Renaissance*. Ithaca: Cornell UP, 1990.

Butler, Judith. *Bodies that Matter: On the Discursive Limits of "Sex."* New York: Routledge, 1993.

———. *Gender Trouble: Feminism and the Subversion of Identity*. New York: Routledge, 1990.

———. "Performative Acts and Gender Constitution: An Essay in Phenomenology and Feminist Theory." *Theater Journal* 40.4 (1988): 519–31.

Caba, María Y. *Isabel la Católica en la producción teatral española del siglo XII*. Woodbridge, England and Rochester, NY: Tamesis Books, 2008.

Calderón de la Barca, Pedro. *Darlo todo y no dar nada*. Electronic text prepared by David Hildner (n.d.), 4 Sept. 2010: <*comedias.org/calderon/DARLO.pdf*>.

———. *La gran Cenobia. Primera parte de comedias de don Pedro Calderón de la Barca*. Ed. A. Valbuena Briones. Vol. 1. Madrid: Consejo Superior de Investigaciones Científicas, 1974.

———. *La hija del aire*. Ed. Francisco Ruiz Ramón. Madrid: Cátedra, 1998.

———. *La hija del aire*. Ed. Gwynne Edwards. London: Tamesis, 1970.

———. *Obras completas*. Ed. Angel Valbuena Briones. Vols 1–3. Madrid: Aguilar, 1959.

———. *The Schism in England (La cisma de Inglaterra)*. Bilingual edition. Trans. Kenneth Muir and Ann L. Mackenzie. Ed. Ann L. Mackenzie. Warminster: Aris and Phillips, 1990.

Campbell, Jodi. *Monarchy, Political Culture, and Drama in Seventeenth-Century Madrid: Theater of Negotiation*. Aldershot, UK: Ashgate, 2006.

Carlos Varona, María Cruz de. "Representar el nacimiento: Imágenes y cultura material de un espacio de sociabilidad femenina en la España Altomoderna." *Goya* 319 (2007): 231–45.

Caro Mallén de Soto, Ana. *Ana Caro: El conde Partinuplés*. Ed. Lola Luna. Kassel: Reichenberger, 1993.

———. *El conde Partinuplés*. *Women's Acts: Plays by Women Dramatists of Spain's Golden Age*. Ed. Teresa Soufas. Lexington: U of Kentucky P, 1997. 133–62.

Carrión, María Mercedes. "Portrait of a Lady: Marriage, Postponement, and Representation in Ana Caro's *El Conde Partinuplés*." *MLN* 114.2 (1999): 241–68.

———. *Subject Stages: Marriage, Theater, and the Law in Early Modern Spain*. Toronto: U of Toronto P, 2010.

Castilla Soto, Josefina. "Tratados para la educación del rey niño." *Carlos II: El rey y su entorno cortesano*. Ed. Luis Ribot. Madrid: Centro de Estudios Europa Hispánica, 2009. 55–79.

Chaucer, Geoffrey. *The Canterbury Tales*. Ed. Frank Pitt-Taylor. London: Chapman and Hall, 1884.

Civil, Pierre. "Le Corps du roi et son image: Une symbolique de l'état dans quelques représentations de Philippe II." Redondo, *Le corps comme métaphore*. 11–29.

Clavería, Carlos. "Gustavo Adolfo y Cristina de Suecia, vistos por los españoles de su tiempo." *Clavileño* 18 (1952): 17–27.

Coello, Antonio. *El conde de Sex. Estudio y edición crítica*. Ed. Donald Schmiedel. Madrid: Colección Plaza Mayor, 1972.

———. *La tragedia mas lastimosa de amor: Dar la vida por su dama ó El conde de Sex*. *Teatro español. Tres flores del teatro antiguo español*. Ed. Carolina Michaëlis. Leipzig: F.A. Brockhaus, 1870.

——— (attributed to Felipe IV). *La tragedia mas lastimosa, El conde de Sex*. *Tesoro del teatro español desde su orígen hasta nuestros días*. Ed. Eugenio de Ochoa. Vol. 5: *Teatro escogido desde el siglo XVII hasta nuestros días. Segundo tomo*. Paris: Librería Europea de Baudry, 1838. 98–127.

Connor, Catherine. "Marriage and Subversion in Comedia Endings: Problems in Art and Society." Stoll and Smith, *Gender, Identity, and Representation*. 23–46.

———. "Teatralidad y resistencia: el debate sobre la mujer vestida de hombr.," Actas XI Congreso de la Asociación Internacional de Hispanistas. Ed. Juan Villegas. Vol. 3: *Encuentros y desencuentros de culturas: desde la edad media al siglo XVIII*. Irvine: AIH, 1992. 139–45.

Córdoba, Fray Martín de. *El Jardín de las nobles doncellas*. Ed. Harriet Goldberg. Chapel Hill: U of North Carolina P, 1974.

Cotarelo y Mori, Emilio. *Bibliografía de las controversias sobre la licitud del teatro en España*. Madrid: Est. de la Rev. de archivos, bibl. y museos, 1904.

———. "Dramáticos españoles del siglo XVII: Don Antonio Coello y Ochoa." *Boletín de la Real Academia Española* 5 (1918): 550–600.

Cowans, Jon. *Early Modern Spain: A Documentary History*. Philadelphia: U of Pennsylvania P, 2003.

Cranston, Jodi. *The Poetics of Portraiture in the Italian Renaissance*. Cambridge: Cambridge UP, 2000.

Cruickshank, Don W. *Don Pedro Calderón*. Cambridge: Cambridge UP, 2009.

———. "Lisping and Wearing Strange Suits: English Characters on the Spanish Stage and Spanish Characters on the English Stage, 1580–1680." *Parallel Lives: Spanish and English National Drama 1580–1680*. Ed. Louise and Peter Fothergill-Payne. Lewisburg: Bucknell UP, 1991. 195–210.

Cruz, Anne J. "Juana of Portugal: Patron of the Arts and Regent of Spain, 1554–1559." Cruz and Suzuki, *The Rule of Women in Early Modern Europe*. 103–22.

Cruz, Anne J. and Mihoko Suzuki, eds. *The Rule of Women in Early Modern Europe*. Chicago: U of Illinois P, 2009.

Danielsson, Arne. "Sébastien Bourdon's Equestrian Portrait of Queen Christina of Sweden—Addressed to 'His Catholic Majesty' Philip IV." *Konsthistorisk Tidskrift* 58 (1989): 95–106.

Davis, Charles. "El tacitismo político español y la metáfora del cuerpo." Redondo, *Le Corps comme métaphore*. 31–9.

Davis, Natalie Zemon. "Women on Top: Symbolic Sexual Inversion and Political Disorder in Early Modern Europe." *The Reversible World: Symbolic Inversion in Art and Society*. Ed. Barbara A. Babcock. Ithaca/London: Cornell UP, 1978. 147–89.

Davis, Tracy C. and Thomas Postlewait, eds. *Theatricality*. Cambridge: Cambridge UP, 2003.

de Armas, Frederick. *The Return of Astraea: an Astral-Imperial Myth in Calderón*. Lexington: Kentucky UP, 1986.

de Lauretis, Teresa. *Alice Doesn't: Feminism, Semiotics, Cinema*. Bloomington: Indiana UP, 1984.

Delpech, François. "De l'héroisme féminin dans quelques légendes de l'Espagne du siècle d'or. Ébuche pour une mythologie matronale." Redondo, *Images de la femme*. 13–31.

Diamond, Elin. "Mimesis, Mimicry, and the 'True-Real.'" *Modern Drama* 32.1 (1989): 58–72.

Donnell, Sidney. *Feminizing the Enemy: Imperial Spain, Transvestite Drama, and the Crisis of Masculinity*. Lewisburg, PA: Bucknell UP, 2003.

Dopico Black, Georgina. *Perfect Wives, Other Women: Adultery and Inquisition in Early Modern Spain*. Durham: Duke UP, 2001.

Earenfight, Theresa, ed. *Queenship and Political Power in Medieval and Early Modern Spain*. Aldershot, UK: Ashgate, 2005.

Edwards, Gwynne. Introduction. Calderón de la Barca, *La hija del aire*. xiii–lxxxiii.

Egido, Teófanes. *Sátiras políticas de la España moderna*. Madrid: Alianza Editorial, 1973.

El Saffar, Ruth (Anthony). "Anxiety of Identity: Gutierre's Case in *El médico de su honra*." *Studies in Honor of Bruce W. Wardropper*. Ed. Dian Fox, Harry Sieber, and Robert ter Horst. Newark, DE: Juan de la Cuesta, 1989. 105–24.

Elias, Norbert. *The Civilizing Process: The History of Manners*. Trans. Edmund Jephcott. New York: Urizen, 1986.

Elliott, J.H. *The Count Duke of Olivares: The Statesman in an Age of Decline*. New Haven: Yale UP, 1986.

———. "Self-Perception and Decline in Early Seventeenth-Century Spain." *Past and Present* (1977): 41–61.

———. *Spain and its World 1500–1700*. New Haven: Yale UP, 1989.

———. "Staying in Power: The Count-Duke Olivares." *The World of the Favourite*. Ed. J.H. Elliott and L.W.B. Brockliss. New Haven: Yale UP. 112–22.

Ellis, Jonathan. "Royal Obligation and the 'Uncontrolled Female' in Ana Caro's *El conde Partinuplés*." *Bulletin of the Comediantes* 62.1 (2010): 15–30.

Espinosa, Juan de and José López Romero. *Diálogo en laude de mugeres*. Granada: Ediciones A. Ubago, 1990.

Falomir Faus, Miguel. "Sobre los orígenes del retrato y la aparición del 'pintor de corte' en la España bajomedieval." *Boletín del arte* XVII (Universidad de Málaga, 1996): 177–96.

Fenster, Thelma S. and Clare A. Lees, eds. *Gender in Debate from the Early Middle Ages to the Renaissance*. New York: Palgrave, 2002.

Féral, Josette. "Foreword." *SubStance* 31.2/3, Special Issue on Theatricality (2002): 3–16.

———. "Performance and Theatricality: The Subject Demystified." Trans. Teresa Lyons. *Modern Drama* 25 (1982): 170–81.

Fernández Santamaría, J.A. *Reason of State and Statecraft in Spanish Political Thought, 1595–1640*. Lanham, MD: UP of America, 1975.

Ferrer Valls, Teresa, ed. *Diccionario biográfico de actores del teatro clásico español* (DICAT). Kassel: Reichenberger, 2008.

———. *Nobleza y espectáculo teatral (1535–1622)*. Seville and Valencia: UNED, 1993.

Findlay, Alison. *A Feminist Perspective on Renaissance Drama*. Oxford: Blackwell, 1999.

Firenzuola, Agnolo. *On the Beauty of Women*. Trans. and ed. Konrad Eisenbichler and Jacqueline Murray. Philadelphia: U of Pennsylvania P, 1992.

Fischer, Susan L. "The Psychological Stages of Feminine Development in *La hija del aire*: A Jungian Point of View." *Bulletin of the comediantes* 34: 2 (1982): 137–58.

Forcione, Alban. *Majesty and Humanity: Kings and Their Doubles in the Political Drama of the Spanish Golden Age*. New Haven: Yale UP, 2009.

Foucault, Michel. *Discipline and Punish: The Birth of the Prison.* Trans. Alan Sheridan. New York: Vintage, 1995.

Fox, Dian. "*El médico de su honra*: Political Considerations." *Hispania* 65.1 (1982): 28–38.

———. *Kings in Calderón: A Study in Characterization and Political Theory.* London: Tamesis, 1986.

Franko, Mark. *Dance as Text: Ideologies of the Baroque Body.* Cambridge: Cambridge UP, 1993.

Franko, Mark and Annette Richards. *Acting on the Past: Historical Performance Across the Disciplines.* Hanover, NH: Wesleyan UP, 2000.

Freedman, Barbara. "Frame-Up: Feminism, Psychoanalysis, Theater." *Performing Feminisms: Feminist Critical Theory and Theater.* Ed. Sue-Ellen Case. Baltimore: Johns Hopkins UP, 1990. 54–76.

———. *Staging the Gaze. Postmodernism, Psychoanalysis, and Shakespearean Comedy.* Ithaca: Cornell UP, 1991.

Frye, Susan. *Elizabeth I: the Competition for Representation.* Oxford: Oxford UP, 1993.

Galino Carrillo, María de los Angeles. *Los tratados sobre educación de príncipes (Siglos XVI y XVII).* Madrid: CSIC, 1948.

Garber, Marjorie. *Vested Interests: Cross-Dressing and Cultural Anxiety.* New York: Routledge, 1992.

García Castañón, Santiago. "La autoridad real en el teatro de Bances Candamo." *Looking at the comedia in the Year of the Quincentennial.* Ed. Barbara Mujica, Sharon D. Voros, and Matthew Stroud. Lanham, MD: UP of America, 1993. 229–34.

Garland, Lynda. *Byzantine Empresses: Women and Power in Byzantium, AD 527–1204.* London and New York: Routledge, 1999.

Goldberg, Harriet. "Queen of Almost All She Surveys: The Sexual Dynamics of Female Sovereigns." *La corónica* 23.2 (1995): 51–63.

González, Lola. "Mujer y empresa teatral en la España del Siglo de Oro. El caso de la actriz y *autora* María de Navas." *Revista sobre teatro áureo* 2 (2008): 135–58.

Goodman, Eleanor. "Conspicuous in her Absence: Mariana of Austria, Juan José of Austria, and the Representation of Her Power." Earenfight, *Queenship and Political Power.* 163–84.

Gracián, Baltasar. *El politico.* Ed. Evaristo Correa Calderón. Madrid: Anaya, 1961.

Greenblatt, Stephen. *Shakespearean Negotiations. The Circulation of Social Energy in Renaissance England.* Berkeley: U of California P, 1988.

Greer, Margaret. Introduction. Calderón de la Barca, *La estatua de Prometeo.* Kassel: Edition Reichenberger, 1986.

———. *The Play of Power: Mythological Court Dramas of Calderón de la Barca.* Princeton: Princeton UP, 1991.

Greer, Margaret Rich and J.E. Varey. *El teatro palaciego en Madrid: 1586–1707. Fuentes para la Historia del Teatro en España XXIX.* Madrid: Editorial Támesis, 1997.

Grieve, Patricia. *The Eve of Spain: Myths of Origins in the History of Christian, Muslim and Jewish Conflict*. Baltimore: Johns Hopkins UP, 2009.
Guevara, Antonio de. *Epístolas familiares*. Ed. William Rosenthal. Zaragoza: Ebro, 1969.
———. *Epístolas familiares. Epistolario español: Colección de Cartas de Ilustres y Antiguos y Modernos*. Ed. Eugenio de Ochoa. Madrid: Rivadeneyra, 1850.
Hammer, Paul E.J. "'Absolute and Sovereign Mistress of Her Grace'? Queen Elizabeth I and Her Favourites, 1581–1592." *The World of the Favourite*. Ed. J.H. Elliott and L.W.B. Brockliss. New Haven: Yale UP, 1999. 38–53.
Hampton, Timothy. *Writing from History: The Rhetoric of Exemplarity in Renaissance Literature*. Ithaca: Cornell UP, 1990.
Hearn, Karen. *Dynasties: Painting in Tudor and Jacobean England 1530–1630*. Rizzoli: New York, 1996.
Hermenegildo, Alfredo. "La responsibilidad del tirano: Virués y Calderón frente a la leyenda de Semíramis." *Calderón: Actas del Congreso internacional*. Madrid: Consejo Superior, 1983. 897–911.
Hernández Araico, Susana. "La Semíramis calderoniana como compendio de estereotipos femeninos." *Iberoromànica* 22 (1985): 29–39.
Hesse, Everett W. "Calderón's Semíramis: Myth of the Phallic Woman." *Bulletin of the comediantes* 38.2 (1986): 209–18.
Hildner, David. *Reason and the Passions in the comedias of Calderón*. Amsterdam/Philadelphia: John Benjamins, 1982.
Hollmann, Hildegard. "El retrato del tirano Aureliano en *La gran Cenobia*." *Hacia Calderón: Cuarto Coloquio Anglogermano*. Ed. Hans Flasche, Karl-Hermann Körner, and Hans Mattauch. Berlin: Walter de Gruyter, 1979.
Howard, Anita. *The King Within: Reformations of Power in Shakespeare and Calderón*. Bern: Peter Lang, 2010.
Howe, Elizabeth Teresa. "Zenobia or Penelope? Isabel la Catolica as Literary Archetype." *Isabel la Católica, Queen of Castile: Critical Essays*. Ed. David A. Boruchoff. New York: Palgrave Macmillan, 2003. 91–102.
Huarte de San Juan, Juan. *Examen de ingenios para las ciencias*. Ed. Rodrigo Sanz. 2 vols. Madrid: La Rafa, 1930.
Huizinga, Johan. *Homo Ludens: A Study of the Play-Element in Culture*. Boston: Beacon Press, 1955.
Hume, Martin. *Queens of Old Spain*. London: Grant Richards, 1906.
Hunt, Lynn. "The Many Bodies of Marie Antoinette." *Eroticism and the Body Politic*. Ed. Lynn Hunt. Baltimore: Johns Hopkins UP, 1991. 117–38.
Jankowski, Theodora A. *Women in Power in the Early Modern Drama*. Urbana: U of Illinois P, 1992.
Jones, Kathleen B. "On Authority: Or, Why Women Are Not Entitled to Speak." *Feminism and Foucault: Reflections on Resistance*. Ed. Irene Diamond and Lee Quinby. Boston: Northeastern UP, 1988. 119–33.
Jordan, Constance. "Feminism and the Humanists: The Case of Sir Thomas Elyot's *Defence of Good Women*." *Renaissance Quarterly* 32.2 (1983): 181–201.

———. *Renaissance Feminism: Literary Texts and Political Models*. Ithaca: Cornell UP, 1990.

Kamen, Henry. *Early Modern European Society*. London: Routledge, 2000.

———. *Spain in the Later Seventeenth Century, 1665–1700*. London: Longman, 1980.

Kantorowizc, Ernst H. *The King's Two Bodies: A Study in Medieval Political Theology*. Princeton, Princeton UP: 1957.

Kaufman, Gloria. "Juan Luis Vives on the Education of Women." *Signs: Journal of Women in Culture and Society* 3.4 (1978): 891–6.

Kelly, Joan. "Early Feminist Theory and the 'Querelle des Femmes', 1400–1789." *Signs: Journal of Women in Culture and Society* 8.1 (1982): 3–28.

Kelso, Ruth. *Doctrine for the Lady of the Renaissance*. Chicago: U of Illinois P, 1978.

Kennedy, Ruth. "*La prudencia en la mujer* and the Ambient That Brought It Forth." *PMLA* 63 (1948): 113–90.

———. *Studies in Tirso: The Dramatist and His Competitors, 1620–26*. Chapel Hill: U of North Carolina Department of Romance Languages, 1974.

———. "Tirso's *La república al revés*: Its Debt to Mira's *La rueda de la fortuna*, Its Date of Composition, and Its Importance." *Reflexión* 2.2 (1973): 39–50.

Kritzman, Lawrence. *The Rhetoric of Sexuality and the Literature of the French Renaissance*. Cambridge: Cambridge UP, 1991.

Kurtz, Barbara. *The Play of Allegory in the* Autos Sacramentales *of Pedro Calderón de la Barca*. Washington: The Catholic U of America P, 1991.

Landy, Marcia and Amy Villarejo. "Queen Christina." *British Film Institute Film Classics*. Eds. Edward Buscombe and Rob White. Vol. 1. London: Taylor and Francis, 1997. 221–48.

Lanza, Diego. *Il tiranno e il suo pubblico*. Turin: Einaudi, 1977.

Laqueur, Thomas. *Making Sex: Body and Gender from the Greeks to Freud*. Cambridge, MA: Harvard UP, 1990.

Lehfeldt, Elizabeth A. "The Gender of Shared Sovereignty: Texts and the Royal Marriage of Isabella and Ferdinand." *Women, Texts and Authority in the Early Modern Spanish World*. Ed. Marta V. Vicente and Luis R. Corteguera. Aldershot, UK: Ashgate, 2003. 37–55.

———. "Ideal Men: Masculinity and Decline in Seventeenth-Century Spain." *Renaissance Quarterly* 61 (2008): 463–94.

Leon, Luis de. *La perfecta casada*. Ed. Javier San José Lera. Madrid: Espasa-Calpe, 1992.

Levin, Carole. *The Heart and Stomach of a King: Elizabeth I and the Politics of Sex and Power*. Philadelphia: U of Pennsylvania P, 1994.

———. "John Foxe and the Responsibilities of Queenship." *Medieval and Renaissance Women: Historical and Literary Perspectives*. Ed. Mary Beth Rose. Syracuse: Syracuse UP, 1986. 113–33.

Liedtke, Walter A. and John F. Moffitt. "Velázquez, Olivares, and the Baroque Equestrian Portrait." *The Burlington Magazine* 123.942 (1981): 529–37.

Linsey, Karen. *Divorced, Beheaded, Survived: A Feminist Reinterpretation of the Wives of Henry VIII.* Cambridge, MA: Da Capo Press, 1996.

Lipmann, Stephen. "The Duality and Delusion of Calderón's Semíramis." *BHS* 59 (1982): 42–57.

Lisón Tolosana, Carmelo. *La imagen del rey: monarquía, realeza y poder ritual en la Casa de los Austrias*: discurso de recepción del ... Excmo. Sr. D. Carmelo Lisón Tolosana y contestación del Excmo. Sr. D. Salustiano del Campo Urbano, sesión del 4 de febrero de 1992. Madrid: Espasa-Calpe, 1992.

Loftis, John. "Henry VIII and Calderón's *La Cisma de Inglaterra*." *Comparative Literature* 34 (1982): 208–22.

Luján, Pedro de. *Coloquios Matrimoniales del Licenciado Pedro de Luján*. Ed. Asunción Rallo Gruss. Madrid: Anejos del Boletin de la Real Academia Española, 1990.

Luna, Lola. "Ana Caro, una escritora 'de oficio' del Siglo de Oro." *BHS* 72 (1995): 11–26.

Lundelius, Ruth. "Queen Christina of Sweden and Calderón's *Afectos de odio y amor*." *Bulletin of the comediantes* 38.2 (1986): 231–48.

Lynch, John. *The Hispanic World in Crisis and Change*. Oxford: Blackwell, 1992.

MacCurdy, Raymond R. *The Tragic Fall: Don Alvaro de Luna and Other Favorites in Spanish Golden Age Drama*. Chapel Hill: North Carolina Studies in the Romance Languages and Literatures, 1978.

Machiavelli, Niccolo. *The Prince*. Trans. Daniel Donno. New York: Bantam Books, 1966.

Mackenzie, Ann L. "Antonio Coello como discípulo y colaborador de Calderón." *Calderón desde el 2000 (Simposio Internacional Complutense)*. Ed. José María Díez Borque. Madrid: Ollero & Ramos, 2001. 37–59.

———. "The 'Deadly Relationship' of Elizabeth I and Mary Queen of Scots Dramatized for the Spanish Stage: [Juan Bautista] Diamante's *La reina María Estuarda*, and [José de] Cañizares's *Lo que va de un cetro a otro, y crueldad de Inglaterra*." *Studies for I.L. McClelland*. Ed. David T. Gies. *Dieciocho. Hispanic Enlightenment Aesthetics and Literary Theory* 10 (1986): 201–18.

———. "Dos comedias tratando de la reina Cristina de Suecia: *Afectos de odio y amor* por Calderón y *Quien es quien premia al amor* por Bances Candamo." *Hacia Calderón*. IV Coloquio Anglogermano. Berlin: Walter de Gruyter, 1979. 56–70.

———. *La escuela de Calderón. Estudio e investigación*. Liverpool: Liverpool UP, 1993.

———. Introduction. Calderón de la Barca, *The Schism in England* (*La cisma de Inglaterra*). Warminster: Aris and Phillips, 1990. 1–44.

MacLean, Ian. *The Renaissance Notion of Woman. A Study in the Fortunes of Scholasticism and Medical Science in European Intellectual Life*. Cambridge: U of Cambridge P, 1980.

Maravall, José Antonio. "La idea del cuerpo místico en España antes de Erasmo." *Estudios de historia del pensamiento español*. Vol. 1. Madrid: Ediciones Cultura Hispánica, 1967. 179–200.

———. "Maquiavelo y el maquiavelismo en España." *Estudios de historia del pensamiento español*. Vol. 3. Madrid: Ediciones Cultura Hispánica, 1975. 41–76.

Mariana, Juan de. *Obras del Padre Juan de Mariana*. Vol. 2. Biblioteca de Autores Españoles 31. Madrid: Rivadeneyra, 1854.

Mariscal, George. "Calderón and Shakespeare: The Subject of Henry VIII." *Bulletin of the comediantes* 39 (1987): 189–213.

Masson, Georgina. *Queen Christina*. London: Secker, 1968.

Mattingly, Garrett. *Catherine of Aragon*. Boston: Little, Brown and Company, 1941.

McKendrick, Melveena. *Identities in Crisis: Essays on Honor, Gender and Women in the Comedia*. Kassel: Reichenberger, 2002.

———. *Playing the King: Lope de Vega and the Limits of Conformity*. London: Tamesis, 2000.

———. *Women and Society in the Spanish Drama of the Golden Age: A Study of the mujer varonil*. Cambridge: Cambridge UP, 1974.

Menéndez y Pelayo, Marcelino. *Calderón y su teatro*. Madrid: Pérez Dubrull, 1881.

Moir, Duncan. Introduction. *Theatro de los Theatros de los passados y presentes siglos*. Ed. Duncan Moir. London: Tamesis Books, 1970.

Monet, Michel. "Deux figures emblématiques: La femme violée et la parfaite épouse, selon le *Romancero general* compilé par Agustín Durán." Redondo, *Images de la femme*. 77–90.

Montoussé Vega, Juan Luis. «Si me buscas, me hallarás»: la configuración del discurso femenino en la comedia de Ana Caro *El Conde de Partinuples*." *Archivium* 44–5. Revista de la Facultad de Letras, Universidad de Oviedo. Web PDF. n.d. <http://www.unioviedo.es/reunido/index.php/RFF/article/view/492/481>.

Montrose, Louis Adrian. "Elizabeth through the Looking Glass: Picturing the Queen's Two Bodies." *The Body of the Queen: Gender and Rule in the Courtly World, 1500–2000*. Ed. Regina Schulte. New York: Berghahn Books, 2006.

———. "Idols of the Queen: Policy, Tender, and the Picturing of Elizabeth I." *Representations* 68 (1999): 108–61.

———. "'Shaping Fantasies': Figurations of Gender and Power in Elizabethan Culture." Stephen Greenblatt, *Representing the English Renaissance*. Berkeley: U of California P, 1988. 31–64.

———. *The Subject of Elizabeth: Authority, Gender, and Representation*. Chicago: Chicago UP, 2006.

Nader, Helen, ed. *Power and Gender in Renaissance Spain: Eight Women of the Mendoza Family, 1450–1650*. Urbana: U of Illinois P, 2004.

Nahoum-Grappe, Veronique. "The Beautiful Woman." *A History of Women in the West: Renaissance and Enlightenment Paradoxes*. Ed. Natalie Davis and Arlette Farge. Vol. 3. Cambridge, MA: Harvard UP, 1993. 85–100.

Navarro, Emilia. "Manual Control: 'Regulatory Fictions' and their Discontents." *Cervante: Bulletin of the Cervantes Society of America* 13.2 (1993): 17–35.
Nieto Soria, José Manuel. *Origenes de la monarquía hispánica: propaganda y legitimación, ca. 1400–1520*. Madrid: Dykinson, 1999.
Novo, Yolanda. "Rasgos escenográficos y reconstrucción escénica de *La gran Cenobia* (1636)." *Teatro calderoniano sobre el tablado. Calderón y su puesta en escena a través de los siglos*. XII Coloquio Anglogermano sobre Calderón. Ed. Manfred Tietz. Archivum Calderonianum 10. Stuttgart: Franz Steiner Verlag, 2003. 359–90.
Oostendorp, Henk. "Cristina de Suecia en el teatro español del siglo XVII." *El teatro español a fines del siglo XVII. Historia, Cultura y Teatro en la España de Carlos II. Diálogos hispánicos de Amsterdam* 8.2. Amsterdam: Rodopi, 1989. 245–59.
Orgel, Stephen. *The Illusion of Power: Political Theater in the English Renaissance*. Berkeley: U of California P, 1975.
Oriel, Charles. *Writing and Inscription in Golden Age Drama*. West Lafayette, IN: Purdue UP, 1992.
Parker, Alexander A. "Henry VIII in Shakespeare and Calderón: An Appreciation of *La cisma de Inglaterra*." *Modern Language Review* 43.3 (1948): 327–52.
———. *The Mind and Art of Calderón*. Cambridge: Cambridge UP, 1988.
Paster, Gail Kern, Katherine Rowe, and Mary Floyd-Wilson. *Reading the Early Modern Passions: Essays in the Cultural History of Emotion*. Philadelphia: U of Pennsylvania P, 2004.
Patterson, Alan K.G. Review of *La hija del aire* by Calderón de la Barca. Ed. Gwynne Edwards. *MLR* 60 (1973): 203–6.
Perry, Mary Elizabeth. *Gender and Disorder in Early Modern Seville*. Princeton: Princeton UP, 1990.
Prieto, María Remedios. "Reaparición en el siglo XVIII del auto sacramental de Calderón *La protestación de la fe* y polémica que originó." *II Simposio sobre el P. Feijoo y su siglo*. Vol. 2. Oviedo: Centros de Estudios del S. XVIII, 1983. 545–74.
Queen Christina. Directed by Rouben Mamoulian. Performed by Greta Garbo, John Gilbert, Elizabeth Young, et al. 1933. DVD, Warner Home Video, 2005.
Quevedo, Francisco de. *Poemas escogidos*. Ed. José Manuel Blecua. Madrid: Clásicos Castalia, 1984.
Quintero, María Cristina. "'The Body of a Weak and Feeble Woman': Courting Elizabeth in Antonio Coello's *El conde de Sex*." *Material and Symbolic Circulation between Spain and England, 1554–1604*. Ed. Anne J. Cruz. Aldershot, UK: Ashgate, 2008. 71–87.
———. "English Queens and the Body Politic in Calderón's *La cisma de Inglaterra* and Rivadeneira's *Historia Eclesiástica del Scisma del Reino de Inglaterra*." *MLN* 113 (1998): 259–82.
———. "Gender, Tyranny, and the Performance of Power in Calderón's *La hija del aire*." *Bulletin of the comediantes* 53.1 (2001): 155–78.

———. "Monarchy and the Limits of Exemplarity in Francisco Bances Candamo's *La piedra filosofal*." *Hispanic Review* 66 (1998): 1–21.

———. "Political Intentionality and Dramatic Convention in the *teatro palaciego* of Francisco Bances Candamo." *Revista de Estudios Hispánicos* 20.3 (1986): 37–53.

———. "The Things They Carried: Objects and the Female Sovereign in Calderón de la Barca's *La gran Cenobia*." *Objects of Culture in Imperial Spain*. Ed. Mary Barnard and Frederick de Armas. Toronto: U of Toronto P, forthcoming.

Redondo, Augustin, ed. *Le Corps comme métaphore dans L'Espagne des XVIe et XVIIe siècles. Du corps métaphorique aux métaphores corporelles. Colloque International (Sorbonne et Collège d'Espagne, 1–4 octobre 1990)*. Paris: Sorbonne, 1992.

———, ed. *Le Corps dans la société espagnole des XVIe et XVIIe siècles. Colloque International (Sorbonne, 5–8 octobre 1988)*. Paris: Sorbonne, 1990.

———, ed. *Images de la femme en Espagne aux XVIe et XVIIE siècles. Des traditions aux renouvellements et à l'émergence d'images nouvelles*. Paris: Sorbonne, 1994.

——— "La métaphore du corps de la république à travers le traité du médecin Jerónimo Merola (1587)." Redondo, *Le Corps comme métaphore*. 41–53.

Redworth, Glyn. *The Prince and the Infanta: The Cultural Politics of the Spanish Match*. New Haven: Yale UP, 2003.

Ribot Garcia, Luis, ed. *Carlos II. El rey y su entorno cortesano*. Madrid: Centro de Estudios Europa Hispánica, 2009.

Ricoueur, Paul. *Memory, History, Forgetting*. Chicago: U of Chicago P, 2004.

Ríos Mazcarelle, Manuel. *Mariana de Austria: Esposa de Felipe IV, 1635–1696*. Madrid: Alderabán, 1997.

Rivadeneira, Pedro de. *Historia Eclesiástica del Scisma del Reino de Inglaterra. Obras escogidas del Padre Pedro de Rivadeneira*. Ed. D. Vicente de la Fuente. Vol. 60. Biblioteca de Autores Españoles. Madrid: M. Rivadeneyra, 1868.

Roach, Joseph. *Cities of the Dead: Circum-Atlantic Performance*. New York: Columbia UP, 1996.

Rogers, Daniel. "'¡Cielos! ¿Quién en Ninias habla?': The Mother-Son Impersonation in *La hija del aire*." *Bulletin of the comediantes* 20.1 (1968): 1–4.

———. "Los monólogos femeninos en *El conde de Sex* de Antonio Coello." *Hacia Calderón: Séptimo Coloquio Anglogermano*. Stuttgart: Verlag, 1985. 175–82.

Ruano de la Haza, J.M. and John J. Allen. *Los teatros comerciales del siglo XVII y la escenificación de la comedia*. Madrid: Editorial Castalia, 1994.

Rubio, María José. *Reinas de España: Las Austrias. Siglos XV–XVII de Isabel la Católica a Mariana de Neoburgo*. Madrid: La Esfera de los Libros, 2010.

Ruiz Ramón, Francisco. Introduction. Calderón de la Barca, *La hija del aire* (ed. Ruíz Ramón). Madrid: Cátedra, 1998.

Rupp, Stephen. *Allegories of Kingship: Calderón and the Anti-Machiavellian Tradition*. Philadelphia: U of Pennsylvania P, 1996.

Saavedra Fajardo, Diego. *Idea de un príncipe político-cristiano, representada en cien empresas. Obras de Don Diego de Saavedra Fajardo y del licenciado Pedro Fernández Navarrete.* Biblioteca de Autores Españoles 25. Madrid: M. Rivadneyra, 1853. 1–267.

———. "Política y razón de estado del Rey Don Fernando el Católico." *Obras de Don Diego de Saavedra Fajardo.* 423–42.

Said, Edward. *Culture and Imperialism.* New York: Vintage, 1994.

San Juan, Rose Marie. "The Queen's Body and Its Slipping Mask: Contesting Portraits of Queen Christina of Sweden." *ReImagining Women: Representations of Women in Culture.* Ed. Shirley Neuman and Glennis Stephenson. Toronto: U of Toronto P, 1993. 19–44.

Sánchez Belén, Juan. "La educación del príncipe en el teatro de Bances Candamo." *Revista Literaria* 49.97 (1987): 73–93.

Sánchez Escribano, F. and Alberto Porqueras Mayo. *Preceptiva dramática española del Renacimiento y el Barroco.* Madrid: Gredos, 1965.

Sánchez, Magdalena. *The Empress, the Queen, and the Nun: Women and Power at the Court of Philip III of Spain.* Baltimore: Johns Hopkins UP, 1998.

———. "Pious and Political Images of a Habsburg Woman at the Court of Philip III (1598–1621)." *Spanish Women in the Golden Age: Images and Realities.* Ed. Magdalena Sanchez and Alain Saint-Saëns. Westport, CT: Greenwood Press, 1996. 91–107.

Sanz Ayán, Carmen. *Pedagogía de Reyes: El teatro palaciego en el reinado de Carlos II.* Madrid: Real Academia de la Historia, 2006.

Saxonhouse, Arlene W. *Women in the History of Political Thought: Ancient Greece to Machiavelli.* New York: Praeger, 1985.

Shergold, N.D. and J.E. Varey. *Representaciones palaciegas: 1603–1699. Estudios y Documentos. Fuentes para la historia del teatro en España I.* London: Tamesis Books, 1982.

———. *Teatros y comedias en Madrid: 1687–1699. Estudios y Documentos. Fuentes para la historia del teatro en España VI.* London: Tamesis Books, 1979.

Silverman, Kaja. *The Threshold of the Visible World.* New York: Routledge, 1996.

Simón Palmer, María del Cármen. "Cuidado del cuerpo de las personas reales." Redondo, *Le Corps.* 113–22.

Smith, Dawn L. "Women and Men in a World Turned Upside-Down: An Approach to Three Plays by Tirso." *Revista canadiense de estudios hispanicos* 10.2 (1986): 247–60.

Soufas, Teresa Scott. *Dramas of Distinction: a Study of Plays by Golden Age Women.* Lexington: UP of Kentucky, 1997.

———, ed. *Women's Acts: Plays by Women Dramatists of Spain's Golden Age.* Lexington: UP of Kentucky, 1997.

Stallybrass, Peter. "The World Turned Upside Down: Inversion, Gender and the State." *The Matter of Difference: Materialist Feminist Criticism of Shakespeare.* Ed. Valerie Wayne. Ithaca: Cornell UP, 1991.

Stoll, Anita K. and Dawn L. Smith. *Gender, Identity, and Representation in Spain's Golden Age.* Lewisburg, PA: Bucknell UP, 2000.

———. *The Perception of Women in Golden Age Drama.* Lewisburg, PA: Bucknell UP, 1996.

Stoneman, Richard. *Palmyra and Its Empire: Zenobia's Revolt Against Rome.* Ann Arbor: U of Michigan P, 1992.

Storrs, Christopher. *The Resilience of the Spanish Monarchy 1665–1700.* Oxford: Oxford UP, 2006.

Stradling R.A. *Philip IV and the Government of Spain 1621–1665.* Cambridge: Cambridge UP, 1988.

———. *Spain's Struggle for Europe 1598–1668.* London: Hambledon Press, 1994.

Strong, Roy. *Gloriana: The Portraits of Queen Elizabeth I.* London: Pimlico, 1987.

———. *Splendor at Court: Renaissance Spectacle and the Theater of Power.* Boston: Houghton Mifflin, 1973.

Tate, Robert B. "Mythology in Spanish Historiography of the Middle Ages and the Renaissance." *Hispanic Review* 22.1 (1954): 1–18.

Taylor, Scott. *Honor and Violence in Golden Age Spain.* New Haven: Yale UP, 2008.

Templin, E.H. "Another Instance of Tirso's Self-Plagiarism." *Hispanic Review* 5.2 (1937): 176–80.

ter Horst, Robert. *Calderón. The Secular Plays.* Lexington: UP of Kentucky, 1982.

Tirso de Molina (Gabriel Téllez). *La república al revés. Obras de Tirso de Molina.* Ed. María del Pilar Palomo. Biblioteca de Autores Españoles. Madrid: Atlas, 1971. 57–112.

Turner, Victor. *From Ritual to Theatre: the Human Seriousness of Play.* New York: Performing Arts Journal Publications, 1982.

Varey, J.E. and N.D. Shergold. *Comedias en Madrid: 1603–1709. Repertorio y Estudio Bibliográfico. Fuentes para la Historia del Teatro en España IX.* London: Tamesis Books, 1989.

———. *Teatros y comedias en Madrid: 1600–1650. Estudios y documentos. Fuentes para la Historia del Teatro en España III.* London: Tamesis Books, 1971.

———. *Teatros y comedias en Madrid: 1651–1665. Estudios y documentos. Fuentes para la Historia del Teatro en España VI.* London: Tamesis Books, 1973.

Vázquez García, Francisco and A. Moreno Mengíbar. *Sexo y razón: una genealogía de la moral sexual en España (siglos XVI–XX).* Madrid: Ediciones Akal, 1997.

Vega Carpio, Lope de. *El animal de Hungría.* Web PDF file. 12 December 2010. <http://humanidades.uprrp.edu/smjeg/libretos/V/Vega,%20Lope%20de/animal%20de%20hungria,%20el,%20lope%20de%20vega.pdf>.

———. *Corona trágica: vida y muerte de la serenísima reina de Escocia María Estuarda.* Ed. C. Gianffreda. Firenze: Alinea, 2009.

———. *La vengadora de las mujeres. Obras de Lope de Vega.* Vol. 13. Biblioteca de Autores Españoles. Madrid: Galo Saez, 1930. 615–46.

Villalón, Cristobal de. *El Scholastico.* Ed. Richard J.A. Kerr. Madrid: Consejo Superior de Investigaciones Científicas, 1967.

Vindel Pérez, Ingrid. "Política y teodicea: una disertación de *La cisma de Ingalaterra*. *Calderón 2000. Homenaje a Kurt Reichenberger en su 80 cumpleaños*. Ed. Ignacio Arellano. Vol. 2. Kassel: Edition Reichenberger, 2002. 383–96.

Vives, Juan Luis. *Instrucción de la mujer cristiana*. Trans. Juan Justianiano. Introduction, revision, and annotation by Elizabeth Howe. Madrid: Fundación Universitaria Española, 1995.

Walthaus, Rina. "Classical Myth and Legend in Late Medieval and Renaissance Ideas of Gender: The Use of Classical Examples in Spanish Treatises for Women." *Critica Hispánica* 18.2 (1996): 361–74.

———. "La comedia de Doña Ana Caro Mallén de Soto." *Estudios sobre escritoras hispánicas en honor de Georgina Sabat-Rivers*. Ed. Lou Charnon-Deutsch. Madrid: Castalia, 1992. 326–41.

———. "*Femme forte* y emblema dramático: la Jezabel de Tirso y la Semíramis de Calderón." *Actas del V Congreso de la Asociación Internacional Siglo de Oro* (Münster, 1999). Ed. Christoph Strosetzki. Madrid/Frankfurt am Main: Iberoamericana Vervuert, 2001. 1361–70.

———. "La fortaleza de Cenobia y la mutabilidad de Fortuna: dos emblemas femeninos en *La gran Cenobia* de Calderón." —*Que toda la vida es sueño, y los sueños, sueños son: homenaje a don Pedro Calderón de la Barca*. Ed. Ysla Campbell. Ciudad Juárez, México: Universidad Autónoma de Ciudad Juárez, 2000. 109–28.

———. "'Representar tragedias así la Fortuna sabe.' La representación de Fortuna en dos comedias tempranas de Calderón (*Saber del mal y del bien* y *La gran Cenobia*)." *Calderón 2000. Actas del Congreso Internacional IV Centenario del nacimiento de Calderón (Universidad de Navarra, 2000)*. Ed. Ignacio Arellano. Vol. 2. Kassel: Reichenberger, 2002. 397–409.

Wardropper, Bruce. "The Dramatization of Figurative Language in the Spanish Theater." *Yale French Studies* 47 (1972): 189–98.

Warnicke, Retha M. *The Rise and Fall of Anne Boleyn*. Cambridge: Cambridge UP, 1989.

Weimer, Christopher B. "Ana Caro's *El conde Partinuplés* and Calderón's *La vida es sueño*: Protofeminism and Heuristic Imitation." *Bulletin of the Comediantes* 52.1 (2000): 123–46.

———. "A *Comedia* Re-Viewed: An Alternative Reading of Tirso's *La república al revés*." *Looking at the* Comedia *in the Year of the Quincentennial*. Proceedings of the 1992 Symposium on Golden Age Drama at the University of Texas, El Paso, March 18–21. Ed. Barbara Mujica and Sharon D. Voros. Lanham, MD: UP of America, 1993. 219–25.

———. "The Oedipal Drama of Tirso's *La república al revés*." *Bulletin of the comediantes* 47.2 (1995): 291–309.

Weissberger, Barbara F. *Isabel Rules: Constructing Queenship, Wielding Power*. Minneapolis: U of Minnesota P, 2004.

Williamson, James A. *The Tudor Age*. London: Longman, 1979.

Woodall, Joanna. "An Exemplary Consort: Antonis Mor's Portrait of Mary Tudor." *Art History* 14.2 (1991): 192–224.

———. *Portraiture: Facing the Subject*. Manchester: Manchester UP, 1997.

Wright, Elizabeth. *Pilgrimage to Patronage: Lope de Vega and the Court of Philip III 1598–1621*. Lewisburg: Bucknell UP 2001.

Zabaleta, Juan de. *El Emperador Commodo. Historia discursiva según el texto de Herodiano*. Madrid: Andrés García, 1668.

Zayas y Sotomayor, María de. *Tres novelas amorosas y ejemplares y tres desengaños amorosos*. Ed. Alicia Redondo Goicochea. Madrid: Editorial Castalia, 1989.

Zuese, Alicia R. "Ana Caro and the Literary Academies of Seventeenth-Century Spain." *Women's Literacy in Early Modern Spain and the New World*. Ed. Anne J. Cruz and Rosilie Hernández. Farnham, UK: Ashgate, 2011. 191–208.

Index

Note: **Bold** type indicates illustrations

Álamos de Barrientos, Baltasar 27–8, 143, 165
Alfonso I (the Wise)
 Segunda Partida 26
Allen, John 8
Álvarez García, Belén 199n24, 200
Álvarez Osorio 50
Ana of Austria (daughter of Philip III) 34, 43
Andrachuk, Gregory Peter 138, 146n18
Andrade, Alfonso 140
Anthony, Ruth (El Saffar) 2n4, 7, 142, 221
Aparicio Maydeu, Javier 11n1
Aram, Bethany 30, 31n23, 106n14
Arbella Stuart 162
arbitristas 10, 50–51, 53, 83, 191, 221
Arellano, Ignacio 46n44, 49n5, 52n9, 53n12, 78n27, 78n29, 86, 199n24, 209n31
Aristotle 4, 92

Bakhtin, Mikhail 48n4, 78
Bances Candamo, Francisco 1, 49, 50, 51, 210
 Calderón and 179n6, 200–202, 210
 Como se curan los celos 46
 loas 46, 199
 La piedra filosofal 3, 207–10
 ¿Quién es quien premia al amor? 43, 46, 179n6, 199–207, 212
 Theatro de los Theatros de los passados y presentes siglos 48, 49, 150–51, 205
Baños de Velasco, Juan 50
Barahona, Renato 188n16
Barcia y Zambrana, José 15, 18
Barrera y Leirado, Cayetano Alberto de la 148, 148n22

Barrionuevo, Jerónimo de
 Avisos 35, 178, 184, 185, 196, 198
Bass, Laura 2n4, 45n43, 106n15, 169n3, 193n22, 219n5
beauty
 in kings 59–61, 84
 neoplatonism and 58
 in queens 57, 61–2, 64–5, 173
 as power (authority) 57–8, 59, 61, 81
 in women 12, 57–9, 84–8, 95, 98, 119, 135–6, 139
Belsey, Andrew and Catherine 152n30
Bennassar, Bartolomé 37
Berkeley, George 16
Bernis, Carmen 171
Boccaccio, Giovanni
 De Claris mulieribus 20, 52, 53, 91, 101, 114
body politic (*see also* monarchy, queens, women) 26–37, 88, 98, 104, 105, 122, 204
 body natural and 19, 116, 118, 119, 134, 141, 142, 152, 153, 164, 165, 181, 204–5, 210
 king's body and 26–9
 women and 29–30, 40, 46, 84, 131, 156, 174, 222
Boleyn, Anne 135, **136**, 144
 in Calderón's *La cisma de Inglaterra* 15, 38, 128, 133, 138–42, 146, 166
 in Pedro Rivadeneira's *Historia eclessiastica* 125, 126, 133–8, 143–4
Botticelli, Sandro 64
Bourdon, Sebastien 176–9, **177**, 181, 183, 197–8
Brown, Jonathan 5, 18, 47, 169, 171
Buckley, Veronica 176n5, 179n7, 211n34
Bushnell, Rebecca 17, 18, 55, 73, 82n36, 103, 110–11, 112, 117, 154
Butler, Judith 11n1, 15, 77, 117, 222

Caba, María Y 38
Cabrera, Alonso de 41
Calderón de la Barca, Pedro 2, 3, 38, 40, 41, 44, 45
  calderonistas (*escuela de*) 50, 148–50
  as court playwright 47–51
  as *homo strategicus* 48, 51, 180, 189
  Machiavelli and 4n6, 51, 55, 74, 118n22
  Rivadeneira and 123–9, 131–9, 143–5, 147
  Tirso de Molina and 88–9, 94
  works
    Afectos de odio y amor 9, 38, 41, 169, 176n4, 180–99, 200, 201, 214, 219, 221
    autos sacramentales 46, 138, 179, 180, 185, 188n15, 197, 198, 199
    Las cadenas del demonio 92n6
    La cisma de Inglaterra 9, 15, 38, 40, 119, 123–47, 148, 160, 165, 166, 190, 199, 221
    Darlo todo y no dar nada 50n6
    La estatua de Prometeo 8n13, 45n42
    Fieras afemina Amor 42, 45
    Las fortunas de Andromeda y Perseo 45
    La gran Cenobia 9, 18, 19, 47–77, 78, 79, 82, 85, 86, 89, 91–2, 94, 96, 114, 117, 119, 122, 135, 156, 181, 186, 189, 190, 192, 216, 219, 221
    La hija del aire 3, 9, 15, 18, 53n12, 81n34, 91–122, 155, 160, 181, 182, 183, 190, 192, 213, 216
    El mayor encanto amor, 157, 158n33
    El mayor monstruo del mundo 45, 45n43
    El médico de su honra 7, 142, 162n36, 194
    El monstruo de los jardines 92n6
    La niña de Gómez Arias 38
    No hay burlas con el amor 189n17
    El pintor de su deshonra 219
    La protestación de la fe 179, 185, 188n15, 197–9
    Psiquis y Cupido 43
    El purgatorio de San Patricio 55n14
    La púrpura de la rosa 93n7
    La segunda esposa y triunfar muriendo 46
    La vida es sueño 55, 92n6, 100, 142, 182, 194, 207, 211, 216n3
Calderón, Inés (La Calderona) 45, 45n41, 119, 139–40
Calderón, María (actress and sister of La Calderona) 45n41
Calderón, Rodrigo 75n25, 133
Camargo, Ignacio de 17, 116, 150
Campbell, Jodi 2n3
Carlos Varona, María Cruz de 34n25
Caro Mallén de Soto, Ana
  El conde Partinuplés 189, 215–20
Carreño de Miranda, Juan **60**
Carrión, María Mercedes 6n10, 215, 216, 219n6
Castilla Soto, Josefina 121n26
Castillejo, Cristobal de 21
Castro, Francisco de 58
Catherine of Aragon 22, 24, 25, 129, 131, 140n14
  in Calderón's *La cisma de Inglaterra* (as Catalina de Aragón) 38, 128–9, 130–34, 138, 141, 144, 146, 186
  in Pedro de Rivadeneira's *Historia Eclesiástica* (as Catalina de Aragón) 125–6, 128–9, 131–5, 137–8, 144
Cerda, Juan de
  Vida política de todos los estados de mujeres 21, 102
Charles II (King of England) 193
Charles II of Spain (last Habsburg king) 1n2, 9, 35–7, 45, 49, **60**, 77, 120–21, 210, 221
  deficiencies of 9–10, 59–61, 121
  impotence (*see also* succession) 10n15, 203, 207–8
  marriages 41, 43, 46, 54n13, 121, 200, 203, 207
  as spectator of *comedias* 44, 46, 54n13, 75n26, 77
Charles V (Holy Roman Emperor) 30, 61n19, 85, 106n14
Charles Stuart I of England (Prince of Wales) 146

Chaucer, Geoffrey 67
Christina of Sweden 176–85, 188, 193–4,
    196–200, 202, 210, 221
  in Bances Candamo's *Quien es quien
    apremia amor* 199–207
  in Calderón's *Afectos de odio y amor*
    38, 180–99
  in Calderón's *La protestación de la fe*
    179–80, 197–9
  equestrian portrait of 176–8, **177**,
    183, 197–8
  in Mamoulian's film *Queen Christina*
    179, 210–14
Civil, Pierre 27, 28, 165, 169n3
Coello, Antonio
  Calderón and 148–50, 156, 162n36
  El conde de Sex 40, 148–67, 194, 206
Coello, Luis 148
comedia (*see also* theater)
  actresses (*see also* Calderón, Inés;
    Garbo, Greta) 13–15, 18–19, 44,
    65, 116–17, 152–3, 181, 188n15,
    211, 220
  comedias de capa y espada 151, 152, 188
  comedias de enredo 151, 182, 196, 197
  comedia de fábrica 202, 207
  comedia histórica 202
  comedias de privanza 133n9
  corrales 6, 9, 13, 42, 222
  Count Duke of Olivares (*see* Olivares,
    Count Duke of)
  María's critics of 13–19, 116, 150, 181
  dance in 14, 42, 48, 140–41
  denouement 6–7, 14–15, 19, 77, 86, 88,
    138, 146n18, 166, 196, 199, 201,
    207, 217, 220
  female characters in 2, 11–13, 15, 19,
    20n14, 25–6, 41, 117, 222
    mujer erudita 67, 197, 210, 216
    mujer esquiva 41, 182, 192, 197,
      208, 210
    mujer guerrero 41, 66, 197
    mujer varonil 41, 99n11, 182, 183,
      187, 192, 197, 213, 220
    mujer vestida de hombre 11, 116,
      117, 181, 210, 213
    queens (*see also individual plays*)
      3, 9, 1, 26, 38–41, 81–2, 221
  feminizing effect on audience 16–17
  gender and power in 1–3, 5, 10, 50–51,
    53, 78, 116–17, 220–22
  gender in 2, 5, 11–19, 46, 68, 88, 92,
    124, 181
  kings as spectators of 5–6, 7, 8–9, 10,
    44, 46, 54n13, 75n26, 77, 119,
    123n2, 157
  kings in (*see also individual plays*)
    5–6, 7
    doubling of king's body 5
    feminization of 3, 7, 17, 221
    tyrants 5, 44
  mythological plays 6, 8n13, 42, 45,
    207–10
  palace theater 1, 3, 9, 10, 18, 42–3,
    48, 51, 54, 77, 118–19, 133, 180,
    185n12, 199, 200, 222
    audience 9, 54
    Cuarto de la Reina 42
    didactic and pedagogical
      dimension of 9–10, 118
    king in the audience 5, 6, 7, 54,
      77, 119
    queen(s) in the audience 6,
      41–2, 77
  queens as participants in 41–4, 199
  queens as spectators 26, 41, 44, 54n13,
    77, 123n2
  relationship to political theories and
    arbitristas 50–51
  as response to societal crisis 1–3,
    50–51
  as *speculum principis* 3–4
Connor, Catherine 6n10, 116n19
Córdoba, Fray Martín de
  El Jardín de las nobles doncellas
    20, 91
Cotarelo y Mori, Emilio 13–17, 19, 116,
    140, 150, 153, 181
Cowans, Jon 36
Cranston, Jodi 170n3
Cromwell, Oliver 193–4
Cruickshank, Don W 45n41, 47n3,
    151n28
Cruz, Anne J. 2n4, 12, 22, 30, 31,
    148n20, 215
Cuervo Arengo, 200

Danielsson, Arne 176n5, 183n11, 198
Davis, Charles 27, 143
Davis, Natalie Zemon 64n20, 78, 116
Davis, Tracy C. 18n8
de Armas, Frederick 52n9, 56
de Lauretis, Teresa 102
de regimine principium (*see also speculum principis*) 4, 22–3, 50, 118
decir sin decir 50n6, 51, 89
Delpech, François 114–15
Descartes, René 185, 210
Devereaux, Robert (*see* Elizabeth I of England)
Diamante, Juan Bautista
   La reina María Estuarda 38n28
Diamond, Elin 5
Díaz Castañón, Carmen 209n31
la doncella guerrera 114–15
Donnell, Sidney 17n7
Dopico Black, Georgina 2n4, 7
Dudley, Robert, Earl of Leicester 162

Earenfight, Theresa 12, 22, 31, 32
Edwards, Gwynne 91, 93n7, 99, 118, 120
Egido, Teófanes 113n17
El Saffar, Ruth (*see* Anthony, Ruth)
Elias, Norbert 48
Elizabeth I of England 24n17, 61, 144, 150, 156, 162, 166
   absence in *comedia* 38, 124, 126, 146–7, 148, 167
   androgyny and virile behavior of 40, 41, 122, 127, 221
   Anne Boleyn and 126, 144, 147
   in Antonio Coello's *El conde de Sex* 148–67
   Armada Portrait 152, **153**
   doctrine of king's two bodies and 28n21, 40, 165
   in Lope de Vega's *Corona trágica* 151
   in Pedro de Rivadeneira's *Historia Eclesiástica* 124–8, 133, 144, 147
   as possible inspiration for *comedia* 41, 122, 124, 147, 216
   Robert Deveraux, Earl of Essex and 149–50, 142, 156, 157, 162, 164
   speeches 40, 165, 167

theatricality and self representation 40, 154, 180n9, 197
virginity and 129n7
Elliott, J.H. 1n2, 5, 18, 31, 47, 50, 156n32, 157n33, 158n35
Ellis, Jonathan 215, 216, 220
Elyot, Thomas
   Defence of Good Women 22
equestrian portraits (*see* portraiture, equestrian portraits)
Erasmus, Desiderus 24, 41, 131
Espinosa, Juan de
   Diálogo en laude de mujeres 21, 91
exemplarity 125, 126
   in the *comedia* 3–4, 51, 53–4, 79, 82, 85, 91, 157
   female 20–26, 82, 84–5, 91
   Spanish treatises on 20–22, 53, 91

Falomir Faus, Miguel 169n3, 193n22
Fenster, Thelma S. 20n11
Féral, Josette 5, 6n9, 15, 217
Fernández Santamaría, J.A. 87n42, 118n22
Fernando of Aragon 39–40, 125, 132, 216
Ferrer Valls, Teresa 8n12, 42–3, 119n23
Findlay, Alison 127, 162
Firenzuola, Agnolo
   Dialogo delle bellezze delle donne 58
Fischer, Susan L. 92n5, 94, 105, 106
Florencia, Jerónimo 31
Forcione, Alban 2, 56, 153
Foucault, Michel 72, 118
Fox, Dian 2, 3–4, 7, 8, 50n8, 87n42, 118n22, 142
Foxe, John
   The Book of Martyrs 144
Fragoso, Juan Bautista 13, 181
Franko, Mark 7, 8, 48
Freedman, Barbara 6, 217–18, 219
Frye, Susan 40n35, 167

Gaines, Jane 211
Galino Carrillo, María de los Angeles 121n26
Garber, Marjorie 11n1
Garbo, Greta 179, 210–14, **212**, **213**, **214**
   Barthes, Roland on 213
García Castañón, Santiago 49n5, 209n31

Garland, Lynda 79n32, 79n33, 86n41
gaze
    male 64, 66, 70, 217
    in painting 174, 178, 198
    scopophilia 64, 70, 156
    societal 3, 58, 77, 116
    in theater and *comedias* 6, 15, 64, 66, 70–71, 137, 140, 142, 156, 217–19
gender (*see also* body politic; *comedia*, gender in; masculinity; monarchy; women)
    theories of 15, 17, 88, 102–3, 117
    transgressions in the *comedia* 84, 93, 105
Gibbons, Edward 65
Gilbert, John (actor) 179, 211, **213**, **214**
Goethe, William 91
Goldberg, Harriet 20n12
Gómez de Sandoval y Rojas, Francisco (*see* Lerma, Duke of)
Gómez Suárez de Figueroa 162n37
González, Lola 19n10
Goodman, Eleanor 120, 121n25
Gracián, Baltasar 39
Greenblatt, Stephen 159n35
Greer, Margaret 5, 6, 8n12, 8n13, 45, 47
Grieve, Patricia 40n33
Guevara, Antonio de
    Epistolas familiares 21, 52–3, 65
    Relox de príncipes 11, 28
Guillen de Castro
    El curioso impertinente 8
Guzmán, Gaspar de (*see* Olivares, Count Duke of)
gynocracies 2, 24n17, 210, 215, 221

Hammer, Paul E.J. 156n32
Hampton, Timothy 51
Hearn, Karen 61n19
Heathe, Nicholas (Archbishop of York) 165
Henry VIII 24n17
    in Calderón's *La cisma de Inglaterra* 15, 130–47 *passim*, 160, 166, 190, 221
    marriage to Catherine of Aragon 24, 129, 131, 143
    in Rivadeneira's *Historia Eclesiástica* 125, 128, 132
Hernández Araico, Susana 117n20

Hesse, Everett W. 100, 106
Hildner, David 50n6, 52n9, 56n16, 76
Hollmann, Hildegard 52n9
homo clausus 48
homo ludens 48n4
homo strategicus 48, 51, 88, 180, 189
Howard, Anita 2n3
Howe, Elizabeth Teresa 21n15, 25
Huarte de San Juan, Juan 36, 59, 61, 86, 102, 106, 185
Huizinga, Johan 48n4
Hume, Martin 34
Hunt, Lynn 135

Irene, Empress of Byzantium 53, 78, 79, 86n41
    in Tirso de Molina's *La república al revés* 19, 78–89, 109n16, 114, 186, 211, 216, 219, 221
Isabel I of Castile (la Católica) 20–21, 22, 24, 25, 30, 38, 39, 40, 67, 125, 216
    ambivalent attitudes toward 39–40
    in *comedia* 38–9
    marriage to Fernando I of Aragon 21, 39
Isabel of Bourbon (wife of Philip IV) 41, 77, 133, 148n22, 169n2
    childbearing 36–7
    and *comedias* 41, 54n13, 77, 123n2, 157–8
    equestrian portrait of 169, 171–4, **171**, 178, 199
    and Olivares 133, 158
    political role of 31, 36–7, 77
Isabel of Portugal 30
Isabel of Valois 34–5, 41, 42

Jankowski, Theodora A. 40n35, 162n37
Joanna of Aragon, portrait by Raphael 61, **63**
Jordan, Constance 20n14, 22n16, 24n17
Joseph Ferdinand of Bavaria 203n29, 209n32
Juan José de Austria (illegitimate son of Philip IV) 45, 119, 121, 140
Juana I of Castile 22, 25, 30, 106n14
Juana Inés de la Cruz 22, 187
Juana of Portugal (Juana de Austria) 30, 42

Kamen, Henry 1n2, 22, 31, 36, 186n14
Kantorowizc, Ernst H. 29n21
Kaufman, Gloria 24
Kelly, Joan 20n11
Kelso, Ruth 33
Kennedy, Ruth 38n28, 53n11, 88
Kritzman, Lawrence 65
Kurtz, Barbara 197

Lacan, Jacques 5, 70
Landy, Marcia 210n33, 211
Lanza, Diego 54
Laqueur, Thomas 102
Lees, Clare A. 20n11
Lehfeldt, Elizabeth 3, 17, 39, 50, 83, 84n38
Leon, Francisco de 84
Leon, Luis de
   La perfecta casada 11, 32–3
Leopold I 44n40, 77, 120n24
Lerma, Duke of (Francisco Gómez de Sandoval y Rojas) 45n43, 75n25, 133, 157
Levin, Carole 40n34, 40n35, 122n27, 129n7, 144, 154, 156, 165
Liedtke, Walter A. 169, 174
Linsey, Karen 129n6
Lipmann, Stephen 99, 103n13, 106, 107
Lisón Tolosana, Carmelo 50, 191
Loftis, John 124n4
Louis XIV 44n40, 48, 77
Lucena, Juan de 39
Luján, Pedro de
   Coloquios Matrimoniales 32–3, 81, 176
Luna, Alvaro de
   Libro de las virtuosas e claras mujeres 21
Luna, Lola 215
Lundelius, Ruth 176n4, 179, 182, 184, 187, 188, 197
Lynch, John 120

MacCurdy, Raymond R. 133n9, 148, 162n36
Machiavelli, Niccolo
   The Prince 55, 56n16, 74, 85, 87, 112
Machiavellianism in Spain 87, 132, 143, 205
   anti-Machiavellianism 4n6, 51, 85, 88
   in Bances Candamo 205
   in Calderón 55, 56n16, 74, 118n22, 143, 207
   in Tirso de Molina 85, 87–8
Mackenzie, Ann L. 123n2, 124n4, 128n5, 133n8, 139, 146, 147, 148, 149, 150n26, 179n6, 200, 201, 207
Maler, Bertil 200, 201n27, 202n28, 203n29
Maravall, José Antonio 28n20, 87, 88, 118n22
Margarita de la Cruz (daughter of Empress María) 31
Margarita of Austria
   and the *comedia* 43
   death 133
   equestrian portrait of 169–74, **170**, 178, 199
   marriage to Philip III 31, 41
   political role 31, 36, 133
Maria Anna of Neuburg
   childbearing potential 203, 207–8
   and the *comedia* 43–4, 46, 200
   marriage to Charles II 41, 200, 203, 207
Maria Antonia of Austria 54n13
Maria Luisa of Orleans
   childbearing potential 35–6, 46, 203
   death 200, 203
   marriage to Charles II 35, 41, 54n13, 77, 121, 203
   participation in *comedia* 43–4, 54n13
Maria of Austria (Empress) 22, 31, 41, 67, 142n15
Maria Teresa (Infanta) 44n40
Mariana, Juan de
   De rege et regis institutione 23, 24, 29, 51, 54, 55, 79, 108, 137, 190
Mariana of Austria (second wife of Philip IV)
   and the *comedia* 42, 43, 45–6, 54, 120, 200, 207
   marriage to Philip IV 35, 41, 77, 120, 207
   political role of 44–5, 54, 77, 120–21
   pregnancies 35, 120n24
   regency of 9, 31, 121
Marie Antoinette 135
Mariscal, George 124n4, 141
Martín Rizo, Pablo
   Norte de Príncipes 160, 190
Martínez de Toledo, Alfonso
   El Corbacho 20
Mary, Queen of Scots 150, 162, 163

Mary Tudor
  in Calderón's *La cisma de Inglaterra*
    38, 131, 142, 144–6, 166
  daughter of Henry VIII and Catherine
    of Aragon 24
  marriage to Philip II 61n19
  Mor portrait of 61, **62**
  in Rivadeneira's *Historia Eclesiástica*
    131, 145n17
masculinity (*see* body politic; *comedia*,
    gender; monarchy; women)
  in Calderón's *Afectos de odio y amor* 191
  in Calderón's *La gran Cenobia* 54, 68,
    70, 72
  in Calderón's *La hija del aire* 99, 100,
    105, 109, 111
  in Caro's *El conde Partinuplés*
  in *comedia* 2, 5
  crisis of 3, 7, 9–10, 17, 50, 83–4, 221
  theories of 102, 218
Masson, Georgina 179, 194
Matos Fragoso, Juan de 148
Mattingly, Garrett 129, 132
Maximilian II (Habsburg Emperor) 33, 67
Maximilian II Emanuel (Elector of
    Bavaria) 203n39, 209n32
McKendrick, Melveena 1n1, 2, 7, 11n1,
    41, 50n7, 52, 88, 99n11, 116n19,
    137, 182, 215
McKim Smith, Gridley 169n3
McLean, Ian 92
Medici, Catherine de' 34, 47
Mendes Silva, Rodrigo 22, 67
Menéndez y Pelayo, Marcelino 169, 182
Merola, Jerónimo 26
Michaelis, Carolina 148n21, 148n22, 149
Moffitt, John F. 169, 174
Moir, Duncan 49n5, 207
monarchy (*see also* body politic, *comedia*,
    queens, women)
  in *comedia* 2, 4–5, 7, 9, 41, 46,
    180–81, 221, 222
  comedia as aesthetics of 3, 51
  as corporate entity 32, 120, 216, 222
  corpus mysticum 28
  crisis in Spain (*see also arbitristas*) of
    1, 9–10, 18, 50, 52, 89, 115, 147,
    208, 222

doctrine of two bodies 28n21, 40, 165
feminization of 3–4, 7, 18, 77, 81, 88,
    112, 119, 209–10, 221
gender and gendering of 2, 39,
    61, 117
inherited 23, 104, 193, 203
institution of 1, 48, 54, 147, 180, 208
masculinity and 6, 9, 18, 122,
    124, 221
and portraiture (*see also* portraiture)
    173, 180–81
succession 10n15, 23, 24n17, 32–3,
    36–7, 89n43, 120, 140, 202–3,
    207–8, 209n32, 216
symbols of 82, 164
tyrants 4, 17, 18, 54–6, 73, 75, 79, 82,
    103, 112, 117, 154, 160
women and (*see* queens, women)
Monet, Michel 29
Montoussé Vega, Juan Luis 215, 216n3
Montrose, Louis Adrian 29n21, 40n35,
    47n1, 61n19, 122n27, 174, 180
Mor, Antonis 61, **62**, 170n3
Moreno Mengíbar, A. 14n5, 16, 58
mundus inversus 78–9, 88

Nader, Helen, 11n2, 12
Nahoum-Grappe, Veronique 64n20
Navarro, Emilia 33n24
Nieto Soria, José Manuel 28n20
Novo, Yolanda 56n16

Ocampo, Florián de
  Crónica General de España 208
Ochoa, Eugenio de 65n21, 148n21, 148n23
Olivares, Count Duke of (Gaspar de
    Guzmán)
  comedia and 88, 119, 157
  equestrian portrait of 170, 174,
    175, 178
  influence on Philip IV 9, 18, 88, 119,
    140, 157–8
  relationship with Isabel of Bourbon
    133, 158
Oostendorp, Henk 179, 185, 200
Orgel, Stephen 102
Oriel, Charles 124n4, 139n13, 146n19
Ornstein, Jacob 20

Parker, Alexander A. 123n3, 124n4, 126, 140n14, 146
Patterson, Alan K.G. 119
Pellicer del Tovar, José 4–5
Pérez de Guzmán, Fernán 22, 52
Pérez de Moya, Juan 21
Pérez de Oliva, Fernán 39
performance (*see comedia*, theater, theatricality)
   vs. law of the theater 5–6, 7, 14, 19, 77, 88, 217, 220
   as repetition 221
   as surrogation 46, 208
   theories of 5–6, 8
Perry, Mary Elizabeth 12, 99n11
Philip II 30, 37, 41, 42, 43, 61, 67, 145, 169n2, 171
Philip III 22, 31, 34, 41, 43, 67, 75n25, 88, 133, 157, 169, **172**, 173, 178
Philip IV 40, 53n11, 146
   and *comedia*
      comedia doubles for 190
      involvement with theater 9
      as playwright 148–9
      as spectator of the *comedia* 54n13, 119, 123n2, 157, 200
      theatricality of 18
   Count Duke Olivares and 9, 88, 140
   death of 42, 54n13
   equestrian portrait of 158, 173–4, **173**
   illegitimate son, Juan José of Austria, and 121
   and La Calderona 45, 119, 139, 140
   marriage to Isabel of Bourbon 31, 37, 41, 77, 157
   marriage to Mariana of Austria 35, 41, 46, 120
   perceived as weak monarch 9, 18, 52, 89, 113n17, 119, 221
   and Queen Christina of Sweden 176, 178–80, 182, 193, 196, 198, 200, 212
Philip of Anjou 203n29, 209n32
Pimentel, Antonio de (Spanish ambassador to Sweden) 179, 196, 198, 200n26
   as character in Bances Candamo's *¿Quién es quien premia al amor?* 203
   as character in Rouben Mammoulian's film *Queen Christina* 211–14
   and Sebastien Bourdon's painting of Queen Christina 198
Pineda, Juan de 15
Plato 17, 55, 59, 82, 82n36, 103
political treatises and theorists (*see also arbitristas*) 50, 53, 87, 79, 108
Porqueras Mayo, Alberto 4
portraiture 61–2, 64, 106, 152, 180–81, 183, 184, 193, 197, 212
   in *comedia* 50n6, 217, 219
   equestrian portraits 169–78, 181–3, 193
Postlewait, Thomas 18n8
Prieto, María Remedios 188n15, 189
privados and *privanza* 9, 18, 110, 119, 133, 156, 157
   in *comedias* 216, 133n9, 157

Queen Christina film directed by Rouben Mamoulian 179, 210–14
queens (*see names of individual queens,* body politic, *comedias*, monarchy, women)
   beauty in 57, 61–2, 65
   body of 20, 26, 33, 174, 176
      reproductive body of 33–7, 46, 106, 120, 193, 203, 207–8
   portraits of 61, **62**, **63**, **136**, 152, **153**, 169–74, **170**, **171**, 178, 199
   prejudice against 30
   Salic laws 186n14
   Spanish 30–32
Quevedo, Francisco de 50n7, 98, 108, 158, 190
Quintero, María Cristina 46n44, 49n5, 56n16, 91n1, 209n31

Raphael 61, **63**
Redondo, Augustin, 21, 26, 27n19, 169n3
Redworth, Glyn 146n18
Ribot Garcia, Luis, 9n14, 60n18
Richards Annette 7, 8
Ríos Mazcarelle, Manuel 35, 37n27
Rivadeneira, Pedro de, 53, 102, 160
   comedia criticism 14, 16–19, 153
   Historia Eclesiástica del Scisma del Reino de Inglaterra 123–9, 131–8, 143–4, 145n17, 147

Roach, Joseph 6, 9, 14, 46, 116, 217
Rodríguez del Padrón, Juan 91
Rogers, Daniel 116, 162n36
Ruano de la Haza, José María 8
Rubens 170
Rubio, María José 31n23, 34, 43, 44, 77, 121n25, 158
Ruiz Ramón, Francisco 92n6, 118n21
Rupp, Stephen 3, 4n6, 46n45, 87n42, 118n22

Saavedra Fajardo, Diego de 4n6, 27, 29, 40, 50, 53, 56, 79, 86, 87, 108, 109, 115, 119, 121, 160, 190, 191
Saenz de Aguirre, José 14, 15
Said, Edward 147
San Juan, Rose Marie 176, 178, 179, 193, 194, 196n23
Sánchez Belén, Juan 49n5, 209n31
Sánchez Escribano, F. 4
Sánchez, Magdalena 22, 31–2, 34, 36, 67, 102, 133n10, 142n15
Sander, Nicolas (*see also* Rivadeneira)
De origine ac Progressu Schismatis Anglicani 123n3, 135
Sanz Ayán, Carmen 9, 42, 43, 50n8
Saxonhouse, Arlene W. 26n18, 85, 87
Schmiedel, Donald 148n21, 149n25, 158n34
Semiramis, Queen of Assyria 20, 22, 38, 53, 81, 91
  in Calderón's *La hija del aire* 3, 15, 81n34, 91–122, 181–3, 185–6, 206, 211, 213, 216, 219, 221
Shakespeare, William 114, 129, 141, 159, 197
Shergold, N.D. 5, 8, 42, 44n39, 119n23, 123n2
Silverman, Kaja 70
Simón Palmer, María del Cármen 43
Smith, Dawn L. 20n14, 78n27, 85n39
Socrates 17, 82n36
Soufas, Teresa Scott 2n4, 13, 15, 25, 102, 189n18, 215, 216, 218
Spanish Match 146
speculum principis 52, 77, 89
speculum reginae 20, 128, 133
Stallybrass, Peter 78, 88, 100
Stoll, Anita K. 2n4, 11n1
Stoneman, Richard 52n10, 65, 67

Storrs, Christopher 1n2, 9n14, 121n25
Stradling R.A. 1n2, 4, 18, 31, 37, 121n25, 174
Strong, Roy 170n3, 180
succession 36, 89n43, 120, 140, 202, 203, 207–8, 209n32, 216
Suzuki, Mihoko 12n3, 30, 31n23

Tate, Robert B. 208n30
Taylor, Scott 188n16
Templin, E.H. 78n28
ter Horst, Robert 2, 38, 189
theater (*see comedia and* performance)
  as feminizing influence 16–17
  as law 5–6, 7, 14, 19, 77, 88, 217, 220
  vs. performance 6, 15, 220, 222
theatricality 6n9, 15, 17–18, 44
  in Calderón's *Afectos de odio y amor* 192, 196
  in Calderón's *La cisma* 140
  in Calderón's *La gran Cenobia* 72–3, 75
  in Calderón's *La hija del aire* 103–5, 107, 108, 109, 115, 117
  in Calderón's *La república al revés* 85
  in Caro's *Conde Partinuplés* 220
  in Coello's *El conde de Sex* 154
  Elizabeth I of England and 40, 154, 197
  of tyrants 17–18, 103, 107, 108, 117
  of women 15, 17–18, 40
Thomas Aquinas 4
Tirso de Molina (Gabriel Téllez) 1, 38n29, 219n5
  Calderón de la Barca and 88–9, 94
  La mujer que manda en casa 85n39
  La prudencia en la mujer 3, 38n28, 52n9, 53n12, 78, 85n39, 88, 89n43
  La república al revés 19, 51, 53, 78–89, 94, 109n16, 114, 190, 216
  El vergonzoso en palacio 219
Titian 179
tragedia di lieto fine 207
Turner, Victor 92

Valera, Diego de
  Tratado en defensa de las virtuosas mujeres 21
Varey, J.E. 5, 8, 42, 44n39, 119n23, 123n2
Varona de Castilla la 114–15
Vázquez García, Francisco 14n5, 16, 58

Vega Carpio, Lope de 1
   El animal de Hungría 33
   Corona trágica 151
   Fuenteovejuna 38
   La hermosa Ester 45n43
   El mejor mozo de España 38–9
   El niño inocente 38
   Peribáñez 219
   El premio de la hermosura 43
   La reina Juana de Nápoles 2n5, 3, 38n28
   La vengadora de las mujeres 21
Velázquez, Diego de
   equestrian portraits 169–74, **170, 171, 172, 173, 175**, 176n5, 178, 212, 214
Victor Amadeus II of Savoy 209n32
Villalón, Cristobal de
   El Scholastico 21–2
Villarejo, Amy 210n33, 211
Vindel Pérez, Ingrid 143n16
Virués, Cristóbal 41, 91n4, 122
Vives, Juan Luis
   Instrucción de la mujer cristiana 11, 12, 22, 24, 25, 29, 30, 33, 52, 57, 58, 59

Walthaus, Rina 20n14, 52, 53, 54, 59n17, 64, 69n22, 74, 75n25, 79, 91n3, 215
Wardropper, Bruce 98n10
Warnicke, Retha M. 129n6, 135, 136, 140n14, 144
Weimer, Christopher B. 53n12, 78, 82n35, 89, 216n3
Weissberger, Barbara F. 21, 39, 40n33, 79
Williamson, James A. 129n6

women (*see also* body politic, body natural; *comedia*, actresses; exemplarity; queens)
   attitudes toward body of 3, 16, 18–19, 25, 30
   beauty and 57–8
   body politic and 29–30, 40, 46, 84, 131, 156, 174, 222
   conduct books for 3, 11, 12, 33
   early modern attitudes toward 3, 12, 25
   enclosure and containment of 12, 14, 15, 16n6, 86, 95, 99, 114, 153, 172
   exemplarity and 20–22
   maternity and childbearing 34–7, 131, 106
   and power 2–3, 4, 20, 22, 26, 30–32
   reign of (*see* queens) 2–3, 22–5, 29–32, 222
   representation in *comedia* of 2, 3, 4, 10, 13
   and succession 23, 24n17, 32, 37
   visibility of 15–16, 25
Woodall, Joanna 61, 170n3
Wright, Elizabeth 45n43, 47n2

Ximénez de Rada, Rodrigo 208

Zabaleta, Juan de 60–61, 84
Zayas y Sotomayor, María de 22, 187
Zenobia, Queen of Palmyra 20, 22, 38, 52, 53, 58, 59, 65, 67, 79
   as character in Calderón's *La gran Cenobia* 19, 47, 52–7, 62–77, 79, 82, 86, 89, 114, 181, 186, 216, 219, 221
Zuese, Alicia R. 215n2

CPSIA information can be obtained
at www.ICGtesting.com
Printed in the USA
BVHW042246140519
548274BV00010B/97/P